SILK STALKINGS

When Women
Write
of Murder

SILK STALKINGS

When Women Write of Murder

A Survey of
Series Characters
Created by
Women Authors
in Crime
and Mystery
Fiction

Victoria Nichols
Susan Thompson

BLACK LIZARD BOOKS · Berkeley · 1988

For information contact:
  BLACK LIZARD BOOKS
  Creative Arts Book Company
  833 Bancroft Way
  Berkeley, CA 94710

Typography by Renée King—Creative Arts Center
Cover Design by Charles Fuhrman
Text Design by Lynn Meinhardt

Library of Congress Cataloging-in-Publication Data

Nichols, Victoria, 1944–
    Silk stalkings: when women write of murder / Victoria Nichols
and Susan Thompson.
        p.   cm.
    Includes indexes.
    ISBN 0-88739-096-X (pbk.): $16.95
    1. Detective and mystery stories, English—Women authors—
Stories, plots, etc. 2. Detective and mystery stories, American—
Women authors—Stories, plots, etc. 3. Detective and mystery
stories—Women authors—Bibliography. 4. Bibliography—Books
issued in series. 5. Women and literature. I. Thompson, Susan,
1946–
II. Title.
PR830.D4N54 1988
823′.0872′089287—dc19   88-10491
                                                                CIP

Printed in the United States of America

To Mom in all her forms and manifestations,
in particular,
Nell Sorensen and Betty Shumaker.

ACKNOWLEDGMENTS

A book the nature of *Silk Stalkings* is far more than just the fruits of the labors of its authors. Over the four years it has taken to bring our work to this stage of completion, we have been aided by countless friends, acquaintances, and total strangers interested in crime and mystery fiction who were willing to talk with us about their interest. Our knowledge on the subject has been enhanced by each and every conversation we've had. Thank you all.

Our deepest gratitude for other, more tangible, assistance given to us by many friends and an occasional relative or two goes to: Dorothy Fadiman, mentor for years of preparation before the fact, the timely introduction and years of encouragement throughout the project; Dania Gamble, matron of art for foundation, walls, and roof, among other things; Al Young for seeing what we had and letting all the right people know about it; Ruth Cohen, Agent Extraordinaire; Creative Arts Books, Inc., and all the Black Lizards—Don Ellis, Publisher Nonpareil; Peg O'Donnell, Managing Editor; and Lynn Meinhardt, Editor, for the careful copyediting and elegant design of the finished product; and Barry Gifford for not saying no—Genie and Talbot Bielefeldt, our earliest critics who laughed only in the proper places; Jim Fadiman, for consultation and general Wizardry; Janet Rudolph of *Mystery Readers of America* for information, contacts, friendship, and much more; Meredith Phillips of Perseverance Press for solid critique, quarts of tea, and no small amount of good wine; Don Surath, KFJC Radio Personality for our first on-the-air appearances; the staff and resources of the Palo Alto Library system; Kim Parker of Words Expressed for processing our words so well; Lori Parker, cosmetologist who coiffed, styled, and made us presentable when we emerged from our lair; Chris Kruss, photographer for our flattering cover portrait; Sherry Boulton for making a corner of our vision manifest; Hugh Thompson for leaving his native test tubes and retorts to do research for us at the New York City Public Library and the New York City branch of Mystery Writers of America; Dean E. Wooldridge, Jr., for rest and recreation at his Ojai oasis; Grounds for Murder, San Diego, for their valuable newsletter and wonderful stock of old and new mysteries; MicroTech Exports for space, supplies, equipment, and the deus ex machina; Xerox Corporation for their fine copying equipment and facilities; Carl Schmitt and all the other wonderful people at The University National Bank and Trust Co., Palo Alto; The London Tea House, Palo Alto, for good food, the proper ambiance and Old Peculier; and The Salon and all its members for companionship and reality; and, above all, Scott Weikart and Peter Norton for their Saving Graces and High Magic.

For general support and enthusiasm throughout the years it took to research and write *Silk Stalkings*, we thank: Wendell Milburn, Sarah Milburn, Al Milburn, Karen Arko, Elizabeth Thompson, Timi Hobbs, Marian Slattery, The Resource Exchange Work Group, Bob and Betty Hilmer, Ben and Meredith Benner, Janis Mark, Doris Killam, Willis and Margaret Miller, Opal Nichols, Richard and Patty Nichols, Richard and Lorraine Kruss, Apple Dog aka Bob Shumaker, River master Dave Offen, Matt and Joanna Offen, Bill and Wendy Kubow, Cherie Crandall for sixteen beautiful and courageous Japanese students, and the Mystery Group of the Menlo Park Library.

Our deepest gratitude goes to our respective husbands for assistance far beyond that of spousal support: Corwin, for saying in the first place, "You read so many of those things you should write about them," for providing the computer we've used, for making special modifications to the data base in which we created, stored, and sorted the master list and appendixes, and the countless hours of helping us make everything work; Geoffrey, for taking Susan to England for research on the factual and fictive, giving us a working title we could live up to, and spending the long, late hours over a hot copy machine for each of the many revisions.

Special thanks for our partnership, Nichols/Thompson, for providing an edifice to contain our joint creativity and conjurations and making it possible for us to spend a lot of time together having fun.

Along with our thanks for the things provided, we add kind words to all for never letting us know how tired you were of hearing about motive, means, mayhem, and murder.

CONTENTS

PREFACE

Silk Stalkings began as a personal shopping list. The authors—true dyed-in-the-wool mystery fans—discovered a common taste for mystery fiction, particularly mysteries written by women. We investigated each other's libraries to find books as yet not read. Enthusiastically, we traded titles and soon exhausted our personal stashes and the "other titles by the same author" lists on the inside covers of our books. Still, we craved more. We went to the library. There we discovered a wealth of information on the subject of crime and mystery fiction. Several formidable-looking reference works listed every writer of this type of fiction from Edgar Allan Poe through contemporary authors. There were also assorted biographies, critical essays, and historical texts. With these riches spread before us, we found that what we were looking for did not exist. What we wanted was a book which listed only the women authors of crime and mystery fiction and titles of their works.

Combing through the various reference books, we were astounded by the vast number of women writing in this genre. Though researchers by trade, we found ourselves slightly whelmed. Undaunted, we contemplated the task of completing our shopping list—which had outgrown several notebooks by this time. We decided to limit our selection of authors to those who had created ongoing series characters such as Agatha Christie's Hercule Poirot and Jane Marple and Elizabeth Daly's Henry Gamadge. For us, the entertainment of these novels lay not only with the author but with the featured character. We love these stories about people, their strengths, weaknesses, and most of all, their relationships. The fact that characters appearing in more than one book have a greater opportunity to develop these qualities adds to our reading pleasure.

As we talked with friends about our discoveries, it became clear that there were other mystery fans who wanted this information as much as we did. Our shopping list became _Silk Stalkings_, which we gladly share with you. Happy reading.

PROLOGUE

In 1941, on the Centennial of the Detective Story, Howard Haycraft wrote what is still considered the definitive History of the Mystery. Since that time, a number of excellent reference books in this field have been written. These include wonderful large volumes listing every author since the dawn of this genre to the present day, such as those works by John M. Reilly and Allen J. Hubin. We are indebted to Mr. Haycraft and all of the other writers who have taken time to research this literary form. Our deepest appreciation and thanks, however, go to all the women authors of mystery series which make our book possible.

The authors we have chosen to focus on are primarily women. Exceptions to this primacy are men writing under a female pseudonym and male members of mixed writing teams. All have written series—two or more titles—featuring a particular detective. Though most fans are familiar with books and characters by well-known women authors such as Agatha Christie and Dorothy L. Sayers, there are many more women whose works provide entertainment and enjoyment and merit attention.

While it can be dangerous to generalize, in our reading we have found that a woman's style of story telling tends to focus less on the actual crime and more on the relationships of the characters involved with the case. The real mystery in these novels lies in the combination of multifaceted human natures which lead some to commit crime and others to solve it. This distinctive style incorporates a certain sense of how the world works and includes practical, often domestic, details in the lives of the characters. Generally, women do not write scenes of exploitative sex, gratuitous violence, or excessive gore. (Meredith Phillips of Perseverance Press states that she will not consider a manuscript for publication from either men or women if it contains any of these three elements.) Some of the women writers whose characters practice in the more hard-boiled school of detection even exclude these elements in their stories.

Murder and mysteries are fascinating when viewed from a safe distance. All crime is an antisocial act. Far more than crimes against property, however, murder is an outrage to society. No effort can be spared in bringing the perpetrator of this ultimate deed to justice. Crime and mystery fiction capitalizes on this effort and sets scenes in which unlikely people are drawn together. A semblance of intimacy develops, out of which comes a certain, often unusual, camaraderie. Murder cuts across class barriers and allows both amateur and professional detectives to probe private lives and ask personal questions as few other circumstances permit.

A popular form of this type of fiction is that of the puzzle. The Whodunit pits the reader's sagacity against the criminal's cunning. Throughout the story, pieces of the puzzle are spread like ground bait for the reader. The author often makes the innermost thoughts of the characters, including those of the perpetrator, available as further clues to the solution of the mystery. The puzzle is a challenge to the reader, an opportunity to test one's powers of observation and deduction.

While the puzzle aspect is intriguing to some readers, others enjoy mystery fiction for its escapist qualities. If the term escapist means to take one out of one's self, the epithet fits. We can think of no better way to take the mind off of a twenty-four-hour bug, a house full of exuberant children, or just a case of the blahs, than to curl up with a good mystery for a few hours.

Most mystery fiction books are short—around two hundred pages —and are generally easy to read. These stories have a beginning, a middle, and an end. Unlike life in the world in which we live, there is almost always resolution and between the covers of the book, justice is usually served. Real life is the backbone of these novels and the reader can be immersed in death and deception vicariously.

Mysteries are not simply puzzles. Many of these works are novels with depth and character which just happen to use a crime of one sort or another as a theme. Readers—not already committed mystery fans—are waking up to the fact that there is literature hidden away in that long-ignored section labeled Mystery. Human nature in all its permutations is the foundation for the mystery metaphor. Often the authors' values are subtly reflected in the story line. Anne Perry's choice of setting for her series is London during the Victorian era—in a social climate which closely parallels our own. The differences lie mainly in the conventions of the period, but the actual crimes and the motivations behind them are the same. By situating events in another era, the author is able to focus on contemporary issues using history as an additional perspective. Emma Lathen places John Putnam Thatcher in an investment banking house in New York. This gives him a wide-angled view of the worldwide business community. Ethics are at issue here in a variety of settings ranging from the automotive industry to church real estate.

The author's personal viewpoint can also be expressed through her characters. Dr. Basil Willing, portrayed by Helen McCloy in a book written shortly after WWII, expounds on the dangers of exploiting children in a country's war efforts. Marital conflict and the question of women's independence provide a counterpoint to the criminal investigations carried out by Dorothy Simpson's Inspector Luke Thanet.

Personal and professional interest and knowledge of a particular field can add depth to a tale. In several of her books, Ngaio Marsh uses her familiarity with the theater to create a stage for a killing in a literal sense. Sister Carol Anne O'Marie is a Catholic nun who has spent thirty years in convent life and has chosen to feature a detecting sister in her new series.

The series character is a device used by many authors of this genre and enjoyed by many readers. It provides both context and continuity for the development of the detective. In our opinion, some of these sleuths exert such influence on the story that one book is simply not sufficient to contain them. Lucy Ramsdale, a sprightly senior citizen, dominates the series as well as the lives of those around her. Some featured characters are simply the key to a successful formula. Fleming Stone, a professional detective, invariably appears late in the story and solves the baffling crime with deceptive ease. A few detectives such as Albert Campion begin with one personality and, in the course of the series, develop another. Other characters never change much at all. Dame Beatrice Bradley is introduced as old, leathery, and saurian, and remains the same after decades of investigations.

In some series, the evolution of these detectives is reflected in their private lives. Tommy and Tuppence Beresford enter their series as brash youths reeling from the effects of WWI. Their last adventure finds them as grandparents in the 1970's, still serving Crown and Country. Superintendent Hannasyde and Sergeant Hemingway, on the other hand, are only known through the scope of their work with Scotland Yard.

It is said that Dorothy L. Sayers fell in love with her creation Lord Peter Wimsey. She is not alone. Several generations of female readers would willingly trade places with Harriet Vane. Lord Peter is an aristocrat whose wealth, position, and education have only enhanced his innate abilities. Handsome Roderick Alleyn has won the admiration of his colleagues, as well as his fans, for his brilliant mind and sensitive demeanor. On the distaff side we find Kate Fansler, an intellectual force within the academic community. Beyond her professional qualifications, she is respected for her down-to-earth views and sympathetic consciousness of the concerns of others.

Fictional figures we find ourselves emotionally drawn to possess a number of admirable aspects. Male and female, they bring capability and a full range of experience to the art of detection. As Coleridge points out, "The truth is, a great mind must be androgynous."[1] We find that we prefer an intelligent character who uses brains before brawn, is self-reliant, independent, and resourceful. Detectives who can find humor in most any situation and are capable of laughing at themselves are also appealing. A strong, yet tender and compassionate, nature completes the portrait of those detectives we would most like to know.

In these novels of murder and mayhem, humor often acts as an anodyne. It lightens up a grim situation and adds an extra measure of entertainment. Johnson Johnson's silliness catches people off guard and makes tense situations tolerable. Sarah Kelling is surrounded by eccentrics—friends as well as family. Their often bizarre behavior either gets them killed or makes them prime suspects. Hercule Poirot never laughs at himself. Though his affectations and monumental ego do have comic qualities, murderers learn, to their regret, that there is more to M. Poirot than meets the eye. Laughter is the best medicine and since murder is a bitter pill to swallow, some of these series provide an antidote.

This book is a survey. With nearly six hundred characters and over three thousand titles, the scope of this particular work can be nothing else. There are samples of detectives from many eras, and a variety of sleuthing styles as well as different professions and disciplines are depicted. We have been reluctant to draw any conclusions based on the data we have collected. It is enough for us now to simply compile this list to the best of our abilities.

Whether captivated by a detective's style of ratiocination, or a particular personality, we are often reluctant to have a story end. A series gives us more of whatever we enjoy and prolongs the entertainment. Mysteries are well known to be addictive. Let the reader beware: to feed your habit, it will be necessary to polish your own detective skills, as many of these golden oldies are hard to find.

INTRODUCTION

*T*he first section of this book consists of chapters in which a selection of series characters have divided themselves rather nicely into categories according to profession, vocation, or the inclination which draws them into the investigation of crime. Some characters, by all rights, belong in more than one category. Where this occurs, suitable comments are made. These chapters contain characters we abhor as well as characters we adore. Many are our old favorites. Some are pleasant discoveries made as we did our research. Some are outstanding simply because they are dreadful or boring.

Each chapter introduces a variety of characters. For example, a number of detectives of different types appear in the category of academic investigators. Professor Pennyfeather, a mild-mannered sleuth of the late 1940's, is drawn into investigations close to his southern Californian home. For readers with a taste for adventures farther afield, the world travelers Professors Glendower and Spring may be just the ticket. Some readers may find they enjoy mysteries with a certain ambiance, style of life, or work. For them, we provide a brief listing of books within series which feature these elements.

A BLOT IN THE COPYBOOK

ACADEMIA

*T*he world of academia provides a wonderful setting for crime, murder, and deception. Personal and professional passions often run high among scholars. Staff and students alike can fall victim to jealousy, avarice, and pride. Aside from professional similarities, the most notable quality the following characters have in common is the fact that all are in their middle years and all are, in general, quite satisfied with what life provides them. These professors seem particularly gifted in using their scholarly methods for purposes of detection. Whether cloistered within the hallowed halls of ivy, or working in the field, these scholars are exemplary citizens of their world—academia.

DR. PENELOPE SPRING and SIR TOBIAS GLENDOWER
1979-1983   7 books   English/American
Margot Arnold (Petronelle Cook)

Dr. Penelope Spring is an American anthropologist who teaches at Oxford University, England. Her partner, Professor Tobias Glendower, is an eminent archaeologist at the same illustrious institution. They share an office, a secretary, a taste for exotic places, and a talent for adventure.

Their first foray into detection takes place in Turkey, in *Exit Actors, Dying*. Two members of a film company on location there are murdered. Unimpressed with the progress being made by the Turkish police, Toby decides that to save what remains of their vacation, he and Penny must solve the crime themselves. When Penny demures on the grounds that they haven't the faintest idea of how to go about it, Toby replies,

> "Why not?" Toby was positively complacent. "We are two highly intelligent human beings, trained to observe and deduce things. The methods used in both archaeology and anthropology are extremely similar to those used in criminology. Besides, if, as we suspect, the crimes are connected with a group of foreigners, *we* are more likely to find out what is going on than the Turks are."[1]

They do in fact solve the crime and return to England in time for Toby to receive the Order of Merit for outstanding services to the British Empire from Her Majesty Queen Elizabeth II and become Sir Toby. The grapevine picks up the tale of their success and it isn't long before their presence is required in other faraway places, as much for their detective skills as for their more legitimate professional ones.

Each of the seven books in the series takes place in a different location and, with a few exceptions, features a different cast of characters. In *Death of a Voodoo Doll*, Toby and Penny encounter gris-gris on the old plantation and the revelries of Mardi Gras. In *Lament for a Lady Laird*, Penny's friend, the title character, is threatened by ghostly intruders. *Zadok's Treasure* takes place in the Holy Land where a colleague of Toby's seems to have disappeared. There, Toby and Penny encounter secrets of an ancient tomb and a major archaeological discovery—quite possibly, the hidden treasure of the Temple of Jerusalem. The stories are entertaining and fast paced. Magic, witchcraft, legends, and lore play major parts in all the books. The humor is dry and mild and the relationship between the two professors is admirable. We would enjoy working on a dig supervised by either or both of these perspicacious professors.

PETER SHANDY
1978-1987   6 books   American
Charlotte MacLeod

Peter Shandy is a down-to-earth professor at Balaclava Agricultural College, Balaclava Junction, Massachusetts. He is perhaps best known in the academic world as the codeveloper of the Balaclava Buster, a giant rutabaga which has brought fame and renown to the college, and fortune to its developers.

In Peter's first murder case, *Rest You Merry*, the victim is Jemima Ames, wife of his closest friend, Professor Timothy Ames. Peter discovers her body behind his living room sofa, where it is assumed she has accidentally fallen during an attempt to modify the less than tasteful decorations Peter has erected for the annual college Christmas Illumination. Peter's powers of observation and his well-known penchant for counting things leads him to believe that Jemima has in fact been murdered. After the initial furor around the discovery of the body has died down, Peter tells the victim's husband of his numerical suspicions.

> "Er—at any rate, I've always kept this bowl of marbles here on the whatnot. There were thirty-eight."
>
> Ames nodded perfunctorily. He took it for granted Shandy would know.
>
> "When I got home this morning, the marbles were scattered over the living room floor and out into the hall. I might not have noticed, since I was cold and hungry and in a state of—er—general perturbation, but one of them tripped me up. So I went hunting for the rest. At first I didn't think to look behind the sofa because it seemed impossible any could have got there. The base is solid right down to the floor, as you can see, and besides, the floor slants a bit in the opposite direction. It's an old house, you know. But I knew I was one short and I'd looked everywhere else, so—"[2]

The apparently natural death of Dr. Ben Cadwall, the college comptroller, not long after Mrs. Ames' demise, further suggests foul play to Peter. Medical evidence confirms his suspicions, and acting under stern orders from President Thorkjeld Svenson to "clear this mess up immediately," Peter wends his way through student revelers and false clues to the solution of both murders. It is in this novel that Peter meets librarian Helen Marsh who has come to help out Timothy Ames as a temporary housekeeper. In the course of Peter's investigation, he and Helen fall in love and their courtship begins as the book ends.

With one exception, the action in these novels takes place on the campus, in the Balaclava Junction community, and the surrounding countryside. The author gives us a view of the inner workings of an institution dedicated not only to education but to practical living as well. MacLeod accords equal respect to common sense and academic excellence. Her campus setting provides undercurrents to the story, such as the plight of the small farmer faced with takeover by agribusiness, or the value of scientific hog breeding to the nation's economic well-being. One gets the feeling that if there were really places like Balaclava, this country might be much better off. Far from being dry social commentary, all of the Shandy novels are liberally laced with humor. Murder is central to each story, and after their marriage—which takes place off the page between the first and second books—Helen joins Peter as a sleuthing partner as well as his spouse.

Peter and Helen's world includes both a transient and a stable population. We meet Professor Ames, Peter's close friend and codeveloper of the Balaclava Buster; Ames' wife, son, and daughter-in-law; the Enderbles; Police Chief Fred Ottermole; the Shandy's housekeeper, Mrs. Lomax; and, of course, President Svensen, his wise and beautiful wife, Sieglinde, and several of their seven daughters—each more beautiful than the last. Reading this series is like returning to a favorite place for another good visit.

JACQUELINE KIRBY
1972-1984   3 books   American
Elizabeth Peters (Barbara Mertz)

Conventional standards of beauty cannot be applied to Jacqueline Kirby, whose fierce intelligence and piercing wit are facets of this paradoxical character. A university librarian and specialist in art history, Jacqueline looks the part to those who see her behind her desk... "glowering impartially on all comers from behind her heavy glasses."[3] Those sufficiently stalwart to withstand the intimidation of the gaze, the glasses, and the severe tailoring are invited to notice her emerald green eyes, thick auburn hair, and youthful slender figure.

She is often drawn into detecting by her literary inquisitiveness.

"I'm going to a writers' conference," she announced.

"Business deduction?"

"Naturally."

"But you aren't a writer."

Jacqueline indicated the briefcase. "We're writing a textbook, aren't we?"

"Slowly," James said. "Very slowly."

"Anyway, I am a librarian. Library, books, writers...Even the fascists at Internal Revenue can follow that connection."

James grinned. Jacqueline's feud with the local IRS office was a campus legend. Once she had tried to deduct her new television set on the grounds that her professional duties required her to watch writers being interviewed on the *Today* show.

"What conference are you attending?" he asked diplomatically.

Jacqueline flourished a newspaper clipping. "The Historical Romance Writers of the World. It's the only one I could find. The ABA meetings were last month, and the ALA is meeting in Birmingham. I wouldn't be caught dead in Birmingham."

"The Historical Romance Writers," James repeated. "Ah. I see....Have you read any historical romances lately?"

"Not lately, no. I loved them when I was young. *The Prisoner of Zenda, Gone with the Wind, Forever Amber.*"

"Ah. *Forever Amber.*"

"It's not a bad book," Jacqueline said.

"No."

"What's the matter?" Jacqueline looked at him suspiciously. "You're smirking, James. I know that smirk."

"I'm not sure the IRS will buy it, that's all. University libraries don't stock many novels. Especially romantic novels."

"Then I'll have to write one," Jacqueline said. "Actually that's not a bad idea. Someone told me they are selling very well these days."[4]

No matter what disguise she has assumed, Jacqueline's capacious handbag is her constant companion. She readily admits that it is a much more suitable accessory with her well-tailored working clothes than with a fifteenth century gown or yards of lavender voile and Brussels lace. However, she adamantly refuses to be parted from it.

Student rumor has it that she can produce anything she wants out of it.

As a librarian, Jacqueline has colossal amounts of information in her mind and at her fingertips. She frequently checks her facts and is thorough in all she does. Her research is not limited to her profession. She is a lusty woman with great appetites—one who believes in the hands-on method of investigation.

Practical jokes at a gathering to rectify the vilification of Richard III, in *The Murders of Richard III*, add confusion to murder and place Jacqueline in the interesting position of knowing the potential criminal without having any idea of the proposed crime or its victim. Working backwards, she solves the mystery, though not until the killer has completed his self-appointed task. Historical data is deftly woven through this story, giving readers insights into the 1500's and information on the penchant some early recorders had of altering events to suit the end desired by the reigning monarch of their period.

Jacqueline is the first of three series characters created by Elizabeth Peters. Under another pseudonym, this author has written numerous gothic romances. *Die for Love*, second in the Kirby series, is a takeoff on that industry with an insider's practiced eye. Peters' other characters include art historian Vicky Bliss and the archaeological team of Amelia Peabody and Radcliffe Emerson.

AMELIA PEABODY and RADCLIFFE EMERSON
1975-1986   4 books   English
Elizabeth Peters (Barbara Mertz)

Miss Amelia Peabody was the youngest child and only daughter of her parents. Her brothers all left home to become successful merchants and professional men. After the death of her mother, Amelia—a proper daughter of the Victorian Age—remained behind to keep house and assist her father, a scholar and antiquarian, with his research. This quiet life suited her and enabled her to pursue her own interests in languages and scholarship. It came as no surprise to anyone in the family that when their father died, he left Amelia all of his property. The discovery that Papa's estate was in reality a fortune of one half million pounds astonished those same family members and caused no small amount of consternation. Rather than sit at home enjoying the discomfort of all her relations and laughing up her sleeve at their efforts to sweep her (and her fortune) into the bosom of the family, middle-aged spinster Amelia sets forth to travel to the places she and her father studied over the years.

Her travels take her to Rome where she meets a young woman of noble birth, fallen on hard times. Evelyn Barton-Forbes becomes the outspoken Amelia's companion—without which few Victorian ladies, respectable or otherwise, would think of traveling—and together they make their way to Egypt. In Cairo they meet Radcliffe Emerson, an eminent, though unsponsored, archaeologist, and his brother Walter. The appearance of what seems to be a walking mummy provides Peabody and Emerson with a clue that there is more to be investigated than simply ruins. Amelia and Evelyn continue their travels by boat down the Nile where their paths cross that of the Emersons at the site on which they have been working. The mummy reappears and creates a mystery which must be unraveled so that the workers, believing in the mummy's curse, will return to assist with the excavation.

Snapping and snarling at one another, Amelia and Emerson proceed to solve the mystery and restore a good name and lost fortune to their rightful heir.

> I set off without another word, not waiting to see whether they obeyed me. By the time I found Emerson, I had worked myself up into quite a state of anger. He was squatting on the ground, his tan clothing and dusty helmet blending so well with the hue of the sand that I did not distinguish his form until I was almost upon him. He was so preoccupied that he failed to hear my approach. I struck him, not lightly, on the shoulder with my parasol.
>
> "Oh," he said, glancing at me. "So it's you, Peabody. Of course. Who else would greet a man by beating him over the head?"[5]

All ends well. Amelia and Radcliffe marry as do Evelyn and Walter. Love for her husband and the lure of the desert combine to make Amelia a welcome part of the archaeological team. Even the arrival of a son, named for his uncle Walter, does not slow down the Emersons. In *The Curse of the Pharaohs*, young Walter—aptly nicknamed Ramses—is left in England while his parents return to Egypt and their work. Besotted with his precocious son, Emerson proposes to add him to the expedition, and, in the third book, *The Mummy Case*, Ramses and The Cat Bastet journey to Egypt and take part in the excavations. It is a lively family, devoted to one another and to the job of locating and preserving antiquities. The identification of the master criminal in *Lion in the Valley* sets readers up for the next installment of the adventures of Amelia, Radcliffe, Ramses, and their friends and assistants.

Author Peters is a graduate of The Oriental Institute, University of Chicago. Trained in historical research, she has written a number of nonfiction books on Egyptology and weaves this specialized knowledge all through these mysteries.

KATE FANSLER
1964-1986   8 books   American
Amanda Cross (Carolyn Heilbrun)

Kate Fansler, Professor of Literature at a New York City university, is well-to-do, well dressed, and well educated. Kate has been raised in an atmosphere of privilege and has a clear sense of her self-worth. She teaches for the love of it and enjoys the company of most of her colleagues. Her life is comfortable and well ordered and as the series opens, she is more than a little content with her un-married status.

In the first novel featuring Miss Fansler, *In the Last Analysis*, Kate becomes involved with murder when a former student of hers is found stabbed on the analytic couch of the top-notch psychiatrist Kate has recommended. Dr. Emanuel Bauer, a close friend and former lover of Kate's, is charged with the murder of his patient and Kate is determined to clear him. In this book we also meet Reed Amhearst, another of Kate's close friends who just happens to be an assistant district attorney. Kate may be a bit vague about exactly what Reed's duties are but she does not hesitate to ask for his assistance in getting her the official information she needs to pur-sue her inquiries. Only slightly shaken by Reed's news that the police have received an anonymous letter accusing her of the murder, Kate presses on with even more determination.

Throughout the series the ultimate clue for this professor is often a literary one. In the first book, armed with little more than a feel-ing she has about an individual who has been affected by a particular passage by D. H. Lawrence, Kate formulates an improbable and seemingly unprovable scenario. She asks Reed to help her get the evidence to prove her literary-based intuition. His agreement is reluc-tant and qualified.

"Will you help if I promise?"
"I won't even continue this conversation until you promise.
I want your word. All right. Now, let me call hospitals. They

will tell me none of their clerks works on Sunday. No one works on Sundays, except you and your friends. I will then threaten and cajole. But we may have to wait even so. I don't know to what degree the New York Police Department is willing to flex its muscles. Now stop evolving schemes. I'll call if and when I get any news. And remember your promise."

Kate had to wait until the afternoon when Reed called again.[6]

Reed does obtain the one piece of physical evidence needed to clinch the case. The mystery is solved and both Kate and Dr. Bauer are exonerated.

There are eight Fansler novels. In each, we learn a little more about Kate, her family, her colleagues, and, of course, her relationship with Reed Amhearst—which eventually leads to their marriage. She appears in a variety of settings, from the hallowed halls of Harvard to an isolated cabin in Berkshire Wood. We discover that her wit and erudition are as well suited to rural simplicity as they are to urban elegance. While Professor Fansler takes scholarship seriously and has earned the respect of both students and colleagues, she takes herself a bit more lightly and can even laugh at her tendency to use seven syllables where two would do.

A Ph.D. in English amply qualifies Amanda Cross for writing about her fictional counterpart. Carolyn Heilbrun is currently Professor of English at Columbia University, New York, and the author of several nonfiction works as well as the Fansler series.

MANDRAKE
1949-1959   3 books   American
John and Emery Bonett (Felicity and John Coulson)

In 1949, the writing team of John and Emery Bonett introduced their first series character, Professor Mandrake. Though an anthropologist by profession, in his later years, the professor has become a radio and television personality. His brilliance is often hidden behind his countenance—described as quite strikingly ugly—and his meddlesome, muddling manner. Aware of his shortcomings, he takes his position in the academic world seriously.

Mandrake looked at his hairy, spatulate-fingered hands rather sheepishly. "It is a part of my profession," he explained, "to know why human beings do as they do."[7]

It is this knowledge which invariably leads him to the solution of crime.

The settings of the three books are varied, as are the combined villains and victims. In *Dead Lion*, the beautiful and ruthless Cyprian Druse, London literary critic, is killed by a falling window. Suspects abound, including several women involved with the murdered man. Mandrake's first foray into detecting comes about at the request of Simon Crane, Druse's nephew and narrator of the story. In the second novel, *A Banner for Pegasus*, the Coulsons drew upon their own experience in the British film industry. A film crew has invaded the small English village of Steeple Tottering, bringing intrigue, jealousy, and murder with it. A young woman whose boyfriend Peter is suspected in the death of the film's director, prevails upon the professor to help prove Peter's innocence. *No Grave for a Lady* takes place on one of the Channel Isles where Lotte Liselotte, a German actress, is murdered and buried in the sand. As in all three books, there is a love interest and Mandrake's involvement is as much on behalf of young love as it is a desire to see justice done.

Mandrake's method is meddlesome rather than methodical but he gets to the heart of the matter nonetheless. Using human beings as his raw material, the professor reaches his final conclusion by applying what he knows about human behavior and the individuals involved. Sometimes there is a dangerous confrontation at the denouement of both the case and the book, but Mandrake remains rather detached from any violence, preferring to maintain his position as observer rather than participant.

A Banner for Pegasus is considered by many to be the Bonett's finest work and a classic in the genre. We find all three of the books to be well worth reading and only wish the series continued. The Bonett's apparently abandoned Mandrake when they moved to the Spanish Costa Brava. They did not give up mystery writing however, as they developed a new series character, Salvador Borges, who appeared in six novels.

A. PENNYFEATHER
1945-1952   6 books   American
D. B. Olsen (Dolores Hitchens)

An English professor with a classical education, Pennyfeather sometimes finds himself inveigled by relatives or friends into investigating murders. The good professor may note objects or things out of place as potential clues, but the foundation for this character's detecting is his classical education and his genuine erudition. Early books in the series are located away from the campus but the last three take place on and around the Clarendon campus and bring up issues of morality in intriguing fashions.

Physically unassuming, the professor nevertheless takes his fair share of knocks in the course of unraveling the mystery.

> She was stretched out, breast down on the top of a pile of trunks. A nice high hiding place—he almost didn't see her in time. There was a question as to whether the muffler and the coat collar would have done him much good against the neat, professional little lead-loaded sap she must have brought in her purse. He ducked as her arm lifted and swept down, then snatched her wrist. She wriggled forward trying to transfer the sap to her other hand, and so huge and vigorous was her fury that she almost pulled Mr. Pennyfeather to the top of the trunks with her struggling.[8]

Most of the time, Pennyfeather is content to sit quietly, reading Milton and an occasional mystery thriller and living up to his legend as the college's leading absentminded professor.

Author D. B. Olsen also created the Murdock sisters, Rachel and Jennifer. Both series were penned from the mid-forties through the fifties and take place in southern California. Olsen has captured the ambiance of both time and place and has drawn characters who fit their scenes well. This prolific author wrote another series featuring Jim Sader, Private Operator, and with her husband Bert, developed two more series.

USING METHODS OF SCHOLARSHIP, these academicians make excellent detectives. Their knowledge, not only in their field of study but of human nature in general, provides them with insights and perceptions not always apparent to law enforcement officials. Their prestige in the world of higher learning often makes it possible for them to reach individuals in positions of power for answers to questions and even assistance and direct intervention. While these characters deal seriously with the problems that confront them in matters of murder and mystery, all of the books in the various series mentioned here are full of laughter and good humor. These are not stuffy souls locked up in ivory towers. They are warm, witty, and above all, human.

Outside investigators, police, and private detectives are frequently called to look into acts of crime and murder on the campus. Other books involving academicians include:

Catherine Aird, *Parting Breath*, 1977
Josephine Bell, *Death at Half-Term*, 1939; *The Summer School Mystery*, 1950
Gwendoline Butler, *Dine and Be Dead*, 1960; *Coffin in Oxford*, 1962; *A Coffin for Pandora*, 1973
Edward Candy, *Words for Murder Perhaps*, 1971
David Frome, *Mr. Pinkerton Finds a Body*, 1934
Martha Grimes, all books in the series
P. D. James, *An Unsuitable Job for a Woman*, 1972
Elizabeth Lemarchand, *Death of an Old Girl*, 1967; *Light Through Glass*, 1984
Gladys Mitchell, *Laurels are Poison*, 1942; *Tom Brown's Body*, 1949; *Faintley Speaking*, 1954
Anne Morice, *Murder in Outline*, 1979
Sister Carol Anne O'Marie, *A Novena for Murder*, 1984
Dorothy L. Sayers, *Gaudy Night*, 1935
Nancy Spain, *Death Before Wicket*, 1946
Margaret Yorke, *Grave Matters*, 1973; *Cast for Death*, 1976

BEHIND THE BADGE

*P*olice within the literary genre of crime and mystery fiction can come as no surprise to readers. This type of story deals, after all, with the breaking of those laws which bind the architecture of society. The enforcement and preservation of the laws of the land are essential ingredients to the general comfort, health, morals, safety, and prosperity of that land's citizenry. The force entrusted with these tasks is, ideally, a body of men and women trained to maintain public peace and order while, at the same time, preventing and detecting crime. A police officer bears the authority to influence and command both opinion and behavior within a given community under its standards.

The number and variety of fictional police detectives is astounding. The gamut from hard- to soft-boiled is well and truly run. Some go by the book while others throw the book away and follow their noses—even if their noses sometimes lead them outside the bounds of the law. There are staunch supporters of The System, and there are those who ultimately serve only Justice in all her blind wisdom. No matter what their detecting style, these are the officials responsible for gathering evidence, tracking criminals, and bringing them in to stand accused. There are sufficient number and variety within this category to suit the broad range of readers' tastes.

Running throughout all the categories of detective in this book are officers of law—the last bastion between the criminal and the society their criminal acts affect. Lord Peter's good friend and eventual brother-in-law is Inspector Charles Parker of Scotland Yard. Albert Campion lives above a police station. Sister Kimberly, amanuensis to Sister Empty Dempsey, is blood sister of Richard Moriarty of the Chicago Police. Elena Oliverez is romantically involved with Lieutenant Dave Kirk of the Santa Barbara Homicide Squad. Broadway actress Jocelyn O'Roarke dates Detective Sergeant Phillip Gerrard of the NYPD and Kate Fansler eventually marries Reed Amhearst, an assistant district attorney of New York.

The long arm of the law reaches through and across all societal boundaries. The men and women behind their badges of office support and enforce the agreements among civilized peoples: that there is right and wrong and that wrongs must be redressed. The police, in pursuit of their duty, must of necessity cause apprehension.

Because of the sheer number of characters in this category, we introduce these professionals by agency.

MAJOR METROPOLITAN FORCES

Those charged with the maintenance of public order, safety, health, and the enforcement of laws in a metropolitan area have big jobs cut out for them. A city is an amalgamation of personal elements. Neighborhood pockets exist where the same people live next door to one another year after year and friendship exists between neighbors and shopkeepers, while in other districts, wealth serves to insulate people from one another. In still other areas, the population is transient and unknown, either from the pride and problems of poverty or the fact that business lives compel some people to work in the city while their private desires allow them to live in the suburbs. Residents may get to know the cop on the beat but in these days of slashed budgets and substandard forces, the beat cop is rapidly becoming a thing of the past. Patrol cars have replaced him, and who can relate to an automobile for safety? There is an impersonality to city life and an anonymity for those who choose it. Random killers, reasonless violence, and senseless crime are daily occurrences and command more resources than a hard-pressed force can possibly provide.

The police officers in this section are a breed apart. Knowing that they are handicapped by lack of funds and person power, they nevertheless persevere and carry on with routine and special duty as best they can. Often the offenses can be bigger than the mind can imagine, having well-established roots in highly organized crime and tendrils reaching from the highest power to the lowest echelon. The fact that there are individuals willing to lay their bodies on the line for the protection and well-being of others is a validation of a vibrant human spirit.

EBENEZER GRYCE, New York Metropolitan
1878-1917   12 books   American
Anna Katharine Green

One hundred ten years ago, Anna Katharine Green introduced Ebenezer Gryce to an enthusiastic public. For twenty years, the series featuring this New York policeman and his pursuit of wrongdoers entertained and titillated readers for whom crime and mystery fiction was an enticing, new literary form. While not the first female author of a mystery nor even the first to produce a series character, Green is known as the author of the earliest American best-seller and holds, among others, the title of Mother of Detective Fiction.

The Leavenworth Case, first in the Gryce series, marks the debut of a police detective and presents a young attorney in the role of evidence gatherer and narrator of the tale. Gryce has, in his own mind, ample reason for employing the young lawyer. He feels that he is forever excluded from one of the very elements of society he must serve.

> "Mr. Raymond," he cried at last, "have you any idea of the disadvantages under which a detective labors? For instance, now, you imagine I can insinuate myself into all sorts of society, perhaps; but you are mistaken. Strange as it may appear, I have never by any possibility of means succeeded with one class of persons at all. I cannot pass myself off for a gentleman. Tailors and barbers are no good; I am always found out."
>
> He looked so dejected I could scarcely forbear smiling, notwithstanding my secret care and anxiety.
>
> "I have even employed a French valet, who understood dancing and whiskers; but it was all of no avail. The first gentleman I approached stared at me,—real gentleman, I mean, none of your American dandies,—and I had no stare to return; I had forgotten that emergency in my confabs with Pierre Camille Marie Make-face."
>
> Amused, but a little discomposed by this sudden turn in the conversation, I looked at Mr. Gryce inquiringly.
>
> "Now you, I dare say, have no trouble? Was born one, perhaps. Can even ask a lady to dance without blushing, eh?"
>
> "Well,—" I commenced.
>
> "Just so," he replied; "now, I can't. I can enter a house, bow to the mistress of it, let her be as elegant as she will, so long as I have a writ of arrest in my hand, or some such professional matter upon my mind; but when it comes to visiting in kid gloves, raising a glass of champagne in response to a toast— and such like, I am absolutely good for nothing." And he plunged his two hands into his hair, and looked dolefully at the head of the cane I carried in my hand.[1]

The upper regions of society may need these lawful guardians but, in the day and age these stories were written, were unwilling to accept them as one of their number. Manners and gentle reticence intrude to confound the investigation. Class, bearing and loyalty keep servants mutely in their appointed places. Gryce chooses his surrogates with care; young Everett Raymond in the first book, and, from the fifth book on, Miss Amelia Butterworth—a social order unto herself.

Science has not yet been admitted as an adjunct to investigation though Green has experts in one field or another called to give their pertinent opinion. Despite the lack of what modern law enforcement takes for granted in the way of forensic data, Gryce and his minions are not altogether careless. Clues are gathered and evidence which could lead to conviction is held. Like his professional successors, Gryce is a reader of character. Without prejudice, he understands the limitations of emotions as well as their power. Though constrained in ways today's police are not, he toils and moles along to the successful conclusion of his cases.

Despite the popularity of her books when they first appeared and the continuing eminence of her contemporaries, e.g., Sir Arthur Conan Doyle and Wilkie Collins, Green's books, with the exception of *The Leavenworth Case*, are out of print. Those which remain in existence are collectors' items with correspondingly high price tags. Over the years, Green's fiction has been relegated to the less than prestigious rank of romantic mystery. There are strong elements of romance and other personal connection in these stories but the detection is solid and the detective eminently believable. Green has been sadly underrated and overlooked for too long. We would like to see all of her works back on the shelves for instruction, entertainment, and, above all, an accurate glimpse of life at the turn of the century.

CHRISTOPHER MCKEE, Manhattan Homicide
1930-1962   31 books   American
Helen Reilly

There are touches of the gothic in this series which opened in 1930. These include dark secrets, brooding mansions, damsels in distress, imprudent—often passionate—emotional attachments and true love requited. While New York City is the venue for most of the action in these stories and McKee himself is the head of the Manhattan Homicide Squad, the problems are not those of city squalor but of the upper classes within their well-defined circles.

Over the series' thirty year span, McKee grows in stature within the ranks of the New York Metropolitan Police. His Scots ancestry and his tweedy, uncitified appearance make the appellation of the "Scotchman" apt as well as descriptive.

So he had called the Scotchman, and McKee had promised to look in. Christopher McKee was not at this time the prominent figure he later became. He had joined the police after special work done during the war, first as unofficial assistant to Commissioner Denby, lingering on during two subsequent administrations, grumbling and growling at the life he led but really enjoying it beneath that savage girding. They had wanted to make him a deputy commissioner after the Harkness case, but he clung to the title of inspector—said he hadn't so far to fall.[2]

This canny Scot often detects by instinct. His attention may be caught by the one clue out of many which leads him to the solution of a knotty problem or he may be visited by a persistent hunch which carries him to a successful outcome. McKee is a perceptive reader of character and possesses a broad understanding of human behavior. His canniness is an integral part of his personality and while it can be described as a flair, rarely causes him to operate outside the bounds of his calling.

There is an emphasis on police procedure which seems dated by today's standards. McKee is a thorough investigator and gathers evidence and interviews tirelessly, winding cases up neatly and seeing young hearts' desires realized. At times, he propels the reader along as he uncovers and discovers elements to the case. At others, he keeps his thoughts to himself and readers must arrange the clues and information on their own.

The very dated and gothic qualities of these novels hold a curious appeal. It may be that the appeal is for a time of innocence gone by and a genteel way of living which is only a faint memory for some and a matter of fiction for most. The books are difficult to find. For readers wanting a taste of New York in the thirties and forties, they are worth a conscientious search.

TOBIN, NYPD
1940-1942   3 books   American
Dorothy B. Hughes

Although there are only three books in this series, each is the sort that is impossible to put down once started. A published poet, Hughes' first effort at mystery writing was *The So Blue Marble*. It featured Tobin, a Princeton-educated New York homicide inspector, and brought its author acclaim as a great new talent. Two more books featuring Toby followed in rapid succession. Hughes went on to write more highly acclaimed mystery novels but Tobin never appeared again nor did she develop another series character to replace him.

Written during the war years, all three stories revolve around complex plots which include espionage, hidden treasure, betrayal, and murder, and involve the upper stratum of New York society and members of the glittering, wealthy international set. We wondered why Hughes had chosen a policeman on whom to depend her series and concluded that she a) needed someone in authority to sanction some of the action of the stories, and b) along with the rest of the country was under the "loose lips sink ships" stricture, so could not use an official spy or government agent.

Due to the nature of the times and his connections, Tobin is peripherally involved with the FBI, the Foreign Affairs Office, and people in high places in New York and Washington, D.C. Toby works primarily offstage setting events and people in motion. His position makes him a logical guardian of secrets and he appears on the scene at the end to arrest the perpetrator of murder and to turn traitors over to the proper authorities. We never see him at home and his personality is only suggested by his acquaintances.

In each of the stories, there is a primary character who is drawn into a web of violence and deceit due to—in one case, quite literally—holding one piece of the grand puzzle. These protagonists are young and idealistic while having knowledge of the evil afoot in the wartime world and some understanding of the dangers facing them. They are clearheaded, resourceful individuals, unsure of whom to trust and forced to make decisions and to take action on their own. They are courageous and their actions stem from their beliefs and convictions.

In answer to a question about a treasure he is determined Hitler shall not have, Kit McKittrick, the hero of *The Fallen Sparrow* replies:

> "Once they meant little to me, priceless and legendary as they were. They weren't more than a nice trinket for Geoffrey, my stepfather, a slight repayment for all he'd given me through the years. That and the thwarting of a man whose chin I didn't like."
> His jaw hardened and the white mold of her face grew more white, fluttered to despair. "Through the years that they tried to force me to give them up, they meant life to me. My hold on existence." His nostrils flared. "Now they mean more to me than life. Now they are the symbol of all the right and justice and beauty that should be the heritage of man on this earth, that

would be our heritage if the false god were slain and his proph-
ets ground to dust."[3]

The books are timely for their day. There is still innocence, a desire
for the good life, and a rising sense of horror of the rapidly growing
German menace. The New York locale is well portrayed. Hughes'
excellent visual sense may explain why several of her books,
including *The Fallen Sparrow*, were made into movies. These works
fall easily into the category of classic, not for the brilliance of the
ongoing character and his detective abilities, but for the complex,
well-plotted story line and the statement each makes about individuals caught in events with global consequences.

RICHARD TUCK, LAPD
1942-1952   5 books   American
Lange Lewis (Jane Beynon)

We were only able to locate one book from the middle of this
series; however, we were struck by the character of Tuck and the
clear portrayal of Los Angeles in the forties. We recommend the
series on the basis of this one novel and will let Tuck's author
describe him here.

Richard Tuck, of the Los Angeles Homicide Squad, was
regarded by his colleagues as being a rather queer duck. Concerning his own understanding of crime, he possessed a humil-
ity against which their glib cynicism rang hollow and empty.
He seemed careless of achieving a record for speedily winding
up cases in which he was involved, and showed instead a
disinclination to make an arrest without substantial evidence.
The result of this odd quirk was that no case of his which had
come to trial had ever been lost by the state. This gave him a
definite standing with Gufferty, the head of the Homicide
Squad, and, which was more important, with the District Attorney's office. A number of detectives were jealous of him. And
yet his convincing unconcern robbed their jealousy of much
point, and left many of them with a sense of most annoying
frustration regarding all six feet five inches of Richard Tuck.
They could never understand why when violent death left
its usual haunts on the wrong side of the tracks and entered a
home in Beverly Hills, a Los Angeles University or other such
genteel places, it was Tuck whom Gufferty placed in charge,

rather than one of themselves. It certainly wasn't that he was a smooth man; he was a slow man, and his inevitable brown suit was apt to want pressing. He took down his own notes in a strange private shorthand. He was grudging in giving information to reporters, yet somehow managed to retain their liking. They called him "The Moose." His final report of a case was long, involved, painstaking, watertight, and written in a flawless, if rather pedestrian, English prose.[4]

The plot of *The Birthday Murder* is well conceived and all the clues are present for the readers' edification. Tuck carries one along in his process of detection and the surprise at the end seems fair. The glamour and tinsel-draped side of southern California is present yet tempered with the fragility of careers built on air and the fickle nature of a public clamoring for excitement. Five Tuck books in ten years and one other nonseries work are the only mysteries author Lewis penned. We wish there were more and that the other titles were more readily available.

KNUTE SEVERSON, Boston Police
1966-1977   15 books   American
Tobias Wells (DeLoris Forbes)

The setting for the series featuring Detective Severson is Boston, Massachusetts, during the sixties and seventies. Civil rights activity, draft card burning, protests against American involvement in Vietnam, and massive power outages are hallmarks of the times, but, aside from serving as background and scene setting, none of these elements enter into the stories. Odd names and stereotypes salt the tales adding confusion though not much flavor.

Bland, blond Knute himself is of Swedish descent. His colleagues at Division Two view him as a lady's man and he does seem to have a way with the fair sex. It is, however, a way which never gets him anywhere. He lives alone with his cat, Mein Hair, and midseries, discovers Dutch beer. Insufficient as the above information may be, that's about all we can find to describe this representative of Boston's finest.

Knute's detecting skills are equally unremarkable. In *Dead By the Light of the Moon*, the connection between murder and a series of small robberies is vital to the outcome and is only made through Severson's whimsical hunch. *Die Quickly Dear Mother* takes place primarily in the courtroom, and while the detective does come up with the answer as to whodunit, and actually gets the perpetrator to confess, the case is never properly concluded, and on the last page the wrong suspect is still on his way to the electric chair.

Tobias Wells is the pseudonym for DeLoris Forbes who writes under several other pseudonyms as well. Knute is her only series character. In general, Forbes/Wells work is highly praised, though we can't find much to recommend in any of the Severson stories we read. What does arise for us are questions. Why choose to make her character a cop of Swedish descent in a locale which is stereotypically policed by the Irish? And why doesn't she do anything with what could be an interesting ethnic juxtaposition? Why, given Boston's history, color, and period, isn't more made of those elements in the novels? And, above all, why did she choose to center her stories around the police without using more in the way of procedural information?

All of this author's works were popular when first released and, more than twenty years after their initial appearance, are still favorably reviewed. Based on what we've read, we don't understand why. The Severson books are hard to find. We think we know the answer to that one.

LUIS MENDOZA, LAPD, Homicide
1960-1987   38 books   American
Dell Shannon (Elizabeth Linington)

Suave, elegant, expensively tailored, soft- and well-spoken Lieutenant Luis Mendoza has been a fixture in American crime literature for over twenty years. Eighteen years on the force when the series opens, Mendoza has risen up through the ranks from regulating traffic, through the vice squad, to homicide—first as sergeant and now as lieutenant. A poor boy originally from the Los Angeles barrio, Luis supplemented the family income from the time he was seventeen years old by running a Spanish Monte game, then later, by out-sharping the card sharps in a casino. Even then, he had class, a certain style, and an awareness beyond his years, of who he was and what he knew.

Some years after Luis joined the LAPD, his grandfather died, and far from being a pauper, the miserly old man had been rich beyond the family's wildest dreams. There was no longer a need for Luis to work. He could live well, even lavishly, on the income from all of those gilt-edged securities and investments in real estate. He's a good cop and takes pleasure in his job, less out of a need to serve justice but more a desire to find all of the pieces to the puzzle each case presents, to contemplate each separate piece, and finally, to contemplate the completely assembled puzzle in its entirety. The challenge of his job is what Mendoza needs. His salary as a cop wouldn't even buy his shirts.

All of the books in the series are of the police procedural type and some have a keen, hard-boiled edge to them. Shannon can write convincingly of sociopaths, giving the full measure of gore and horror to the crimes they commit and a smaller measure of authenticity to their compulsions in committing them. She can also craft believable accidental murderers and those for whom the act of murder is simply incidental. The hard-boiled edge of her stories is sometimes dulled by a formula approach. At those times, Mendoza and his colleagues act as functionaries and crime—even the most horrific sort—is just part of the job. The main attractions for readers clearly are Mendoza the man, his family, his pets, his various associates, and their personal lives. These are the primary features which keep readers coming back to this series again and again.

Mendoza is an instinctive detective. He does not simply sit and cerebrate, however, but often prefers to view the scene and the evidence himself. He delegates his subordinates' attention to the inevitable routine and usually sifts through the mountain of paperwork each case generates to find frequently disguised pieces of the puzzle. Mendoza relies on his understanding and appreciation of the natural order of things. He knows that the most complex problem can only have a simple solution and he knows that few problems facing the police are ever really complex. For this officer, it is a matter of collecting the pieces, arranging them, rearranging them as often as necessary until the picture emerges. And it always does.

In the first book of the series, *Case Pending*, Luis Rodolfo Vicente Mendoza meets Alison Weir. Always successful with the fair sex, he is set to enjoy her as he has the others. He is only a little surprised to find that she is more than any of the others and that he is ready to choose and to allow himself to be chosen. They marry, build a home on Royo Grande (Great Thunderbolt) Avenue and start a family. Bast, Luis' Abyssinian cat, adds to hers as well, producing El Señor, Sheba, and Nefertite. The twins and four cats create confusion and it is only when Mairi MacTaggart takes on the task of housekeeper that order is restored and maintained.

The series is chronological and elastic. In 1977, in *Appearances of Death*, Luis is forty-six years old and a twenty-five-year veteran of the force. Alison is expecting their third child and looking for a bigger house. In 1985, *Chaos of Crime* has Luisa, the Mendozas' third child still an infant, a fourth on the way and the twins angling for a swimming pool. Mairi still holds things together.

Dell Shannon has two other series under the pseudonym Lesley Egan and one under her real name, Elizabeth Linington. All of the series began in the early sixties and have run concurrently. A staunch supporter of law and order and a self-stated conservative in her political leanings, Shannon has, in Mendoza, created an almost completely anarchistic detective who serves law and order for his own reasons.

> And there are always, in any efficient city police force, the policemen like Luis Mendoza, single-mindedly, even passionately concerned to bring some order and reason, some ultimate shape, to the chaos. Not necessarily from any social conscientiousness—Mendoza cared little for humanity *en masse*, and was a complete cynic regarding the individual. Nor from any abstract love of truth or, certainly, of justice—for all too often the criminals he took for the law evaded punishment, this way or that way; and Mendoza sometimes swore and sometimes shrugged, but he did not lose any sleep over that. Being a realist, he said, *Lo que no se puede remediar, se ha de aguantar*—what can't be cured must be endured. Nor from ambition, to gain in rank and wages through zeal—Mendoza desired no authority over men, as he resented authority over men, as he resented authority himself.[5]

CHRISTIE OPARA, New York County District Attorney's Office
1968-1970   3 books   American
Dorothy Uhnak

In this three-book series, Uhnak describes a whole and very multidimensional character while leaving readers guessing just who Christie Opara really is. Opara works in the New York County District Attorney's Special Investigations Squad. She is the only woman assigned to the squad and a first-grade detective. She is there because she is good at her work and has established herself among her colleagues as a competent and reliable partner.

Casey Reardon, supervising assistant district attorney of New York County, leads the squad which investigates the interconnecting crimes which occur in and around the city. Organized crime in one form or another is the crux of the investigations carried out by Reardon and his staff. Links between narcotics dealings at the highest level, prostitution, religious charisma, and the student movements of the late sixties are made by the District Attorney's Office. The goal is to use the links to build strong cases against the lords of these underworld domains. Opara, Stoner Martin, Marty Ginsburg, Tom Dell, and Bill Ferranti detect at the instigation of Reardon. He holds the master plan of their actions and often has his minions carry out his instructions without explanation. Knowing and using the weaknesses as well as the strengths of his officers is one of Reardon's tactics. Opara is the only one who ever requires (or gets) a full explanation.

"Ah, come on Christie, didn't you ever play good-guy bad-guy before?"

"Is that what we were playing?"

"Think about it for a minute," he told her. His thumb jerked toward himself, his index finger pointed at her. "Bad-guy, good-guy. Elena watched you a hell of a lot closer than she watched me. She reacted to *your* reaction, not to what I said."

It made sense, yet Christie felt there was still something lacking in his explanation. It was a perfectly acceptable technique but there was a difference in the way Reardon used it.

He answered before she could state her objection. "I didn't set it up in advance for one very good reason. I didn't think you'd be able to carry it off." He grinned. "Honey, I'll go so far as to credit you with being one hell of a good detective, but I don't think you'd ever be good as an actress. For instance, right now. You should be playing the role of competent detective, agreeing with the boss that he had the right instincts on that particular score. Instead, you're glaring at me like a sore-headed twelve year old who's been kept out of part of the game. Come on, baby, grow up."

"That envelope *might* have slipped from your fingers," she said. "It just *might* have and..."

Casey Reardon tapped the edges of the papers together without taking his eyes from her. "You know, Christie, sometimes I wonder why the hell I feel that I owe you explanations of any kind."[6]

Personal tensions between Opara and Reardon add dimension to each book. The lives of other characters may seem more apparent as the stories unfold but the thread connecting Christie and Casey is strong and depends as much on who each is in relation to the other as on their professional designations.

Christie, widow of a police officer killed in the line of duty and mother of a young son Mickey, lives with her mother-in-law Nora, who cares for them both. They are a family, and the love, affection, and respect between them are obvious. Christie's job is central to her and to who she is. She occasionally feels bitter over her husband's untimely death but does not act from any sense of vengeance. Hers is rather a practical desire to be rid of the menace responsible for his death and the countless other deaths brought about by the organizers of crime.

Uhnak, herself a detective for the New York City Transit Police is no stranger to police procedure and the realities of justice. She writes what's true about crime, investigation and relationships from the perspective of a woman charged with maintaining order in a man's world with men's rules. After 1970, all of Uhnak's work has been non series crime fiction. In 1985, she wrote *Victims*, featuring Detective Miranda Torres. This could be a new series and we hope it is.

NORAH MULCAHANEY, NYPD
1972-1987   12 books   American
Lillian O'Donnell

Neither a desire for revenge nor a feminist chip on her shoulder have compelled Norah Mulcahaney into police work. Rather, a combination of family and economic factors have placed her in the ranks of the New York City police force and her innate sense of right and wrong has propelled her up the professional ladder to her position as a homicide detective.

When the man charged with raping a young neighbor of Norah's is acquitted of the crime in *Dial 577 R-A-P-E*, Norah is outraged. Determined to bring the perpetrator to justice, she effects a special assignment transfer to the new Rape Analysis and Investigation Squad where she uncovers evidence that the rapist may also be responsible for an as yet unsolved murder.

Still on special assignment, Norah moves to the Third District, where the murder has occurred, to work on the case. Her prospective colleagues, all male, are less than enthusiastic at the prospect of working with a woman. Reporting for duty, Norah firmly introduces herself.

"I'm Norah Mulcahaney," she announced and looked them over as frankly as they would have her if she hadn't beat them to it. Of the three she picked out the youngest—a short, chunky, broad-shouldered, heavily muscled redhead—Captain Blake had shown great concern for her personal safety. He wore a knit pullover with a turtleneck that came right up to the end of his chin and the loudest plaid sports jacket she'd ever seen. "You must be Detective Robert Hoff." She held out her hand.

Hoff gulped and took it. "How come you knew me?"

"You're the only one who blushed when I identified myself."

The other two smirked, and Hoff's face turned an even deeper red. The freckles disappeared in the wash of red; even his wavy red hair bristled.

"Score one for the lady." Voice number two took a step forward and offered his hand. "I'm Sal Parisi."

Number three did the same. "Nate Oberlander. Glad to have you with us."

"Thanks." Norah turned again to her newly assigned partner. "In case you're wondering how much I heard, I got to the door just when you were saying you hadn't joined the force to take orders from a woman. I think it's only fair for you to know the advance info I got about you."

"From the captain?" Hoff's high color faded, and his chubby face was creased with worry.

"I can't reveal my source, but it wasn't the captain. The word I got is not to underrate you."

Parisi and Oberlander gaped.

Norah went on coolly. "I also heard that you talk loud, but you're real cool in a crisis. I was told I could count on you."

"That's score two for the lady," Parisi said and let his admiration show.

"Thank you." Norah smiled politely. "About Detective Schonbar...he didn't miss a thing. The possible break in the Russo case wasn't anything he overlooked but a result of the investigation of a crime committed after he retired."

"Score three for the lady," chortled Hoff. "OK, Detective Mulcahaney, what's on the schedule?"

"My name's Norah, and I was just going to ask you."

Hoff beamed. "Well, I guess we ought to start at the beginning. Go back to the scene."

"Whatever you say."

"Lets go, then." Hoff sprang forward and reached for the door.

"We're partners, so I'll open my own doors and I'll pay for
my own coffee or beer or whatever. OK, Detective Hoff?"

"Call me Bobby."[7]

By defusing a confrontation she has actually set up, Norah
demonstrates one of her strongest abilities—that of using insight and
empathy together to prove her point while maintaining another's
self esteem. It is a technique she uses successfully with colleagues,
victims, and suspects alike.

The police procedural aspects of Mulcahaney's work are highly
apparent in each of the well-plotted stories. This is balanced by
Norah's personal life which is also an integral part of every book.
As the series progresses, Norah is courted by fellow officer Joe
Capretto, marries him, and is widowed. Norah's outspoken Irish
father and Joe's large Italian family are well portrayed and are at times
involved in the course of her cases. Solid detective work, loyalty,
and personal responsibility are hallmarks of this series. Mulcahaney
is portrayed as a whole person: woman, daughter, wife, and competent police officer.

The feminist movement opened doors of opportunity for women
in the seventies. Author O'Donnell has taken advantage of this opportunity to create a strong and believable female character in the
role of hero. O'Donnell occasionally has Norah react in a more obvious, almost stereotypical, feminine fashion. In doing so, however,
she casts Norah as Everywoman which only adds to this character's
validity. Stereotypes are, after all, patterned on archetypes.

JILL SMITH, Berkeley Police Department
1984-1987   5 books   American
Susan Dunlap

Graduate school at University of California, Berkeley, was the
draw for the professorial aspirations of Jill Smith's husband, Nat.
Looking for a job to support them while he finished his studies, Jill
took and passed the Berkeley patrol officer's test. The couple's stay
in Berkeley was to have been a temporary one, but four years locked
in less than blissful matrimony concluded that state, and after some
rather acrimonious bickering over objects acquired together, they
divorced and stayed on.

But I had come to love Berkeley, with its warm winters and
dry summers, its street artists, the coffee houses, the campus

haranguers, the Telegraph Avenue freaks, and the atmosphere that gave them freedom. I enjoyed the pottery studio that was open till midnight, where on my nights off I could throw lop-sided bowls and call them artistic. I liked my friend Sarah, who worked part-time and shared a tiny house because she wasn't willing to sell any more of her time, and Lydia, who designed and sewed wild and wildly expensive vests and dresses, and Jake at Super Copies, the poet—all the people who would never become staid and grown up. I wasn't willing to leave Berkeley, or my friends, or my career.[8]

Jill takes a room—actually a converted back porch— in a house belonging to her landlord, Mr. Kepple. Jalousied windows on three sides of the room provide light, air, and the sensation of camping out. Jill's lack of furniture and decorating intentions reinforce that ambiance; domesticity is clearly not her highest priority.

Lieutenant Davis, Jill's watch commander when she joined the force, has sponsored her rise up the ranks. It was he who insisted she go to homicide school and approved her promotion to the homicide detail. Seth Howard, six-foot-six and red haired, is Jill's closest friend both on the force and off. They often worked as part-ners until promotion for each moved them into different divisions. Their friendship and playful rivalry are not cluttered by romantic attachment. Connie Periera, beat officer, has a rather astonishing grasp of things of a fiscal nature and aids and supports Smith in her investigations. Herman Ott adds local color to Jill's cases. He is a shabby, secretive private detective who can be persuaded—for a price—to give Jill information. Many of his clients are addicts or dealers and he walks a fine line between his felonious clients and the police.

Jill Smith would not describe herself as an instinctive cop. Instead, she relies on legwork and facts rather than hunches or intuition. She has taken her training seriously and counts on that to protect her in unavoidable, threatening situations. She takes risks but they are calculated— no *macha bravada* here. Common sense, resource-fulness and an honest liking for her job are all that compel this character. The stories are of the procedural sort and author Dunlap has done her homework on both the city of Berkeley and the police who patrol it.

Jill Smith is a staunch representative of the new breed of indepen-dent women. Unlike Detectives Opara and Mulcahaney, she does not have to constantly prove her worth in a predominantly male world, therefore she takes the acceptance of her position for granted and is admired and respected by her colleagues. Jill has managed to set aside many of the day-to-day considerations most women contend with, such as husband and domestic routine, and in the process, finds that she prefers this level of independence. She possesses compassion and empathy but these virtues do not, in any way, compromise her judgment about people. Strong without being tough, Smith is the kind of officer we would want to find on any force in any city.

Susan Dunlap is an East Bay Area resident familiar with the color and oddity of the city of Berkeley. Her picture of the city and its inhabitants is clear, accurate, and entertaining. On the edge of the San Francisco Bay, on the westernmost edge of both the state of California and the North American continent, Berkeley is a city in the vanguard. The free speech movement was born there in the 1960's and People's Park was an issue worthy of the National Guard's attention. It is the home of the Gray Panthers, a senior citizens' activist group, and the Center for Independent Living, a disabled citizens' activist group. In her stories, Dunlap includes members of all these diverse walks of life. There is no sensationalism surrounding these people or locations any more than there is sensationalism surrounding Smith's work as a cop. All in all, this is a well-done series and we look forward to more. Dunlap has also created another series character, Vejay Haskell, a meter reader for PG&E in the Russian River area up the north coast of California. While the Haskell tales are entertaining and well written, Jill Smith remains our favorite.

THOMAS PITT, London Metropolitan
1979-1987   8 books   English
Anne Perry

Although this series is eight years old, the stories themselves take place in the late eighteen hundreds. Thomas Pitt is a member of the London Metropolitan Police and so serves as an effective bridge between those forces and the fabled Scotland Yard.

The times and the nature of the teeming city of London decree the necessity of an active police force. Its members, whose primary charge is to preserve the peace, often find themselves providing a rougher justice for the lower segments of society while protecting the upper classes as much from distasteful knowledge and intrusion as crime itself.

Married to the daughter of a quality family of the city, Pitt's investigations involve Charlotte and her friends and relations to an unusual degree. A loving husband and father, Pitt's natural inclination is to be protective of wife and children. His respect for Charlotte's intelligence and his desire to redress some of the wrongs perpetuated in part by a strictly classed society cause him to involve her both in his discussions and some of the more active aspects of his investigations.

The gentry prefer to remain uninformed of the more vile features of life and Pitt often finds himself—always an unwelcome caller in his official capacity—obliged to apprise them in a seemingly brutal fashion.

> "My wife, Mr.—er." He waved aside the necessity for recalling a name for a mere policeman. They were anonymous, like servants. "I'm sure there is no need for you to concern yourself. Arthur is sixteen. I have no doubt he is up to some prank. My wife is overprotective—women tend to be, you know. Part of their nature. Don't know how to let a boy grow up. Want to keep him a baby forever."
>
> Pitt felt a stab of pity. Assurance was so fragile. He was about to shatter this man's security, the world in which he thought he was untouchable by the sordid realities Pitt represented.
>
> "I'm sorry, sir," he said even more quietly. "But we have found a dead boy whom we believe may be your son." There was no point in spinning it out, trying to come to it slowly. It was no kinder, just longer.[9]

Power is held tightly by the upper classes and Pitt's superiors are at the mercy of those who hold the reins. They must preserve law and order but must refrain from making waves in high places. Pitt's own position, by virtue of his marriage connections, is supported by a segment of the higher echelon of society which has a growing awareness of social conditions. His integrity allows him to operate regardless of the restraints placed on him by those in authority. Not only does Pitt serve as a bridge between the metropolitan forces and Scotland Yard, he serves as a bridge between classes and centuries as well.

SCOTLAND YARD

Although the building is no longer reached via the gate through Scotland Yard, the name has remained, bringing instant recognition to almost everyone around the globe—even those who disdain mystery novels. Unlike the FBI in the United States, Scotland Yard is not a national police agency. The Yard's services include forensic science laboratories and the central criminal records office. Local forces throughout the United Kingdom may solicit assistance from Scotland Yard officers in the investigation of murder but are not required to seek their aid. This fact gives the Scotland Yard inspector enormous latitude in an investigation. Authors are well aware of this arrangement and take full advantage of both the rights *and* prohibitions under which these detectives operate.

SEPTIMUS FINCH
1938-1977   21 books   English
Margaret Erskine (Margaret Williams)

Margaret Erskine capitalizes on her character Septimus Finch's standing as a Yard officer to *prevent* him from having any official connection in the cases in which he gets involved. Finch falls over unexpected dead bodies in odd, out-of-the-way places throughout the British Isles. His standing as a Scotland Yard officer is either unstated or unwelcome to the local police officials. Each case usually involves: The House, The Storm, The Secret, The Ghost, The Muffled Whispers, and The Furtive Footsteps. These tales are frankly gothic in nature. Septimus himself, the seventh son of a Cornish family, is a student of sleight of hand and legerdemain, and well endowed with extrasensory perceptions. Operating ex officio, Finch has the opportunity to give his sixth and seventh senses free reign during an investigation. His reputation as one of the Yard's "Bright Boys" provides an amount of the necessary cachet with the local police superintendent and allows him more privileged information from reluctant locals than that available to the ordinary citizen.

The strong gothic overtones of this long-lived series hold little appeal for today's mystery buff. The stories do provide interesting glimpses of a certain segment of British society and are indicators of a standard of popularity present in the thirties and forties.

MACDONALD
1931-1959   47 books   English
E. C. R. Lorac (Edith Caroline Rivett)

This long-lived series opened in the early thirties and continued—often at the rate of two books per year—through the fifties. Author Lorac, under the pseudonym Carol Carnac created two other short series featuring, Inspector Ryvet and Inspector Julian Rivers. Few of these books are available today. In fact, we have never found Ryvet or Rivers and only three Macdonalds. Nevertheless, the books we did find are captivating little tales, less for the main character than for the individuals populating the stories and providing the action for the Scotland Yard detective.

Macdonald himself is a Londoner by upbringing but a Highlander by both birth and inclination. At the end of the series, the superintendent has bought a farm, Fellcock, above the village of Crossghyll to which he plans to retire. The action in *Dishonour Among Thieves* takes place in and around Crossghyll and its neighboring industrial town of Lunesdale. Unprepossessing in looks and manner, Macdonald is a man of both conviction and compassion with an understanding and appreciation of human nature and its potential.

> Macdonald was, essentially, a humane man. Though it had been his lot to arrest murderers and other evildoers, he had never forgotten that a criminal may suffer, and the sight of intense suffering is ill for any humane man to witness. Macdonald stood there while the seconds ticked away, and then he said quietly: "What's the matter?"[10]

This humanity permeates his investigations and interrogations. Victims and suspects speak willingly to him as they see in him a fairness which insures that their words will not be misinterpreted nor used against them, out of context. The quality most prominent in this detective is that of guardian rather than that of hunter.

Macdonald's personality does not intrude into his cases though it is clearly he who directs things to their outcome. It is the vitality of the other characters and their relationships to one another which provide the fascination and tension to these relatively short books. Macdonald comes in, does his job using his authority appropriately, and leaves only a faint wake as the case concludes.

We want to read the entire series and, if the books are really no longer available in the original, hope they are soon reissued.

HANNASYDE and HEMINGWAY
1935-1953   8 books   English
Georgette Heyer

The series featuring Superintendent Hannasyde and Sergeant Hemingway can best be described as drawing room crime. The suspects are invariably related to one another and the scene is the country home or London house of a wealthy individual or family. The related suspects are usually eccentric. The heir may disdain his anticipated wealth or be brusque to the point of rudeness toward his benefactor. Other members may be vague and flighty or their nerves so highly strung that when the crime—always murder—is discovered, they dissolve into tears and remain prostrate for most of the rest of the novel, except for meals. There is a liberal dose of romance, as a rule, between two people who haven't the slightest idea that they are attracted to one another. They spit and snap at each other but the threat of incarceration for one of the pair brings out the other's true feelings. The unknown beloved is defended and at the end true love is recognized for what it is and the happy couple are united.

The first four books feature the detecting duo of Hannasyde and his sergeant, Hemingway. The last four have Hemingway, now promoted to inspector himself, on his own. Hannasyde's appearance is limited to brief conversations over the phone with either his former sergeant or the chief constable of the locality which requires expert assistance. These detectives are personifications of the Yard and their personalities rarely intrude upon the case. They are pleasant and have great appreciation for a good lie. Hemingway tends to favor a psychological approach to suspect and victim alike. His flair leads him toward the belief that when a case seems most hopelessly confused, it is near its conclusion. Hannasyde is more prosaic and gives Hemingway's theories short shrift. Both men are methodical though not to the point of tedium. Their lives outside the investigation seem nonexistent.

Locked rooms, missing weapons, and airtight alibis for all potential suspects provide the necessary bafflement. The solution requires some solid knowledge on the author's part of pathological motivations and infernal devices. These stories are neat puzzles, in the classical form, with the emphasis on character and well-devised plot. The victim is well out of the way and the perpetrator deserves all he gets in consequence of his crime. Love is requited and all ends happily.

BURNIVEL
1953-1971 3 books English
Edward Candy (Barbara Alison Neville)

The first two books in this series have medical themes and feature Fabian Honeychurch, Professor of Child Health in the University of London and President of the Royal College of Pediatricians. When it becomes necessary to call in Scotland Yard, Honeychurch prevails upon his acquaintance with Inspector Burnivel who arrives as the official investigator. Together, these two professionals conclude the cases in which they are mutually though separately involved. The third book takes place in the same location as the second, the town of Bantwich. The Yard, personified by Burnivel, is called in as there is a multiplicity of murder far beyond the scope of the local constabulary. Honeychurch is not present in this last investigation.

Burnivel is small, compact, and dark haired. He is a neat if uninspiring-looking gentleman whose dedication to his calling sometimes makes him impatient with his lack of progress towards a solution. This impatience manifests itself in frustration, an almost childish temper, and infantile tendencies.

> Burnivel sucked his knuckles: this was not the undiscarded, comfortable habit of his nursery days, but an action dictated by sheer necessity as a consequence of premeditated violence. Convention and law alike having denied him the chance of relieving his feelings by punching Garside's shapely jaw, he had waited only till the doors of the lecture theatre closed behind the erect, fastidious figure to punish the bench before him with a mighty blow from his clenched fist.[11]

Inspector Burnivel is almost a convention in this short series. What makes these books worth reading is not the presence of a Scotland Yard detective, but intricacies of plot and well-presented narratives. Characters do not really shine forth, though Fabian Honeychurch and Gregory Roberts are very effective focal points for the action in the books in which they appear. Burnivel could almost be any detective whose name had reached the top of the rota, but Candy has chosen this particular official of the force of law and order on which to hang the series. The authority of the Yard must have been seen by this author as necessary to conclude the cases. The books have all been recently rereleased. This is, no doubt, due to their classic form and enjoyability.

WILFRED DOVER
1964-1980   21 books   English
Joyce Porter

The series featuring Detective Chief Inspector Wilfred Dover must be read to be believed. Like some of his literary colleagues, Dover's resemblance to a policeman eludes most people, though not for the usual reasons.

> "So you're the detective from London, are you?" he rasped, eyeing Dover up and down with ill-disguised surprise. Most people, it must be confessed, evinced a certain amount of simple disbelief when they saw Chief Inspector Dover for the first time. He chimed so ill with the popular romantic image of a senior policeman. He was too fat, too shabby and too surly-looking. Adding to which he had a paunch, chronic dyspepsia and acute dandruff. Where were the keen grey eyes, the high intelligent forehead, the wide generous mouth crinkling slightly at the corners in a benevolent smile? Not, it was only too obvious, in Wilfred Dover's lowering, heavy-jowled mug.[12]

His appearance does not belie his abilities. If anything, he is even less apt than his description would lead one to imagine. It is only the fact that Dover's quarry is even more repellent and bungling than he is, that justice is ever served.

Detective Sergeant Charles Edward MacGregor is Dover's long-suffering assistant. Where Dover is gross and uncouth, MacGregor is elegant and polished. Dover will cast aside any piece of evidence which does not square with his preformed view of the case. MacGregor carefully and conscientiously collects and reviews clues to the case and follows his superior's blundering charge with solid detective procedure. Eating and sleeping are Dover's primary activities and the stories are punctuated with his snores and belches. A more odious figure is hard to imagine (though readers are invited to meet Porter's two other series characters before forming a final judgment on repugnance).

Dover is the antithesis of all that Scotland Yard stands for. His presence on the force is a continuing embarrassment, but his prejudicial views and slipshod methods have a measure of merit as Dover always gets his man. Neither the character nor the series are among our favorites. We must admit a grudging admiration for the author who, if nothing else, is one of the most consistent in the genre.

HENRY TIBBETT
1959-1987   18 books   English
Patricia Moyes

Henry Tibbett's special interest is in international drug traffic. His work over the years has given him connections with the police of countries all over the continent and the United States and provided strong ties with Interpol.

His professional dedication becomes obvious as the series progresses though this professionalism never gives lie to his gentle nature. Mild-mannered and likable, Henry is a comfortable sort of fellow, rather avuncular in nature. He makes friends easily and people find themselves talking openly with him, even after they discover that he is a police officer. Henry fits into most surroundings as an unobtrusive part of the landscape. He possesses no special chameleon qualities. He is just Henry Tibbett, a man who knows who he is and has no need to prove it to himself or to others. Henry does possess a "nose." That he feels some small discomfort at the recognition of this intuition demonstrates that this is no Super Cop. Discomfort aside, Henry trusts his nose and uses his intuitive ability in conjunction with his professional training to successfully conclude his cases.

One of Tibbet's greatest assets is his wife, Emmy. They pass easily for innocent and interested tourists as they travel, picking up friends and acquaintances as they gather clues and information concerning Henry's cases. At home, Emmy provides Henry with a haven from the rigors of duty and a warm, inviting place to entertain their many friends. In the field, she does more than simply provide her husband with cover. She assists him in gathering data and occasionally acts as decoy or bait.

In all of the novels, Henry Tibbett comes across as a complete and very whole personality. Moyes does not withhold information about this man in either his professional or his private capacities. Small domesticities abound and are not irrelevant to the story being told. The partnership between Henry and Emmy is obviously a loving one. It is also one of mutual respect and support. These elements are apparent in their dealings with friends and relatives as well. We wouldn't mind being courtesy nieces of this warm pair.

Moyes' plots are intriguing and her locations interesting and inviting. Characters featured in one book can appear in another. These readers want more of the wonderfully eccentric Manciple family which includes among its scatty members the Bishop of Bugolaland

and his crossword brain. While this series can be described as lightly humorous, the detecting is solid and the stories well told.

TOM POLLARD
1967-1986   16 books   English
Elizabeth Lemarchand

Inspector Tom Pollard is the solid sort of bedrock material upon which the Yard is founded. Large and ordinary looking, Pollard walks into a room and its occupants know that The Police have arrived. Detective Sergeant Toye, the inspector's assistant in all stories, is equally unremarkable in appearance but possesses a disarming quality which takes people's minds off of the fact that they are being interviewed by Authority. Together, these two have been bringing criminals to justice for twenty years. Their method of detecting can only be described as methodical.

> Jane Pollard called her husband a compulsive tabulator. When on a case his invariable method was to get the results of fieldwork on to paper as quickly as possible. In this way the confused mass of statements and impressions which, in the raw, merely gave him mental indigestion, was reduced to assimilable columns of related facts. These lists, made on sheets from pads which he carried round with him for the purpose, were known to his colleagues and subordinates as Pollard's washing bills, and had become a standing joke. As a case progressed they were duly amended or rewritten. Sergeant Toye, trained in the technique, was now equally addicted to it.[13]

Pollard is portrayed as a family man with strong and tender feelings for his wife Jane, and their twins, Andrew and Rose. Like Emmy Tibbett, Jane is an asset to her husband's investigations though less of a presence on the actual scene. Most of Jane's assistance is rendered over the phone in the automotive code she and Tom have developed over the years. An artist and art historian whose career was suspended during the twin's early years, Jane has given Tom some basic information on pictures and painting technique which he puts to good use in a couple of stories involving fine art forgery and theft. Though infrequently together, Jane and the twins are always in Pollard's mind and readers are kept aware of Rose and Andrew's growth and progress throughout the series.

These novels are distinctive for their superfluity both of characters and coincidence. Plots and subplots abound and red herrings are freely strewn about the landscape. Pollard's timetable is essential not only for the detectives but for the readers as well. Recurring themes include: convoluted inheritances, illegitimacy, purloined documents, and art treasures. The ultimate clue is often a piece of information casually thrown out by an individual unconnected with any aspect of the investigation to that point. Oddly enough, what could be seen as drawbacks to a successful series are things that Lemarchand makes work in her characters' favor. Solid and foursquare, Pollard and Toye gather and sift evidence and clues, and devise an airtight case against the perpetrator. Lemarchand gives readers all the information necessary to arrive at the same conclusion as her detectives. Sometimes there is a twist at the end of the tale but one which is always fairly given.

ADAM DALGLIESH
1962-1986   8 books   English
P. D. James

In the course of an investigation, Scotland Yard detective Adam Dalgliesh lays bare parts of many personalities.

"...It certainly looks like a small cut but it's ridiculously small. In two days it won't be visible. Are you sure you don't want to photograph it?"

"No thank you," said Dalgliesh. "We've had something rather more serious to photograph upstairs."

It gave him considerable satisfaction to watch the effect of his words. While he was in charge of this case none of his suspects need think that they could retreat into private worlds of detachment or cynicism from the horror of what had laid on the bed upstairs. He waited for a moment and then continued remorselessly.[14]

A combination of provocation and patience form a single nameless element in this character. An element which enables Dalgliesh to absorb an enormous amount of datum and then, within himself, distill it down to its very essence of truth. Out of the morass of information emerge clues and out of the clues arise the pattern. This pattern is, for Dalgliesh, the signature of the criminal. Not incidentally, this element serves him both as a detective and as a poet.

Unlike most other detective novels, readers are given additional insights into character through the individuals connected to the case. There is a certain honesty in many of these self-revelations, which give even the most minor character in the story substance. These insights often include the suspects' view of the detective himself. While some are rather predictable reactions to a policeman and his duty, others are remarkably accurate in the reading of this remote, and somewhat obsessed, inspector.

The person of Adam Dalgliesh emerges slowly over the series' span of twenty-four years. Details about this enigmatic detective are sparingly woven into the narrative of the eight novels in which he appears. Only son of a canon of the Church of England, Adam's upbringing was one of isolation and introspection. The death of his wife in childbirth is at first a sadness, and later a liberation for Dalgliesh. Tall, dark, and handsome is the convenient, stock phrase which describes his physical appearance. As the series evolves, he is seen to be ruthless and rather unorthodox. That he is a successful poet is ironic. How, one asks, can such a reserved and private person expose so much in such a public fashion?

This series and its main character are difficult to summarize. There are similarities to other Scotland Yard detectives, beyond the job of investigating crime, that Dalgliesh shares with his fictional counterparts. Characters from one book appear in others. Dalgliesh suffers a crisis of faith, brought about by ill health and stress. And, in one story, works ex officio to solve a crime which would never have been seen as one had he not appeared on the scene quite incidentally.

There, however, the similarity ends. James' emphasis is less on the acts of crime and more on the effects of crime on people and their society. This does not diminish her qualities as a master of the genre. Plot and puzzle are there for those who enjoy those aspects. Her presentation of the complexities of human experience and foibles of human nature enhance these aspects and allow these books to be read again and again. It comes as no surprise when critics aver that James has taken the traditional detective novel and elevated it to the status of the mainstream.

RICHARD JURY
1981-1987   9 books   English
Martha Grimes

When Richard Jury walks into a room, women auto-matically take out their mirrors. At six-foot-two, with reddish brown hair and eyes the color of old, well-cared-for pewter, his effect upon the fair sex is hardly surprising. Jury is another Scotland Yard detective whose resemblance to a policeman is almost nonexistent. His low, well-modulated voice is ideal for soothing bereaved victims as well as for disarming the suspects he questions.

> In the expanding silence, Riddley tapped ash from his cigarette and said, "Superintendent, I confess in the face of your relentless questioning."
> Jury smiled. "To what?"
> "Anything, anything. You've asked exactly two questions since you walked in the door. No, three, with that last one. You've simply let me yammer on and on..."[15]

Where Dalgliesh is provocative, Jury is compassionate. Like Dalgliesh, Jury is gifted with a boundless patience and a relentless approach to the truths in a case. Unlike Dalgliesh, Jury likes small children and communicates well with them. In almost every one of the nine books in this series, a child or an adolescent, often in the company of an animal, is one of his allies and informants. His own early life has inclined him towards introspection and it is from a point of self-reference that he views the world and its inhabitants with understanding and empathy.

Jury's hypochondriacal sergeant, Wiggins, is a constant test of Jury's compassion. A young man made old by a variety of symptoms, both real and imagined, Wiggins is, nevertheless, an efficient and talented officer. Jury accepts and overlooks the long list of ailments and complaints under which Wiggins labors and en-courages that young man to rise above his considerations and get on with the job at hand. Oddly enough, the handkerchiefs and lozenges with which Wiggins is always amply supplied, can have moments of valor of their own. Jury's life is saved by some cough drops—though not by their ingestion—which Wiggins provided at the first hint of catarrh in his superior's nasopharyngeal passages. While there are times when Jury wishes he were assigned another sergeant, as the series progresses he comes to terms with the fact that he and Wiggins do work well together and that this particular sergeant is a valuable and valued partner.

Superintendent Racer is Jury's superior at the Yard. Eager to get work off his desk by giving it to someone else, Racer is a vain and preening peacock of a man who rests on the laurels of his title and the accomplishments of his subordinates. His unsubtle disparagements are designed to keep Jury under his thumb and out in the field where he will be a less obvious threat to Racer's position. Fiona Clingmore, secretary, and Cyril, the office cat, keep things running in the frequent absence of the superintendent and provide unnecessary, though always welcome support for Jury in his encounters with his titular superior.

Wealthy and aristocratic Melrose Plant is Jury's closest friend. They meet in the first book, *The Man With a Load of Mischief*, when Jury arrives in the village of Long Piddleton to investigate the murder of a guest at the Jack and Hammer Pub. Long Pid, as it's known to its inhabitants, is the village nearest to Ardry End, seat of the earldom which Melrose has renounced. Each man strikes a chord in the other and at the end of the story, Plant writes to Jury, bringing him up to date on the events in the lives of mutual acquaintances and expressing a polite and uncloaked desire to be included in another investigation—which of course he is. It is usually Melrose's connections that put him in the neighborhood of Jury's detectings and while Jury is perfectly capable of holding his own with members of the aristocracy and landed gentry, he is always gladdened by Plant's presence and insights into the personae involved.

While Jury the man is similar to Dalgliesh in manner and method, the stories themselves have more the flavor of Moyes' work featuring Henry Tibbett. There is a lightness present in these tales which make them enjoyable reading. Like the Tibbett series, settings and characters provide much of the charm and appeal. There is a recurring cast of Plant's eccentric neighbors, relatives, and staff. Jury lives in London and provides still another set of regulars—other residents of the building in which he lives: Mrs. Wasserman, afraid of her own shadow and of the mysterious, perhaps imaginary stranger who lurks in wait for her, and Carole-anne Palutski, a nineteen-year-old topless dancer whose charms are wasted on Jury. She declares him to be her first failure. Jury states that he may be her first success.

Jury and Plant form a frame. Within this structure, other characters and the events in their lives, including murder, are displayed—bordered and defined by the aspects of perspective provided by Grimes' protagonists. Well plotted, well told, and well peopled, these books can be read in any order and read often.

RODERICK ALLEYN
1934-1982   32 books   English
Ngaio Marsh

Roderick Alleyn of the Criminal Investigation Division of Scotland Yard is one of the few aristocrats officially connected to the forces of law and order. Second son of a baronet, Alleyn was educated at Eaton and Oxford (Lord Peter Wimsey's alma mater) and trained for the diplomatic service. At the age of twenty-two, he left the corps to become a police officer for reasons never explained though described as a remarkable story.

Alleyn's brother, Sir George, ranks high in diplomatic circles, if low in his brother's opinion. Lady Alleyn, their mother, makes frequent appearances in the books and has great respect and admiration for her younger son. Other characters appear with some regularity in the thirty-two books of this well-known series. Journalist Nigel Bathgate opens the first book, *A Man Lay Dead*, as a member of a houseparty where the murder of his cousin, Charles Rankin, occurs. Dismissed as a suspect by Alleyn early in the case, Bathgate becomes the detective's confidante and aid in solving the murder and fulfills the same function in subsequent stories.

Alleyn's usual cohort in investigations is Inspector Fox—a man who looks like a policeman and comports himself with the almost ponderous dignity of his calling. He must have a first name but is generally referred to by his superior (in rank only) as Br'er Fox or Foxkin. A master of understatement and truly welcomed below stairs, Fox is an effective counterweight for Alleyn. Detective sergeants Bailey, the fingerprint expert, and Thompson, the police photographer, are early on the scene of most cases. Their presence may be only functional as they rarely have much dialogue nor do they appear often, but Alleyn himself admits that he would be all at sea without their valuable contributions. Mr. Rattisbon is the archetypal family lawyer, dry as the ancient documents entrusted to his legal care. In this long series, it is possible for the ancillary characters to develop along with the primary character. Marsh's theatrical attention to setting, detail, and cast makes these people real to readers, and their continuing presence is a clever way to open the world and provide new vistas and perspectives to the major player in the scenario.

Alleyn is described as a cross between a monk and a grandee. Where Fox is ponderous, Alleyn is elegant and moves with streamlined grace, from English drawing room to New Zealand sheep station. When the upper classes are involved in crime, the presence of this gentleman is a comfort. One can almost forget that this tall, slim, well-tailored person is a member of His/Her Majesty's finest. In writing up his cases, the press often refer to him as Handsome Alleyn—a name he deplores but one which provides the lower classes with a form of satisfaction. H-A somehow seems approachable. Although his fount of British reserve seems endless, he has his moments of true humanity as when he discovers that the body of a murdered cab fare is that of an old and valued friend.

> "Mr. Alleyn?"
> But Alleyn did not answer. He was alone with his friend. The small fat hands were limp. His feet were turned in pathetically, like the feet of a child. The head leant sideways, languidly, as a sick child will lean its head. He could see the bare patch on the crown and the thin ruffled hair.
> "If you look froo the other winder," said the driver, "you'll see 'is face. 'E's dead all right. Murdered!"
> Alleyn said: "I can see his face."
> He had leant forward and for a minute or two he was busy. Then he drew back. He stretched out his hand as if to close the lids over the congested eyes. His fingers trembled.
> He said: "I mustn't touch him any more." He drew his hand away and backed out of the taxi. The sergeant was staring in astonishment at his face.
> "Dead," said the taxi-driver. "Ain't he?"
> "—you!" said Alleyn with a violent oath. "Can't I see he's dead without—"
> He broke off and took three or four uncertain steps away from them. He passed his hand over his face and then stared at his fingers with an air of bewilderment.[16]

Unlike many of his fictional counterparts, Alleyn courts and marries in the course of the series. The couple first meets in *Artists in Crime*, on a cruise ship bound from New Zealand. As the story progresses, painter Agatha Troy becomes a suspect in the murder of the artists' model posing for a class she teaches. Reserve and reticence prevent Alleyn from pressing his suit for some time and when he does begin wooing Troy in earnest, his progress is painfully slow. Raymond Chandler notwithstanding, the love interest Marsh adds to this series is not a distraction. It furthers the development of the detective as a person and allows another dimension of his personality to be brought forth. Alleyn's feelings for Troy and, later on, their small son Ricky permeate his investigations giving him both respite from and insight for his deliberations.

ALAN GRANT
1929-1952   6 books   English
Josephine Tey (Elizabeth MacKintosh)

> If Grant had an asset beyond the usual ones of devotion to duty and a good supply of brains and courage, it was that the last thing he looked like was a police officer.[17]

Alan Grant is a gentleman. An inheritance has made it unnecessary for him to work for a living. The work he does, however, is what he loves and that for which he is well suited. Little is known about Grant's origins. He describes a grandfather as a renegade Scot and never speaks of his parents. He lives in a comfortable flat and is cared for by devoted housekeepers (Field and Tinker). Most of his life is lived among his colleagues and through his investigations. Grant is well thought of by both his superiors and his subordinates. He and Sergeant Williams, Grant's faithful Watson in all cases, provide a balance for each other and share a high, mutual regard.

Along with the advantage of not looking like a policeman, Grant possesses "flair." Like Tibbett's nose, this flair is an intuitive grasp of information beyond the normal limits of conscious thinking. However, what Grant knows intuitively is not always born out by the evidence in a case. At times, his colleagues and his own professionalism force him to disregard his flair. It is a powerful force of its own though and worries away at Grant's thinking until he is compelled to do something to acknowledge its significance. In *The Man in the Queue*, his flair acts as a double-edged sword, first leading Grant to the discovery and capture of a fleeing suspect, then acting preconsciously to make him uncomfortable with a too neatly concluded case.

Grant was introduced in 1929 as a developed personality, and over the twenty-three years the series spans, this remains consistent. In the third book, *The Franchise Affair*, written twelve years after the second, Grant makes only a token appearance as Scotland Yard personified, yet even in this brief role, his flair is mentioned. Grant is in charge again in *To Love and Be Wise*, and continues to grow in stature (quite literally from medium height in 1929 to six-foot-plus in 1950).

The Singing Sands, published the year Tey died, is, in every sense, the last book in the series. On leave from his job, Grant is feeling the effects of overwork manifested by severe claustrophobia. Leaving the train which has taken him to the Scots Highlands, where he has gone to recuperate, Grant is confronted with the dead body of a young man in a sleeping compartment. Something in the young man's countenance and the few lines of poetry scribbled in the margin of a newspaper compel Grant to investigate what evidence and authority declare to be an accident. The ex officio investigation is at once Grant's salvation and the means to bring his career at the Yard to an end.

Tey is a true master of her craft. There is a cohesiveness to this short series despite the twelve-year gap between the second and third books, the intervention of two nonseries mystery novels and the apparent attempt to write Grant off as a minor character in *The Franchise Affair*. The success of Tey's novels does not lie in the presence of a dead body and the detection of the perpetrator of murder. She effectively demonstrates, through the perceptions of her main character, that what seems one thing is often, in reality, quite another, and that the other is not necessarily less a crime than the act of murder. Tey's mastery is the ability to use character and setting to subtly guide the reader to precisely the conclusion she has drawn, while keeping the reader unaware of being led. These books can be read as good, escapist mystery stuff. Don't be surprised however, to know more after you've read a Tey novel than you thought you had learned.

THE PROVINCIALS

Our dictionary gives one definition of *province* as:

> an administrative district or division of a country, all of a
> country except the metropolis.[18]

All of the following characters come from areas which fit that
definition to a *T*. Most of them were born in or near the district in which they now pursue their profession and all feel
strong ties and obligations to their particular domains and its
indigenes.

Within this category, there are contrasts. England's shires and
counties are long settled and have been well ordered for centuries.
Canada is bursting with raw power and energy and the American
West still has an untamed air about it. For all the differences these
localities represent, the tasks with which their guardians are charged
are similar: understand the territory, and be a friend to and defender
of the populace.

The metropolis can be a place of anonymity. The country rarely
is. One is known to one's neighbors in small towns, villages, and
on farm or ranch land. Strangers are always obvious. It takes a
special sort of soul to make a good provincial peace officer—one
who can use information which the combination of position and
long residence in one place provides, while suspending judgment
over some of the information and the informants. Town and
country each has its needs and these country crime fighters meet
the needs of their respective regions commendably.

COCKRILL
1941-1968   8 books   English
Christianna Brand

Some of the crime and mystery genre's best-contrived
puzzles have been crafted by Christianna Brand in her series featuring Inspector Cockrill of the Kent Constabulary. The plausibility
of cases built up against a small, select number of suspects is amazing. Clues, red herrings, and clues disguised as red herrings are
skillfully woven through each tale and are carried by the dialogue
and behavior of those involved. It is possible to figure out who the
murderer is as Brand lays the true trail as carefully as the false ones.

One is not, however, surprised at being surprised when the killer is unmasked at the end of the story.

Kentishman Cockrill is not as much a man of the land as some of his successors in the profession. He has lived in the region long enough to know most inhabitants, many from their childhoods. A sort of universal uncle, the inspector arrives at the scene of the crime and provides everyone with a mixture of avuncular reassurance and admonishment.

> Inspector Cockrill was a little brown man who seemed much older than he actually was, with deep-set eyes beneath a fine broad brow, an aquiline nose and a mop of fluffy white hair fringing a magnificent head. He wore his soft felt hat set sideways, as though he would at any moment break out into an amateur rendering of 'Napoleon's Farewell to his Troops'; and he was known to Torrington and in all its surrounding villages as Cockie. He was widely advertised as having a heart of gold beneath his irascible exterior; but there were those who said bitterly that the heart was so infinitesimal and you had to dig so deep down to get to it, that it was hardly worth the trouble. The fingers of his right hand were so stained with nicotine as to appear to be tipped with wood.[19]

This inspector has a great deal of personality. However, all manifestations of this quality are limited to his professional life. Clues to his history can be found in early books but this historical background seems irrelevant to the investigations. Cockrill is not limited to operations within his home territory. Two of his cases take place in London where he works together with one of Brand's other series characters, Inspector Charlesworth of Scotland Yard, and the last novel in which Cockie appears takes place on the imaginary Mediterranean island of San Juan el Pirata.

The series is consistent in several regards. The puzzle aspect is always foremost, enhanced by good, believable dialogue and action between a small cast of suspects. An interesting consistency is that the murderers are often tainted with some form of mental aberration, though this is not made clear until the case is finally resolved. There is evidence of wit and humor in the earlier books but in *Tour de Force*, the setting is almost comic opera and there is rampant silliness right up to the end. *Three Cornered Halo*, featuring Cockie's sister, Harriet, takes place on this infernal island paradise though the inspector himself does not appear. This island is also mentioned in *The Rose of Darkness*, which features Inspector Charlesworth.

Brand's literary crime career spans the years from 1941 up to the present. Nearing eighty now, she manages to bring touches of the modern to her tales while holding on to a sense of morality more prevalent in the society of years-gone-by. The Inspector Cockrill series has been recently reissued in paperback. Not surprising for these classic puzzlers.

MALLETT
1938-1959   18 books   English
Mary Fitt (Kathleen Freeman)

The series featuring Superintendent Mallett fits the category of the English classic in that the setting is invariably the country manor home and the cast is made up of those from the upper classes, either monied or aspiring to wealth and usually related by blood or marriage. The tales are hardly cozy though, as fear, loathing, and jealousy are the compelling forces behind the murders which bring the superintendent and his unofficial partner, Dr. Fitzbrown, on the scene.

Large, with a florid complexion, red hair, luxuriant moustache, and green eyes, Mallett is The Police personified.

"In short, they have a definite suspicion against someone?"
"I wouldn't go so far as to say that. Let us say they are exploring the possibilities—which may be several—and leave it at that. Mallett is in charge of the case, you know. He's a good man—a dangerous customer, because he's unorthodox in his approach; and yet he looks so much like a policeman that people are apt to underrate him."[20]

Mallett does not seem to adhere to one particular method of detecting. Sometimes he questions suspects extensively, at other times, he leaves the questioning to Fitzbrown as people often talk more easily to doctors than to policemen. The superintendent winds up his cases and gets full credit for solving the crime but the solution is frequently delivered by one of the suspects or brought about by the confession of the guilty party.

The characters which appear in the stories are united in misery— not necessarily that brought by murder in their midst. There may be a love interest or two but it is unrequited, thwarted, misdirected, or unregarded emotion. Parents and siblings conspire together against other family members and accusations against all and sundry are hurled in the general direction of Mallett who catches and juggles all of the evidence—circumstantial and factual. Mental instability and a marvelous ability to keep secrets characterize at least one individual in each case and compound the welter of clues and suspects.

Fitt began the Mallett books at the end of the thirties and the series holds the flavor of those times even though it spans twenty years. There is a keen intelligence behind the creation of these confusing tales. Fitt plays fair by laying out enough clues for the reader to arrive at the correct answer. Her detective, Mallett himself, does not provide much in the way of distraction. In most books, there is a twist at the end which, while explicable and fair, can be somewhat of an anticlimax. For readers who enjoy drawing room crime with psychological overtones, Fitt fits the bill.

CHARMIAN DANIELS
1962-1981   8 books   English
Jennie Melville (Gwendoline Butler)

Even though books in this series are hard to come by, and the only one we located is the next to last novel, we have included this character because she is one of the few fictional female police officers and the only one we found who is both English and provincial.

In *A New Kind of Killer*, Daniels is on leave from the Deerham Hills Police Force and attending the University of Midport to earn a diploma in criminology. The university is feeling the effects of the sixties and seventies and is plagued by student rebellion and uprisings. Along with her tasks as a student, Daniels is lecturing to policewomen cadets in their training course and simultaneously operating undercover to find the real leaders of the student activities. Although representing law and order—the other side of chaos—Charmian, too, is a product of the era. Her professional experience has focused her attention on some of the apparent changes in the crime statistics. In conversation with a former police colleague, now lodgings officer to the university, she says,

> "...What I want to do on my own is a study of the new patterns of crime."
> "There is one?" asked Alda skeptically.
> "Yes, Alda, think about it," said Charmian. "Haven't you been following what's been happening? There's been a

tremendous increase in violent crime in the young age groups, the under twenties."

"Well, I know that."

"But, Alda, you see what it means. The population is growing younger all the time. And with more young *men* in it than young women. So there's going to be more young criminals. What's more there's going to be more of them relative to the rest of the population. Give us a decade or two and the statistics say that about one man in three will have a violent act in his past."

"Yes, that's bad," said Alda.

"It's worse than that," said Charmian. "Already only four cases out of ten in every violent crime, like murder, are cleared up. That's a bad clear-up rate," she said seriously. "What's society going to look like if that's the way it goes."

"Well, how is it going to look?"

"Violent," said Charmian. "Full of young, casual violence. Why we're going to have to recognize that we're creating a new kind of killer. Boyish, casual, and committing murder almost without thought."

"And undiscovered," said Alda wryly.[21]

Daniels deals with this new kind of killer in her positions as lecturer and undercover agent. A young policewoman who attends Charmian's classes is killed in the line of duty by one of the new breed and the violence directed towards the university and its members is generated by others of just this sort as well. While she is aware of a trend in the direction of crime and criminals, Daniels is unprepared to deal with the effects it has on her personally. Her professional position and the insight she has gained on the job carry her over the rough spots and she is able to solve the murder of her friend Alda as the book closes.

It is difficult to judge Charmian Daniels, either personally or professionally, on the basis of one book. Our conclusion is that this is a young woman with strong intentions, a clear head, and a resourceful nature. We would like to read more about her and to see her operate at home in Deerham Hills.

Jennie Melville is the pseudonym of Gwendoline Butler, creator of the Inspector John Coffin series. The Coffin books are equally hard to find even though the fifteen-book series has run for nearly thirty years and is well received in Butler's native England.

RUDD (Finch in England)
1971-1987   12 books   English
June Thomson

Rudd is an Essexman. Large, rumpled, and comfortable, he looks like a farmer. His ties to the land reinforce this vision. This is a man operating in home territory, among familiar folk. Rudd has turned the landsman's skill toward his own trade.

> "In that case, wouldn't he suspect the real identity of the person who's threatening his life?" Bravington asked. "The man's no fool."
>
> "Possibly," agreed Rudd, "although he may, to ease his own conscience, prefer to accept the idea that it's someone connected with that train-load of prisoners. All of us are capable of self-deception if it's kinder to our esteem to fool ourselves rather than face up to an unpleasant truth."
>
> Bravington looked at him with interest and respect.
>
> "You have a good knowledge of human nature," he remarked.
>
> "It's my job," Rudd replied. "Like a carpenter gets to understand wood, I get to know people. It's my stock-in-trade you might say."[22]

While Rudd bears the appearance of a rustic, his mind is not locked into a pastoral mode of thinking. As *Case Closed* begins, Rudd has been tailed for three days by an unknown man. Rather than collaring the suspect, Rudd prefers to wait—even to deceive his shadow—in order to learn what is behind his surveillance. In *The Long Revenge*, the tables are turned and Rudd is the follower. His quarry, a successful spy for over twenty years, knows Rudd is watching him. Each story becomes a game in which wit and experience are well matched and both situations require skill and subtlety not normally present in the agrestic personality.

Rudd's cases often involve those who have, for one reason or another, removed themselves from normal social intercourse. Max Gifford, an aging arthritic painter in *Portrait of Lilith*, has retreated from a world which has never recognized his talent. The father of a murdered girl in *Case Closed* looses his tenuous hold on village life after his daughter's death and moves onto a boat moored in a slough. This self-exile is opposed to the strong ties and loyalties present in small communities. It provides an interesting counterpoint to the usual village interconnections and gives Rudd fascinating raw material with which to construct his cases.

The man at home is rarely visible. Never married, Rudd lives with his widowed sister Dorothy, who serves as his housekeeper. It is a comfortable enough arrangement for both of them but one which lacks even familial intimacy. Subordinates Boyce and Kyle appear frequently in investigations and are suited in their roles as underlings. The focus of these novels is Law and Order and Rudd is the focal point in each book.

All twelve novels in the series are well plotted and peopled with a variety of characters from varied walks of life. Countrywoman Thomson writes what she knows and does it with accuracy and perception.

C. D. SLOAN
1966-1987   12 books   English
Catherine Aird (Kinn Hamilton McIntosh)

Banter between experts, authorities, and erudite persons characterizes this series, which is another of those which sneak up on the reader. The detecting is solid and the results unpredictably correct. However, Sloan's methods and all of his circumlocutions prevent this from being a straight police procedural. Landlore, tradition, forensic science, and character study provide both foundation and background for Sloan the man and his investigations. The people with whom he works and those he encounters in the course of the case possess intelligence, both native and educated. Their informative statements and Sloan's often amusing thoughts resulting from them wind through these tales like a meandering river.

The cast of characters is set out fully in the first book, *The Religious Body*: Superintendent Leeyes; Dr. Dabbe, the pathologist; Burns, his silent assistant; Detective Constable Crosby; Inspector Harpe of the traffic division; the never-present Sergeant Gelven; and Sloan's wife Margaret. All assume their respective places. They and their relationships to one another remain constant—though not by any means static—throughout the twelve-book series. What grows is the reader's appreciation for these characters, their interconnections with one another and the cases upon which they work together. Their methods are well established. There is respect and consideration for the role each plays in the drama and, even though there is some dissension, it provides relief rather than dismay to those involved.

Like Pollard and Rudd, Sloan is a man in his place. Born and raised in Calleford, Calleshire, he is with and of the land and his position as guardian and protector of that land and its inhabitants is taken seriously and in depth by this inspector.

> Sloan wasn't listening. He was looking across at the thirteenth Earl of Ornum with new eyes. He, Charles (sic) Dennis Sloan, Detective Inspector in Her Majesty's County Constabulary of Calleshire, was the natural heir and successor to the Earl in this matter of law and order. Where once the Earl had kept unruly villains obedient so now did he. Sloan, too, had taken an oath of allegiance. And he hadn't realized until now how ancient was his duty.[23]

The county encompasses a variety of venues and a host of habitants. It boasts seats of both a duke and an earl, an active convent, and many churches noted for the great antiquity of their towers and apses or their well-maintained records, a University which houses the impressive Greatorex Library, and a multiplexity of villages and towns surrounded by rich verdant farmland and bounded on one side by the sea.

The peace of village, meadow, and field is frequently disturbed by murder. The county of Calleshire seems to abound with those who do harm to another for gain or for concealment. Deaths which at first glance appear to be brought about by, if not natural causes, at least innocent ones, prove under the careful scrutiny of Dr. Dabbe to be most unquestionably unnatural. Sloan and his colleagues, associates, and subordinates go about the business of unraveling the tangled skein of clues leading to the perpetrator of demise, well and efficiently. Dispatch by drowning, poison, and the proverbial blunt instrument are well represented here.

Sloan's "A Ha" moments are quiet ones. He does not possess a particular flair but somewhere in his thinking process the legwork and questions begin to pay dividends.

> The door opened. Crosby brought in two mugs of tea.
> There had been something, too, that the gardener woman, Miss Paterson, had said about the dinner party...the dinner party for the new Mrs. Washby. Something about a fertility rite. And then there was something Richard Renville had told him, too. That they had talked about blood donors after dinner, while the port was going round. A picture was beginning to take shape in Sloan's mind. A different picture from the one they had all been looking at.

That was it. They'd been trying to do the wrong puzzle with the right pieces. Oh, they'd got the pieces all right—all of them—they'd had them all the time, but put together differently they made a very different picture.

"Tea, sir," said Crosby, plonking down the mug.

Sloan didn't even see it. In his mind's eye he was looking again at the broken statue of the God of Love, and hearing Dr. Dabbe's ironic detached voice saying, "The devil was a fallen angel, Sloan."[24]

Sloan's personality is not a driving force in this series. Readers learn that he is happily married but his wife remains off the page in most books. He grows roses and enters them in local exhibitions but we never see him working in his garden. He is, first and foremost, a policeman— a thoughtful and insightful one at that.

LUKE THANET
1981-1986   6 books   English
Dorothy Simpson

Luke Thanet was born and raised in the village of Sturrenden, Kent. Now, as an inspector in the CID, he lives there still. Married to his school sweetheart, Joan, Thanet feels a strong attachment for the beautiful Kentish countryside and those who inhabit it. His job is to protect and defend these people and this place and it is one which he willingly shoulders.

Thanet and his sergeant Mike Lineham are a methodical and effective team. Much of their work on a case involves reading and re-reading reports and statements. Thanet believes that accurate, well-written reports are the very foundation of good police work and is somewhat of a Tartar toward his subordinates and colleagues to insure this accuracy. He is far from a desk-bound detective though. He and Lineham do a lot of fieldwork and conduct personal interviews themselves. Intelligent and thorough, though lacking the self-confidence to easily rise up in rank, Lineham is a good partner for Thanet. Thanet has an eye for detail and files in his mind an enormous amount of seemingly unimportant data. At various points in a case some of these pieces coalesce to provide him with a different perspective or a new line of inquiry. Lineham's view of the world follows more rigidly pragmatic lines and it is often necessary for him to ask Thanet to explain exactly how he has reached a particular conclusion. Thanet's explanation often further clarifies his own thinking, and conversation with his sergeant is an integral part of the process of solving the crime.

As the series progresses, readers become more familiar with Thanet's family life. His children, Bridget and Ben, grow from toddlers to teens. As they grow, Joan, his wife, finds less satisfaction in being a housewife and desires a career. Thanet is reluctant to lose any of the comfort she provides and is worried that the children will suffer if she takes an outside job. Prompted by the events and personalities of a case he is working on, Thanet goes through a process of honest self-analysis before forming a final judgment. Joan does go away to college and her mother, Mrs. Bolton, comes to care for Luke, the children, and the house.

Luke's relationship to and feelings for his family color his view of the victims and suspects he confronts in the course of his work. He is a compassionate man and while he possesses a knowledge of evil and inhumanity, is distressed at its manifestations.

> And there she was.
> Thanet always hated this moment. No matter how often he experienced it, no matter who the victim was, he could never quench this initial pang of pity, of regret for a life cut short. Almost at once he was able to become detached again, aware that emotional involvement could cripple his judgement, but this moment could never leave him unmoved and he was not sure that he would want it to. As he lowered himself gingerly to kneel beside the body, however, his face remained impassive. Many of his colleagues, he knew, would regard such feelings as weakness.[25]

This officer is an embodiment of authority but his personality is not limited to definition by job. He is a complete and complex human being, as much at the mercies of his fears and vanities as most men and fully aware of these as potential limitations.

Author Dorothy Simpson, herself a resident of Kent—perhaps even the Isle of Thanet—knows the area and its populace well. Familiarity here breeds no contempt. Simpson respectfully translates her knowledge onto the page of each of the mysteries featuring Thanet. All places have their dark side and Sturrenden, Kent, is no exception. Simpson conveys this darkness and puts Thanet on the scene to bring light. There is a complete cast of recurring characters whose natures continue to develop and unfold, on their own and in relation to Thanet himself. Simpson even uses very minor characters to deepen the dimensions of her primary character.

DOUGLAS QUANTRILL
1978-1986   6 books   English
Sheila Radley (Sheila (Mary) Robinson)

The action of what may be described as the dark side of the force takes place in the northern uplands of Suffolk. The divisional police headquarters in Breckham Market sits on the dividing line between the old town and the new. Quantrill himself maintains an uneasy seat between these apparent opposites as well, and in this series manages a remarkable balancing act.

> The market was busy. Quantrill had a wide acquaintance, and he tipped his hat impartially to the wife of the Methodist minister and to a retired prostitute who, feeling the lack of an occupational pension, tried to supplement her social security by selling information.[26]

As the series opens, in *Death in the Morning*, Quantrill has just been promoted. His longtime assistant, Police Constable Godbold, bemoans the loss of the old ways and Detective Sergeant Martin Tait, brash young college graduate, embraces the new. Quantrill captures the dynamic tension between the push and pull of these two, and synthesizes it into his vision of authority which must acknowledge both.

The six novels quite literally depend upon the scope Quantrill provides. Full of human imperfections himself, he does not pretend to have the answers and is as puzzled by some of the aspects of human behavior as the nonprofessional might be. His reliance on his knowledge of the old and an appreciation for the new permits him to rise above the quandry presented by the varied elements of the human puzzle. He often reaches a solution without fully realizing—or caring—how and why he has done it.

> Chief Inspector Quantrill was too old a detective to think in terms of tying up loose ends. Life was too short, and the list of undetected crimes in the division too long, to allow him the luxury of tidying up as he went. He was reconciled to the fact that, in many of the inquiries he conducted, he would never know exactly what had happened. The Nether Wickford incident was a time-waster, but he persisted with it because he had nothing else that looked remotely like lead in the A135 murder investigation.[27]

Radley creates strong characters, particularly women. Often, however, these strong individuals are skewed and whatever powers they possess are misdirected causing untold harm and damage to themselves and to the social fabric itself. It is unusual to have stories populated by such an amazing number of powerful, well-developed, yet casual, characters. Readers see these characters as Quantrill sees them and as Quantrill does *not* see them. In the early books, the strong women are the destroyers and there is little balance with strong women who are also builders. It is to Radley's credit that, as the series and the ongoing characters develop, Quantrill is given potent female allies as well as worthy female opponents.

Douglas Quantrill is married and the father of two girls and a boy. Married at an early age, with a baby on the way, Doug and Molly have reached a marital understanding over the years while managing to avoid the honesty vital to most solid unions. Their difficulties lie less in deception than in the inability to speak their true feelings and an ingrained hesitancy to touch outside the most intimate of connections. These familial habits affect all the relationships between husband and wife, parents and children and siblings. While Quantrill feels as though something is missing in his family life, he knows that he is not capable of changing to meet any discovered needs. He observes, notes, and acts on the home front in much the same fashion he does on the job.

Luke Thanet's investigations may bring light to the situation under scrutiny. Quantrill's method seems to allow more shadow play and there are areas in each story which remain completely in darkness. Quantrill uses his authority to impose order on chaotic situations and to set limits on his subordinates' behavior. Order and limits may not provide the ultimate solution to the crime or the problems underlying the crime, but these are what he is charged with doing and he carries out his tasks well.

KELSEY
1981-1987   5 books   English
Emma Page (Honoria Tirbutt)

Neither Chief Inspector Kelsey nor his sergeant, Lambert, seem to have first names, and facts on just who these men are, when they're at home in Cannonbridge, are hard won by the reader. Kelsey is a large, florid soul with carroty red hair who was married at one time. When that didn't work out, he decided to never repeat the experiment. Lambert simply fades into oblivion outside of his work. In this new series Kelsey's method of detection can best be described as interrogative.

> Kelsey banged it straight over the net. "We're not mind-readers," he said sharply. "And we're not magicians. We have to have the information, all the information, never mind picking and choosing what folk think is important. Anything else that occurs to you, never mind how insignificant or trivial it may seem to you, you come along and tell us, pronto. We'll decide what's important and what's not important."[28]

In *Every Second Thursday*, first book in the series, Kelsey is introduced as a CID officer with a strong intuitive flair. This flair leads him to look further into an officially closed case of apparent suicide. The investigation, carried out by Sergeant Lambert, must be conducted ex officio. Questions put to the various parties connected to the victim during her life could prove embarrassing to the department should Kelsey's intuition prove false. Clues to the nature of the suspects lie far afield of the city of Cannonbridge. At one point, Kelsey and Lambert evade their superiors to journey some distance to Norfolk in pursuit of their inquiries. Questions are asked, rephrased and asked again. The solution arises out of the right question asked of the right person at precisely the right moment.

In subsequent stories, there is less focus on Kelsey's intuition but the method of detection-by-query remains the same. Information is not only gleaned by questions put to individuals in the course of the investigation, but by the author's vivid description of people and places in the stories. *Last Walk Home* begins with vignettes of at least twenty people before the crime is even committed. Kelsey makes his first appearance in chapter eight. Once the investigation is under full steam, readers learn much more about the twenty or so, plus several others turned up as the plot literally thickens.

These books work as straight novels. Page draws wonderfully colorful characters and scenes. The detectives and the crime seem to exist as the only fine, tenuous thread which binds together a disparate group of suspects, informants, and innocent bystanders. The ultimate clue is often serendipitous and delivered at the eleventh hour. Other authors, notably Lemarchand and Simpson, can carry off works with a plethora of plot, an abundance of actors, and a cloud of coincidence. We're not sure why this doesn't work for Page as well.

REG WEXFORD
1964-1985   13 books   English
Ruth Rendell

That Chief Inspector Wexford should be sitting at his
rosewood desk reading the *Daily Telegraph* week-end sup-
plement on a Friday morning was an indication that things in
Kingsmarkham were more than usually slack. A cup of tea was
before him, the central heating breathed deliciously and the
new blue and grey folk-weave curtains were half-drawn to hide
the lashing rain. Wexford glanced through a feature on the
beaches of Antigua, pulling down an angle lamp to shed light
on the page. His little eyes, the colour of cut flints, held a mock-
ing gleam when they lighted on a more than usually lush advertisement for clothes or personal furnishings. His own suit was
grey, double-breasted, sagging under the arms and distorted
at the pockets. He turned the pages, slightly bored. He was
uninterested in aftershave, hair-cream, diets. Corpulent and
heavy, he had always been stout and always would be. His was
an ugly face, the face of a Silenus with a snub nose and wide
mouth. The classics have it that Silenus was the constant companion of Bacchus, but the nearest Wexford ever got to
Bacchus was an occasional pint with Inspector Burden at the
Olive and Dove.[29]

Sussexman Wexford is a husband and father as well as a competent police officer. Staid and middle-aged in the first book, *From
Doon With Death*, he manages to grow and change as the series
progresses and he is confronted with the results of the changing
economics and morality of his native country.

There is nothing very special about the town and the people of
Kingsmarkham. Granted, there are some who are very rich and
some who are very poor but most are more or less ordinary citizens,
many from the working class. One of the most notable aspects of
all of these books is the way in which all of this apparent normalcy
embraces violence and death. The odd coincidence, a slight mis-
judgment, or a moment's hesitation can propel the most average
of these ordinary citizens into the maw of murder.

On the page, the lives of Reg Wexford and his working partner
and friend, Mike Burden, incorporate private relationships as well
as ones created by their jobs. Reg's wife Dora is a homemaker
and enters the stories only as wife of the policeman and mother
to their two daughters, Sylvia and Sheila. Burden's wife is away

at the seashore in most of the early books, then dies of cancer, leaving her husband in unbearable grief. Left to cope with his children on his own, Burden nears the brink of despair. The wives and children of these two men form the backbone of subplots to the central one of murder and provide interesting parallels and perpendiculars to the main theme.

Rendell writes other, nonseries mysteries which are darker in nature and fraught with psychological under- and overtones. The books featuring Wexford are lighter in tone while maintaining a high tension of suspense and possessing a good twist at the end. Plots are well crafted and almost too believable. Characterization is an important element in all of Rendell's works and the minor players have the same quality of depth as that of the permanent cast. Wit is one of Wexford's hallmarks and one which provides relief from the terror and sadness which accompanies murder.

MADOC RHYS, Royal Canadian Mounted Police
1980-1986   3 books   Canadian
Alisa Craig (Charlotte MacLeod)

Everybody knows what a Royal Canadian Mounted Policeman looks like. He is lean, bronzed, straight-backed, steel-jawed, handsome as all getout, and stands six-foot-four in his socks. He wears a dashing red tunic, shiny boots, and blue jodhpurs with yellow stripes up the side. Mounties are most apt to be found either astride magnificent stallions, singing, "Rose Marie, I Love You," or else driving strings of huskies across frozen wastes of snow with the aurora borealis flashing behind them and repentant renegades lashed to their sleds.

Janet Wadman had no trouble whatever passing off Detective Inspector Madoc Rhys of the RCMP as Annabelle's cousin from Winnepeg. He looked like an unemployed plumber's helper. After a short but surprisingly reassuring interview, she left him to study the family album for background, and stepped across to the Mansion.[30]

Here, as is often the case, looks are deceiving. Welshman Rhys stacks up against the best of the Mounties in his abilities to always get his man. This is all to the good, for his tone deafness renders him unfit for the family trade, which is, of course, music.

This new series is penned by Alisa Craig, better known as Charlotte MacLeod, creator of the Sarah Kelling/Max Bittersohn, and Peter Shandy series. Craig seems to be the name MacLeod has chosen for her series with Canadian settings as there is another featuring The Grub-and-Stakers, a gardening club.

Like all the other books Craig/MacLeod has written, the Rhys series is a lighthearted romp through murder and mayhem with diversion and complications provided by zany families full of individual eccentrics. The crimes—always murder—are a bit bizarre themselves. Botulism is the agent employed in the first book, and poison—possibly in the wassail—in the second. Clues are diverse, such as cut versus snapped beans and a missing set of false teeth.

As in MacLeod's other books, the hero finds his true love early on and their courtship involves crime and the requisite detection. This combined with the cold Canadian winters, provides opportunities for the couple to get to know one another as few other situations permit. Love flourishes, generating enough heat to keep the lovers comfortable in spite of felonious escapades and chilling temperatures. Rhys the Mountie continues to get his man—and his woman.

Readers fond of MacLeod's work will enjoy this foray into what are the true provinces.

MOSS MAGILL
1956-1963   3 books   American
Dorothy Gardiner

Happy at finding a Western sheriff to round out this section, we were a little dismayed when the only book we located is set in Scotland. Undaunted, we pressed on and discovered that the good sheriff is written as a real Son of the Old West whose knee-high cowboy boots and ten-gallon hat are as much badges of his office as is the star he wears.

Hailing from Notlaw, Colorado, Magill is a native of the area and relates fervently to both the country and its widely scattered inhabitants. Eccentricity is more often the rule than the exception in these wide open spaces and wealthy Harriet Orchard, erstwhile resident of Rowanmuir, Scotland, is a fine example. Her last will and testament charges Magill with hand delivering her ashes—in a suitable container—to her birthplace and laying them to rest on top of the local mountain, Bein Biorach, on her birthday. Further caveats to her testament require that all of her beneficiaries be present at the interment and on the journey to Inverness which immediately precedes. Absence of any participant in these rites equals forfeiture of that individual's share.

Reluctantly, Moss Magill undertakes the task motivated not by the prospect of inheritance but by a deep respect for the late Hattie Orchard. In preparation for his journey, Magill unearths information pointing to crime and fears for the safety of Lizzie Farquhar, Hattie's older sister. Murder by lorry, the possible presence of *Amanita phalloides* in one or more evening meal, odd potshots as Magill strolls in the gloaming, and several bizarre characters cast in the roles of mourners add up to a tale which should be absolutely awful, but is, in our opinion, a witty one. Author Gardiner takes her characters to the heights of absurdity then pushes them up a few more notches. What plot exists is convoluted, full of holes, and generally unbelievable.

Magill, in hat, boots, and flamboyant flannel shirts, discovers not only the murderer but his own Scots heritage and knows he will follow the drone of the pipes anywhere they may lead him.

> Now the pipes affect different men in different ways. Some men, and strong ones at that, run miles to escape them or hide quivering heads under pillows to shut out the sound; others consider the music mere noise, pleasant or unpleasant as the case may be. But other men will jump from moving trains, parachute from airplanes, to follow the pipes, and to this breed, although until this day he had not known it, belonged Sheriff Moss Magill of Notlaw, Colorado.[31]

Gardiner has created one other two-book series featuring Mr. Watson and one nonseries mystery. None of these may be every reader's cup of tea but we are looking forward to finding and reading every one of these books.

FOREIGN

American readers have little difficulty relating to the systems which exist in England if for no other reason than there is a common language. Differences which do exist can be overlooked as they are close enough to the model of reality most of us hold. These foreign series drop readers into the center of much different systems, with different languages and sets of customs and traditions. Both the similarities and differences between other countries and the United States are remarkable and reinforce the fact that crime and justice are not defined by national boundaries. Detection in one locale is carried out in much the same fashion as it is in another.

MARTIN BECK
1967-1976   10 books   Swedish
Maj Sjowall and Per Wahloo

The series featuring Chief Detective Inspector Martin Beck is written by Swedes, originally in the Swedish language, and takes place primarily in Sweden. Those Americans who rely only on mass media for their information don't have much idea of just what goes on in this northern foreign country. The general impressions of that place seem to imply simply that all Swedish women are tall, blond, and beautiful and the society supports free love. Some may know that Sweden has a Royal family. The worldwide popularity of Sjowall and Wahloo's mysteries go a good distance to enhance one's geographic, political, and social education.

Martin Beck is only one of a number of Swedish citizens readers get to know in the course of the ten novels in this series. Neither the strongest nor the wisest among his colleagues, Beck seems to represent Everyman in a way his more noteworthy associates do not. He is a good policeman and is not carried away by an inflated sense of dedication nor the trappings of power. He simply does his job and it is the best thing he does.

His marriage and family life are dismal. Wedlock for Martin and Inga came about as a consequence of raging adolescent hormones. As the years go by, and he realizes that he and Inga have nothing in common beyond their two children, he discovers that he was unprepared for the full responsibilities of marriage in the long term, has done nothing to increase his understanding of the institution, and the marriage comes to an end.

Beck became a policeman to avoid entering the army during WWII without realizing what policework held in the long term either. The rewards and successes Martin enjoys from his profession match the talent, intuition, and effort he puts into his work and he is supported by strong colleagues. Unlike his marital relationship, Beck's understanding of the responsibilities his position entail grows. Out of that understanding comes a greater appreciation of human needs—his own included.

Sweden in the mid-sixties was in a state of transition. The police force had been nationalized in 1964 and changes in both the police and the political system are reflected in *Roseanna*, the first Beck book. The American involvement in Vietnam, increased drug use, its resultant traffic, and a sharp rise in crime for gain within the country, combine to add confusion to that transition. Authors Sjowall and Wahloo devised this series at this particular time as a way to make a larger social statement.

These are true police procedurals. Beck of the Stockholm Homicide Squad, works in a methodical and familiar way to solve crimes. He and his colleagues divide their time between footslogging fieldwork and the tedium of writing and reading reports.

> The police had appealed to the public for help through the press, radio and television, and over three hundred tips had already come in. Each item of information was registered and examined by a special working group, after which the results were studied in detail.
>
> The vice squad combed its registers, the forensic laboratory dealt with the meager material from the scene of the crime, the computers worked at high pressure, men from the assault squad went around the neighborhood knocking on doors, suspects and possible witnesses were questioned, and as yet all this activity had led nowhere. The murderer was unknown and still at large.
>
> The papers were piling up on Martin Beck's desk. Since early morning he had been working on the never-ceasing stream of reports and interrogation statements. The telephone had never stopped ringing, but in order to get a breathing space he had now asked Kollberg to take his calls during the next hour or so. Gunvald Larsson and Melander were spared all these telephone calls; they sat behind closed doors sifting material.[32]

There is violence—even brutality—in every book. However, these elements are not provided exclusively to satisfy reader's blood lust but rather as information on the social climate as much as on the scene of the crime. The authors only go so far with this savagery and balance it with a sense of compassion and excellent timing. Stockholm and other Swedish towns and cities are accurately portrayed and the lack of equilibrium between the traditional old and the technological new of the country is well presented.

GUARNACCIA
1981-1987   5 books   Italian
Magdalen Nabb

This series featuring Marshal Guarnaccia of the Italian Carabinieri takes place in and around Florence. It is written by an English woman who has resided in Florence since the mid-seventies. Magdalen Nabb has done a marvelous job of capturing the essence of Florence, the Florentine people, and the surrounding countryside. She may well have done an equally good job in her treatment of the Italian forces of law and order. However, as we are unfamiliar with the finer points of justice in this Latin country of contrasts, we can't be too sure.

There are several different and distinct branches of both national and municipal law enforcement agencies in Italy. The Carabinieri is a militarylike body whose members must answer to any of several higher authorities. Officers in this corps are not necessarily natives of the area in which they serve, and Sicilian born Salvatore Guarnaccia is assigned to the barracks of Stazione Pitti in Florence.

Carabiniere Bacci did not like the Marshal. In the first place because he was Sicilian and he suspected him of being, if not actually Mafia, at least *mafioso*, and he knew that the Marshal knew of his suspicion and even encouraged it. He seemed to think it was funny. He disliked the Marshal in the second place because he was too large and fat and had an embarrassing eye complaint—embarrassing to Carabiniere Bacci—that caused him to weep copiously during the hours of sunlight. And since he continually mourned the absence of his wife and children who were at home in Syracuse, his rolling tears often seemed distressingly real—distressing to Carabiniere Bacci. The Marshal himself would fish unperturbedly for the dark glasses that were always in one of his voluminous pockets and explain to anyone and everyone, "It's all right, just a complaint I have. It's the sunshine starts it off."[33]

In general, though, the marshal is well regarded by most of his colleagues. His large size is the mark of a contented man who loves good food. He is an excellent cook himself, and one who enjoys a placid, congenial nature. With no strong personal ties to the locality in which he serves, Guarnaccia is nevertheless an admirable representative of the force he does serve.

Unable to rely on local knowledge, Guarnaccia instead relies on his knowledge of human nature and his instinct for moral correctness. He is observant and has a retentive memory. His deductions are a mixture of hard evidence and remembered details which could fall into the category of intuition, though he is not credited with possessing any particular flair. Perseverance wins through, and after a crime has been solved, the marshal often finds himself feeling empathy and compassion for the miscreant as a victim of circumstance or simple human folly.

There is an international flavor to all of the novels in this series. The English, the Germans, the French, and the Americans are all frequent visitors to this warm, benevolent climate. Sardinians graze their sheep on the lush hillsides and play their bagpipes in the cities in exchange for coins from tourists and shopkeepers. The Florentines remain, apparently tolerating the influx of foreigners and sharing the Tuscan wonders of mountain, sea, and beautiful cities with the outsiders.

As with the Swedish novels, the names of places and people can be confusing for one unfamiliar with the country. In this series, the confusion is compounded by a wealth of titles and designations that must be crystal clear to the author but which elude these readers. There are substitute prosecutors, sublieutenants, captains, vigili and digos liberally mingled with the carabinieri and all of their internal ranks. The differences between Italy and the United States are every bit as remarkable as the similarities between Sweden and the United States and equally reinforce the fact that crime and justice are not defined by national boundaries.

But it was vague; it was grey. That safe full of illegally imported money, that stolen bust with an indisputable government seal around its neck were like a tonic to him. The man was a villain. The rules were in operation; if they were Italian rules and not English, at least they were rules.[34]

A POLICE OFFICER ONCE TOLD US that he enjoyed reading the police procedural mystery for its sheer fiction value. However, he added, a cop could get bounced from the force for conducting an investigation the way some of these characters do. It appears that authors of this type of mystery often take a healthy measure of poetic license in crafting their tales. They can, in other words, get away with murder. This should give little cause for complaint. After all, we're talking about crime and mystery *fiction*. For factual accounts of real crime, readers must turn to nonfiction books or their daily newspaper.

Readers will find law enforcement officers in almost every book within this type of fiction. Obviously there is no need to list other titles.

THE BLOOD RUNS BLUE

ARISTOCRACY

Webster defines the word *aristocracy* as follows:

> 1. Government by the best individuals or a small privileged class.
> 2. A governing body or upper class usually made up of an hereditary nobility.
> 3. The aggregate of those felt to be superior.[1]

In some countries, there is a nobility whose titles and lands are bestowed for service and passed on to successive generations through lineage. However, not all members of the aristocracy come from countries which rank their members by hereditary titles. Some individuals attain this status by virtue of wealth, ability, athletic prowess, order of arrival, and/or creed. Nevertheless, a noble title implies that its bearer possesses the qualities of dignity, honor, and distinction.

Aristocratic sleuths use rank and class privilege as armor against the dragons and evil sorcerers of crime. They share a nobility of spirit and if the detective is a latter-day hero and the true successor of Arthur's knights, then the chivalrous aristocrat who pursues the quest of following clues and detecting the wrongdoers fills the bill aptly—our contemporary champion.

SARAH KELLING
1979-1987   7 books   American
Charlotte MacLeod

With the American Revolution, the colonies declared their independence from British rule and created a society with no apparent class divisions. It only took a few generations for those who had been among the first arrivals on these new shores to declare their superiority over latecomers and those with less land and/or money. The caste system had arrived.

Lineage, location, lucre, religious and political affiliation combine to give Charlotte McLeod's Sarah Kelling, by Boston standards, blood of the bluest hue. As the series opens, we find the young Sarah living with her older husband, Alexander, and his mother in a Kelling family house on the proper side of Beacon Hill. Events of the first story substantially alter the quality of Sarah's life, and at the end of the book, readers find her planning to turn the Kelling family home into a boardinghouse.

> "I'd be a lot more crackbrained to let the High Street Bank grab my property without a struggle, wouldn't I?" Sarah was, after all, a Kelling by herself, both by birth and by marriage to a fifth cousin once removed. "What's so crackbrained about a boardinghouse, anyway? Lots of perfectly respectable people have done the same. Look at Mrs. Craigie."
>
> "Mh'h. I'd forgotten about Mrs. Craigie. Cambridge woman, right? And that Longfellow chap stayed with her. Wrote poetry, of course, but his people were all right, and he married an Appleton. Well, I suppose if you make sure to take the right sort—"[2]

In spite of her reduced circumstances, the multitudinous Kelling relations are still very much a part of Sarah's life and her new household. Family members and several of the residents of the boardinghouse appear in subsequent books. Max Bittersohn aids Sarah in her first foray into investigation and moves into the basement. Mariposa Fergus and her friend Charles C. Charles, a resting actor, make up the staff. Mrs. Theonia Sorpende, a magnificent figure of womanhood, frequently serves as hostess in Sarah's absence. She is admired and rather decorously pursued by the male members of Sarah's family and one or two of her fellow boarders.

DEARBORN V. PINCH
1977-1982 3 books American
Edith Piñero Green

High Society is yet another aspect of American aristocracy. Money can buy a place in this stratum, though having the right family connections doesn't hurt. Dearborn V. Pinch has both. A certain latitude is granted to members of this class, and their antics are often written off as simply high-spirited behavior.

> "And then," Stella continued, "when Arthur Howe got into difficulties—"
> "What kind of difficulties?" Dearborn asked.
> "Transvestite," Fannie said, lowering her handkerchief. "Picked up in Times Square wearing his wife's evening gown."
> "Could have been a terrible scandal," Stella confided. "He was always so belligerent. But he called and we all exchanged clothes and went down there."
> "Told them it was a masquerade party," James explained. "We might have all ended up behind bars."
> "I still remember what you looked like in Dolly's bloomers," Fannie reminisced. "And Louise. Remember Louise? She cut off some of her hair and pasted it onto her upper lip."[3]

Dearborn capitalizes on this latitude; he takes advantage of his position, his wealth, and his age to bully his way around officialdom as he deals with his friends' problems and the inevitable murder.

Benjamin, Dearborn's son (Princeton, summa cum laude), is a professional basketball player, currently out of work. As an athlete, he is used to running interference for his teammates and often finds himself in that role with his father.

Readers may not find Edith Piñero Green's Dearborn V. Pinch a particularly sympathetic character. Clearly his friends do not, though they depend upon him to get them out of difficulties. Dearborn is the centerpiece of the three novels in which he appears. These stories are well crafted with tight plots and delightful characterizations. Humor runs high on every page and one can almost forgive D. V. P. most of his eccentricities.

HIRAM POTTER
1955-1970   11 books   American
Rae Foley (Elinore Denniston)

Each of the Dell paperback issues of Rae Foley's books has on its cover the picture of a troubled young woman, and over the title, the words, "A Novel of Danger and Romance." Readers should be reminded to not judge a book by its cover. At the same time, the writing style and story lines do hold the flavor of the era (the fifties and sixties) in which they were penned. Miss Foley was best known for her nonmystery romances before she created the sleuthing Hiram Potter. There is always a puzzle and a limited time in which to find the solution. Mr. Potter is a quick-working and capable detective in the best tradition.

At first glance, Hiram himself looks "rich, idle and harmless."[4] Here, too, appearances can be deceptive. It is accurate to say that Mr. Potter is rich, but behind this fair, somewhat innocuous facade lies a keen mind and a great sense of moral responsibility which prompts Mr. Potter to get involved in criminal investigations. He considers publicity vulgar and goes to extreme lengths to avoid it.

> Mr. Potter liked people; essentially he was as friendly as a puppy, but for the entity called the Public he felt only a single loathing. The Public was a collective peeping Tom without respect for privacy or human dignity.[5]

Hiram resides in the house in which he was born, an elegant manse in Gramercy Park, New York City. He and the family home are cared for by the housecouple Tito and Angela, who, along with several other characters, appear in most of the books in the series.

MISS AMELIA BUTTERWORTH
1897-1917   6 books   American
Anna Katharine Green

Another denizen of Gramercy Park, though of an earlier era, is the very proper Miss Amelia Butterworth, created by Anna Katharine Green in 1897. While demonstrating a strong talent for detective work and an admitted fascination with the crime of murder, Miss Butterworth is the embodiment of the Victorian model of feminine rectitude. Upon being summoned to the office of police detective Ebenezer Gryce she declares,

> "But I shall have to explain my purpose not to find myself at too great a disadvantage," she replied with grim decision. "Not that I like to display my own weakness, but that I recognize the exigencies of the occasion and fully appreciate your surprise at finding that I, a stranger to Mr. Adams, and without the excuse which led to my former interference in police matters, should have so far forgotten myself as to be in my present position before you. This was no affair of my immediate neighbor, nor did it seek me. I sought it sir, and in this way. I wish I had gone to Jericho first; it might have meant longer travel and much more expense; but it would have involved me in less humiliation and possible publicity. Mr. Gryce, I never meant to be mixed up with another murder case."[6]

Miss Butterworth appears in six of Green's novels. Her impeccable social standing makes her an ideal foil for Gryce who often feels at a disadvantage in his dealings with the upper classes. Miss Butterworth's intuition coupled with her inherent knowledge of codes, customs, and mores, aid Gryce in bringing criminals to justice and exonerating the innocent.

At the turn of the century, when these novels were first published, they achieved a popularity which remained undimmed for over two decades. Today's readers will find the language stilted and the melodrama rather excessive with a full quota of swooning ladies and honor-bound gentlemen. The stories are good reading for just those reasons. Miss Butterworth is an interesting character, both for her willingness to involve herself in matters considered outside the bounds of "a refined woman's natural instincts,"[7] and as the predecessor of Miss Jane Marple and Maud Silver.

Unfortunately, only one of Green's books, *The Leavenworth Case*, has been reissued and the other novels are hard to find.

CHARLOTTE ELLISON
1979-1987   8 books   English
Anne Perry

Anne Perry has given us Charlotte Ellison, the second daughter of an upper class English family which resides in a pleasantly large house outside of London. The world is in the process of change in 1881: women are admitted to universities, gaslights illuminate the city streets, and the British empire spans the globe. Charlotte's family, however, still adheres to a rigid social structure. Because of her startling inquisitiveness and honest outspoken nature, Charlotte is an oddity and, at times, an embarrassment to her family. Her parents despair of their daughter ever finding anyone who will marry her.

Waiting to be called in from an entirely different, though parallel, world is Inspector Thomas Pitt. This tall, untidy policeman with the melodious voice arrives at the Ellison home to investigate the grisly murders occurring in their neighborhood. Pitt intrigues Charlotte and successfully undermines her cool facade. As the second book begins, Charlotte and Pitt have been married for two years.

According to the customs and manners of polite Victorian society, there were things which were unsuitable for ladies to know. The men took care of those things.

> "I'm sorry. I shouldn't have told you that."
>
> "Why?" she demanded, moving suddenly. "Isn't it true?..."
>
> "Yes, of course it's true, but I shouldn't have told you..."
>
> "Why not? Do you think I need to be protected, politely deceived like some child? You used not to treat me so condescendingly! I remember when I lived in Cater Street, you forced me to learn something of the rookeries, whether I would or not—"
>
> "That was different! That was starvation. It was poverty you knew nothing of. This is perversion."
>
> "And ought I to know about people starving to death in the alleys but not about children being bought and used by the perverted and the sick? Is that what you're saying?"
>
> "Charlotte—you can't do anything about it."
>
> "I can try!"[8]

Many women were aware of these unsavory issues; their social consciences and actions were guided by that knowledge. These women were, however, wise enough to ruffle the feathers of convention in discreet, though effective, ways.

Incest, rape, abortion, homosexuality, and child abuse are among the issues which surface in the course of Pitt's murder investigations. While we tend to think of these as modern problems, Perry makes us aware of the fact that there have always been victims—of convention as well as crime.

THE HONORABLE CONSTANCE ETHEL MORRISON-BURKE
1970-1979   5 Books   English
Joyce Porter

Noblesse oblige is the watchword of this gentlewoman. "Not the world's most perceptive aristocrat,"[9] the Hon. Con, by virtue of birth, considers it her moral duty to improve the lot of others less fortunate. After unsuccessfully trying to alter the structure of every organization in her district, she is thrown back on her own resources and opens Connie's Advice Bureau.

> "It's my bounden duty to give a helping hand to these poor nitwits, isn't it? People look on me as a sort of father-figure—see? But soon as I join one of these societies or organizations or what-have-you, the plebs all gang up to thwart me, don't they? So, I've just got to strike out on my own."
> "On your own dear?"
> "It's the obvious solution. I should have thought even you would recognize that. I've just got to open my own advice bureau."[10]

Her peerless lack of tact does bring results and crimes are solved, because of, or in spite of, her efforts.

Joyce Porter has created two other series characters: Inspector Wilfred Dover and Edmond Brown. Though their areas of speciality differ from the Hon. Con's, all three share the same jaundiced view of the world and its inhabitants and have similar personality quirks. Some readers may find this entertaining.

MELROSE PLANT
1981-1987   9 books   English
Martha Grimes

What do Old Peculier and French literature have in common? Melrose Plant,

> one of the most eligible men in the whole of the British Isles. He had intelligence, looks, character, warmth. Whether Jury had enough of those himself, he didn't know. But he knew damned well he didn't have the rest of it, like money. Melrose Plant was filthy rich. And titles. Though Plant had given them

up, his titles trailed after him like the wake of a ship. The Earl
of Caverness. Lord Ardry. Twelfth Viscount in the Ardry-Plant
line—[11]

The aristocracy, quite frankly, bores Melrose and to keep boredom
at bay, he holds the Chair of French Romantic Poetry at the University of London, "where he teaches for about four months out of the
year leaving echoes of himself to reverberate for the other eight."[12]

In the first book of the series, Plant is on the scene when a body
is discovered. Richard Jury of Scotland Yard finds Plant's insights
and keen sense of observation invaluable tools to aid him in his
official investigation. Sparks of friendship and camaraderie between
these two are ignited and glow warmly in succeeding tales.

Martha Grimes writes with wit, humor, and definite style. She
plays fair with her readers by setting forth all the clues to the mystery
in the course of the story. Her characters come alive on the page,
from Plant's nemesis, Agatha, his American-born aunt by marriage,
to the unattainable Vivian Rivington, to Mrs. Witherby, known
affectionately as the Old Trout by the frequenters of the Jack and
Hammer Pub in Long Piddleton, where she chars part-time for her
drinking money. Each of the nine books featuring Plant and Jury are
titled with the name of an English pub and are a pleasure to read again
and again. Though Grimes is an American, she is a staunch
Anglophile and travels to England frequently. We didn't discover
her nationality until we had finished several books in the series. We
were pleasantly surprised to find that a fellow countrywoman could
write in such a convincing traditional English manner.

LORD and LADY TINTAGEL
1951-1952   2 books   England
F. Draco (Julia Davis)

The aristocracy was brought down a peg or two when Lord
Robert Tintagel and his American wife Ginger came on the scene.
Their manor house is Chillstone, their village Creighton Buzzard,
and an ancient family curse hovers over Lord Robert.

Newly arrived, Lady Robert proposes a houseparty in order to get
acquainted with the neighbors. An odd assortment of guests from
the village attend. Crazy Aunt Cordelia and the omnipresent butler,
Frothingham, add to the mystery of the Devil's Church. Murder in
the manor house, foreign espionage, and the occult are liberally
mixed to provide a confusing though unique contribution which

poses no threat to the art of detective fiction. Fortunately, there are only two books in this series by F. Draco. We didn't read the second.

LORD PETER WIMSEY
1923-1972   17 books   English
Dorothy L. Sayers

No discussion of the aristocratic sleuth could be complete without Lord Peter. Elegant, urbane, impeccable, and witty are only a few of the adjectives which can be applied to this quintessential noble detective created in 1923 by Dorothy L. Sayers.

As the second son of the fourteenth Duke of Denver, Lord Peter is free from the responsibilities of the dukedom. Wealthy in his own right, he wears both his affluence and his title with ease, indulging himself in fine wines and the pursuits of a bibliophile. From the first book of the series, it is clear that another of his abiding interests is murder and that he is already considered—by his mother, the dowager duchess, and Inspector Charles Parker of Scotland Yard—to be a proficient amateur.

Wimsey's accomplishments are legion. He plays Scarlatti with the touch of a master and can ring changes on church bells. He could, should the need ever arise, support himself by writing advertising copy, and is known by some of the fair sex to be a considerate and generous lover. He can even be rude gracefully.

> "...Now don't you worry Mr. Appledore. I'm thinkin' the best thing I can do is trundle the old lady down to my mother and take her out of your way, otherwise you might be findin' your Christian feelin's gettin' the better of you some fine day and there's nothin' like Christian feelin's for upsettin' a man's domestic comfort. Good-night sir—Good-night dear lady—it's simply rippin' of you to let me drop in like this.''[13]

Wimsey and his man Bunter make a formidable duo in a murder investigation. Lord Peter's title and family connections provide entrée into a world in which the police and Scotland Yard are about as welcome as a rabid dog at a garden party. Inspector Parker is a close friend (who later becomes his brother-in-law) and often relies on Lord Peter's position almost as much as his detective skills in bringing an investigation to a successful close.

Lord Peter is clearly the star of the series, though scattered throughout all of the stories is a host of satellite characters: family, friends, and professional acquaintances who crop up from time to time to add to the overall enjoyment. The stories themselves are fascinating, not only for the excellent plotting around the crimes, but for the highly accurate details on somewhat esoteric subjects with which the author laces her detective fiction.

Sayers was a scholar, an Oxford graduate at a time when women were allowed to study but were not granted degrees. It has been said that she created Wimsey only to make money for herself and that his success in doing just that for her was all that kept the series going through twelve novels and several collections of short stories. The fact that Sayers wrote over fifty books that have not a whisper of Wimsey seems to support that contention.

We can be glad that, whatever the reason, Lord Peter exists and while we envy any reader who has yet to discover this most distinguished detective, these are books which can be read often.

ALBERT CAMPION
1929-1973   26 books   English
Margery Allingham

Though reputedly close to the throne by birth, Albert Campion does not use his family name nor his title. Who he really is, is never really known, though hints to his actual identity are dropped throughout the series. Albert's demeanor in the early books is that of a charming, bumbling Zany hiding behind horn-rimmed glasses. His quick wit and artfully misleading erudition are captivating, creating a story line which is almost secondary to the capricious antics of the avuncular Albert. The various guises of this lanky, fair-haired young man and his general affability win him many friends in strange and lofty places: royalty, vicars, gypsies, and crooks. But who is Albert when he's home? Only Lugg, irrepressible valet, housekeeper, and ex-con might know Albert through and through.

Lady Amanda Fitton, a brilliant young aircraft designer, is introduced in the fifth book. Gifted with a straightforward and quick-witted way about her, she upstages the unflappable Albert and becomes his perfect foil. She understands him so well that his reticence becomes eloquent. Their marriage as well as the birth of their son, Rudolph, take place off the page.

When Campion and his sister Val appear together there is a silent and appreciative meeting of the minds. Val, a successful designer for the fashion house of Papendeik, has need of Albert's sleuthing services in more than one story. These are the black sheep of their blue-blooded family—nobles who have chosen to pursue careers and forsake their family names.

In post WWII stories, Albert becomes more serious and withdrawn. As a personality, he almost fades into the background though his creator does use him as a vehicle for delivering social commentary, artfully woven into the story line.

> Mr. Campion resumed his spectacles. "It must be something to do with officialdom," he said. "Everything in the free world is, today. It'll pass, but at the moment we're in the midst of it. I know. I've lived through the Jazz Age, the Age of Appeasement, the Battle Age. Now it's the age of the Official. By the law of averages we ought to move on to something more cheerful next time. Meanwhile, my sweet, I fear we have a more immediate problem."[14]

Margery Allingham's fluent prose invites the reader's interest in Albert and his mysteries. Making Mr. Campion's acquaintance is, however, only one of many pleasures. Each book in the series is an immensely readable, complete story to which the actual crime is almost incidental. These works stand on their own as novels outside the mystery genre.

As Allingham changed and grew in real life, Albert's paper life changed, too. By reading the entire series, one has a unique opportunity to observe the development of both a character and his author over a span of some thirty years. This collection is one of our favorites and we recommend that readers start at the beginning and follow it through to the end. The printing history of the various titles in the series makes it obvious that the reading public is always ready for more of Mr. Campion.

WHILE NOT ALL OF THESE CHARACTERS possess titles, all possess true nobility of spirit. The advantages of family, class, education, and money give these aristocrats an edge over less privileged detectives. They are at home with the forms and manners of the more rarified strata of society. At the same time, they bring a certain undeclared authority to their dealings with the lower classes. Wit, style, grace, and humor are trademarks of most of these characters. Their creators have had a good time skimming the cream off the top for the reader's delectation.

Scotland Yard can claim a member of lesser nobility for its ranks. Roderick Alleyn of the Criminal Investigation Division is one of the few aristocrats officially connected to the forces of law and order.

Other books involving the aristocracy and their residences include:

Catherine Aird, *The Stately Home Murder*, 1969
Margot Arnold, *Lament for a Lady Laird*, 1982
Ann Bridge, *The Portuguese Escape*, 1958
Agatha Christie, *Lord Edgware Dies*, 1933
Margaret Erskine, *The Voice of the House*, 1947
Antonia Fraser, *The Wild Island*, 1978
Ngaio Marsh, *Death of a Peer*, 1940
Helen McCloy, *The One That Got Away*, 1945
Elizabeth Peters, *The Murders of Richard III*, 1974

CRIME AND THE CORPUS DIVINE

RELIGION

Crime comes as no surprise to the religious. They are familiar with sin. The sacred calling to this vocation places its members in direct conflict with the devil and his manifestations in the everyday stuff of life. Priests and ministers christen the young, nurture the souls of the living, and bury the dead. The sisters and brothers of the church teach our children and heal our sick. They've been privy to the innermost secrets and desires of many of us through our confessions. This knowledge of human nature and a natural inclination towards the triumph of good over evil can create a formidable foe against crime.

BROTHER CADFAEL
1977-1987   14 books   English
Ellis Peters (Edith Pargeter)

Perhaps the most unique of the religious detectives is Ellis Peters' Brother Cadfael. He leads a quiet life as a Benedictine Monk in the harsh world of England in the 1100's. As a young man, Cadfael traveled as a crusader to Venice, Cypress, and the Holy Land. He has turned from a life of wandering and adventure on the open road to the contemplative life at the Abbey of Saint Peter and Saint Paul in Shrewsbury where he enjoys tending his herb garden, one of the finest in the Benedictine world.

The present day Cadfael is a thickset, stout fellow in middle years whose early career is a great curiosity to his fellow brothers. His rumored past encounters—amorous and otherwise—contrast with the celibate, quiet monk who now brews potions for the sick. Brother Cadfael's background is, however, an asset to the process of detection. Besides being a man with a keen mind and a naturally great gift of logic, he can draw upon his worldly past to help him put two and two together to solve the crime.

> "...Letting the devout voices slip out of his consciousness, Cadfael congratulated himself on having made as many people as possible happy, and drifted into a dream of a hot knife blade slicing deftly through the thick wax of a seal without ever disturbing the device. It was a long time since he had exercised some of his more questionable skills, he was glad to be confirmed in believing that he had forgotten none of them, and that every one had a meritorious use in the end."[1]

Brother Cadfael's Welsh charm and clerical anonymity enhance his abilities, too. He does not refrain from sharing a companionable cup or two with friendly folks and listening to their gossip. People feel free to pour out their hearts to him, to ask for his help and to call upon him at all hours to take care of their sick. As he is the only healer for miles around, he is free to travel far from the walls of the Abbey.

In the first book, *A Morbid Taste for Bones*, Cadfael is attached as an interpreter to a group of monks from his abbey as they venture into Wales. Their purpose is to bring the blessed bones of the Welsh Saint Winifred back to their Benedictine house in Shrewsbury. Usually though, his activities keep him closer to home. In Cadfael's second adventure, *One Corpse Too Many*, he is drawn into a web of political intrigue in Shrewsbury as the town provides a site for the opposing forces of King Stephen and the Empress Maud who vie for the throne of England. Cadfael's medical skills take him away to the priory of Bromfield in *The Virgin in the Ice*, and again he becomes personally involved in murder.

In the second book, Brother Cadfael and Deputy Sheriff Hugh Beringar are introduced to one another as formidable adversaries. They grow to respect each other's talents though and become allies as the story draws to a close. The sheriff and Cadfael work together in other novels. The tales are also populated with the satellite characters of the monastery. Abbot Heribert looks after the brothers of the abbey with love and tenderness. Prior Robert Pennant, second in command, is handsome and aristocratic—and well aware of it. Other brothers are mentioned throughout the series and usually Brother Cadfael is assisted in his detecting by one young man or another who has been assigned to learn herb gardening from him.

A published author since the mid-thirties, Peters began writing mysteries in the fifties with her first series characters, Inspector George Felse and his family. Brother Cadfael came on the scene in 1977, and fourteen books now chronicle his adventures. Peters' choice of the twelfth century as the setting for murder mystery is fascinating. She provides readers with a rich tapestry of characters, scenes, and settings, deftly woven into the pattern of a morality play. Good always triumphs! Her own seven-year experience as a chemist's assistant adds accurate and delicious detail to the arts of herbal healing and herbal murder. We look forward to further installments.

FATHER SIMON BEDE
1975-1979   4 books   English/American
Barbara Ninde Byfield

Barbara Ninde Byfield's detective, Simon Bede, is an Anglican priest and aide to the Archbishop of Canterbury. His responsibilities with the church take him to parishes all over the globe. In the first novel, *Solemn High Murder*, Father Bede arrives in the winter rain of New York City reminiscing about the last few weeks spent in the warm Caribbean. He has come to work on the agenda for the important international Anglican Consultative Conference, and also to personally assess the character and abilities of the Reverend Dunstan Owsley, who is under consideration for a new position within the hierarchy of the church.

As the reverend's guest at the rectory of the Church of Saint Jude the Martyr, Bede's first glimpse of both the church and Father Owsley is at evening prayer.

> He caught his breath and stood quietly for a moment, adjusting his eyes to the sparse light that came from soft floods cleverly buried in the Gothic vaulting ninety feet above him. Although he had never set foot in St. Jude's before, he felt immediately at home. The unmistakable smells of damp stone, votive candles, incense cured wood and what he always swore was pure prayer were as comfortable and familiar as the cracked wooden handle of the shaving brush he had used for twenty-five years.[2]

Reverend Owsley is murdered—elevating him to a position beyond his highest aspirations. This event serves as the introduction of Simon to Helen Bullock, a Pulitzer Prize winning photographer and his future companion-in-crime. After the murder at Saint Jude's, she takes a shaken Simon under her wing. Bede and a young priest gladly follow Helen to her apartment where she is able to have her first good look at Simon as they collapse and sip drinks. She admires his wonderfully blue eyes, his square and solid frame, and his quiet nature; and as these two get to know one another, romance blooms. Bede's familiarity with religious ritual and Helen's artist's eye enable them to recognize the key clues to this crime. Fortifying each other with warmth and amiable humor, their further investigations often extend beyond the scope of detection.

Bede's son Fergus, a struggling free-lance filmmaker, resides in the family's dilapidated country home in Kent, England—fondly named Crumbles. Though Simon is absent from the action in *A Parcel of Their Fortunes*, which takes place in Marrakech, Fergus joins Helen in adventures there. Helen is really the star of this series. Her strong feeling for Simon and all his position with the church represents, provides her with a sea anchor—steadying, never restricting. They detect together in several books and these readers always look forward to the good father's appearance.

SISTER MARY TERESA DEMPSEY
1981-1986   5 books   American
Monica Quill (Ralph McInerny)

Monica Quill's set of successful detectives live in downtown Chicago in an old Frank Lloyd Wright house. They are the last three nuns of the Order of Mary and Martha, founded by the Blessed Abigail Keinesweigs. Among the few nuns who detect, these sisters are worth their considerable weight in gold. The venerable Sister Mary Teresa Dempsey, a nun for over sixty years, stands not much more than five feet tall and weighs close to 200 pounds. She is affectionately and alternately known to her sisters as Attila the Nun or Emtee Dempsey.

The intimidating Sister Mary Teresa prefers to retain the habit and starched headdress designed by the Blessed Abigail centuries earlier. Cloistered in the house on Walton Street, Sister Mary Teresa continues the work she began while teaching at the order's college years ago. She writes about the monastic movements in southern France in the twelfth century, investigating life as Brother Cadfael must have lived it in his own niche in England. The remaining two members of the order are in their mid-twenties and dress as ordinary people. Sister Joyce presides over the kitchen in jeans and sweatshirt and attends to the most menial chores in the convent—while sneaking a pack and a half of cigarettes a day. Sister Kimberly does research at Northwestern University for Emtee Dempsey's opus magnum.

Sister Kimberly's brother, Richard Moriarty, is a policeman. Though they are exasperating to him, Richard relies on these sleuthing sisters. Sometimes he sets up situations which involve them in his cases; and when he does, it is often to take advantage of what Sister Mary Teresa might have gleaned through conversation and observation. To Richard's consternation these sisters straddle the law adeptly. While they are tracking clues and criminals outside the convent, they are capable of granting sanctuary to gangsters in their basement.

"...Mr. Murphy, you are in grievous danger, and I suspect your lawyer will see it more quickly than you. Meanwhile, you can hide here."

He laughed, a merry, full-throated laugh. "You would give refuge to a fugitive?"

"I would consider it an almost religious obligation to do so."

"But what if I'm guilty?"

"The right of sanctuary is not reserved for the innocent, Mr. Murphy."

If he had reacted to the offer as to a joke, within minutes he was more than interested, following Kim's description of the basement apartment with undisguised fascination.

"Hidden in a convent? It sounds like one of Geoffrey Chaser's plots."[3]

Sister Mary Teresa only adds to Richard's exasperation by her insistence that nearly fifty years as an historian qualifies her—even better than the police—to reason out a crime using common sense as opposed to routine.

For a layman, writing about the life of a nun must present certain obstacles but these entertaining mysteries flow from the pen of Monica Quill with ease. Ralph McInerny received his education at Saint Paul's Seminary in Minnesota, has been an instructor in philosophy at Creighton University, Nebraska, and is currently the Director of the Medieval Institute at Notre Dame University, Indiana.

SISTER MARY HELEN
1984-1986 2 books American
Sister Carol Anne O'Marie

A feisty seventy-five-year-old nun is the star of Sister Carol Anne O'Marie's new series. Sister Mary Helen, a retired professor, has come to Mount Saint Francis College for Women in San Francisco as research assistant to the head of the History Department.

"Welcome, Sister." He ushered her inside. "We are so glad to have you." He ran his hand over his straight hair. "Your wisdom will be a real asset to our history department."

Mary Helen knew bunk when she heard it. Why, the man had just met her. How in the world would he know whether she was wise or not? Unless he thought it came with age. She wanted to tell him that someone had once said, "The older I grow, the more I distrust the familiar doctrine that age brings wisdom." Instead, she threw back a little bunk of her own. "I'm looking forward to working in your department, Professor."[4]

Fearing a dull life, the sister's expectations are shaken during a simple game of cards which is interrupted by an earthquake and the death of her new boss, Professor Villanueva.

Kate Murphy, a young San Francisco homicide officer and graduate of Mount Saint Francis College, is assigned to the case after it is determined that the professor's death was not accidental. Kate and Sister Mary Helen find an early and mutual respect. The sister feels free to call on Kate with information as the case progresses while Kate seeks Mary Helen's advice on a more private aspect of life—her relationship with Jack Bassetti—an impetuous and voluble Italian with a large, equally vocal family. Kate's Irish heritage and strict Catholic upbringing have raised specters of doubt in her mind over the wisdom of a somewhat mixed marriage and she turns to the sister for advise and counsel.

An ardent mystery fan, Sister Mary Helen often refers to Saint P. D. James—especially when one of her colleagues discovers that the religious cover on the book Mary Helen often carries, disguises that author's latest paperback novel. Detecting appeals to Mary Helen and it is not difficult for her to instigate her own investigation. A firm background in historical research gives the sister further information on possible aspects of the murder. However, it is only in the cold early morning, when, unable to sleep, the sister goes for an ill-advised and solitary walk and literally stumbles into the final piece of evidence.

In *Advent of Dying*, murder strikes a little closer to Sister Mary Helen when her secretary is killed. The same gentle, persistent inquisitiveness leads her to the solution of the second crime. Thirty years in convent life have given Sister Carol Anne O'Marie the inside track and an edge on knowing how a Catholic sister's mind might work. A third book in the series is due in 1988. These readers offer Hails to both Mary and Sister Carol Anne for this septuagenarian newcomer to the mystery scene.

REVEREND MARTIN BUELL
1949-1965   6 books   American
Margaret Scherf

The rectory of Christ Church in Farrington, Montana, is the home of the Reverend Martin Buell. Margaret Scherf's character is a portly, middle-aged Episcopalian priest who views life with a jaundiced eye.

> If then, to some readers Martin appears to devote an undue
> portion of his time to events outside the realm of parish duty,
> let them remember that he does so in a strictly vertical manner,

and that he is using time which other less cerebral clergymen would devote to sprinkling the lawn or taking vitamins. Let these readers consider too, if it is not a mark of restraint and good taste for Martin to enjoy his crimes vicariously rather than to follow the natural inclination of every clergyman to murder a select few of his parishioners.[5]

For a man of the cloth, the Reverend Buell holds some harsh and uncharitable thoughts about some of his parishioners. It may be that this is true for all clergymen but Martin is a bit more outspoken than many of his brothers in Christ. When the vestry of Martin's parish tear down the creaky old house that has served as residence for Martin and Mrs. Beekman and replace it with a prefabricated structure which resembles a corsage box, Martin is not at all dismayed to find the body of Barry Collins, instigator of the plan, murdered and stuffed into the works housing of a grandfather clock. Ill will toward his fellow man aside, Martin is compelled to get to the bottom of murder, and with the help and support of Sheriff Hunnicut and Doc Campbell, launches forth on his investigation.

His housekeeper, Mrs. Beekman, and his loyal companion Bascomb, a Chesapeake Bay Retriever, take turns hounding him throughout the series which is populated with a full cast of amusing, recurring characters. Henry Beaver, Martin's next-door neighbor, assists the reverend with his gardening—the harvest at least—gives advice and offers some assistance to Martin on murder cases. Hattie Kettlehorn, another neighbor, is the nosy sort and keeps a close watch on both the rectory and the rector. Her frequent advice is delivered with an acid tongue and mixed intentions. As a widower, Martin ranks high on the list of eligible men, but most of the women in town have given up all thoughts of snagging this catch. Helen Kettlehorn, Hattie's daughter, is one of these, though her friendship for Martin remains steadfast and loyal.

Gossip is coin of the realm in Farrington, and Martin's parishioners render it up to him along with the more acceptable tithings for the collection plate at Christ Church. Martin receives this offertory with a grain of salt while storing data away in his mental, human nature file. The Reverend Buell encounters murder both in town and on his travels, away from his home parish. His long and intimate exposure to the vagaries of life among his flock translates to any place the crime of murder has occurred.

Margaret Scherf is responsible for the creation of some of our favorite characters, Dr. Grace Severance, with her no-nonsense views of life, and the rather scattered and whimsical husband and wife team of New York City interior decorators, Henry and Emily

Bryce. Martin Buell and the Big Sky of Montana are well suited to one another—vast and uncompromising.

THESE RELIGIOUS DETECTIVES bring to crime investigation a fine sense of reason bolstered by logic. They are all highly intelligent individuals who are able to weigh the pros and cons of a case to solve the crime. Each has a vocation in the world other than the religious which adds dimension to their mental prowess. Being in the world but not of it, these detectives pair objectivity with powers of reason to reach their conclusions.

The police and private detectives have either stumbled over or into the religious body in other ways. Other books involving the religious and their lives include:

Catherine Aird, *The Religious Body*, 1966
Margery Allingham, *Mystery Mile*, 1930; *Tiger in the Smoke*, 1952; *The Mind Readers*, 1965
Christianna Brand, *The Three-Cornered Halo*, 1957
Agatha Christie, *The Murder at the Vicarage*, 1930
Mary Fitt, *Death and Mary Dazill*, 1941
Antonia Fraser, *Quiet as a Nun*, 1977
Martha Grimes, *The Man With a Load of Mischief*, 1981
P. D. James, *Cover Her Face*, 1962; *A Taste for Death*, 1986
Emma Lathen, *Ashes to Ashes*, 1971
E. C. R. Lorac, *The Organ Speaks*, 1935; *Policemen in the Precinct*, 1949
Ngaio Marsh, *Death in Ecstasy*, 1936
Gladys Mitchell, *St. Peter's Finger*, 1938
Sara Paretsky, *Killing Orders*, 1986
Sheila Radley, *A Talent for Destruction*, 1982
Dorothy L. Sayers, *The Nine Tailors*, 1934

CRIME ON CUE

STAGE, SCREEN, AND TELEVISION

*T*he world of the performing artist is one of make believe and illusion. Reality must, however, be the foundation in order for the illusion to succeed. The stage actor needs enough believable reality in his role to capture and convince audiences, performance after performance. Screen actors, appearing larger than life, play to an invisible audience and their imagination must encompass the reality of both the role and the viewer.

Successful performers actually enter other lives. An actor embodies the character. An interviewer is empathetic with the subject of the interview. Years of training cause a sixth sense to develop—an awareness to surroundings, mood, lighting, and interpersonal tension. This sense may be applied to life off the stage as well and serves these professionals in the equally subtle art of detecting.

MERLE (MERLIN) CAPRICORN
1975-1981   6 books   English
Pauline Glen Winslow

> Capricorn had become a policeman because he loved tradi-
> tion, order, stability, and he had made it his life's work to pro-
> tect them. Through that work he had come to realize no order
> was a mechanical structure that could be imposed and forced
> to remain. Order was a living thing, based on tradition but
> created each day by living men and women.[1]

To Scotland Yard and the profession of law enforcement,
Capricorn brings the unusual tradition of theatrical magic. Scion of
the Great Capricornus and nephew of the Magic Merlinos, Merlin
was raised and trained to take his place in the family trade. From the
age of three, he had been schooled by his father in the art and trickery
of their craft. Young Merlin could easily escape from small confined
spaces and was dexterous with any implement. Even though Merlin
turned his back on his family and his heritage, his fingers retained
the memory of his training and he often found this memory useful
in his service of law and order.

The three remaining Merlino sisters, Dolly, Nelly, and Tilly, continue to live the high life they'd always known. From third-rate performers on the music hall stage, they made the transition to the
television screen and in the 1970's, emerge as dazzling stars. Again,
as at the beginning of his police career, Capricorn finds himself living down his family's notoriety with his colleagues. Even though
each affects to despise the other's way of life and trade, Capricorn
and his aunts share a mutual measure of respect for their differences.

Not only his early training but his father's words of wisdom come
to him from time to time, the wisdom which transcends the trick
and enhances his detective perceptions.

> "It's always in front of you, if only you look," he would say
> with a cunning wink. "Anything that seems solid, heavy, like
> it don't move—the floorboards even might be part of the trick.
> Take the last thing you'd ever think of, and watch it like a
> woman trying to get in your trouser pockets. That'll be it."[2]

Pauline Glen Winslow has crafted a fascinating series. Her books
have a certain ambiance—a sense of shifting perspectives—with a
shimmering illusive quality to both characters and plots alike.
Readers are tantalized with snippets of information often carried

through from other books. Characters reappear irregularly, sometimes in only one sentence, nevertheless one has the feeling that these are familiar people. "Flash" Copper, Happy Delaney, Joss Parker, and the ephemeral Rose are featured in one or another of the six novels. With fine literary legerdemain Winslow captures and releases their essence through Capricorn's memory scape.

There is a chronological sequence to these novels though it is not apparent in the order in which they were published. To fully appreciate Winslow's stylistic chicanery, we recommend reading from the first book published to the last.

JOCELYN O'ROARKE
1983-1984   2 books   American
Jane Dentinger

With only two books in this series, Jane Dentinger has created a full-blown, well-developed, and believable character. Jocelyn O'Roarke is the product of an Irish Catholic upbringing and a survivor of parochial school. An actress in New York, she is neither starving nor struggling. Rather, she is a competent professional with confidence in her talent and a willingness to practice her trade on both sides of the footlights—on stage, in classroom settings, and in the more lucrative though less prestigious world of television advertising.

O'Roarke's introduction to sleuthing coincides with her near debut on Broadway and her meeting with Detective Sergeant Phillip Gerrard. Together, they bring the mystery to its denouement and as the second book of the series opens, are working toward meshing their professional lives as nicely as their personal lives have done.

"There's nothing the matter with you...nothing at all," he said, gently stroking her wrist and feeling like an ass. He was furious with himself for not fully appreciating the compromised position their relationship placed her in. It was true; she was one of his best sources of information on a case like this. Hopeless at remembering birthdays and anniversaries, Jocelyn was a gold mine of knowledge about theatre people, their past peccadilloes and present follies. She studied people the way a jeweler studied gems, critically but with enormous affection for their various facets. How could he forget that her shrewd, analytical mind was simply the protective coating for a kind and empathetic nature?[3]

As within other close communities defined by profession, everyone in these stories has the goods on everyone else whether through intimate contact or by word of mouth. Dentinger's own theatrical background provides fertile ground for the development of her characters and their settings. We look forward to more of Jocelyn's performances both as an actress and as a detective.

MICHAEL SPRAGGUE
1982-1986   4 Books   American
Linda Barnes

Tall, handsome, and possessing presence on both stage and screen, Michael Spraggue is also the descendant of Robber Baron Davison Spraggue of Boston. Schooled at the Royal Academy of Dramatic Arts in London, Spraggue has done off-Broadway work and appeared in the movies. One day, he shocked his family by applying for his private investigator's license but let it expire when he realized that hurt people stayed hurt. Friends still call on him to help them solve problems, and in the four books in which he appears, these problems lead to murder.

> "And what's your other offer—"
> "And you could play him, Michael." Darien rode over the interruption. "You're an actor. The years away from the profession don't matter. You're back now. God, I envy you that face, that adaptability. Your nose is a nose, your mouth is a mouth. Nothing outstanding but those cat's eyes. You've got that wonderful variety. You remind me of Lawrence Olivier when he was young."
> Spraggue lifted one eyebrow. The very best butter, he thought. The hidden half of the deal must be pretty raw.[4]

Michael lives in Boston, not far away from the Spraggue family mansion on Chestnut Hill. Though it belongs to him, he refuses to live there. He has, however, convinced his aunt, Mary Spraggue Hillman, to make what he usually refers to as the mausoleum her residence and command post for managing the Spraggue empire. Aunt Mary is equal to both tasks ably assisted by Pierce the butler and Dora the cook.

Birth and training have given Michael connections in a variety of settings: real estate, viticulture, politics, business and finance, law enforcement, and, of course, the worlds of film and theater. His activities span the continent and require him to apply his skills and call upon his connections as he works to solve a case.

Author Linda Barnes' own theatrical background gives this character insights and technique for both acting and detecting. We'd go to Michael's movies any day and want to read more about this dashing hero with amber cat's eyes.

KENNETH CARLISLE
1929-1931   3 books   American
Carolyn Wells

Out of the five series characters devised by Carolyn Wells, Kenneth Carlisle is one of the lesser known and the last created. When Carlisle was introduced, Wells had been writing mysteries around her best-known character, Fleming Stone, for twenty years. While Stone continued for another thirteen years, Carlisle lasted only a total of three.

A very different type than The Great Detective Stone, Carlisle is young and has turned to detection from a different discipline.

> A cinema hero, a movie idol, he had won all hearts from managers to fans, and from critics to flappers.
>
> His work was of the best grade—sincere, talented, finished. He had put his honest efforts into it and had made a reputation that was hailed from coast to coast.
>
> And then, surfeited with success, tired of praise and flattery, he had withdrawn from the game, and no offers of glory, fame, or lucre could tempt him to take part in another picture.
>
> But what did happen was this. Owing to the popularity of crime plays and detective work Carlisle read and pictured much of that sort of literature.
>
> And it got him at last. The game intrigued him, the field called to him, and unable to resist, he became a detective and went into the work with his whole soul.[5]

Carlisle made a clean break with Hollywood and moved to New York. His wide circle of acquaintances includes Police Sergeant Downing who appreciates Carlisle's talents in solving the insoluble case. A star before the advent of ''talkies,'' Carlisle's training taught him to pay attention to the subtleties of manner and motion. In his detective work, he most often looks for the clue that isn't there.

The plots are convoluted and some are improbable. Wells doesn't play quite fair with her readers; she certainly doesn't adhere to the strictures laid down by The Detection Club of London exhorting against gangs, Chinamen, and lunatics. Nevertheless, this three-book series is a delightful departure from Wells' other formula works.

SIR JOHN SAUMAREZ
1928-1932   2 books   English
Clemence Dane and Helen Simpson (Winifred Ashton with Helen Simpson)

Sir John Saumarez, famous actor-manager, is the star of the short-lived series created by Clemence Dane and Helen Simpson in 1928. Sir John enters and reenters the world of crime in two books and then, presumably, retires from detection to manage his theater, the Sheridan.

Born Johnny Simmonds, Sir John earned his knighthood through his work in the theater and won his wife, the lovely and regal Martella Baring, through proving her innocence at the end of the first book.

Fretted over by Mr. Foulkes, his business manager and factotum, and Mr. Boyd, his faultless manservant, Sir John manages to epitomize all that is conceited, stylish, handsome, and urbane.

The study to which a man servant admitted Novello was an apartment so perfect, so like the study of any stage ambassador, that Novello at once felt at ease, as though it were, indeed, one of those three-walled rooms in which so much of his working life had been spent. And Sir John, standing by his own fire, was the same faultless Sir John of the photographs, familiar as his setting—and as unreal. Little Markham discovered, to his surprise, that he had got his stage-fright over; and he had a fleeting sense of relief that he had refused to put on the blue suit. For Sir John was in blue—a creation to which Novello's mere coat and trousers were as rushlights to the moon.

Sir John did not advance to meet him; but his expression was considerate and welcoming. They shook hands.

"Sit down, won't you?" said Sir John indicating a chair.

Novello obeyed. Sir John continued to stand, looking down on his guest, taking in details with a lazy glance or two. Novello would have been surprised to learn how accurately, though as yet superficially, he had been assessed.[6]

Winifred Ashton, writing as Clemence Dane, and Helen Simpson collaborated on only one other mystery book (between the two Sir Johns). Miss Simpson's untimely death in the London air raids unfortunately ended their writing partnership.

TESSA CRICHTON
1970-1987   20 books   English
Anne Morice (Felicity Shaw)

Theresa Crichton treads the boards in London and the provinces and makes occasional appearances in film and television drama as well. Whether acting or resting—usually at Cousin Toby's Oxfordshire retreat, Roakes Common—Tessa is inevitably drawn into investigating a murder.

> "You mustn't mind Tessa," Robin told him, "she takes a burning interest in crime and always hopes that the prime suspect will turn out to be innocent."[7]

Loquacity and dry wit are hallmarks of this character offstage. Readers must assume that she is competent onstage, for we never see her there. Clues to Tessa's age and appearance are harder to find in these stories than clues to the murderer.

The theater is familiar territory for Anne Morice. Father, daughter, brother-in-law, and two nephews are all involved in this histrionic profession. Morice uses her knowledge of staging as the medium for murder. She gives readers fluent behind the scene information and rich descriptions of the cast members.

> This arrangement, like the invitation card, was in sharp contrast to Elsa's normally casual brand of hospitality, but I was unable to ask her whether it was for Millie's benefit, or whether she had been taking a course in social climbing. By the time I arrived she was tearing around in a frenzy, issuing commands and countermands to the hired staff and evidently on the verge of a nervous breakdown. Small wonder either, for, as Marcus confided in a muttered aside, the torrential rain which had fallen during the morning had not only brought down one section of the marquee, wrecking the most spectacular flower piece of all, but had also transformed the meadow which was doing duty as a car park into a slimy bog.

In addition to this, it had now turned out that the hem of Millie's dress, which measured approximately four miles, had to be turned up before she would consent to wear it, and some of the more raffish guests had started rolling up at five o'clock, apparently under the impression that their arrival was the signal for the party to begin.[8]

Robin Price, Tessa's husband and Chief Inspector of the CID of Scotland Yard, plays a supporting role in her offstage dramas. He brings his professional expertise to Tessa's less than orthodox methods of detecting and often plucks her from the very brink of disaster, which she has reached through her curiosity, nosiness, and penchant for gossip. Robin is willing to become involved because Tessa is very often right and he has come to trust her intuition.

Morice plays fair with readers in a classic "cozy" style. Locations and characters become familiar old friends and while nothing much ever changes in this twenty-book series and the plotting is rather predictable, it is enjoyable nevertheless.

JEMIMA SHORE
1977-1986   7 books   English
Antonia Fraser

As a performing reporter, her screen title is Jemima Shore Investigator. As a working reporter, she has won respect for her coverage of issues ranging from birth control to poverty to euthanasia. Jemima is a Television Personality and is recognized as such by an admiring public which finds her programs both entertaining and instructive. Her abilities are also recognized by her peers, colleagues, and personal friends. Among those are individuals who ask Jemima for help in getting to the root of their difficulties—all involving a murder or two.

In school, Jemima was known for her talents in the debating society. Professionally, she has become a trained and practiced interviewer and a thoroughly competent researcher. Jemima also possesses the actor's skill—which some people simply call instinct—in reading people and situations.

Jemima Shore, for her part, wished she could feel so totally convinced about the guilt of James Roy Blagge. It would have made life so much simpler. Instead, her instinct was troubling her; that famous instinct, merrily castigated by Cy Fredericks

('Your lady's instinct, my dear Jem, always so expensive, what
is it asking for this time?') and Pompey of the Yard ('My wife
suffers from the feminine instinct too; you could say we both
suffer from it.') But Jemima knew by experience that this instinct
was not to be derided.

The single word 'instinct,' drawing the fire of such quizzical
males as Cy Fredericks and Pompey, was in fact not quite accurate. It was more that Jemima possessed a very strong instinct
for order. This would not let her rest so long as the smallest
detail was out of place in the well-regulated pattern of her
mind.[9]

Her reputation precedes her and Jemima has little difficulty in
gathering information for those who obviously respect her very visible abilities. People in general are eager to talk with her and while
working on a mystery for a friend, she collects conversational clues
which lead her to the correct conclusion.

Jemima Shore is a multifaceted character. Committed to excellence in her work, she remains uncommitted in her personal relationships with the men in her life. Marriage interested her at one time
though now she is careful to keep her affairs firmly casual. Here, too,
her status provides her with a seemingly limitless supply of members
of the opposite sex to serve as escorts and companions of a more
intimate nature. Jemima has many friends from many walks of life.
Those to whom she is the closest seem all to be male. Flowering
Cherry, as she is affectionately known at Megalith Television, is
Jemima's private secretary and sometimes confidante. Theirs is less
a friendship though than a working partnership with clear-cut lines
of responsibility.

Antonia Fraser is well known as an historical biographer. Although
her mystery series character is a departure from the subjects of her
other works, Fraser's knowledge of history and her own abilities as
a careful researcher are apparent in all seven of the Jemima Shore
novels.

THESE DETECTIVES with their theatrical connections, give proof
to the statement that "all the world's a stage." As life imitates art,
they apply aspects of stagecraft and "business" to the lively art of
detecting. While not all of these detectives perform their craft before
an audience, all use their theatrical training and experience in solving murders. The writers of these series, themselves, are adept at the
skills of deception to the delight of their readers.

It is fitting that many of Ngaio Marsh's detective novels take place on and around the stage. A theatrical producer in New Zealand and honorary lecturer in Drama at Canterbury University, Dame Marsh had a theater named for her there in 1962.

Other books involving actors and the stage include:

Margery Allingham, *Dancers in Mourning*, 1937
Margot Arnold, *Exit Actors, Dying*, 1979
Caryl Brahms and S. J. Simon, *A Bullet in the Ballet*,
    1937; *Murder a la Stroganoff*, 1938
Elizabeth Daly, *Unexpected Night*, 1940
Leslie Ford, *The Devil's Stronghold*, 1948
Jane Langton, *The Memorial Hall Murder*, 1978
Charlotte MacLeod, *The Plain Old Man*, 1985
Helen McCloy, *Cue for Murder*, 1942
Ruth Rendell, *Death Notes*, 1981
Josephine Tey, *The Man in the Queue*, 1929
Anna Mary Wells, *Sin of Angels*, 1948
Carolyn Wells, *Prillilgirl*, 1924
Sara Woods, *Bloody Instructions*, 1962; *Dearest Enemy*,
    1981
Margaret Yorke, *Cast for Death*, 1976

CURE IT OR KILL IT

MEDICINE

*T*he healing arts are populated by individuals dedicated to alleviating pain and suffering. Both victims of crime and those unjustly accused of crime's commission can be said to be suffering pain. Our medical detectives are skilled at tracking down elusive microbes and wandering the mazes of the mind. Crime and illness are both aberrations and must be either thwarted or eradicated. Using their training and skills these professionals fill the prescription to remedy ills— both social and physical.

DR. GRACE SEVERANCE
1968-1978   4 books   American
Margaret Scherf

A pathologist studies human physiology to discern structural and functional changes brought about by disease. Any deviation from an assumed normal state of the nonliving or nonmaterial is also fair game for pathological study. Grace Severance, a pathologist newly retired from active practice, finds herself uncomfortable and at odds with the usual pastimes of retirees.

"Bullshit," Dr. Severance said softly, and felt better. There was no more difficult role than being the object of benevolence. The more powerful the benefactor, the greater the hazards. Look at the people who had to have their houses burned down to save them from the enemies of democracy. Myrtle was continually doing things for her that she didn't want done, and taking her to places she didn't want to see, like that trip last week to the date palm festival in Indio. Acres of grapefruit laid out on gold paper, thousands of hot tired people eating hamburger and spun sugar, or looking at slides on the sex life of the date palm.

For twenty-five years she had looked forward to the moment when she could stop teaching anatomy to unruly young medics and take her ease. The moment had come, and what was she doing? Reading treatises on cactus, listening to retired insurance men talk about their grandchildren, pretending to admire the rocks hauled in off the desert daily by people obsessed by rock hauling. For moments of high excitement she attended a class in ceramics and made leaves.

"Retirement is one hell of a bore," she said, and lay back on her pillows. She could hear Myrtle snoring gently in the room across the hall, building up strength to take on her job of managing everything. Dr. Severance wondered on what day, at what hour and second, she had allowed that fatal crack in her armor to show— the crack of serious age, age that made it advisable to tell someone where you were going when you went out, and to have someone phone you each morning to see how you were and if you were. Once you let that crack show, you were in for it. A mere chance acquaintance would give you advice on everything from cascara to corns, while a relative, like Myrtle, burdened with an iron sense of responsibility—[1]

The study of medicine and a full life provided by its teaching gives Grace a substantial body of knowledge which remains undimmed by the passage of time. If anything, her senses are made even more acute by the boredom her retirement has brought.

In the first novel, she is drawn into detecting by the advent of an unconscious young girl in need of medical attention. Though Grace is far more familiar with patients who are beyond any form of assistance, she knows how to cope with a situation which deviates from her norm. In the three books which follow, she becomes much more assertive, and, in one, actually discovers a body when no thought of murder had yet arisen.

Tracing down the elusive disease which has killed a patient is not much different than tracing the elusive human murderer. Curiosity and responsibility are essential qualities of this character. She does not leap to conclusions and does whatever is necessary to gather information for her diagnosis.

From the first book in this series of four, Grace is a fully developed character. One advantage to having an older protagonist is that these individuals begin with a history which can be woven into the story. Scherf has done this deftly and in the process has presented a warm, competent, and humorous woman we wouldn't mind meeting.

Margaret Scherf's writing career began in the mid-forties and spanned over thirty years. Author of several nonseries mysteries, she is best known for books featuring ongoing characters, including Reverend Martin Buell, and Emily and Henry Bryce.

NURSE HILDA ADAMS, "Miss Pinkerton"
1932-1942   3 books   American
Mary Roberts Rinehart

Mary Roberts Rinehart is best known as the mother of the had-I-but-known school of mystery writing. Nurse Hilda Adams is Rinehart's sole series character and appears in only three books written between 1932 and 1942.

Romantic terror is the central theme of all of Rinehart's stories. Murder does occur to be sure, but this is almost incidental to the plot in which a young, beautiful heroine is terrorized and thwarted in achieving her heart's desire.

Called to cases by Inspector Patton (in the first book, Fuller in the third), this attractive, thirty-eight-year-old is all that a good nurse should be.

And then I had made that alliance with Inspector Patton and the Homicide Squad. By accident, but they had found me useful from the start. There is one thing about a trained nurse in a household: she can move about day and night and not be questioned. The fact is that the people in a house are inclined pretty much to forget that she is there. She has only one job ostensibly, and that is her patient. Outside of that job she is more or less a machine to them. They see that she is fed, and if she is firm that she gets her hours off-duty. But they never think of her as a reasoning human being, seeing a great deal more than they imagine, and sometimes using what she sees, as I did.[2]

Nurse Adams has a gun, a snub-nosed little automatic which the inspector gave her for protection. At home, she keeps it in the jardiniere with the Boston fern which her housekeeper never remembers to water. A canary named Dicky lives in a cage in the living room, which is—in all books—newly done in chintz. "Miss Pinkerton" doesn't get to spend much time at home, though. The inspector does not hesitate to call upon her at all hours in her professional capacity to tend a patient, and, unofficially, to assist him with behind-the-scenes investigation.

Danger, bordering on the supernatural, lurks in the houses Nurse Adams attends. The stories are veiled with an eerie quality designed to build suspense for the reader.

> It was midnight when he went away. Miss Juliet had wakened by that time, and so I went down at half-past twelve and heated a glass of milk for her. But I must admit I was not comfortable down there. A wind was blowing outside, and the kitchen wing seemed to be even more out of repair than the rest of the house. It creaked and groaned, and once I would have sworn that the tea-kettle moved right across the stove! If it had been possible to gallop upstairs with a glass of hot milk in my hand I would have done it! As it was, I went up with my head turned over my shoulder, until I got almost to the top of the stairs. Then I fixed my eyes on the landing, and if Miss Juliet had appeared there at that minute in her white nightgown I dare say I would have died of heart failure.[3]

The Nurse Adams stories are not up to Rinehart's classic standard of terror and foreboding. They have a lighter, more humorous touch than many of this author's other works. The device of the nurse as the central character is clever. She is a respected professional, upon whom the inspector relies. The suspense is well done, if a bit melodramatic and follows a tried and true formula. Fans of Rinehart are urged to seek out these books.

NURSE SARAH KEATE
1929-1954   7 books   American
Mignon Eberhart

In a crisp uniform and starched white cap, Sarah Keate ministers to the ailing and infirm as a private duty nurse. Her patients invariably inhabit dark, brooding mansions.

> No one spoke. There lay over them all a tense, determined quiet that seemed to restrain hysteria. I lingered for only a few moments. Gray daylight was beginning to filter in pallid streaks through the shutters.
> At the muffled sound of the hall door closing I started back to the tower room. From the window in the hall, beyond the wet path and dreary iron gate, I caught a glimpse of an ambulance. It loomed coldly white through the dismal, gray dawn. The sleet was turning again to heavy fog. The shrubbery, bare and brown and dripping, mingled indistinctly with the shadows of the fog. Toward the north of the house, the dense thickets of evergreens made black blotches. And all about the place reared that solid wall, hemming in the evergreens and the shadows and the lifeless garden and the grim old house in which I stood, where murder had walked that night.
> It was a world of its own. And I, Sarah Keate, hitherto a respectable and respected spinster, was involved in that dreadful world and, by virtue of my profession, forced to stay there![4]

A selection of old family retainers and servants with strange names and stranger habits make up the household staff and help or hinder Nurse Keate in the pursuance of her duties. A variety of friends and relatives are also on hand to wish the patient well or ill, depending on the inheritance question.

Introduced in 1929, Sarah usually appeared with Lance O'Leary, a young, independent private investigator.

> He was a slender young fellow, not very tall, his features clear and finely cut, his head well shaped and thoughtful, and his eyes a clear cool gray that saw everything. His light brown hair always shone smoothly; he was immaculately groomed and

must have spent more money on his clothes, quiet though they were in style and color, than any man should spend. He had a partiality for gray and liked a thin scarlet stripe in socks and tie, drove a long gray roadster of a make that I did not recognize, kept a manservant with the most discreet and secretive voice I have ever heard, and—well, beyond these few facts, I knew little of him.

But if, as I went about my duties in the tower room, I felt that with Lance O'Leary in the house the fearful thing the night had held was at an end, I may as well admit here and now that I was never more mistaken in my life.[5]

Mignon Eberhart has chosen the had-I-but-known style for this seven-book series. Romance, requited and un-, is a major feature in each story. Family secrets, lost wills, and German spies add up to forgettable, soap-opera melodrama.

DR. DAVID WINTRINGHAM
1937-1958   14 books   English
and DR. HENRY FROST
1964-1966   2 books   English
Josephine Bell (Doris Bell Ball)

As a practicing general physician herself, Josephine Bell is well qualified to write about the realm of medical practice. It is not surprising that two of her series characters are physicians nor that the settings of many of her other mysteries are hospitals, nursing homes, and doctors' offices.

The first two books of Miss Bell's series, featuring a young Dr. David Wintringham, were released in 1937. In *Murder in Hospital*, he is joined by an equally young Inspector Steven Mitchell of Scotland Yard. Over the ensuing twenty years, these two were frequent collaborators in detecting. Each appeared on his own in one or two novels, and, after the Wintringham series came to an end in 1958, Inspector Mitchell joined the retired Dr. Henry Frost in solving murder cases.

Though he is a featured character in fourteen books, Wintringham is not The Great Detective. Miss Bell seems to use him more as a scene setter and one who provides the opportunity for the investigation of probable foul play. His wife Jill appears in most of his stories and does not appear to be at all encumbered by domestic routine nor the activities of the couple's four children.

Jill laughed, and Tom joined in. He had lost some of his shyness, and was recovering from the shock of finding his misconceptions proved both false and ridiculous. He sat back in the comfortable armchair, sipping his sherry and wondering why it was so easy to talk to Mrs. Wintringham, whom he did not know at all, and so difficult to get on with Mrs. Felton, the mother of his friend Christopher, whom he had known for several years.

"What exactly does—Dr. Wintringham—do? It is Dr., isn't it?"

"Yes, it is. He is head of the clinical research department at St. Edmund's Hospital. He organizes the research done, and he does some himself. He gives lectures on medicine to the students and he takes them round on his visits to his own cases. He used to take out-patient sessions, but he has given that up now."

"He sounds a pretty important bloke," said Tom, as casually as possible.

"He is one of the senior consultants at the hospital. *I* think he is very important, naturally." And Jill smiled at Tom so frankly that he found himself smiling back, and wishing he had pencil and paper at hand to record her charming devotion.[6]

The couple's devotion is mutual but they are not one of the Golden Age's fun detecting duos. Jill serves as David's sounding board and sometimes paves the way for him to question individuals involved in murder. While this pair is not particularly memorable, the stories in which they appear—usually puzzles—are enjoyable. The author gives all the clues in fair fashion and the outcome is not easily predicted.

Dr. Henry Frost appears in only two novels between 1964 and 1966. In the first book, he and his family are directly involved in uncovering (literally) a crime and the complicity of the population of the entire village where the Frosts have moved in retirement.

Henry Frost was a large, white-haired man who looked older than his sixty years. He had retired from his exhausting general practice in London in January, having endured the rigours of the National Health Service for fourteen and a half years and before that a mixed practice from two years after the time he had qualified in 1927. He need not have retired for another five years, but as his colleagues kept reminding him, his pension, for which he had only begun making contributions in 1948 and which was computed on Civil Service lines, would be negligible in any case, so why kill himself over minor ailments and injuries, emergency calls to children whose parents wanted to shift their responsibility, not to mention endless paper work, for the sake of a few shillings a year more? Far better to secure now the compensation money for his former excellent practice that the Government had bought in and buy himself a place in the country or a flat in London where he could sit back and laugh at them all still struggling with the disease-conscious health-hag-ridden general community....

...Jean, his wife, insisted upon making their new home in the country, in the south rather than the east or west. The north they did not consider at all, having no ties there of any kind. But in the south their two sons, one a surgeon, the other an engineer, would, with their families, be available for visits. Their daughter, Judy, an occupational therapist at a London hospital, must be able to come to them for weekends. So the south it was, Sussex for preference.[7]

Secure in his knowledge and former position, Dr. Frost makes a tenacious and formidable adversary to the perpetrator of murder and others involved in the conspiracy of silence. His wife Jean and their daughter Judy take active roles with the doctor in detecting.

Bell has created two other nonmedical series characters as well: Claude Warrington-Reeve, a London Barrister (Inspector Mitchell also appears here), and the elderly Amy Tupper, a former actress.

DR. JEFFREY and ANNE MCNEILL
1936-1954   19 books   American
Theodora M. DuBois

Jeffrey is a doctor at the local medical school where he is enormously well liked and admired by colleagues and staff. His adoring wife, Anne, oversees their beautiful home, maid, nurse, and two small precocious sons. Their days seem all too full with the wonderful stuff of life: Jeffrey busy lecturing at school and Anne at home planning luncheons and dinner parties or well-deserved vacations. They are, however, often called upon to provide their discreet services in dealing with the more dark and sordid aspects of the world.

"It's the McNeills, on their *Thetis*," Perry Fisher said.

A dark, authoritative-looking man sat at the sloop's tiller, and a lithe woman in gray slacks and sweater waved at them from where she stood with the rope in the bow. Her corn-colored short hair was blown by the wind.

Her husband called to her, "We'll have to go up the river a bit, Anne, and come into the dock against the tide."

"That's the way one should do it," Linden said approvingly.

"The McNeills know everything," Fisher said, but without envy. "Linden, honey, here we've opened to exactly the right page at the back of the book to find all the answers. As soon as they've docked we'll tell them the whole story and turn it over to them."

"But Perry, they're making this waterway cruise on a vacation. They'd simply hate to be involved with another body, and everything hectic."

"They're used to it," he said firmly. "The crime detectors supreme. Come on. Catch their ropes."[8]

There are nineteen books in this series, written between 1936 and 1954. Anne and Jeffrey are forerunners of other witty, fun detective couples popular during this genre's Golden Age. The stories are, on the whole, lighthearted. Romance flourishes, honor prevails and the McNeills keep moving from one success to another. Unfortunately, the writing is heavy-handed and long-winded. Miss DuBois does not play fair with her readers. She throws in superfluous characters with the missing explanation at the last minute and, in one story, gives us a central character who does not even recognize her own fiancé as the murder victim.

Fortunately, the books are hard to find.

DR. GORDON CHRISTY
1983-1985   2 books   American
Barbara Moore

In the first book of this new series, Gordon Christy is a recent graduate of Colorado College of Veterinary Medicine in Fort Collins. He has decided that the mountains are where he wants to be and is on his way to serve as locum for Dr. Potter, a Vail veterinarian. On the way up the mountain, Christy is run off the road by the driver of a black MGB. The passenger in the sports car is a Doberman. Almost as soon as he arrives at Dr. Potter's clinic, Christy is whisked off to a condominium where he encounters the Doberman once again, this time, guarding a murdered body, the driver of the black MGB.

The practice of veterinary medicine is a challenge. One deals with patients unable to tell how they are feeling or what hurts. Solid anatomical knowledge is essential. Beyond that, an instinct for reading behavior, to indicate a line of diagnosis, is invaluable. As Dr. Potter points out, this training is similar to that of a detective's.

> "I'm no detective, Dr. Potter. I'm a doctor of veterinary medicine. I figured the patients would come before anything else."
>
> "So they do. So they will. And as for your not being a detective, come, come. What are they teaching you young people over at the vet school if not to follow clues and arrive at a solution? It's basic scientific method, Dr. Christy. You collect data and see where they lead you. Now this nine-thirty appointment, a cat with feline urologic syndrome. It so happens that I know the patient but you don't. What would you do before you initiated treatment? You'd evaluate the symptoms. You'd obtain a history, including diet, right? Has the cat dysuria? Hematuria? In your physical exam, you'd determine whether the old boy is obstructed or nonobstructed. You'd collect a urine sample, and you'd keep looking for abnormalities there. Finally you'd arrive at a diagnosis. That's all you have to do to be a detective, Dr. Christy. Isolate your symptoms, evaluate them, and make your diagnosis."9

Keeping Dr. Potter's words of wisdom in mind, and with a little help from Gala, the Doberman, Christy solves his first murder mystery. At the end of the story, Christy finds himself the owner of Gala and a partner in the clinic with Dr. Potter.

In the second book, Christy is called by a friend to help with a family problem involving a werewolf. Sam Benally, a Navajo with a Ph.D. in Geology, works for the Council of Energy Resource Tribes. Sam's family lives on a Navajo Reservation in New Mexico. A rancher living adjacent to their property has been killed—his throat ripped out by large, canine teeth. Superstition and a somewhat reluctant belief in witches and ghostly spirits has forced the neighbors to lay the blame for the murder on the Benally family doorstep. Sam wants Christy's help in catching the animal and clearing his family of suspicion.

There is an interesting balance of folklore and modern science in this story. Once again, Christy's knowledge of medicine and animal behavior leads him to the human agent directing the canine killer. A respect for the natural order of things and the true nature of beings—canine, feline, reptile or human—gains Christy respect in return from the Indian community. He does not rely on macho tactics in any of his dealings and he makes it easy for the officials—both Indian and Anglo—on the case to accept his assistance.

Information on canine physiology, animal care, and training is slipped into these stories in an easy, narrative fashion. Without resorting to anthropomorphism, Moore also gives readers an idea of what might go on in the mind of a domesticated dog abandoned in the wild. She actively demonstrates the ferocity and unpredictability of a highly trained, though abused and mishandled attack dog.

Barbara Moore is a staunch animal advocate. Her book jacket blurb tells readers that she raises and shows Dobermans. It makes sense that one of the main characters in her series is a Dobe and further, that a veterinarian is another.

We like Dr. Christy. We want more of him and more of his friends and colleagues and the animals he meets professionally and socially.

DAME BEATRICE ADELA LESTRANGE BRADLEY
1929-1984   68 books   English
Gladys Mitchell

In spite of an incredibly long and productive career, Mrs. Bradley is not as well known in this country as she is in her native Great Britain. It may be that the focus which author Gladys Mitchell placed on folklore, mysticism, and superstition—intimately linked with British history—was felt to be just too English for American tastes.

A practicing psychiatrist with a small clinic of her own, Mrs. Bradley is also a consultant to the Home Office. She has earned renown and, in at least one book, is described as "one of the most famous of modern women."[10] Competent and well respected by her professional peers and police and government officials, she is treated with both affection and fear by more ordinary citizens.

Introduced in 1929, she burst on the scene, a woman of great age and much experience. Variously described as reptilian, shriveled, and cronelike, Mrs. Bradley leers, shrieks, and cackles her way through life and criminal investigations without seeming to age beyond her already advanced years.

> Mrs. Bradley changed the subject. Resting her clawlike hands on the arms of her chair, she smiled by stretching her lips sideways until her yellow countenance resembled that of a chameleon, blinked her bright, beady, little black eyes several

times in quick succession, and observed in the voice which always startled strangers by its richness and beauty—it startled me, of course, the first time I heard it:

"What do you consider the most amazing sight on earth, Mr. Wells?"

There was a silence, while she darted her quick glances from one to another and then back to me. I could feel myself sweating, and I began to realize what birds feel like when snakes watch them. There was something saurian about Mrs. Bradley—about her eyes, about her lips, about the brain behind those eyes and the tongue behind those lips. She passed the tip of a small red tongue over the lips and then pursed them into a little beak, and I remember being rather surprised to note that the tongue was not forked like a serpent's tongue. "So this," I thought to myself, "is a psychoanalyst." Mrs. Bradley apparently read my thoughts.

"Quite so, my dear," she said. "And, moreover, one who is old-fashioned enough to consider Sigmund Freud the high priest of the mysteries of the sect. Kindly refrain from making the obvious and heart-rending pun, for there should be no jesting upon sacred subjects except by Dean Inge."

She concluded the remark with a startling scream of mirth, and, to my acute embarrassment, she pinched my cheek playfully.[11]

Married three times and mother of grown sons, Mrs. Bradley is also the beloved aunt to various nieces and nephews who drop in and out of the stories, sometimes as partners in whatever adventure is at hand, and at others, merely as decoration. Oddly enough, children number her most ardent admirers and, as a rule, eagerly do her bidding without being put off by her unnerving appearance.

Hers is a large and affectionate family by extension as well as by birth and through marriage. Laura Menzies meets Mrs. Bradley in 1942, assists the "Old Trout" in her investigations, and from then on rarely leaves her side. Serving as secretary, confidante, and general dogsbody, Laura's life proceeds along more conventional chronological lines than does her employer's. After a long engagement, she marries Detective Inspector Robert Gavin, gives him a son and a daughter, and is a grandmother by the end of the series.

Hints throughout the series indicate that Mrs. Bradley is descended from a long line of witches and may have inherited arcane powers. None of the books we have found give much information regarding her early life or education. That she was an established, practicing psychiatrist in 1929 indicates that her academic pursuits must have taken place around the turn of the century, a period which coincides with the new dawn of scientific inquiry. Perhaps the gift of second sight is what enables Mrs. Bradley to use her penetrating mind to recognize the deeper pattern of events. Without her formidable education, she might simply be considered another village eccentric, however, her inherited gift and her academic background allow her inquiring intellect to suspend judgment when investigating either fact or fantasy.

The stories themselves are rather unconventional. Morris Dancers, Roman ruins, the Green Man, a cousin of the Loch Ness monster, and all the beliefs and superstitions which surround them are treated with the same nonjudgmental, intellectual curiosity by Mrs. Bradley as are more contemporary issues such as smuggling, women's rights, education, and murder. Though apparent opposites rarely meet, Mrs. Bradley—in all her paradoxical glory—blends and makes use of both scientific fact and supernatural supposition. Even though the topics and their treatment are unusual, these are well written and believable tales.

As an early member of the Detection Club, Mitchell is committed to playing fair with her readers and does so by laying all the clues to the mystery before them. At times, however, Mrs. Bradley is privy to insights which enable her to reach a conclusion no one else could have done, even one possessing all the facts. Her understanding of human nature is such that she is able to predict actions and events with uncanny accuracy. Where a hypothetical explanation is often enough to satisfy authority, "Mrs. Croc" is not above manipulating lives, fiddling with fate, and meting out her own form of retribution. Criminals are not always brought to justice by law and during her career she actually admits—if only to herself and to those near and dear—to committing three murders.

As so few of these books were originally published in the United States, older copies are hard to find. There is a resurgence of interest in these classics and it is to be hoped that the entire series will be reissued in this country.

DR. BASIL WILLING
1938-1980   13 books   American
Helen McCloy

Introduced in 1938, Basil Willing is one of mystery fiction's first American psychiatric detectives. Willing uses psychiatry to delve into an individual suspect's unconscious to uncover motive. He also uses it to discover physical clues to the crime as well. Assistant Chief Inspector Foyle of the New York City Police Department has availed himself and the department of Willing's services over the years. Willing tells him,

> "You gave me my first chance to apply psychology to the detection of criminals. Now I'm supposed to be applying it to the detection of spies and saboteurs. But I ought to be with some medical unit. I'm under forty-four, I have no wife or children, and I've been in the Medical Reserve Corps ever since the last war. I went straight from Johns Hopkins to a casualty clearing station and it was through shell-shock cases that I first became interested in psychiatry.[12]

Born around the turn of the century Basil Willing ages at the same rate as the era. When the series opens, psychiatry is a relatively new and untrusted science. McCloy makes fascinating links with history, prevailing thought, and the constant human condition. She presents a strong, competent leading character who understands the practical application of these links and is capable of explaining psychological phenomenon. Willing enables individuals to investigate their own motivations and to view life from a slightly altered perspective.

> "For a man's past and future are not just things that happen to him. They are as much a part of him as the shape of his face or the color of his eyes. That is why a man's life always has a consistent pattern, and depth. Psychologists find that each of us throughout life tend to repeat the same mistakes over and over again. Our mistakes are a part of us. Without them we would be different people.
>
> "When you seek a murderer among people who are superficially incapable of crime, the answer must lie in the long body of one of those people—the true shape of a character as it is revealed over a long period of time. That's why you felt suddenly that your relatives and friends were strangers to you. You were suddenly aware that you were seeing them in cross-section, not as they really were extending in time as well as space."
>
> "In other words," said Alice, "the roots of this crime are deep in the past?"
>
> "Put it this way: The past is an invisible part of the present that is already shaping the future."[13]

Settings are accurate and carefully chosen to showcase Dr. Willing's speciality in the context of location. The actions of young soldiers on patrol along the Texas–Mexican border in 1918 have an effect on lives over the following thirty years. Scotland immediately after WWII makes an unlikely setting for repercussions of that war. Satellite characters are well drawn and believable, not only in action, but in thinking as well. McCloy combines these elements, in complex permutations to make an exciting and readable story.

Perhaps the most interesting aspect of some of the Willing novels is the foray into paranormal psychiatric phenomena. Doppelganger, poltergeist, Hindu mystical philosophy, precognition, and multiple personality provide subtle counterpoints to straightforward detective fiction.

There are only thirteen books featuring Dr. Willing. They span forty-two years and the most recently released appeared in 1980. Earlier works are hard to come by and well worth the effort a search takes. We trust that this is a series which will be reissued in the near future.

DR. WILLIAM AMES
1971-1975   3 books   American
Lucy Freeman

When Lucy Freeman decided to try her hand at writing mystery novels, her choice for a detective was the natural outgrowth of her previous writing. Ms. Freeman is the author of over thirty-five books in the fields of psychiatry and psychology. Dr. William Ames seems to be just the sort of psychoanalyst someone familiar with the trade would design. Delving into the unconscious in the long, drawn out process of psychoanalysis means that the doctor must listen to a lot of rambling drivel from the patient without lapsing into unconsciousness and missing key information. With his patients, Dr. Ames is Johnny-on-the-spot and terrifically Freudian.

In the first book, sex is the entire issue. If the scenes themselves are not gratuitous, the long-winded explanations of the acts and their meanings—overt and covert—certainly are. Dr. Ames ascribes Oedipal and Electral complexes to all of the suspects of the murder of his patient. One gets the uncomfortable feeling that the entire world population is a seething mass of repressed, libidinous desires and that our children are all going to hate us.

The names given the various characters in this story are interesting. We wondered whether Ms. Freeman had deliberately chosen them, or if, perhaps, they were seepages from her own unconscious: Dr. Ames = aims (and goals? for the target?), Mary Ames = the perfect Mary and mother of one, Jonathan Thomas = Jon Thomas (euphemism for the male member?), Elaine, his wife = Lancelot's abandoned spouse? and Detective Lonegan = a lone gun.

Dr. Ames is drawn into detecting when Lonegan asks him to interview suspects in the case.

These two sleuths meet in three books. While Dr. Ames manages the clues of the psyche, Lonegan manages the physical clues and at the end, the cases are wrapped up—too neatly—with no loose ends. Lonegan gets all the credit as Ames feels his involvement in detecting wouldn't go over too well with the New York Psychiatric Association. We think he's right. What really puzzles us though, is how such a sympathetic, aware, and likeable character as Dr. William Ames could arise from the bog of psychobabble Ms. Freeman has wrought.

The series featuring Dr. Ames is advertised as the first to use a practicing psychiatrist as a sleuth. This is not quite accurate as both Dr. Basil Willing and the following character clearly demonstrate.

DR. HILLIS OWEN and MISS POMEROY
1942-1948   3 books   American
Anna Mary Wells

With a comfortable office on Park Avenue and a thriving practice, Dr. Hillis Owen is only slightly taken aback when he is approached by Mrs. Jerome Meredith, a widow recently acquitted of her husband's murder. She has come to him for professional advice because, in spite of her acquittal, she isn't sure that she didn't pull the trigger which ended her husband's life. Reluctantly at first, Dr. Owen agrees to take the case and, as the therapy proceeds, finds it impossible to declare her innocence on psychiatric grounds, though he is personally convinced that she did not commit the crime.

After discharging her as his patient and advising her to hire a detective to provide the information she needs to clear her mind, Dr. Owen confides to his nurse, Miss Pomeroy that he wishes he could do more.

> Miss Pomeroy took off her glasses and sat back in her chair.
> "She didn't respond to hypnosis, then?"

"She responded too damned well—beg pardon, Pomeroy.
She acted it all out both ways. She did and she didn't. We're
right back where we started from."

"But you don't believe now that she did it, do you, doctor?"

"Touché. No, I don't. And in April I did. I told her that, for
what consolation it may be to her. She's a game kid. She got
under my skin."

"I like her too," Miss Pomeroy said. "What will she do now?"

"I advised her to hire a detective, but I don't think she
will. She's afraid of picking up somebody innocent and putting
'em through the mill. Besides, she says it's too late. The clues
are all gone. Damn it, if I was a detective, I'll bet I could turn
one up."

Miss Pomeroy looked hard at him until he flushed and
laughed.

"Not so hot at my own job, but I could sure do the other
fellow's."

"Well, why don't you?" Miss Pomeroy asked.

"Why don't I what?"

"Investigate it yourself. There's no law against prying as long
as you don't take a fee for it."[14]

Dr. Owen continues the investigation along more conventional
lines of detecting. He checks facts and both he and Pomeroy interview the people involved in the case. The solution finally comes
through the doctor's particular expertise in delving into and
understanding the human psyche.

Unfortunately, only the first two books have been reissued and
the third in the series seems to have fallen off the planet. In the second book, Dr. Owen is serving in the army and Miss Pomeroy takes
a job with a detective agency. While Dr. Owen makes a brief
appearance, this is really her story. Dr. Owen and Miss Pomeroy are
intelligent, warm, and caring people. The stories are well written
and well plotted— real psychological thrillers. There's good action,
suspense, and danger and the endings are believable surprises.

FOR THE MEDICAL PRACTITIONER unable to hold death or
madness in abeyance by the application of healing skills, the call to
serve Hippocrates is perhaps best answered by unmasking the
perpetrating organism—the cause of death. From hospitals through
consulting offices to private homes, these detecting doctors and
nurses are dedicated to relieving dis-ease.

Other books featuring medical personnel include:

Catherine Aird, *A Late Phoenix*, 1970
Josephine Bell, *A Well-Known Face*, 1960
Christianna Brand, *Green for Danger*, 1944
Edward Candy, *Which Doctor*, 1953; *Bones of Contention*, 1954
R. B. Dominic, *The Attending Physician*, 1980
E. X. Giroux, *A Death for a Doctor*, 1986
P. D. James, *A Mind to Murder*, 1963; *Unnatural Causes*, 1967; *Shroud for a Nightingale*, 1971; *The Black Tower*, 1975; *Death of an Expert Witness*, 1977
Emma Lathen, *A Stitch in Time*, 1968
Ngaio Marsh, *The Nursing Home Murder*, 1935
Dorothy L. Sayers, *Whose Body?*, 1923
Sara Woods, *Tarry and be Hanged*, 1969; and others

KILLINGS ON THE MARKET

*F*amiliarity with business procedure and financial protocol gives this group of characters an edge against the competition—both professional and criminal. Much of what they know comes from years of experience, and, over time, each has developed a sixth sense which alerts them to the fact that things aren't "adding up right."

The small business owner exhibits independence. Time is her own, but within that apparent temporal freedom is the responsibility for doing the job well and satisfying the customer. Business professionals must often manage people as skillfully as other assets. The best managers hold an overview of particular situations and deal with the individuals in each situation within its context. Bankers have access to privileged information about individuals and companies which gives them clues to a case not readily available to officers of the law. Those in sales frequently possess strong powers of observation and perseverance which are important in successful detecting.

As the *Salesman's Handbook* points out:

Don't trust to luck, but be exact and verify the smallest fact.[1]

JOHN PUTNAM THATCHER
1961-1982   19 books   American
Emma Lathen (Martha Henissart and Mary Jane Latsis)

The Sloan is the third largest investment bank in the world. Staffed by a group of highly trained experts in the financial aspects of business, the Sloan is a major force, not only on Wall Street, but around the globe. John Putnam Thatcher, senior vice president of this august institution could easily be the subject of a painting entitled, *Portrait of a Banker*. Silver-haired, well and conservatively tailored, Thatcher respects the power of the "almighty dollar" while remaining unimpressed by the mere trappings of wealth.

Experience and expertise enable Thatcher to find the bottom line of the most complex financial statement. He also applies these fiscal talents to solving murders which arise to complicate the Sloan's normal, steady course of business.

Executive offices, boardrooms, limousines, fine restaurants, country clubs, and mansions are the usual milieu in which John Thatcher operates. He is, however, equally at ease in factories, dealer's showrooms, and the Chock Full O' Nuts on lower Broadway. Wherever his duties take him, he is always appropriate. Banker's gray provides excellent cover for Thatcher's investigations. His position gives him authority and a great deal of latitude to pry into affairs both pecuniary and personal.

John Putnam Thatcher's personal life is far less apparent than his professional one. A widower with three grown children and numerous grandchildren, he lives alone in a residential hotel in downtown Manhattan. His work is his life and the stories find him in his office on the sixth floor of the Sloan building or traveling in the service of the bank.

> Important events demand important men. Let Australia expand her nickel capacity and Thatcher would find himself on Macquarie Street, Sydney. If Battle Creek planned to saturate Scandinavia with cornflakes, Thatcher would get to Copenhagen before the cereal salesmen.
>
> It was inevitable, therefore, when the Sloan decided on a major reshuffling of its European credits, that John Thatcher, supported by his second-in-command, Charlie Trinkam, should expect to spend several weeks on one of the most heavily trafficked extensions of Wall Street—the Bahnhofstrasse in Zurich, Switzerland.[2]

The banking community provides Thatcher with a variety of subordinates and colleagues who assist him—ostensibly, in his banking business—though their aid often helps him unravel the clues leading to a killer. The eccentricities and foibles of these satellite characters provide fertile ground for the humor which runs throughout the series. Tom Robichaux, the much-married partner of Robichaux and Devane, is one of Thatcher's oldest friends. Bradford Withers, president of the Sloan, is decidedly unpresidential. He is usually to be found anywhere other than the bank. When he is there, it is to redecorate his office and to confuse any issue at hand. Everett Gabler, the most senior of Thatcher's section chiefs is both particular and persnickety. He carefully tends his weak digestive system with the same assiduity he gives Rails and Industrials.

In the first Thatcher novel, readers learn that the banker was graduated from Harvard some forty years earlier, which would make him over sixty in 1961. Nineteen books later, in 1982, he and his colleagues are still the same respective ages.

Each book in the series covers a different aspect of business and finance. Emma Lathen is the joint pseudonym of two women eminently qualified to write on these subjects. Mary Jane Latsis is a former economist and Martha Henissart holds a law degree. Together they have given readers a twenty-year chronicle of American business along with humorous, well-plotted mysteries. Under another pseudonym, R. B. Dominic, they have created a character who operates in the arena of national politics.

RICHARD TRENTON
1980-1982   3 books   English
Anne Burton (Sara Hutton Bowen-Judd)
STEPHEN MARRYAT
1980   2 books   English
Margaret Leek (Sara Hutton Bowen-Judd)

Sara Bowen-Judd writing as Sara Woods, created the well-known London barrister Antony Maitland. When we discovered that under other pseudonyms she had created other series, we were naturally curious. We found that within the span of two years, 1980 to 1982, she published fifteen mystery novels, six featuring Antony Maitland, and the complete series of Trenton, Marryat, and Jeremy Locke. Richard Trenton and Stephen Marryat belong in this chapter by virtue of their association with business and finance. Maitland, Locke, and Anne Marryat can be found among the legal eagles.

Richard Trenton is a controller in the Advance Department of the Northumberland and Wessex Bank in London where he has been employed for over twenty years. Trenton's responsibilities to the bank involve the review and approval of loan applications for his section. After he successfully solves a murder in the first of this three-book series, his superiors do not hesitate to take him away from his desk to look into questions not directly connected to the financial side of banking.

Richard and his family live in a flat on Eden Place in The City, London's legal and financial district. This rather unusual residential location puts him within an easy stroll of the Bread Court office of his friend, solicitor Jake Fulford, with whom he consults on points of law.

Richard's most valued consultants are, however, his wife and son. Red-haired Maggie administers Scotch and sympathy while serving as a sounding board for Richard's ideas and hypotheses. Although she is mother of three—Hugh and Jane are away at school and never enter the story—she is Richard's wife first and foremost. While Maggie soothes her husband, Ricky—a precocious eight-year-old—spends his time in the kitchen perfecting his artistic skills. When he does join his parents, he actually contributes suggestions which aid Richard in finding lost children and documents and unmasking murderers.

Stephen Marryat is an estate agent and occasional appraiser and auctioneer in Broadcombe, West Midshire, in the English countryside. He and his wife Anne live in the house in which he grew up, in the village of Ashfield. Anne is a solicitor with a background in criminal law and the stories are told from her point of view. The two novels in the series take place within the Ashfield-Broadcombe communities and involve the Marryats' friends. By applying his intuition and personal knowledge of the area and its inhabitants, Stephen is instrumental in solving Anne's cases.

We find most of Bowen-Judd's characters somewhat wooden and predictable. Maggie is *always* there with the Scotch. Ricky is *always* either painting or confounding his parents. Richard is *always* in conflict with Detective Chief Inspector Denby. Stephen and Anne frequent the Fighting Cock Pub where they are often reminded by the other regulars that while Anne is accepted as Stephen's wife, she remains slightly beyond the pale due to her London upbringing and her profession.

Readers familiar with the Maitland character may share our curiosity about other characters created by this author. That is the only reason we can suggest for reading them.

MONTAGUE EGG
1933-1939   2 books   English
Dorothy L. Sayers

There are no Montague Egg novels. He exists only in eleven short stories. A commercial traveler for Plummet & Rose, Wines and Spirits, Piccadilly, Egg is a firm believer in each and every maxim in the *Salesman's Handbook*. He relies on his powers of observation and business acumen to solve murders which are mainly of the timetable variety.

Young and fair, he pales by comparison to Sayer's famous Lord Peter Wimsey. While Lord Peter detects from a sense of duty arising out of noblesse oblige, Egg's sense of duty stems from the desire to serve—the public as well as his company.

> He supposed it must be murder to terrify an old man to death; he was not sure, but he meant to find out. He cast about in his mind for a consoling motto from the *Salesman's Handbook*, but, for the first time in his life, could find nothing that really fitted the case.
>
> "I seem to have stepped regularly out of my line," he thought sadly; "but still, as a citizen—"
>
> And then he smiled, recollecting the first and last aphorism in his favourite book:
>
> To serve the Public is the aim
> Of every salesman worth the name.[3]

These are good stories. Tight, little vignettes of detection with definite beginnings, middles, and ends. Monty, himself, is an amusing, though minor, character.

EMILY and HENRY BRYCE
1948-1963   5 books   American
Margaret Scherf

Manhattanites Emily and Henry Bryce are decorators by trade. As the series opens, they are not as yet married. Their studio, the Lentement Decorating Company, is located on Lexington Avenue and their respective apartments are around the corner on East 62nd, just across from one another.

Emily, bubbleheaded about most things and incapable of turning down a job, knows most everything there is to know about paint.

> "Miss Murdock," Burgreen interrupted, "take a look at this overcoat, will you? It has some red paint on it. I'd like to know if it's the kind of paint you were using on Bryce's kitchen."
> Emily bent over the sleeve, examined the stiff stains. She scrambled through the worktable drawer for a reading glass, took the coat to the light. "It's pigment," she decided. "Pure, dried-up pigment."
> "You mean it isn't wall paint?" Burgreen demanded.
> "No," Emily said. "It's coloring."
> "Is she right?" Burgreen asked Henry.
> "Better take her word for it. On any other subject I'd rather believe an intelligent horse, but on paint—Emily knows."[4]

She is nicely offset by Henry, an amiable, gentle soul with a good, if not hard, head for business. He is Emily's employee until they marry when he becomes her partner in business as well as detecting.

The standing cast of characters includes Roscoe, Emily's longtime and worshipful employee whose one bad habit is using his own judgment; Link Simpson, a purveyor of antiques who proposes to Emily at least twice a year; Hilda Leghorn, proprietress of a neighborhood beauty parlor and Emily's barb-tongued best friend; and Mr. Gottlieb, owner of the local deli and Emily's devoted admirer. He appreciates her hearty appetite.

These are humorous books with the silly, sophisticated wit of the late forties. They are well up to the standard of Scherf's other series featuring the characters of Dr. Grace Severance and the Reverend Martin Buell.

JENNIFER CAIN
1984-1987   4 books   American
Nancy Pickard

The small coastal town of Port Frederick, Massachusetts, has become a dichotomy. Economically depressed since the demise of its mainstay industry, Cain's Clams, it remains the home of some of the East Coast's richest families. In 1968, one of these families, having no offspring to inherit its accumulated wealth, established the Port Frederick, Massachusetts, Civic Foundation and encouraged their friends to make substantial contributions and bequests to the fund in order to

> protect and promote the well-being; the cultural, spiritual and mental development and the superior achievement of all kinds of the citizens of Port Frederick, Massachusetts.[5]

Jennifer Cain is an apt representative for this split community. Daughter of the wealthy James Damon Cain III whose inability to manage the family canning business brought about its collapse and with it the town's economic recession, she serves as the well-qualified executive director of the foundation.

> Thanks to the foresight of my grandfather—or maybe to his disappointed understanding of his son's deficiencies—my sister and I had long ago been provided with hefty trust funds. So even after the closure, she and I could still afford to move among the country club set into which we'd been born. (Perhaps I should say here that I'd like to able to claim that I won my job on the basis of my sterling qualifications alone, but the truth is that my upper crust connections didn't hurt me none, as they say in Texas.) Even my father had trust funds on which to support my mother and enable him to live out the rest of his lazy days in California.
>
> Of course, the people he put out of work were not so lucky. It was they who suffered the most from the collapse of Cain Clams. I don't know if my father ever allowed himself to admit that fact—it isn't like him to take any blame for anything—but it shamed my sister and almost killed my already sick mother then and there. As for me, it was probably that incident as much as anything that propelled me toward this strange combination of high finance and social work. I guess I thought that through my good deeds I might make partial payment toward the debt my family owes this town.[6]

The mysteries in this series arise out of Foundation business. In the first book, the "Big Five" of potential donors are being systematically disposed of. In the second, plans to breathe life into the town by developing the harbor are sabotaged. Jenny is drawn into the mysteries from her position as the foundation's director. Her M.B.A. from a Pennsylvania University gives her the knowledge and expertise necessary to map her way through the maze of financial complications inherent in a charitable organization. As a member of the wealthy and privileged upper stratum of Port Fred's social structure, she has cachet with her peers who are, not incidentally, active supporters of the foundation. No dilettante heiress with time on her hands, Jenny puts in a full day at her office and at home in her spare time works at her computer on a book on the games of high finance.

Geof Bushfield has his feet in both camps of the town as well. A police detective, he is also a son of the family which owns Bushware, Inc., third or fourth largest plumbing supplier in the country. At the age of seventeen while in the throes of a juvenile delinquent phase, he fell in love with fourteen-year-old high-school cheerleader Jenny Cain. Half her lifetime later, they meet over murder and appreciate a now mutual attraction.

The stories, told by Jenny, deal with many interesting aspects of finance, business, and the law. Readers also get glimpses of Jenny's family and her somewhat uneasy relations with its members. Her mother is the victim of what doctors describe as a rather common sort of chemical imbalance. Unfortunately, this was not diagnosed before she had been branded an alcoholic. Mrs. Cain has become a permanent resident of Hampshire Psychiatric Hospital where she lives out her days in a comforting, drug-induced haze. Jenny's father lives in another sort of haze.

> It was a lovely land my father inhabited, and one where no one else was admitted.[7]

Insulated by wealth and upbringing, handsome Jimmy Cain breezes through life, from yacht to resort to exclusive club, blissfully unaware of the havoc his actions have wreaked. Sherry Guthrie, Jenny's sister is the victim of their ill-starred parents. She uses her beauty, money, and an icy demeanor as weapons against a life which has caused her great pain.

Within this four-book series, Nancy Pickard has created a complex yet believable set of characters. Readers should not be misled by any soap-opera aspects of the stories. These are well-crafted puzzles and Ms. Cain seems to be an admirable amateur detective.

IF THE LOVE OF MONEY is the root of all evil, these fiscal and enter-prising sleuths have their work cut out for them. The fields of cut-throat finance and business are fertile places for the seeds of murder to be sewn. Readers reap the benefits of these experts' forays into the world of crime.

Other books featuring business and finance include:

Margery Allingham, *The Fashion in Shrouds*, 1938
Geraldine Bonner, *The Black Eagle Mystery*, 1916
Christianna Brand, *Death in High Heels*, 1941
Patricia Moyes, *Murder à la Mode*, 1963
Sara Paretsky, *Indemnity Only*, 1982; *Deadlock*, 1984
Dorothy L. Sayers, *Murder Must Advertise*, 1933
Margaret Scherf, *The Banker's Bones*, 1968

LEGAL EAGLES

*T*he practice of law, for these jurists, involves much more than pleading a case before a judge and jury to prove innocence or gain a client's freedom. With their legal training and knowledge of the judicial system, the lawyers, solicitors, and barristers alike make formidable detectives. As officers of the court, they are constrained to act in a proscribed fashion. Some of our eagles fly beyond these bounds however and even put their own careers at risk in the pursuit of justice for both the innocent and the guilty.

A few of our characters never appear in court between the pages of their novel adventures. Their expertise in that arena is taken—by the reader at least—on faith. Others do some of their work before the bar and the courtroom scenes have a fascination all their own.

A strong, personal sense of equity compels these advocates. If their actions at times exceed the letter of the law, the spirit is well and truly upheld.

ANTONY MAITLAND
1962-1987   48 books   English
Sara Woods (Sara Hutton Bowen-Judd)

The British court of criminal law forms the backbone of all of these books. The conduct of all officers of the court is carefully proscribed and Sir Nicholas—senior member of their chambers in the Inner Temple—frequently reminds his nephew Antony of this fact as well as the constraints under which he must prepare and conduct his cases. Barrister Antony Maitland does not simply rely on the information contained in the brief given him by his client's solicitor. He prefers to personally interview everyone he possibly can who is in any way involved in the case. As far as Sir Nicholas is concerned, Antony always exceeds his instructions.

"You don't think he'd do a thing like that," said Sir Nicholas, snatching the words from him savagely. "How many times have you listened to that, and cursed your luck at having a fool for a witness?" He paused, but Antony did not speak. "Well?" he demanded. "On what do you base your opinion?"

"On character, sir."

"A dangerous business, Antony."

"Yes, I know."

"He may have changed; at least, he may have developed aspects to his character of which you know nothing."

"I realize that. But if he *is* telling the truth—"

"Don't tell me," said Sir Nicholas, tight-lipped (for his nephew's passive acceptance of his strictures was having the worst effect on his temper), "another lame dog!"

"Is that so strange, sir?"

"No, not strange, merely pigheaded, and no more than I should expect."

"Well, then," said Antony, still meekly.

"I cannot imagine," said Sir Nicholas, as though goaded beyond bearing, "why you should wish to embroil me in the affair."

"Because I shall have my work cut out, without having to worry about the presentation of the case in court. Don't you see, Uncle Nick—"

"I am glad at least that you realize there may be some difficulty in defending a man who claims to have no memory of his movements during the period in which the crime occurred.

Who does not even know," Sir Nicholas added, with deliberate
malice, "whether he is innocent or guilty."

"Well, I know it's awkward," Antony confessed. "But I can't
leave it where it is, sir, you must see that."

"To my sorrow, I can well believe it." He paused, looking
his nephew up and down, and then added tartly: "Just what are
you proposing to do?"

"Find out what happened," Antony replied without hesitation. "All the things Peter can't tell me." His uncle eyed him
stonily.

"Meddling again," he commented. And added, ungraciously,
"You'd better tell me the rest of the story, I suppose."[1]

In the end, Antony always prevails, his client is always exonerated
and Sir Nicholas always proves to have been of grudging support and
assistance throughout the case.

As a postscript to *Naked Villainy*, the final book in the collection,
readers will find a biographical sketch of Antony Maitland. In ten
pages, Ms. Woods tells us more about this static, predictable
character than we have been able to learn in over twenty years of
reading about him. We recommend that anyone unfamiliar with Mr.
Maitland and his associates begin by acquainting themselves with his
life through this sketch. Throughout the series, readers are given
snippets of information about Antony and others who frequent the
stories. New characters are introduced as the series progresses. Some
become regulars—members of the Harding-Maitland family, as it
were—while others make their brief appearances in only one or two
later books. There is continuity to these literary lives, spanning
twenty-five years. Only by going back into Antony's past, however,
do we get a sense of these characters' depth and an understanding
of their motivations.

The series revolves around Maitland in more ways than one. It is
certainly he who dictates the direction and the rhythm of the investigation. At the same time, his more personal sensitivities make it
necessary for Maitland's wife Jenny, their close friends, and his colleagues to avoid offending phrases and any reference to his war-
injured shoulder in order to keep him on an even keel. As Antony
is unable to lay to rest most of the ghosts from his past, they, of
course, rise up to haunt him at every turn and often serve to hinder
the progress of the case.

Jenny always makes casseroles, curls up in the same corner of the
same worn sofa, and defers to Antony in the same fashion. From time
to time she shows signs of spirit, however, her constant deference
to Antony prevents this from being any more than a glimmer. Sir

Nicholas is a paragon of British rectitude and while there is no deference in his attitude towards his nephew, it is obvious that their relationship has not progressed in spite of their many years of personal and professional connection. It is unfortunate that none of those close to Antony is willing to capitalize on opportunities which might ameliorate his repressed and repressive nature.

Most of the elements of a good mystery are present in each of the books—all of which take their titles from Shakespeare. The cases in this series are interesting, unusual, and pleasantly convoluted. The plots are well crafted and sufficient details are given so that readers can use their own deductive powers to solve the puzzle. These are excellent intellectual exercises and the way in which Maitland arrives at his conclusions is always made obvious to readers at the end. What is missing is any development of the personalities and relationships of the featured regulars. The very predictability of these characters does, however, create a fairly innocuous and constant background against which the mystery can unfold.

Sara Hutton Bowen-Judd has created three other series, two of which portray individuals, Anne Marryat and Jeremy Locke, also connected with the legal profession. These are sufficiently different from the Maitland series to merit reading by those familiar with and fond of that collection though they are not of the same caliber. Published under other pseudonyms, it is clear that the author was not trading directly on the popularity of the Maitland series or the well-known pseudonym of Sara Woods to sell them.

ROBERT FORSYTHE
1984-1987   5 books   English
E. X. Giroux (Doris Shannon)

Like Antony Maitland, Robert Forsythe is a barrister, has an injury he does not like to be reminded of, and, to a certain extent in the opening book, *A Death for Adonis*, is a somewhat repressed character. Unlike Maitland, however, Forsythe is given the opportunity to liberate himself from his old ghosts, takes it and lays them to rest, wiser for the experience. In this series, readers are presented with a well-rounded individual possessing talents and training, who learns and evolves with each case.

"I know all about Robert Forsythe, barrister from a long line of barristers, something of a child prodigy, passed the bar exams at an extremely early age and started to make good predictions of a brilliant career, gave up said career suddenly in his twenty-seventh year and returned to the family home in Sussex, where he has lived as something of a recluse for six years."[2]

"Nevertheless, it was good of you to trust me, to speak so frankly."

Melissa smiled slightly. "I phoned Sir Hilary. I haven't contacted him since the trial, but I still respect his opinion. He's the one who inspired the trust. He told me that you, despite the rumors I'd heard, deserved all the help I could give you. If anyone could uncover evidence to help my brother, he believes it will be you. Sir Hilary has a high opinion of your ability, says you have a devious mind, more suited to a detective than a barrister."[3]

The rest of the series finds Robert back in the fold of his profession ably assisted by Miss Sanderson, a woman of undisclosed age. Sandy had not only been Robert's father's secretary but raised the young Robby after his mother's death, as well. Their relationship is one of warmth, mutual respect, and admiration. Miss Sanderson, known as the most competent legal secretary in London, is also a willing and active assistant for Robert in his detective efforts. In *A Death for a Doctor*, she takes the role of investigator at the behest of Chief Inspector Kepesake and Detective Sergeant "Beau" Brummell.

While they have their differences with Forsythe, Kepesake and Brummell are actually glad to find him and Miss Sanderson at the scene of a crime. Forsythe is good at noticing seemingly unimportant details, both physical and verbal, which in fact hold the seeds of the solution. His manner inspires trust and he gains confidences by encouraging people to speak to him freely. His methods of investigation are mainly cerebral, and although there can be physical action, the plot does not hinge on it. Forsythe's respect for the law is tempered with the belief that justice is often best served by divine intervention. While he will not compromise a case by withholding vital evidence, he will do so when that evidence will serve nothing but blind justice.

Giroux is developing comfortable and interesting characters who, while predictable in action and motivation, are, at the same time, capable of original and innovative thinking. Her plots are original though the situations are often stereotyped. Clues and the obligatory red herring or two are well placed and readers can, if they so desire, arrive at the same conclusion in the same way the detective has.

JULIA LARWOOD
1981-1984   2 books   English
Sarah Caudwell (Sarah Cockburn)

Julia Larwood is one of the junior members of Chambers, at 63 New Square, Lincoln's Inn Fields, where she practices law as a tax expert. Next door at 62, in Chambers referred to as The Nursery, are her good friends and colleagues, Timothy Shepherd, Desmond Ragwort, Michael Cantrip, and Selena Jardine. Of this group of five, Julia is the most obvious by virtue of her somewhat amoral approach to life and her seeming disregard for everything not directly related to the Finance Acts. Julia is quite simply oblivious to the more mundane aspects of day-to-day living except as it regards her profession.

In the first book in this new series, Julia takes a holiday to Venice. She is a full year behind on her income tax payments believing—in spite of her intimate professional acquaintance with the Revenue—that this was not anything that had to do with real life. She has no money with which to pay her arrears taxes, nor can she really afford a holiday. Her logic compels her to take the trip in any event as it will in no way affect her ability to pay her tax.

Julia is the featured character in these books because her native state of oblivion propels her into the midst of murder. Her friends and Timothy's former Law History professor, Hilary Tamar, are required to take heroic measures to extricate their errant friend from her follies. Professor Tamar, on hearing that Julia has gone to Venice, points out that

poor Julia's inability to understand what is happening, or why, in the world about her, her incompetence to learn even the simplest of the practical skills required for survival—these must have made it evident, even in childhood, that she would never be able to cope unaided with the full responsibilities of adult life. She must have been, no doubt, a docile, good-natured child, with a certain facility for Latin verbs and intelligence tests—but what use is that to anyone? Seeking some suitable refuge, where her inadequacies would pass unnoticed, her relatives, very sensibly, sent her to Lincoln's Inn. She is now a member of the small set of Revenue Chambers in 63 New Square. There she sits all day, advising quite happily on the construction of the Finance Acts, and doing no harm to anyone. But to let her go to Venice—I imagine her, wandering alone through those devious alley ways, looking—as, indeed, she does at the best of times—like one of the more dishevelled heroines of Greek tragedy; and I could not forbear to chide.[4]

Sometimes the colleagues act in concert while at others each acts separately. Professor Tamar narrates the tales and is the actual sleuth who pieces all of the information together. With reference to obscure, historical legal precedent, this scholar synthesizes the data and orchestrates the action toward the successful conclusion of the case.

The person, Hilary Tamar, is a bit of a mystery to us. Americans tend to think of the name Hilary as a woman's, and, on first reading, we did just that. On reflection, however, we recalled that the English use the name more frequently for the opposite sex. Rereading the two books brought us no joy in discovering the actual gender of this scholar and so, for us, this professor shall remain pleasantly androgynous.

Anglophyles will enjoy these stories, rich in dry British wit and long, complex sentences in the full bloom of the Queen's English. These are truly scholar's narratives. While the verbosity actually adds to the enjoyment of the stories for some readers, it can detract for others. In the words of Professor Hilary Tamar:

> Some of my readers, perhaps many, having expected to find in these pages diversion rather than instruction, will now hasten back to their booksellers to demand indignantly, it may be with threats of legal action, reimbursement of the sum so ill-advisedly expended. So be it: such readers will give me credit, I hope, for having enabled them by my prompt confession to return the volume unread and in almost pristine condition; and I for my part (for publisher and bookseller I cannot speak) would rather forgo the modest sum which would accrue to me from a sale— very modest, meagre might be a better word, one might almost say paltry—would infinitely rather forgo that sum than think it obtained by deception.[5]

ARTHUR G. CROOK
1936-1974   50 books   English
Anthony Gilbert (Lucy B. Malleson)

Large, untidy, red-haired, and with a penchant for loud, checked suits, Arthur Crook's clients are—according to this worthy solicitor—always innocent. This statement might lead readers to believe that stories featuring Mr. Crook deal with the more obvious criminal type. While society's bad boys and girls do enter into some of the drama, the star client in each of Crook's cases is more often a member in good standing, if not a pillar, of that same society, who finds that circumstances frequently create ideal victims.

> "The man you want is a chap called Crook. Name ring a bell?" he asked, sharply.
>
> Gerald shook his head. "Not that I've had much truck with the law since I came of age..."
>
> "Quite. Well, Lady Silk's dilemma is that she can't tell her defense the truth without breaking the promise she gave to us, and landing us all in the cart, too; and she won't give her defense a chance if she keeps her mouth buttoned up. Crook may get the story out of her, though not the names, but the difference between him and chaps of Morsby's kidney is that he's used to making bricks without straw and producing such an effective substitute you'd hardly know it from the genuine article. The other thing in his favor is his conscience. His professional conscience, he calls it."
>
> "Which means?"
>
> "That he considers his job is to get his client acquitted, not to use his opportunities to set up as a judge, say, I don't believe this statement or that, therefore I can't undertake the case. If he saw a cat eating a canary he'd still undertake the defense and persuade a jury the cat had found the feathers in the garbage can—once he'd agreed to act for the cat, that is. Now you see why I asked how well you knew the Silks."[6]

Crook is a pushover for the damsel in distress though the damsel need be neither young nor lovely. In fact, in a discussion with a young woman about another in her fifties, Crook himself says, "My favorite age for a dame—no offense meant, sugar, but they don't get their sense much younger, and sense is what I'm lookin' for now."[7] His appreciation of ladies of an age runs constant throughout the series and, for us, is one of the prime delights.

Some of the stories begin with Crook and he is involved throughout the entire tale. In others, however, he comes in late and winds things up neatly. Whenever he makes his appearance, his presence and energy pick up the pace of the story. He gets the rest of the cast on the move and propels the plot to his desired conclusion. Crook is an organizer. He can take a handful of disparate facts and string them together in any of a number of creative ways. He does not completely obfuscate evidence but he is not above clouding issues until the climate has become generally more favorable for his client.

Mr. Crook and all of his eccentricities—from his outsized business cards to his vehicular preferences—make this a series well worth reading. Author Gilbert's skillful presentation of other characters as whole people makes it easy for readers to ascribe the potential for violence to any of the suspects. The endings almost always come as a surprise. One thinks one has the solution of the crime and the identity of the murderer and then, with a deft twist of the mechanism, Gilbert turns the spotlight on the true culprit.

JOHN J. MALONE and THE JUSTUSES
1939-1967   14 books   American
Craig Rice (Georgiana Ann Randolph Craig)

"I still say an eminent Chicago attorney should—" Joe paused, possibly overcome by finding and using such a classy word.

But *eminent* might have been laying it on a little thick in Malone's case. There were other descriptive terms. Sawed-off shyster; sneaky mouthpiece; the hood's friend. Call Malone whatever you chose and you'd find that someone in Chicago had said it first.

Still, no one could deny that he was one of the keenest little criminal lawyers who ever gave a judge fits. Once, years earlier, while making his living as a cab driver, he'd become disgusted with his lack of progress in life and enrolled in a law course in night school. He earned his diploma, and passing the bar exam had been the turning point in his life.[8]

Prohibition had been over for six years when this series opened but Chicago was still very much under the sway of gangsters who achieved their power during the fourteen years in which the Eighteenth Amendment was in effect. Malone made his mark as a hard-hitting Chicago lawyer by successfully defending the criminal element of that city during those free-for-all years. This well-earned reputation put Malone in the way of all sorts of contacts and all manner of information which he put to use in solving crime as well as getting and keeping people out of jail.

Malone's boast, "I've never lost a client," is remarkably like Crook's, "My clients are always innocent." Like Crook, too, Malone is rumpled and untidy and, at times, tends toward the flamboyant.

Their view of the law agrees as well. Neither sets himself up as judge but rather, sees justice as a principle to be served.

In this series, Malone is helped and hindered by Jake and Helene Justus who meet in the first novel, court in the second, and marry off the page before the third begins. Jake is variously, a publicist, a television producer, and a night club owner—none too successfully. Helene is an heiress and beautifully blond to boot. The three live the high life and often get involved in crime inadvertantly. With his special skills, Malone could probably solve the cases much more easily on his own but the stories would be much different than they are. Jake and Helene add the comic dash which keeps these from being just hard-boiled crime tales, and the party atmosphere surrounding the trio keeps Malone's liquor consumption from turning him into just another lush.

The last book in the John J. Malone series, was published ten years after the author's death. Supposedly, the manuscript for *But the Doctor Died* was found in a locked trunk. One can't help but wonder if this was truly the work of this well-known author. The characters are there and much the same people they always have been but the tone of the story is different and the plot revolves around espionage rather than murder.

Craig Rice's characters and stories earned her wide popularity in the crime and mystery field. Under the Rice pseudonym, she created another series featuring street photographers Bingo Riggs and Handsome Kusak. As Michael Venning, she wrote a three-book series with Melville Fairr as the principal character, and from 1941 to 1942, she ghostwrote two mysteries for Gypsy Rose Lee.

GAIL and MITCH MITCHELL
1969-1979   2 books   American
The Gordons (Mildred and Gordon Gordon)

Mitch Mitchell—a graduate of the University of Southern California with honors—has practiced criminal law in Los Angeles for five years. His reputation among the city's lawyers is for being honest and shrewd. The night before he is to marry his secretary, Gail Rogers, she is accosted by a stranger hidden in the back seat of her car. The unknown man demands that Gail act as a go-between for him, to pick up two hundred thousand dollars which will be left at an as yet, undisclosed location. He tells her he will know her every move and threatens Gail with the death of her critically ill mother if she does not comply.

The bride-to-be goes to the LAPD. Lieutenant "Hawk" Hawkins is put on the case and, as it develops, calls in the special Heavy Squad. Meanwhile, Mitch is kept in the dark though he knows that things are not all well with his betrothed. Wedding eve jitters? Concern for her ailing mother?

Hawk, the special squad, and Gail work together and at one point Hawk gives Gail a pep talk.

> She was near hysteria, and his quick anger faded. She was in such a damn spot. "About your apartment, those thin walls. Keep your radio on soft. That'll blur anything you say over the phone, if you can't get out and have to call us from there. Now you'd better go back home the same way you came. Barney will take you." To Barney he said, "Better use the paneled pick-up."
>
> He turned back to her. "The time may come when you'll want to run, when he tightens the screws until the threads scream. When that time comes, remember you're doing something for people, not just for yourself and your mother, but the same as if you were helping fight cancer. Remember that, will you? You're helping people."[9]

A frantic chase through the hills and along the fringes of the city of Los Angeles is compounded by helicopter surveillance and various members of the Heavy Squad in full riot gear. Bruised and battered but safe, Gail meets Mitch at the altar the next day and all ends well.

Ten years later, the obvious sequel to this hair-raising adventure, *The Night After the Wedding*, was published. Needless to say, the young couple returns to detecting exhausted, after one of the longest literary wedding nights recorded. Mitch is awakened by a phone call from a young woman urgently pleading for his help. A man has broken into Cathy Doyle's bedroom, demanding that the one million dollars he accuses her of hiding be handed over to him the next night. Cathy swears she knows nothing about the money but is unwilling to go to the police for aid. Eventually the LAPD does get involved and once again, Hawk is in charge of the case. He and Mitch strategize and work against the clock to save Cathy's life. Gail's recent experience with extortion and violence makes her the logical one to hold Cathy's hand and offer comfort.

The husband and wife team of Mildred and Gordon Gordon wrote mysteries for over thirty-five years. The plots of the short-lived series featuring Gail and Mitch as well as their other thrillers follow a well-defined formula. D. C. Randall (a cat) and John Ripley are other characters created by this pair.

ELLIE GORDON
1985-1986   3 books   American
Karin Berne (Sue Bernell and Michaela Karni)

Newly divorced Eleanor Gordon is middle-aged, has been drowning her sorrows in Big Macs, and is rapidly living up to the first part of their name. A friend steps in and sets her straight on her abilities and the fact that there is life after divorce. Ellie goes on a diet, begins an exercise program, gets a new wardrobe and a new job. She signs on as the office manager for the firm of Abbotts, Devlin, and Busch, Attorneys at Law, and soon after she begins working there, discovers the murdered body of one of the partners, Katherine Busch. Ellie is involved in the investigation when her house is burgled. Confronted by the killer, she hits him with a vat of chili, hot off the stove, and concludes her first case.

Well on her way to glamour and liberation, Ellie is reluctant to become involved in any more murder investigations and, in conversation with her friend Betsy, says,

> I was used to being teased about my role in solving the sad and frightening business of Katherine Busch's murder, though there was nothing remotely amusing in finding someone strangled or suspecting that you might be the next victim. "Will you forget that episode? It was just a fluke," I scoffed, "and certainly no way to impress the D.A. with my intellect and *je ne sais quoi.*"
>
> "Hmm," Betsy murmured thoughtfully. "You're a pretty devious character. Somehow I find it slightly unbelievable that you'd cultivate the interest of Joe Corelli without using him as a source to practice your rare talent."
>
> "You can't possibly think I want to make a habit of catching killers."
>
> "It's instinct, Ellie, my friend. You'll never be able to keep your nose out of things if a suitable mystery presents itself."
>
> "So you're calling me a busybody. All right, I'll prove you wrong. If you promise never to recommend another health food salad to me again as long as you live, I will refrain from solving the next murder that comes my way. A deal?"
>
> "You're on, but I predict you'll be eating bean sprouts within a month."[10]

District Attorney Corelli, whom Ellie has been dating, finds himself in the position of prosecuting one of her best friends, Lois, for the murder of her boss. Drake Prescott, head of public relations at the Canyon Escondido nuclear power plant is electrocuted and Lois is the obvious suspect due to her long-standing antagonism toward him. Lois appeals to Ellie for help and Ellie eats bean sprouts at the end of the book.

False Impressions, third book in the series, takes place while Ellie is vacationing in Santa Fe, New Mexico. Away from home and out of her league, she nevertheless is drawn into detecting when she finds the dead body of vitriolic art critic, Jerrold Willett, in the garden of her hostesses' gallery. As in the other two stories, Ellie is in peril as the case draws to a close and saves herself in the nick of time.

Author Karin Berne—the pseudonym used by Sue Bernell and Michaela Karni—has given us a sharp-tongued, wisecracking woman with a developing feminist perspective. The stories featuring Ellie Gordon are entertaining, and the main character herself seems to have potential as a competent sleuth. As women, we are always interested in one who rises from depression and the drudgery of housework and faces the world with a fresh attitude. We look forward to watching Ellie's evolution and, while we don't long for a humorless celibate, hope she can rely a little less on her sexuality and acerbic wit in future stories.

TOM ARAGON
1976-1982   3 books   American
Margaret Millar

This young Hispanic attorney appears in only three novels and is almost a mere convenience in the last two. In *Ask For Me Tomorrow*, however, he is central to the story as much for his ethnic designation as for his profession. A very junior member of the offices of Smedler, Downs, Castleberg, MacFee, and Powell, Attorneys at Law, Aragon is given the tiresome, tedious tasks so often required for clients.

As the story opens, a personal friend of Smedler has asked him—without revealing her reason—for assistance from someone possessing Aragon's qualifications. Smedler complies and Aragon is given the case with his salary and expenses covered by Mrs. Decker. His task involves the search for the woman's first husband. The quest takes Aragon to Baja California—first to the sleepy little village of Bahia de Ballenas and the site of a failed resort development, then into the town of Rio Seco which boasts the jail called La Cantera, The Stone Quarry. While his appearance and linguistic fluency work in his favor in obtaining information, the nature of The Baja operates to frustrate Aragon in his quest and three people are murdered in the course of his investigation. The end of the story contains a surprising twist and, as with many of Millar's novels, ends with no real resolution.

Aragon's personal life plays a very small part in the stories. As the series opens, he's about twenty-five and a recent graduate of law school. His wife Laurie is a pediatric resident in a San Francisco hospital and their marriage is carried on long distance, except for brief, off-the-page vacations. Tall and slim with dark hair and dark eyes behind horn-rimmed glasses, he seems to have a pleasant nature without being prepossessing. Charity, Smedler's secretary, is a series regular as is Smedler himself. Their relationships with Aragon are purely professional though Charity often engages in verbal sparring matches with Aragon just to keep in practice for her main events with Smedler.

> Aragon looked at one of the plants, wondering if Charity talked to it, and if she did, why it hadn't shriveled up and blown away.
>
> "You want to know why I believe you'll make it as a lawyer, Aragon?"
>
> "Not particularly."
>
> "You look dumb. Not dumb dumb, more innocent-like dumb. Any judge or jury would feel sorry for you seeing those calf eyes peering from behind those horn-rimmed glasses. Juries hate a smart-looking lawyer who dresses well."
>
> "Do you talk to your plants, Miss Nelson?"
>
> "No."
>
> "I thought not."
>
> "I'm not a loony. What in hell would I say to a plant?"
>
> "Oh, something soothing, pleasant, complimentary—you know, the way you talk to the new employees."
>
> "I don't talk like that to *any* employees. You trying to come on funny, junior? Better think twice."[11]

Millar's stories fall into the category of psychological thrillers. So gifted is this author, however, that one is rarely aware of the depth of the psychological aspects until the final chapter—often the final line of the book. Plots, subplots, red herrings, and fascinating characters abound. Normalcy and improbability are well mixed and readers may find that they are left with a foreboding sense of unease at the possibility that life is more than we can see or know.

Two other short series were created by Millar. They feature Dr. Paul Prye, a psychiatrist, and Inspector Sands of the Toronto Police Department. She has also written numerous nonseries mysteries.

CASS JAMESON
1983-1986   2 books   American
Carolyn Wheat

Carolyn Wheat's series character deals in life's harsher realms. Cass Jameson is a practicing attorney, a criminal defense lawyer for the Legal Aid Society. *Dead Man's Thoughts*, opens with Cass in a Brooklyn, New York, night court processing bodies through the initial steps of the legal system. Cass' clients are clearly *not* always innocent. Sometimes they are as guilty as hell and it is up to her as their appointed legal representative to give them the best defense she can and get them the best deal possible. This requires quick thinking and fancy footwork, a streetwise understanding of her client, and a professional summation of her opponent and of the individual judge who embodies the court. Cass is aware of a growing sense of being simply a machine with neither empathy nor compassion for the human element of her work. After the court session, Cass and her colleague and lover, Nathan, talk over coffee after a late night dinner.

Why did you go to law school?'' He asked it conversationally, like a guy coming on in a singles bar. Then, before I could answer, he said. ''Because you wanted to save the whales, end the war, and stop pollution, all in your first year of practice?''

''Something like that.'' I smiled in spite of myself; it had been exactly like that. ''After the shootings at Kent, which the legal system did nothing but cover up, I decided to learn the language, get my union card, and do what I could.''[12]

These are not light, humorous stories. Readers are given an accurate view of the realities of the streets and of the system designed to protect the innocent and punish the guilty. As the first story progresses, Cass discovers her lover's murdered body. The killing looks like the result of a sadistic, homosexual frenzy and Cass is convinced it is a setup, designed to discredit Nathan as much as to physically remove him. She determines to find his killer and in the process uncovers a seethe of corruption lying just below the never-placid legal surface. In the second book, divorce, child custody, and politics are mixed with murder. Cass is pushed into detecting out of concern for her murdered client's child whose father is charged with the crime. Violence and brutality are clearly depicted in both books— not only in the killings central to each story but in the streets and halls of the courthouse as well. This is not, however inconsistent with the tales, nor incidental to them. Wheat writes the truth and does it well.

While this is not our favorite sort of reading, we like Cass and see her as an evolving character with a lot of potential. She questions both her personal and professional lives and is moving toward a workable balance between idealism and stark reality which takes humanity fully into account. Beyond that, Cass is willing to own her failures and misconceptions as well as her successes and insights.

> Damn, I thought. Damn, damn, damn, damn—like Henry Higgins. I'm *good* at this! I'm fucking *good*. I began to laugh. Goddamn it, Nathan, I laughed in shocked surprise. I'm good, just as you said I was. What a revoltin' development *this* is. Here I've been spending all this time and energy trying to convince myself that this is not my life, and all the time I'm really good at it. Does that mean that you were right about the other thing, Nathan? Involved is involved. Because I can get it up for Hezekiah Puckett, I have more to put into my photographs? Concentration and compassion strike again.
>
> It was my own personal piece of the moon.[13]

CHARLES SPOTTED MOON
1976-1979   2 books   American
Chelsea Quinn Yarbro

A five-year veteran and partner in the law firm, Ogilvie, Tallant & Moon, Charles is a lawyer with a conscience and a true sense of justice. In a conversation with a client wanting to drop an investigation of murder, Charles explains,

> "Look, when I was a kid, on the reservation, I was very lucky. We had one hell of a teacher there, Etienne de Groote. He'd got- ten out of Belgium when the war started, and he came to Canada. He was highly qualified, but not by Canadian standards of certification, and so, since he couldn't teach in regular schools, he taught on the Iron River Reservation. We learned English and French—I already knew English, having spent my first six years in California—and German and Italian as well. We

read Goethe and Rimbaud and Racine. De Groote was a devoted supporter of the oppressed. He told us that the law was our only hope, which was very much what my grandfather always said. So when the time came to go further in studies, I came back to California, went to McGeorge, and after a while, I was a lawyer. And then I started to learn about the law." His voice had gone bitter and he looked past Ty into the night. As he spoke, his accent had taken on a Canadian twinge, slightly Australian with a faint overlay of Scots. "I learned that the law was a tool, and that in skillful hands it could be made to perform the most wonderful tricks. I've seen my own partners use the law for despicable ends. But I've always believed that justice was an achievable, laudable goal. Justice and the law. They're often strangers to each other.[14]

As a child in Vallejo, Charles' Indian heritage had made him feel an outsider. His lack of connection with his own culture made him feel the same way in his tribe. The teacher, Etienne de Groote had recognized Charles' academic talents and had given him a sense of the value and beauty of learning. His grandfather, the tribal medicine man, recognized Charles' gift of magic and, while Charles was still young, began instructing him further in the ways of magic. At the old man's death, Charles assumed the title of medicine man himself, and now, each year, returns to the reservation for the tribal council. Dual citizenship makes it possible for Charles to reside in many worlds. The practice of magic and the practice of law are not mutually exclusive. His roots are with his people. His home is California.

A malpractice suit against a friend of his brings Charles face to face with murder in the first book, *Ogilvie, Tallant & Moon*. A dead body is discovered outside the clinic where his client works. Questions around the estate of a pharmaceutical manufacturer—for whom the victim was a salesman—put Charles on the trail of clues which he feels may unravel the case against his client. After exhausting more conventional lines of investigation, Charles prepares himself in the traditional manner of his ancestors, links himself to the spirit of the dead man and retraces the man's steps on the last day of his life.

In the course of the stories, Charles' status as the firm's "token minority" is challenged by the arrival of lawyer Morgan Studevant. Assigned to assist him with his case load, Morgan bristles with righteous feminist indignation. The sparks which fly between them are due as much to attraction as to antagonism. Other characters appear regularly including both of Moon's partners, Willis Ogilvie and Alex Tallant. Elizabeth Kendrie, a wealthy philanthropist, is one of

Charles' clients and directly responsible for his second foray into murder.

Music When Sweet Voices Die revolves around grand opera and the volatile personalities and passions of the artists. The dramatic death—onstage, mid-song—of the French tenor during the last act of *The Tales of Hoffmann* may be the result of an inadvertent overdose or a flagrantly staged suicide. Charles suspects murder and views the entire cast with suspicion as each has cause for wishing Feuier dead. As the investigation into the death at the opera progresses, Charles and Morgan are drawn into a frightening confrontation with the brutal husband of one of their clients. The jeopardy the pair survives puts a different complexion on their feelings for one another and while the sparks still fly, the antagonism between them is lessened.

Charles hesitantly tells Morgan about his magic and his position in his tribe. Her acceptance of this information and its giver marks a turning point in trust for both of them. The story ends with Charles facing a moral dilemma. Nothing can be proven against the perpetrator but Charles knows who the guilty party is and why murder has been committed. No resolution is provided. Readers are left with the same questions facing Charles and are nicely set up for the next book which, alas, has not yet appeared.

This series is simply too short. We found the second book in the series first and had to search for over a year for the first one. Yarbro has created a fascinating character and set the scene for a long-running series, then left her Moon fans hanging by their collective toenails after only two books. To this day, each time we drive through San Francisco, we see the building that seems perfect to house the offices of Ogilvie, Tallant & Moon and speculate on whether Charles is at his desk in the room we just know is his.

REBECCA SCHWARTZ
1982-1986   3 Books   American
Julie Smith

Again, San Francisco and Marin are the settings for this new series featuring attorney Rebecca Schwartz. Some of the City's well-known, beloved, and/or notorious features are highlighted in the books, adding pleasure for Bay Area residents, tourists familiar with the City, and armchair travelers alike. In *Death Turns a Trick*, the infamous hooker's union, Coyote (though under another name), is central to the story, and in *The Sourdough Wars*, a starter for the fabled San Francisco french bread is the prize worth murder.

Ambiance isn't all these books have going for them, though. Schwartz herself is an interesting, well-drawn character and her friends and family are equally well-crafted additions to the tales. Daughter of Isaac Schwartz, famed criminal lawyer, Rebecca has her work—making a name and career for herself—cut out for her. She wants to make it on her own merit and, at the same time, has the good sense to call on her father for assistance when it is obviously in the best interest of her client. Mrs. Schwartz is the archetypal Jewish mother worried about her headstrong daughter while frequently accusing her of being the direct cause of her father's imminent demise.

Schwartz's law partner Chris Nicholson is the tall, blond, willowy counterpart to Rebecca's own dark and curvaceous appearance. Their outer office is staffed by male secretary, Alan Kruzick— live-in boyfriend of Rebecca's sister, Mickey. Kruzick takes inordinate pleasure in goading his boss and provides much of the comic relief in the stories. Rob Burns, reporter for the *San Francisco Chronicle*, is Rebecca's boyfriend. His journalistic curiosity is of use in her investigations and if he possesses any clout with his publisher, it is used—not always successfully—to keep Rebecca's name out of unfavorable print.

> Mom turned on him like one of the furies. "You get away from here, Mr. Rob Burns of the *Chronicle*. Look at that bruise on her face! You did that to my daughter, you, you"—she searched for the right words—"newshawk!"
>
> Mickey and I both giggled. It started out as a little tiny ripple of a giggle, and before we could stop it, it was a giggle fit. Mom and Dad just stood there, with the corners of their mouths turned down, looking like a couple of tragedy masks. Several times before, I'd come very close to disgracing the family, and now I finally had, and Mickey and I were yucking it up while Pete Brainard recorded the Fall of the House of Schwartz for the *Chronicle*'s half million readers.
>
> Rob looked as if I'd punched him in the kishkas. He finally managed to speak, in a high, kind of cracked voice. "Rebecca, are you okay?"
>
> The giggle fit blew over, and I was suddenly very mad. "Okay? Okay? No, I am not okay, you newshawk. I have been pistol-whipped, falsely arrested and thrown in a cell, where I have probably contracted a rare venereal disease, and all because you had to phone in your stupid story."[15]

The stories are fast paced and full of a wry kind of witty repartee. Author Julie Smith, a former reporter for the *San Francisco Chronicle*, knows the City and its denizens well. She takes reality and strings it out to limits of improbability which makes for a lively plot. She provides readers with all the necessary clues to the identity of the killer and, at the end, adds a little fillip of surprise. Smith has written another series featuring former *Chronicle* reporter, Paul McDonald.

JUSTICE is a harsh, demanding mistress. Those who serve her must often weigh the spirit against the letter of the law while remaining true to their profession and the ethics it imposes. By involving themselves in the investigative part of their clients' cases, these advocates strive to remove all shadow of doubt which might cloud an individual's future. A keen eye, sharp talons, and the ability to soar above both peaks and valleys gives these eagles strength, tenacity, and perspective, qualities which the blindfolded lady holding the scales accepts as her due.

As the courtroom is the logical terminus for cases of murder and many stories include members of the legal profession, we have not listed titles of books in which some of the more satellite practitioners can be found.

MURDER BETWEEN THE PAGES

WRITERS AND JOURNALISTS

*N*ovelists and reporters are by nature and inclination curious. The craft of writing calls upon its practitioners to carefully hone their powers of observation. Insight and intuition are useful tools of this trade. Novelists need the ability to create plausible situations for their characters and journalists need a nose for news. Both disciplines require an excellent understanding of the human condition and a measure of detective skill to get and tell the *full* story.

The sleuth who lives by wit and pen is well advised to use both the material evidence and the uncertainty of humanity in concert. While irrefutable facts are the superstructure of a news story and are often the backbone of a work of fiction, they must be balanced with the personal and the unpredictable in order to complete the equation.

C. B. GREENFIELD
1979-1986   5 books   American
Lucille Kallen

Sloan's Ford, Connecticut, is the home of the *Sloan's Ford Reporter* and its editor/publisher/sole proprietor, Charles Benjamin Greenfield, a long, lean, somewhat lugubrious-looking gentleman with thick horn-rimmed glasses and a passion for classical music. Veteran of twenty-five years as a NBC News staff writer, Greenfield is an inveterate newshound and

> he made a good gadfly; he was irritating, relentless, stubborn, and waspish—although very few people were aware of these traits, since he walked around in the guise of an immensely calm and soft-spoken man.[1]

> His expression suggested he was resigned to this unaccountable infamy of fate, but, as I've said, the expression of benign and gentle melancholy was totally deceptive. He had been known to cut an ego to ribbons while giving a perfect impersonation of a kindly old country doctor handing out lollipops.[2]

This affluent suburban fastness, redolent with history, is an ideal hideout for this well-disguised crusader.

The remaining staff of the *Reporter*, with one exception, is all female. Maggie Rome, chief reporter and legperson for Greenfield's sleuthing, narrates her adventures and his cerebrations in a fashion both witty and nonchalant. Calli Dohanis, "The Greek," handles paste-up and layout for the weekly while suffering from some ailment or other. Helen Deutsch runs the Justowriter and the Varityper while keeping the office supplied with motherly admonitions and health food. Stewart Klein, odd man out on the staff, works as a reporter for the paper while waiting for *Time/Life* to call him to man one of their far-flung, foreign desks.

Wednesday is the day the *Reporter* makes its appearance. The activity in the old house on Poplar Avenue reaches epic proportions as the paper is put to bed. On Wednesday evenings, Greenfield joins Maggie and—when he's not off engineering in far away places—her husband Elliot for dinner at the Rome home. On Friday, Maggie, Greenfield, and Gordon Oliver, another series regular, gather at the Oliver house to play a little chamber music en trio: Maggie, piano; Greenfield, cello; and Gordon, violin.

Charlie is a change-hating, chauvinistic curmudgeon who intimidates every female within range into doing his bidding. Maggie succumbs to his whims while, at the same time, holding her own and maintaining a semblance of equality in their relationship. The foundation of this partnership is mutual respect. Greenfield is hardly lavish with praise for Maggie's success at some of the quasi-legal tasks to which he sets her, or, for that matter, her cooking. Readers get the sense that his appreciation runs deep, however, and his lack of verbal acknowledgement just another part of his disguise.

In their own way, each is a champion of causes. Maggie is willing to run risks on Greenfield's behalf because she trusts his innate sense of right and correctness. Though he may not always be clear on why he feels the way he does on a given issue, Maggie's intuition coupled with this basic trust puts the issue and Greenfield's perception into perspective and allows her to rationalize her sometimes deceitful activities.

> He was, beyond everything else, a fighter. He had always fought every offense to a civilized and humanitarian way of life that came within his orbit, from the third-grade writing skills of high school graduates to the dumping of toxic materials on an undeveloped tract two miles outside the village, knowing that in the first instance it would take a miracle to resurrect the importance of the written word, and in the second that organized crime might find him enough of a nuisance to send out a man with a fly swatter. He had never before bothered with the odds.[3]

Humor is, for the most part, light-handed though it can grow a little heavy around the bickering between Rome and Greenfield. Author Kallen's background as a television comedy writer comes to the fore here and may even explain her characters' penchants for the one-liner. The laughs do balance the zealous pursuit of justice Greenfield maintains. He has left the mainstream news world out of disgust for the dishonesty and ineptitude of the medium and chosen a seeming backwater arena where he can ply his trade and just maybe make a difference—however large or small.

JIM QWILLERAN
1966-1987   6 books   American
Lilian Jackson Braun

> Since his arrival at the *Fluxion* seven months before—with
> his ample moustache, picturesque pipe, and unexplained
> past—Qwilleran had been a subject for conjecture. Everyone
> knew he had had a notable career as a crime reporter in New
> York and Chicago. After that, he had disappeared for a few
> years, and now he was holding down a quiet desk on a
> Midwestern newspaper, and writing, of all things, features on
> art![4]

This rather large, rather rumpled man with the name that
confounds typesetters has more than a nose for news. His luxuriant moustache acts as a veritable antenna, bristling and prickling
when its owner needs to be especially aware. In his mid-forties,
divorced and a reformed alcoholic, Qwill is a man of modest
means, few possessions, and fewer pretensions. *The Daily Fluxion*
is a far cry from the bustling, big city newsrooms where his career
began, soared and finally crashed. Still, it is a newspaper and,
for a man with printer's ink in his blood, the best possible place
to be.

Qwilleran's first assignment on the *Flux* is that of art writer. His
job is to do feature articles on artists, their environments, and their
motivations. Art critic, George Bonifield Mountclemens III, invites
Qwill for dinner and ends up extending an invitation for him to move
into the vacant downstairs apartment. The critic is murdered. His
Siamese, Kao K'o-Kung, leads Qwilleran to the clues which solve
the crime and, in the best fighting cat fashion, protects Qwill when
he is attacked by the murderer. At the end of the book, Koko and
Qwill mutually adopt one another and proceed to detect murder in
five more books.

With each book, Qwilleran's writing assignment changes and so
does his address. In the second book, Qwill and Koko are joined by
Yum Yum, a delicate female Siamese. The murders in which Qwill
and his feline confederates find themselves involved all take place
in and around wherever they happen to be living. Gathering information for his news assignments provides Qwill with the necessary
credentials to investigate suspicious events, places, and people. His
reporter's intuition enables him to see behind the obvious to the
heart of the story. Lively curiosity and natural stealth are
characteristics people expect cats to possess. Koko is easily

overlooked as he prowls about, often finding just the object or location Qwill needs to wind up the case. The unlikely partnership of the hard-boiled newsman and two feisty and independent pussycats is clever. The author has captured both human and feline qualities and placed them in well-crafted tales. There are six books, to date, in this series which began more than twenty years ago. We look forward to many more.

WADE
1931-1932   2 books   American
Gwen Bristow and Bruce Manning

Only two books featuring Wade were written and are long out of print. In fact, we could only find one of the titles. Nevertheless, this short series is another little gem. Wade, star reporter for *The Morning Creole*, covers the newsbeat in New Orleans. Though Wade is central to the story, the action swirls and eddies around him, involving others—especially Wiggins, cameraman for the paper—much more directly.

The Mardi Gras Murders is filled with local color and information on the events of Mardi Gras. The dialogue sparkles and is laced with the terminology, dialect, and slang of the time and place. The characters may be a little stereotyped but that simply seems to be a hallmark of much of the writing produced through the forties. This is a book of fast, high living. Gambling, blackmail, depravity, and homicide are elements of this story and are added with a matter-of-factness which robs them of their sensational qualities while increasing the sense of evil at the same time.

They saw her face and figure in profile, and apparently she did not hear the opening of the door, because she did not look up as they entered. She still wore her red devil-costume, and one black-gloved hand hung over the arm of the chaise-lounge, dangling her painted mask. She had pushed back the headdress, so that the black and scarlet hood with its fantastic horns lay on her shoulders, and her bright golden hair was rumpled above her forehead as though the headdress had been pushed away in a hurried gesture for freedom. Cynthia looked like one of those women who at one time have been exquisitely beautiful. She was still very lovely, but it was a loveliness crystallized as though in ice; her hard mouth and tired eyes suggested that she had had too much of everything, and that now, though she was still young and still charming, she had arrived at the desert place where life held no more promises.[5]

If you can find this book and its predecessor, *The Gutenberg Murders*, we think you will enjoy them. They're worth a search.

PETER PIPER
1929-1932   5 books   American
Nancy Barr Mavity

Tall, thin, and nearsighted, James Aloysius Piper is known as Peter to his colleagues at the *Herald*, one of San Francisco's daily newspapers. A law student in his off hours, Peter holds a Phi Beta Kappa key. The lure of the hot lead and the fast-breaking story may be enough, however, to keep this young man from practice at the bar.

Intelligent and hardworking, Peter neither under- nor over-estimates the power of the press. In speaking to a young reporter who has expressed some doubts regarding the release of a story, Peter puts the realism of reporting into perspective with its idealism.

"You've got to believe in your job, young man. You said something about a sordid crime sensation in the papers. There are always thin-witted people complaining about the play given to crime news—though I notice most of them seem to read it. But for good or ill, human nature is what it is, and I've a notion it's worth our respect, even if we don't like it. The great stories have been crime stories all down the ages. When Shakespeare wanted to write *Macbeth* and *King Lear* and *Hamlet* he rooted around in Holinshed's Chronicles—which were the bound newspaper files of the day—and hunted up a good crime yarn. Maybe I'm wrong about *Hamlet*, but the principle's the same. Murder mysteries, everyone of them. And there's *Oedipus*—one of the grandest detective stories ever conceived. The Greeks and the Elizabethans responded to those stories—Shakespeare and Sophocles responded to them. And the stuff is still there. Unfortunately, Shakespeare and Sophocles haven't got jobs on daily papers, and the public has to get along as best it can with you and me. But don't you go turning up your nose at crime news."[6]

Peter's first loyalty appears to be to his paper. He is talented, ambitious, perseverant, and loves his job. His loyalty, however, supersedes the sensationalism the public clamors for. Above all, Peter loves the truth and is unwilling, under any circumstances, to stop short of it.

The last of this five-book series is, without a doubt, the best. Sing Wong, an elderly servant in a wealthy household, is charged with the murder of his master. Peter interviews the old man in his cell and is astounded to discover that this humble domestic is a well-educated man, holding several degrees. Wong is an enigma. He does not mind meeting his death for the crime and will say nothing in his own defense. As both the case and story unfold, Peter and the readers learn about philosophy of both the East and West, and personal integrity from the soft-spoken Wong.

Written on the cusp of decades, this series captures the urgency of getting an exclusive, the intensity of the city room, and the flavor of the times with accuracy. San Francisco in the early 1930's is well depicted as a raw, energetic place where almost anything goes and almost everything is possible. Using foresight, Mavity introduces concepts, new to the age, in her books—psychiatry, sociology, ballistics, and forensic medicine—and correctly predicts the importance of these fields to the future of crime detection.

SUSAN DARE
1934   1 book (short stories)   American
Mignon Eberhart

Mignon Eberhart's short series featuring mystery writer Susan Dare is contained in six adventures appearing in one book published in 1934. Miss Dare is invited to detect in the first episode by a new acquaintance, Jim Byrne, a reporter for a Chicago newspaper. He postpones adding certain facts to his story so that Susan has the opportunity to prove her friend's innocence. In succeeding chapters, Jim and Susan collaborate on cases in which an inheritance is at stake or is in jeopardy for the love of an unattainable partner. Sometimes, Susan dons a disguise to gain entrance to fogbound family homes which are often wrapped in a brooding silence. At other times her profession is her calling card.

Randy had turned away and vanished without more words,
and Tryon Welles, strolling across the room with Christabel,
was looking at Susan and smiling affably.

"Susan Dare," he said. "Watching the moonlight, quietly planning murder." He shook his head and turned to Christabel. "I simply don't believe you, Christabel. If this young woman writes anything, which I doubt, it's gentle little poems about roses and moonlight."

Christabel smiled faintly and sat down. Mars, his black face shining, was bringing in the coffee tray. In the doorway Joe Bromfel, dark and bulky and hot-looking in his dinner coat, lingered a moment to glance along the hall and then came into the room.

"If Susan writes poems," said Christabel lightly, "it is her secret. You are quite wrong, Tryon. She writes—" Christabel's silver voice hesitated. Her slender hands were searching, hovering rather blindly over the tray, the large amethyst on one white finger full of trembling purple lights. It was a barely perceptible second before she took a fragile old cup and began to pour from the tall silver coffee pot. "She writes murders," said Christabel steadily. "Lovely, grisly ones, with sensible solutions. Sugar, Tryon? I've forgotten."[7]

Mignon Eberhart also created two other series characters, Sarah Keate and Lance O'Leary. Miss Eberhart's style runs true to form in all of her books, even the nonseries. It is the had-I-but-known school and she does it well. The vernacular in these stories is dated and, to modern readers, atrocious at times. Oddly enough, this does give an example of prevailing thought and mores of the era. Romantic entanglements abound and there's always a happy ending.

JULIA PROBYN
1956-1973   10 books   English
Ann Bridge (Lady Mary Dolling O'Malley)

Young, beautiful, wealthy, and unfettered, as the series opens, Julia Probyn works from time to time as a free-lance journalist for several English weeklies and at least one provincial daily. Readers' first glimpse of Julia is through the eyes of her Scots relatives, the Monros, who initially hold a mildly contemptuous view of her personality and abilities. Nevertheless, her availability, credentials as a journalist, and her linguistic talents combine to make her the ideal person to search for Colin Monro who has not been heard from by his mother and sister for nine months.

The Julia we meet, in *The Lighthearted Quest*, is far from the flighty character described by her aunt Ellen and cousin Edina. She is a complex individual compelled by strong personal loyalties and is often motivated by the conviction that one does all one possibly can for those for whom one cares. It is this attitude, coupled with a strong sense of independence, which causes Julia to find herself in situations calling for far more than family loyalty, friendship, and a desire to be of personal assistance.

The search for Colin takes Julia to Morocco via cargo boat. Her natural amiability and genuine interest in people enable her to easily make the acquaintance of everyone from dock hands to bankers as she pursues her elusive cousin. Without realizing the true nature of the game in which she has become involved nor the stakes of that game, Julia goes about her task in an efficient and practical manner.

The stories are not simply murder mysteries. The plots and premises, involving international secrecy, espionage, and multinational secret services, are as complex as Julia herself. Her forays into the world of spies and intrigue are generally accidental. Julia's class, upbringing, wealth, and the people she knows provide her with entrée to all levels of society. Her innocent, even idle, social exchanges often furnish information which, in another context, becomes vital in unraveling knotty problems facing Julia and the more professional intelligence gatherers. Common sense and resourcefulness enable Julia to make appropriate use of the bits and pieces which come her way. She often surprises herself and the professionals.

> "Well, Miss Probyn, I have to hand it to you," Torrens said. "Reluctantly, I admit! But though I have been on this job for a longish time, and often up against quite powerful organizations, I've never before been brought to a full stop by a single young woman."[8]

On the surface, this series seems to be just another lighthearted romantic romp from one exotic locale to another. Readers looking for this sort of entertainment will not be disappointed. There are, however, other levels that can provoke thought and challenge assumptions. In each book, Julia is confronted with situations and people which induce her to question her own status quo. She learns from these encounters and grows as a character and an individual throughout the series which spans seventeen years. Readers see Julia through several failed courtships, marriage, motherhood, widowhood, and remarriage along with her adventures as a spy without portfolio. Her efficiency grows and matures as she does and as the series progresses, her skill in this high stakes game becomes more artful.

At the end of *Malady in Madeira*, second to the last book in the series, Julia accepts an official position with British Intelligence. In the last book, however, aside from a few personal contacts in the intelligence community, Julia is not involved in spying. *Julia in Ireland* is simply the book which winds up the series so that fans of this compelling character are satisfied with the requisite happy ending.

Ann Bridge is the pseudonym for Lady Mary O'Malley. Her husband is a member of the British Diplomatic Service (retired). Knowledgeable, widely traveled, and fluent in several languages herself, she has created a character who embodies many qualities we find admirable. Like Mrs. Pollifax, Julia uses her native abilities and intelligence in a creative and responsible fashion. Her risks are calculated ones and her solutions logical.

PATIENCE MCKENNA
1984-1986   3 books   American
Orania Papazoglou

Category romance paid my rent. My ego was supported by articles in slick women's magazines like *Sophistication* and alternative newspapers like *Left of Center*. I wrote articles on the growing incidence of alcoholism among working women, the cover-up campaign on the dangers of chemical wastes, the co-optation of women in the executive suite, and the dangers inherent in the growth of the New Right. I would continue to write them as long as no one ever found out I was also writing category romance.[9]

The art and business of romance writing is central to the first two books in the series. As Patience herself says, it does pay the rent. For some writers, it does substantially more. Susan Marie DeFord, aka Myrra Agenworth, for example, purchased and furnished over the years, a magnificent twelve-room New York apartment and draped her substantial figure in jewels and fur with the proceeds from her pen. Phoebe (Weiss) Damereaux has been Pay's best friend since Greyson College days and is also a successful writer in the genre with a ten-room Manhattan apartment and ropes of diamonds.

Sweet, Savage Death, first in this series, opens with Myrra's funeral—apparently murder by a mugger in Riverside Park. After the service, Pay returns to her own one-room apartment on West Eighty-second Street to find it bolted from the inside and a very dead body on the floor of the nine-by-twelve room. The corpse belongs to Julie Simms, literary agent for Myrra.

Patience discovers that Myrra has left her the twelve rooms in the Braedenvoorst and all of their contents. Evidence, including her recent inheritance, keeps pointing to Patience as the probable killer. When she finds the third body, Pay is arrested and charged with murder. It takes some fancy footwork on her part and assistance from Phoebe; Nick Carras, a Greek lawyer; and Camille, the black cat, to extricate McKenna from the district attorney's clutches.

Six feet tall and well beyond slim at 125 pounds, McKenna could be a model were it not for her face. Thick, blond, waist-length hair, unconventional clothing, and a capacious handbag round out the description of a striking and conspicuous character.

Other characters appear throughout the series, including Phoebe Damereaux, who stands four-foot-eleven and outweighs Pay by five pounds. Warm generosity is built into her nature and her loyalty to her longtime friend borders on the devotional. Nick Carras is six-foot-eight, looks like Christopher Reeve, and is well cared for by his mother. He is fascinated by Patience though a bit put off by her intensity and that which seems to surround her. As a friend of Phoebe's (she introduced him to Pay), he is caught up by both his fascination for Pay and Phoebe's loyalty to her.

Luis Martinez, NYPD Homicide, seems somewhat distracted by his first encounter with Patience when it was necessary to consider her as a prime murder suspect. He is, however, actually glad to hear from her when she calls him directly, to let him know that she has found still another body at her new place of work in *Wicked, Loving Murder*, second book in the series. Papazoglou provides the much-maligned craft of romance writing with a sense of integrity in this series. Only moderately tongue in cheek, she writes informatively on the subject and creates solid, believable, if sometimes exaggerated, characters.

BARNEY GANTT
1936–1976   8 books   American
John Stephen Strange (Dorothy Stockbridge Tillett)

The last book in this series came out in 1976. Unlike other writers with long-lived characters, Strange seems to have made the transition to modern times fairly well, though there are some clues that this book may have been penned at an earlier date. The story deals with Black Nationalism, terrorist acts, a wealthy young woman turned revolutionary—à la Patty Hearst—and the residents of a quiet, Connecticut nursing home. All events and activities are of the 1970's, but there is a distinct flavor of a New York of earlier days. Radio and newspapers are still the reigning powers of communication, television is never mentioned, and an occasional word or turn of phrase, popular in days-gone-by, slips into the more contemporary vernacular. Those hints, coupled with the fact that the previous Barney Gantt book came out in 1952, are enough to make these readers wonder and be intrigued.

Barney Gantt was introduced in 1936 in *The Bell in the Fog*. At that time, he was staff photographer for the New York *Globe*. As the series progresses, Barney keeps up his photography but is also billed as the *Globe*'s star reporter.

> Barney, on leaving the Kinney house, went into the first bar he came to, bought himself a highball and retired with it into a quiet corner to think. Going over in his mind the events of the afternoon: Mary Sanderson's death and her queer statement made to him when she was dying, the telephone call warning him to stay out of the affair, Dan Kinney's sudden and opportune illness and the govenor's obvious fear that the old man had been poisoned, there seemed to Barney little room for doubt that he was on the track of a conspiracy that would split the town wide open. Proof, to be sure, was lacking, but every instinct—that sixth sense that made him, indeed, one of the best reporters in the business, something more than a good photographer—told him that chance had thrown in his way a scoop on the biggest story of the season. If he could break it right.[10]

Political bosses are just that, black activists spout all the correct rhetoric, and boatmen are always crusty old salts, but readers should not be put off by stylized, one-dimensional characters. They are all part of a good tale, full of unpredictable twists and turns in which all the clues are laid out fairly for the truly dedicated puzzle fan.

Barney himself is well developed, as is Muriel (Singmaster in *Bell in the Fog* and Masterman in *Rope Enough*), who writes the lonely hearts column for the *Globe* under the byline Dorothy Darling. Muriel and Barney marry and seem as well suited to one another as to the detecting that is at the heart of every book. Louis Hand, the large, Buddha-like city editor, chews cigars, snarls at reporters and copy boys, but knows good work when he reads it, and appreciates the talents of both Barney and Muriel. Little Jimmy Alton, son of John, a waiter at Charlie's, is a smart kid. Introduced in *Rope Enough*, he assists his idol, Barney, in preventing a murder. His ambition is to become a newspaperman like Mr. Gantt and his ambition is realized in later novels.

The real identity of John Stephen Strange was a well-kept secret for over forty years. In reality, he was Dorothy Stockbridge Tillett, who, using that pseudonym, created more than twenty mystery novels.

MAXINE REYNOLDS
1978-1979   7 books   American
Marjorie Grove

Mysteries appear to some to be relatively simple formulae, easy to read—and so it follows—easy to write. All one needs is a victim, a killer, several different scenes, a few scattered clues, and, of course, a detective. The series featuring Maxine Reynolds, gossip writer for a Hollywood daily, is just that. All seven books in the series were released within two years by a company which advertises on the covers of their books, "The novel that lets you be the detective!" and provides readers with a page on which to write their answers before they open the *sealed*, final chapter. Sound awful? It gets worse.

Red-haired, green-eyed Max spends her time dashing about Hollywood, lunching at the Beverly Hills Hotel, attending screenings, cocktail and dinner parties, and mingling with the stars and those who aspire to those heights. When not involved in this mad social whirl, Max is chained to her telephone making dates and appointments and picking up more tit bits for her column. When does she find time to write one might ask? The answer to that is that she rarely does. Her assistant, the veddy, veddy British Pamela Tooth manages that portion of the job. Their relationship is one based on mutual need and, if their banter is a clue, is supposed to be somewhat egalitarian.

Locations, attire, and behavior are described in painstaking detail, less, one suspects, to set the scene and present characters than to impress the reader with an insider's knowledge of the habits and haunts of the rich and famous. While the locations are genuine and the dress and behavior plausible, not much more of the story is. We finished one book because we couldn't believe that anything that bad could be sustained for some two hundred pages. That was an error in judgment. We can't say much more than that readers are well advised to avoid the entire series.

RAIN MORGAN
1985-1986   2 books   English
Leslie Grant-Adamson

Rain Morgan's photo appears beside her byline at the head of her gossip column in the *Post*, a London daily. The paper is widely read and Rain is easily recognized by her fans. This visibility is two-sided. On one hand, it makes it difficult for her to choose anonymity, while on the other, it gives her access to information from people always willing to talk to a media personality.

"...Who'll I say?" she said, looking over her shoulder, already on her way out of the bar. She had a loud voice.
"Rain Morgan."
"Who?"
Again. Louder.
A lot of nudging was going on. "There you are," said the jolly man who had been at the church gate. "I said it was her." He turned to Rain. "I told 'em it were."
Rain smiled back over her glass. There was a bit of banter, no single remark distinguishable. A very old man leaned closer and shouted into her ear. "Now what I've always wanted to know about them gossip columns..."[11]

A borrowed cottage and an absent host in the village of Nether Hampton give Rain her first taste of detecting in *Death on Widow's Walk*. Oliver West, Rain's boyfriend, has assured her that his cousin Adam Hollings has offered him the use of his cottage. Neither Oliver nor any of the neighbors of Withy Cottage seems to know just where Adam has gone nor how long he will be away. The neighbors are friendly, and through inquiries as to Adam's whereabouts, Rain makes their acquaintance and is welcomed into their social circle.

Archaeologist Robin Woodley discovers the first body in the well of Nether Hampton Castle. The second body is that of Joan Murray, one of Rain's new neighbors. Rain's curiosity is piqued by a missing man and murder close by, and she begins to pay more attention to the casual chatter at the local pub, the shops, and post office. Her reporter's instinct leads her along a trail of clues which eventually lead to the identity of the murderer.

Location, again, initiates Rain's second murder investigation. In *The Face of Death*, her assistant Holly Chase moves into a new home and begins to meet her neighbors. It soon becomes apparent that something fishy is happening, and even though there is no corpse in evidence, inquiries are opened by the two journalists. Introduced in the first book, Holly Chase is black, beautiful, and rather outrageous. In the second, it is she who is featured while Rain plays a much more secondary role mainly appearing to tie up loose ends and reinforce Holly's investigative efforts.

These two characters show promise. We will look forward to reading about them as they develop further. The writer, Leslie Grant-Adamson, is a London journalist herself and brings insight and professionalism to her stories.

LETTIE WINTERBOTTOM
1981-1985   3 books   American
Leela Cutter

Eccentric is the word which best describes this series. The characters, the plots, and the dialogue all support oddness. Lettie, herself, is the requisite scatty old lady. She causes those around her to worry about her health and safety as she tends to wander around in a daze of preoccupation from time to time.

> "Auntie, I think it would be wise to use a cab. I hate to think of you injuring yourself—or someone else."
> "Now, it's nothing so serious! Just a little spell of writer's distraction. I will be perfectly all right once I settle down to starting a new one. Don't you remember all those mishaps I had between *The Corpse Took Two Lumps* and *Lambs and Lemmings*? I even wound up with a broken ankle, but it was well worth it because I met that wonderful young surgeon who told me about dermatographia, which was the very idea I needed for a new plot."[12]

This dottiness carefully covers a sharp mind capable of both logic and intuitive leaps. Her niece Julia does most of the legwork, though Lettie herself will take off on a wild chase at the drop of a hat.

Saint Martin's Mere is home for Lettie where she is watched over by long-suffering, but not silent, Phyllis, the housekeeper, and guarded by Tim, the ferocious terrier. Lettie writes mysteries and, in the first book, is in search of a new plot as her adventures begin.

A millionaire electronics wizard and his bizarre family form the centerpiece of this foray into real-life detection for Lettie which involves a mysterious invention, a suspicious death in Spain, and a security specialist from Palo Alto, in the heart of Silicon Valley, California.

In *Who Stole Stonehenge?*, the standing stones themselves, have disappeared in a mighty storm. A prize is offered to the finder and Lettie, teamed up with J. D. Hilsebeck, an impoverished journalist, and Julia, is determined to find them if for no other reason than to spite her nemesis, Gwenna Hardcastle. Lettie and Gwenna have never met but there is a long-standing (on Lettie's part) antipathy and resentment over Gwenna's success as a romance writer.

Gwenna is featured in the third book, which opens with a ball given to honor the opening of the Museum of Historical Romance. Nasty nephew Freddie is found quite dead in the depths of a diorama depicting *Romeo and Juliet*'s balcony scene. At Gwenna's urging, Lettie takes on the investigation which involves a convent, orphans, a bon vivant party crasher, a midnight dash to the Continent, and a wild motorcycle ride.

Leela Cutter is an American who, like Martha Grimes, has chosen to set her tales in England. Not only does she carry off this trans-Atlantic transposition well, she causes readers to effectively suspend their disbelief. Improbable as the plots and stories are, there is a delightfully zany credibility to them.

LIZ CONNORS
1985-1986   2 books   American
Susan Kelly

Susan Kelly has created a character whose skills and background closely match her own. Liz Connors has become a freelance writer after spending a number of years as an assistant professor of English. She still teaches occasionally and, in *Summertime Soldiers*, is teaching report writing at the Cambridge Police Academy. Author Kelly holds a Ph.D. in English literature, teaches at the Cambridge Police Academy, and resides in Cambridge, Massachusetts, as well.

Jack Lingemann, Cambridge homicide detective, is Liz's boyfriend and her entrée into the world of violent crime. Her connections with the police, her assignments, and credentials as a writer give her license to ask questions of people on the fringes and at the center of the action. Though they do not work together officially, Jack and

Liz's respective tasks overlap and they share leads and information with one another.

> "Seriously," I said. "Does what I'm saying about Sandra make sense? I can see, now, what she and Joan saw in Bingham. True, he's a dork. But he does have a certain amount of power and prestige, in addition to his looks, and those things do have an aphrodisiac effect on some women. Especially young ones. But...the guy in Bingham's profile is a *wimp*. A *wimp*. Would a girl like Sandra even look at someone like that? Much less bother to invite him to her apartment and to her bed?"
>
> Jack was quiet for a few seconds after I'd wound up my diatribe. Then he said, "Want a job?"
>
> "Say what?"
>
> He smiled. "I'd like to hire you as an investigator."
>
> My mouth fell open. "Are you serious?"
>
> "Well, I can hardly issue you a badge or a gun. But you would probably be goddamned good at this kind of work."
>
> Bemused, I shook my head. "That's the nicest thing you've ever said to me."
>
> He looked taken aback. "Oh, come now. Surely not the *nicest*."
>
> I smiled. "Well, the second nicest..."[13]

Job offer notwithstanding, Jack gives Liz more information than seems prudent for a civilian to possess. This information is definitely provocative and, coupled with Liz's innate curiosity, gets her into situations beyond her ample capabilities. The murder of a neighbor involves Liz in the investigation of *The Gemini Man*. Asked by Brandon Peters of the *Cambridge Monthly* to do an article on the dead woman, Liz finds herself interviewing friends and associates of the victim, including the murderer. In *Summertime Soldiers*, Peters assigns Liz to write on the theme of "what-ever-happened-to-the-peace-activists?" following terrorist murders claimed by a group which had dropped out of sight some fifteen years earlier.

Both books show us the investigative process of a reporter firsthand and the same sort of process by the police through her relationship with Lieutenant Lingemann. Beyond the procedural aspect of the stories, both are complex and compelling psychological thrillers. The first can be called a whodunit but the why ends up being far more interesting. In the second, the who is known at the outset, the why gets explained as the story progresses, and the tension is held by the threat to Jack's life and Liz's eleventh-hour jeopardy.

Liz and Jack are likeable, their relationship with each other is comfortable and obviously one which includes mutual respect. Though this is not a hard-boiled series, there are scenes of explicit violence and excessive intimidation which serve as a counter for the amiability of the characters.

THE POWER OF THE PRINTED WORD may have diminished slightly with the advent of electronic media. It is, however, still a force with which to contend. Experience can be consolidated in a well-written paragraph in a way few TV news broadcasts or films can match. Words are reflective as well as immediate. They enhance a reader's knowledge of an event, and remain for reference long after the initial occurrence has passed, and express and evoke many different things to many different people.

As a published poet, Adam Dalgliesh deserves mention here as does mystery novelist, Harriet Vane, Lord Peter's light o' love. Nigel Bathgate aids Scotland Yard Inspector Roderick Alleyn, and Jammy Hopkins, who shouts "Jam! Jam!" at the hint of a hot story, appears in several Alan Grant books.

Other books featuring letters and journalism include:

Margery Allingham, *Flowers for the Judge*, 1936
Hildegarde Dolson, *Please Omit Funeral*, 1975
Margaret Erskine, *A Graveyard Plot*, 1959
Joan Hess, *Strangled Prose*, 1986
Patricia Moyes, *A Six-Letter Word for Death*, 1983
Monica Quill, *Sine Qua Nun*, 1986
Sheila Radley, *The Chief Inspector's Daughter*, 1980

MUSEUM PIECES

CURATORS, BIBLIOPHILES, AND ART EXPERTS

*T*he study and preservation of rare and beautiful creations demands concentration, appreciation, and, to be considered an expert in one's field, a high degree of competence. Recognized primarily as authorities in antiquities, the detectives introduced in this chapter also use their skills to uncover contemporary crime.

Some are compelled to detect in order to protect that with which they are entrusted, others use their particular knowledge as an aid in tracing clues to the ultimate solution of a murder. Still others are less well known for their interest in paintings, objets d'art, and manuscripts than for their sleuthing skills. One of these is Lord Peter Wimsey, who, nevertheless, is recognized as a celebrated bibliophile by the Reverend Theodore Venables in Dorothy L. Sayers' *The Nine Tailors*.

> "Lord Peter Wimsey—just so. Dear me! The name seems familiar. Have I not heard of it in connection with—ah! I have it! *Notes on the Collection of Incunabula*, of course. A very scholarly little monograph, if I may say so. Yes. Dear me. It will be charming to exchange impressions with another book-collector. My library is, I fear, limited, but I have an edition of the *Gospel of Nicodemus* that may interest you.[1]

These detectives possess talent and highly specialized skills for their trade. Fortunately, these translate well toward the resolution of crime.

CONAN FLAGG
1973-1984   6 books   American
M. K. Wren (Martha Kay Renfroe)

Introduced by M. K. Wren in 1973, Conan Flagg possesses most of the qualities we find admirable in a detective. Licensed as a private investigator by the state of Oregon, Conan practices detecting only part time and does not advertise his services. He prefers to spend his hours in the small, well-appointed office of his prized possession, the Holliday Beach Book Shop, where he is well attended by Miss Dobie and Meg, a blue point Siamese. As sole heir to the Ten Mile Ranch and its major stockholder, Conan does not have to work for a living.

Tall and good looking, his Nez Percé ancestry shows itself in his straight black hair, high cheekbones, and the faint oriental cast to his dark eyes. Wealth, good taste, and good looks are not the only features to recommend this character. Conan cares deeply about the land and all of its inhabitants.

> Conan watched him go, irritably annoyed at himself; that question could have waited. As the desert silence closed in, he lit a cigarette and watched the burgeoning of stars. He heard Ted's departure on Molly, but afterward the only sounds were distant slammings of doors from the bunkhouse as the hands settled in for the night, and later the eerie harmonic chorus of a coyote pack singing the moon up. A wild sound full of echos of years and millennia past, a cast of mourning in it that unexpectedly brought tears to his eyes for a man who had been vital and alive when the moon last rose. Or perhaps his grief was for the survivors; for the victims of some vicious and senseless game.[2]

Conan's activities as a private eye are what interest readers. A sedentary, contented collector of books—no matter how rare and valuable they may be—is not, generally, the stuff of which adventurers are made. Although Conan's investigations may take him far from home, his thoughts are never far from his bookshop.

> Nearly four hundred miles behind him, across the breadth of the state of Oregon, the sun would be making mist in pine and spruce forests and glinting on silk and cream breakers, but he wasn't there to look out the windows of his house to see them. Nor was he there to walk the two blocks to the ramshackle,

shingled pile that he regarded as his one contribution to the continuity of civilization: the Holliday Beach Book Shop.[3]

VICKY BLISS
1973-1987   4 books   American
Elizabeth Peters (Barbara Mertz)

In the first book in this series, Dr. Victoria Bliss is a history instructor at a small midwestern college. She and a colleague embark—as friendly rivals—on a quest to a castle in Germany to find a lost, jeweled woodcarving created circa 1550. During this adventure, which involves secret passages, the ghost of an armored knight, and several villains and villainesses both historical and contemporary, Vicky meets Herr Schmidt. A potential suspect as the adventure begins, Schmidt becomes Vicky's ally and future employer at the end of the story.

The next two books find Vicky Bliss working for Herr Professor Doktor Schmidt at the National Museum in Munich and writing softcore porn for her boss' weekly entertainment. As a medieval historian with a minor in art history, Vicky is well qualified both for her position at the museum and as an amateur detective. The mysteries she unravels involve lost, misappropriated, and forged antiquities. Murder is not the central issue.

In the second book, Sir John Smythe is introduced and unmasked as a clever con artist who works both sides of the street. Dr. Bliss' feelings toward this elegant and handsome crook with a string of aliases (i.e., Al Monkshood) are ambivalent, to say the least.

John is a thief. He specializes in the objects I am paid to guard and protect—gems, antiques, art objects. He isn't a very successful thief. He's smart enough, and God knows he's tricky, but he is also a dedicated coward. When he hears the heavy footsteps of cops or competitors thundering toward him he drops everything and runs. That may not seem like an attractive quality, but it is actually one of John's more appealing traits. If everybody were as reluctant to inflict or endure pain, there wouldn't be any wars, or muggings of helpless little old ladies.

He has the most atrophied conscience of anyone I know. He also has...But perhaps I had better not be too explicit, since I want this book to appeal to a family audience. When he's engaged in what he does so well, one may be momentarily

bemused into forgetting his true nature, but one would have
to be a damned fool to let him con one at any other time.[4]

Needless to say, the attraction and ambivalence are mutual.

While Vicky's professional qualifications are impeccable,
her physical attributes are equally outstanding. Nearly six feet
tall, her blond hair, dark blue eyes, and shapely figure echo her
Scandinavian ancestry. Vicky considers her pulchritude unfortunate.

> It isn't easy to convince people that you've got a brain
> when all they can see are curves and flowing blond hair.
> Nor is it easy for a woman like me to get a job. Intellectual
> women mistrust me on sight. Intellectual men are just like
> all other men, they hire me—but for the wrong reasons.[5]

Though Vicky views her appearance as a handicap, she clearly rises
above it and allows it to serve her. This is a woman who believes
in herself and her abilities. As a world citizen, we predict she will
go far.

The stories, like the heroine herself, are overblown. They
are entertaining spoofs on the classic romance/thriller, however, underneath the humor and histrionics is a good story, well
told which relies on solid research and historical fact as its foundation. Author Elizabeth Peters has also developed two other mystery series featuring women who are strong and unconventional
academicians. A scholar herself, Peters brings a high standard
of scholarship to this delightfully humorous series.

ELENA OLIVEREZ
1983-1986   3 books   American
Marcia Muller

Santa Barbara is a seaside city of around 75,000, stretch-
ing north along the coast to the University of California,
my alma mater, and south to Montecito, where the rich
people live. The shoreline curves along the Pacific, edged
with beaches and parks. To the east, softly rounded hills
form a protective bowl. The beauty of the natural setting
is further enhanced by the graceful Spanish architecture,
which reflects the town's heritage. Santa Barbara has become one of the foremost vacation areas in California and
is a haven for the wealthy and famous, many of whom

are seeking to escape the cheap glitter of Hollywood to the south.[6]

Marcia Muller's descriptions of Santa Barbara and the surrounding countryside are fluent and accurate. She captures the timeless quality and complexity of a land claimed by various nations over the centuries.

Elena Oliverez lives here in the house in which she grew up. As the series begins, she is the curator of the Museum of Mexican Arts in Pueblo Viejo, Santa Barbara's old town. A degree in art history from the University of California, Santa Barbara, qualifies her for this position. Her Mexican heritage enhances her academic qualifications and should provide an effective means to explore the disparate views of this historically rich area.

Elena is introduced to murder in the first novel when Frank De Palma, director of the museum, is brutally crushed to death by an *arbol de la vida* (tree of life). Lieutenant Dave Kirk of the Santa Barbara Homicide Squad determines that the director's death is not the accident it first appears and Elena is high on his list of suspects. To clear herself, she investigates the killing on her own and uncovers an active smuggling operation. Exonerated from the crime, at the end of the story she is named acting director by the museum's board.

As the second book opens, Elena has been officially confirmed as director. In this story, she is simultaneously, if somewhat warily, courted by both Carlos Bautista, chairman of the museum's board, and Lieutenant Kirk. Wealth and respectability blur class and ethnic barriers for Bautista who is able to give Elena entrée to the upper echelons of Santa Barbara society. In spite of this, Elena rails and kicks against obstacles she still perceives. Carlos' sophistication, his twenty-five-year seniority, and acceptance of the macho tradition count heavily against him in pressing his suit with Elena.

Dave Kirk is a cop and an Anglo. The spark of attraction between him and Elena, ignited in the first book, has dimmed and is only rekindled when murder allows their paths to cross in the second. Kirk asks for Elena's assistance in gathering information from the predominantly Chicano residents of the mobile home park where her mother lives and where the crime has occurred. He feels the residents might speak more freely to ''one of their own'' than to an outsider. Elena's petulant attitude toward the lieutenant has less to do with his profession and racial origins than with his gender.

Other characters are regulars in the series. Gabriela Oliverez, Elena's mother, and her boyfriend Nick Carillo alternately chide and assist Elena as she pursues killers. Susana Ibarra, a spoiled child bride ultimately deserted by her Colombian husband in the first book, is Elena's secretary in the second. Jesse Herrera, a young Chicano artist who creates *camaleones*—fanciful mixes of bird, reptile, and mammal—exhibits at the museum. His artist grandmother, Abuela Felicia, appears in the second story.

While Muller succeeds with her descriptions of the countryside and historical information, she is less successful with some of the people in her stories. Elena herself often comes across as a spoiled child unwilling (or unable) to accept some of the social responsibilities inherent in her position as director of an art museum. There is potential in both the principal character and the milieu in which Muller has placed her. When Ms. Oliverez grows up a bit, learns to laugh at herself, and accepts the rights and privileges of her position, she may be a more fascinating creation.

MAX BITTERSOHN
1979-1987   7 books   American
Charlotte MacLeod

In the first book in their series, handsome Max Bittersohn is introduced to Boston blue blood Sarah Kelling as a writer who is an expert in precious jewels. His literary interest lies in the beautiful and rarely viewed heirloom set belonging to Sarah's aunt/mother-in-law. Actually, this thin disguise conceals a very effective detective. His job is the recovery of stolen art works and jewelry for their distressed owners and/or insurance companies.

Max's detections solve an historic scandal and a series of contemporary mysterious tragedies for Sarah. To protect her, Max moves into the Kelling's basement apartment. He accepts a return engagement in the second book, though as a permanent lodger, to unravel yet another mystery in Sarah's home, now an elegant boardinghouse.

"You need a tenant who's trained to keep a straight face under any and all conditions, right? And I need a place to hang out when I'm in town, don't I?"

"But you already have one."

"Wrong. I've had one. They're turning the building into condominiums and I either have to buy a scroungy apartment I have no desire whatever to own or get out by the first of the month. You wouldn't want to see me sitting in the middle of Bowdoin Street with all my worldly goods, namely two suitcases and a genuine hand-carved teakwood back-scratcher presented as a token of esteem by a grateful client, would you?''

''Of course not, but—I can't believe it!''

''So call up the real estate agents. I'll give you their number. They'd sell you my place this minute, if you don't mind paying an arm and a leg for two crummy rooms overlooking several acres of pigeon droppings. I may be homeless by the time I get back there, for all I know. Mrs. Kelling, I don't smoke, I don't shine my shoes on the bedspread because my mother brought me up right, I don't own any disco records and wouldn't play them if I did. I pay my rent a month in advance because I never know when or for how long I'll be called out of town, and whatever you charge couldn't be any worse than I'm getting stuck for now. I'd need to install a private phone, which of course I'd pay for myself. I sometimes have slightly weird visitors at odd hours, but I could make them come and go by the alley door in order not to tarnish your image. I'd as soon be in the basement because I'd probably feel more at home with the hired help than the paying guests. Do we have a deal or don't we?''[7]

Love blooms for Max and Sarah in book three, and bursts into full flower in book four. They marry off the page and book five has Max working on his own while Sarah wifes the house.

Because of Max's expertise and considerable knowledge, he is often in demand and in pursuit of thieves and objets d'art around the world. His adventures though, much to his delight and amusement, frequently involve him in the increasingly convoluted and eccentric Kelling family affairs.

The murders which Max and Sarah investigate occur within the Kelling family circle. As the clan is extensive, long-lived and combative, a good deal of lethal raw material is at hand. Max and Sarah are sensitive and sympathetic characters. Their wit is dry and they are effective counterfoils for the wilder antics of MacLeod's other characters in these stories.

Writing as Charlotte MacLeod, this author has also created Professor Peter Shandy. As Alisa Craig, she writes about the Royal Canadian Mounted Police officer, Madoc Rhys, and the Grub-and-Stake Gardening and Roving Club. Humor is the trademark of each of these series.

SIMON BRADE
1936-1946   7 books   English
Harriette Campbell

Between 1936 and 1946, Simon Brade appeared in seven novels. So far, we have only been able to track down one of these, which is frustrating as this seems to be a charming, erudite, and somewhat silly character we'd like to read more about. Brade is an expert in porcelain and glass but supports himself by detecting.

"Hobby?" Brade looked at him vaguely. "Oh, I suppose you mean my little excursions into the investigation of crime. That's not a hobby, Mr. Prentice. That's the sinister blot on an otherwise harmless, not to say useful, career. Tell him about it, Jerry. He seems to want to know."

Dr. Jerrold replied to his host's lifted eyebrow.

"Brade regards his collection of porcelain and glass as his justification in life, not as a hobby. As for his work as a detective—"

"What a word, Jerry!" sighed Brade.

"As for that, he does it to earn a living, and he doesn't like it at all. He hates sending a man to prison, and the one or two cases he has had when he has helped to expose a murderer have very nearly killed him. So you can't call that business a hobby either. If he has a hobby at all, it's thinking up ways to make people believe he's even sillier than he is."[8]

The setting in the one book we were able to find is a comfortable old English country home. Politics, hunting, horse racing, and antiquities are elements in the story which seems to present accurate, if casual, social commentary. One of the book's undisputed stars is Chen, a cairn terrier with a distinctive and wordlessly eloquent nature.

We'd like to be able to tell you more about this little colourless antiquarian and will just have to be content to introduce an old character to new readers.

HENRY GAMADGE
1940-1951   16 books   American
Elizabeth Daly

"I suppose you know what I do do. I'm supposed to advise on disputed manuscripts and documents."

"Are you?" The young man looked astonished. "I thought you investigated things for people—quietly."

"I have, sometimes," said Gamadge. "If you want to know my fee for that kind of thing, it's nothing."

"Nothing?"

"I'm not a professional," said Gamadge. "I have no facilities and no license. I only do that kind of thing, very rarely, for friends or their friends, or because I'm interested for reasons of my own."[9]

Henry Gamadge, bibliophile and sometime detective, is one of the most enigmatic characters we've encountered. Throughout the sixteen-book series, readers become familiar with his house, family, friends, and associates and could probably pick Gamadge out in a crowd. On the surface, he appears to be just what he seems. Henry is gentlemanly and urbane. He is fond of cats, dogs, and small children, particularly his own. Though he is open in all of his dealings with people, there is a well-hidden side to this man.

The stories take place in and around New York City of the forties. Elizabeth Daly, herself a native New Yorker, laces her series with the flavors of the city and the times. Gamadge is at home here. He knows the geography well enough to be familiar with its more subtle aspects. Shortcuts and back alleys often provide him with direct and discreet routes to his destinations. His trade puts him in touch with those possessors of esoteric information necessary to his avocation but the mind of this man, where all his data is stored and sorted, remains firmly closed to view. Gamadge is taken on faith by those who seek his assistance with their problems and by those with whom he works.

Though he relies on the assistance of many people, he synthesizes information on his own. Henry doesn't withhold clues. He does, however, withhold his conjectures, and his ratiocinative process is never obvious. Readers may unravel the puzzle before the end of the book by clues Miss Daly makes available. They will seldom arrive at their conclusion in the same way Gamadge reaches his and one is never quite sure just how he has done it.

The crimes in the Gamadge stories involve the upper classes. Murder here seems almost genteel. A strong undercurrent of evil is present, however, and at the denouement, readers may be disconcerted by the contrast between the pleasant facade and the sordid details and reasons surrounding and permeating the case.

Author Elizabeth Daly was sixty-two when the first Gamadge book was introduced. Over the next eleven years she produced sixteen books which were well received by readers. These books are currently being reissued for the enjoyment of a whole new generation.

THESE OUT-OF-THE-ORDINARY PROFESSIONALS are experts in their respective fields. Their creators are to be congratulated on skillfully weaving esoteric and historically accurate information into entertaining mysteries.

Other books featuring antiquarians and bibliophiles include:

Mary Fitt, *Clues to Christabel*, 1944
Anna Katharine Green, *The Golden Slipper and Other Problems for Violet Strange*, 1915
Henrietta Hamilton, *At Night to Die*, 1959
Elizabeth Holding, *Too Many Bottles*, 1951
P. D. James, *Unnatural Causes*, 1967
Susan Kenney, *Garden of Malice*, 1983
Jane Langton, *The Transcendental Murder*, 1964; *Dark Nantucket Noon*, 1975
Elizabeth Lemarchand, *Step in the Dark*, 1976
Frances and Richard Lockridge, *Murder Within Murder*, 1946; *The Drill is Death*, 1961; *Murder Has Its Points*, 1961; *The Distant Clue*, 1963; *Murder by the Book*, 1963
Amelia Reynolds Long, *The Shakespeare Murders*, 1939; *The Corpse at the Quill Club*, 1940; *Death Looks Down*, 1945
Charlotte MacLeod, *Rest You Merry*, 1978
Helen McCloy, *Two-Thirds of a Ghost*, 1956
Lenore Glen Offord, *Walking Shadow*, 1959
Stella Phillips, *The Hidden Wrath*, 1968
Charlotte M. Russell, *Murder at the Old Stone House*, 1935
Norma Schier, *Murder by the Book*, 1979
Phoebe Atwood Taylor, *Going, Going, Gone*, 1943; *Proof of the Pudding*, 1945

Lee Thayer, *Murder Stalks the Circle*, 1947; *Dead on Arrival*, 1960
Alice Tilton, *Beginning With a Bash*, 1937
Carolyn Wells, *Murder in the Bookshop*, 1936
Carolyn Weston, *Rouse the Demon*, 1976

PORTRAITS IN CRIME

THE VISUAL ARTS

*T*he artist's eye is trained to recognize, record, and represent detail. As much attention is paid to the spaces between things as to the things themselves. To the artist, a shadow or an intimation of an outline is sometimes more a definition of an object than the object itself.

> Happily, I am the complete master of my pencil. In seconds it will catch the essence of a motion, the accurate impression of a landscape, the characteristic tilt of a head. And my artist's eye is my pencil's servant, endlessly at work storing away images and impressions, none too neatly but accurately enough so they can be brought out and transferred to paper months and even years later with the freshness of a sight just seen.[1]

Whether the following characters are painting, sculpting, photographing, or detecting, they are gathering information for a finished portrait.

AGATHA TROY
1934-1982   32 books   English
Ngaio Marsh

Painter Agatha Troy is introduced in the sixth book of Ngaio Marsh's mystery series featuring British Inspector Roderick Alleyn. Their meeting is initially inauspicious though not completely without import. Troy's reputation as a painter is well established and Alleyn, after their first abrupt exchange over a canvas on which she is working, recognizes the style and puts the artist's name to the work.

Ngaio Marsh had doubts regarding the marriage of her handsome, aristocratic, bachelor creation. She feared that the result of taking Alleyn off the marital market and domesticating him might lead to the loss of readers. Marriage could clearly reduce the provocative vitality of this dynamic character.

Troy was, however, already a presence in Marsh's mind. She arrives fully developed with a firm personality and a fierce talent.

> There was a kind of spare gallantry about her. She turned quickly before he had time to look away and their gaze met.
>
> Alleyn was immediately conscious of a clarification of his emotions. As she stood before him, her face slowly reddening under his gaze, she seemed oddly familiar. He felt that he already knew her next movement, and the next inflexion of her clear, rather cold voice. It was a little as though he had thought of her a great deal, but never met her before. These impressions held him transfixed, for how long he never knew, while he still kept his eyes on hers. Then something clicked in his mind, and he realized that he had stared her out of countenance. The blush had mounted painfully to the roots of her hair and she had turned away.[2]

Obviously she existed in Alleyn's mind as well. Their courtship is not without complications for these are mature, strong, and independent individuals with separate careers and lives. Not for them a hasty or casual union. Commitment, if it is made, will be total. Happily for the reader, it is, and Troy appears in most of the rest of the books in the series.

JEFF and HAILA TROY
1940-1966   10 books   American
Kelley Roos (Audrey and William Roos)

Jeff Troy is a commercial photographer. "He says he likes his job but he is happiest when he is involved in a nice murder."[3] Jeff and his charming wife Haila form an entertaining detective team. They live and work in the Manhattan of the 1940's, an era which also saw the creation of other married detective teams such as the Abbotts (by Frances Crane) and the Norths (by the Lockridges).

Witty sophistication is a hallmark of the Troys, the times, and the place. The stories, told from Haila's point of view, include casts of zany characters, breezy banter, and minimal violence. The Troys' detection uncovers murders motivated by espionage, family greed, and blackmail.

Haila, a former starving actress, occasionally applies her theatrical talents to create a disguise in order to shadow a suspect. Sometimes she finds herself in jeopardy but rallies quickly and presses on regardless.

> "After this, when I'm unconscious, I'll thank you to keep your damn hands off me and call a physician. Mr. Randall, what time is it?"
>
> "It's nearly eight, Mrs. Troy."
>
> "Damn it, I've missed dinner."
>
> "Mr. Troy," Randall said anxiously, "perhaps we had better call a physician."
>
> "No," Jeff said. "She's always like this after she's been knocked out."
>
> "Has she—has Mrs. Troy been knocked out often?"
>
> "It gets worse every year."
>
> I said, "May I have a cigarette?"
>
> "Now she's all right," Jeff said. He gave me a cigarette, he even lit it for me. "You are all right, aren't you, Haila?"
>
> "I'm fine," I said. "As a matter of fact, the whole thing was a very refreshing experience. How long was I out?"[4]

This amusing series was created by husband and wife Audrey and William Roos. Their puzzle formula in the ten books featuring the delightful young Troys is enhanced by effervescent humor. The Rooses have captured the fin-de-siecle flavor of the 1940's which adds to the enjoyment of this lively series.

HELEN BULLOCK
1975-1979   4 books   American
Barbara Ninde Byfield

Helen Bullock is also a photographer. Her talent is such that she is able to pick and choose among the assignment plums which come her way. She travels widely and apparently never unpacks from one trip to the next. Her wardrobe tends toward the functional and her hair is described as ''some colorist's Terrible Joke or just devil-may-care, practically patchwork.''[5]

A member of the congregation of the Church of Saint Jude the Martyr, Helen is a friend of the Reverend Dunstan Owsley. He has talked Helen into donating her time for a photo series of a year at Saint Jude's for him. On Ash Wednesday of this photographic year, Helen is at work recording images when the Reverend is murdered.

Now the light from the music rack on the organ console lit the passionate absorption in the old man's face, showing none of the querulous pettiness he was known for in his day-to-day contacts. It was the first time she had ever seen him look completely happy.

She was happy herself and would have been surprised if she could have seen her own face at that moment, solid with the tension of a craftsman absorbed in the job at hand, equal to it, and animated with the challenge.[6]

Helen meets Father Simon Bede, an Anglican priest and aide to the Archbishop of Canterbury, at the scene of the crime in the first book of their series. Each is an independent individual in pursuit of an interesting career. Their attraction for one another is strong and they manage to meet in both familiar and exotic places all over the globe. One of the familiar (as in breeds contempt) places is Crumbles, the dilapidated Bede family home in the wilds of Kent, England.

Helen's creator, Barbara Ninde Byfield, is herself a well-known illustrator of children's books. Byfield's artistic perceptions are apparent in both the character of Helen and in the well-drawn scenes of the four books in the series.

PERSIS WILLUM
1977-1985 3 books American
Clarissa Watson

Persis Willum often refers to herself as a starving artist. In truth, she is a noted painter and oversees the complex operation of running a gallery for Gregor Olitsky. Any missed meals are the result of preoccupation rather than poverty.

At the age of ten, after the death of her parents, Persis became the ward of her impressively wealthy aunt, Lydia Wentworth.

> My parents had the misfortune to vanish at sea while cruising the Bahamas.
>
> "Most unfortunate," said my aunt and proceeded to do her duty, shepherding me into adulthood, albeit from a more-or-less safe distance. "I find children alarming," she confessed; and sentenced me to boarding schools round the clock—a sentence sweetened, when she felt particularly robust, by occasional trips to the races in England or Normandy and house parties with assorted nobility in the south of France. "It is important for a young girl to learn the amenities," she had said, and taught me to ride sidesaddle, to curtsy to grownups and, after I was sixteen, to drink a "brut" champagne from the proper flute and to distinguish between a Bordeaux and a Burgundy.[7]

Through Aunt Lydie's connections, Persis has friends in high places, and enemies as well. Murder is at the center of each story. Intrigue and espionage complicate matters and test Persis' perceptive visual skills, good memory and keen intelligence.

Clarissa Watson populates the Willum stories with a wonderful cast of recurring luminaries from the worlds of society, art, and politics. Gregor, art impresario and Persis' boss at the gallery, would do anything for the ravishing Miss Wentworth. Encouraged by Aunt Lydie, Oliver Reynolds, art critic and filmmaker, pursues Persis with unrequited romantic intentions. Persis' own modest home on Long Island is shared with Isadore Duncan, the cat, and overseen by the very capable, devoted, and domineering "houseworker" Mrs. Howard.

Watson's three-book series spans nine years. We hope we don't have to wait another four or five for Persis to make her next appearance.

JOHNSON JOHNSON
1968-1984   6 books   English
Dorothy Dunnett

Bifocals and baggy, nondescript clothing are the first things one notices about this enigmatic character. His droll humor and tendency to overstate the absurd give the impression that one has encountered a harmless eccentric. This innocuous demeanor masks a superb intelligence. Though his eyesight may be poor, his vision is sharp and true.

The female who holds his heart and commands his wealth is *Dolly*. Big, white, and sleek, she carries him to exotic ports around the globe.

> If you know about boats she is a gaff-rigged auxiliary ketch, of about fifty-odd tons, which implies a great deal of money. She had a curious detachable shell fitted over the cockpit, which Johnson slid back without explanation. For the rest she was quietly and expensively fitted, not only with awnings and Neiman-Marcus soft furnishings, but with a depth-finder and R.D.F. unit. I noticed a big-scale radar set which I'd heard one of the lab technicians daydreaming about, over a sputum swab. They cost ten thousand dollars.[8]

In truth, Johnson Johnson is a world famous portrait painter. His subjects include socialites, royalty, and an occasional pope. Even this information doesn't fully describe this unostentatious person who actually has more money than most of his clients.

Painting and sailing provide cover for Johnson Johnson's other activities, he is a spy's spy.

> "What are you, sir? MI-5?"
> "They never gave me a number," said Johnson with regret. "I just knock around with a boat and some paints, and they call me in if anything happens to the genuine men in the field. If they go off the rails or get themselves into trouble or get murdered, for instance."[9]

Each story is narrated by a different young woman: the "bird" in all American titles. Competent and capable at whatever her trade or profession may be, she finds herself caught up in danger and international plots with the intrepid Johnson Johnson at the helm of both the *Dolly* and the case.

Dorothy Dunnett (Halliday in the United Kingdom) crafts a tight, fast-paced story. A professional portrait painter herself, she brings solid working knowledge to these books.

CHRISTOPHER STORM
1940-1949   7 books   American
Willetta Ann Barber and R. F. Schabelitz

Promiscuity, marijuana, and open marriage may be familiar themes to today's reader. In 1941, however, they were shocking aspects of society out of plumb. The writing team of Barber and Schabelitz used these elements less for their shock value than as sound development of an amoral character necessary to a story. They skillfully weave these salacious details into the more ordinary events of life and tell a good tale in the process.

Christopher Storm, known as Kit, is a New York magazine illustrator. Sherry Locke, his fiancée and later, wife, chronicles his detections. Together, they make an effective team. Kit's artist's eye quickly captures tiny, out-of-the-ordinary details which add up to potential clues to murder. Sherry serves as devil's advocate against Kit's recorded images.

"When I walked around the house this morning I noticed that particular window; first, because it was the only one on the entire second floor which hadn't a screen in it, although it was wide open. Second, the curtains were cock-eyed; one hung out over the sill, and the other, inside the room, was dragged aside."

"So you're going to try to make something out of that?"

"Third, and what made me really look twice, was the Boston ivy on the wall below it and the forsythia bush at the bottom."

"They're broken," I said with all the disparagement I could put into it.

"They're broken all right. Neither of them alone would have meant much. But"—his tapering artist finger waggled at the paper in my lap—"the odd thing about it, from where the ivy begins under the window they're broken *in a straight line* to the crushed forsythia on the ground beneath. And, what's more, when I saw them at quarter of seven this morning the leaves weren't even remotely wilted. Douglas told us they'd had Indian summer here until last night. Also, although I'm no gardener, I know that the juice is thicker, has less skin around it, at the end of a vine and runs out quickly. Those leaves would wilt in three hours after they were broken. *So they were O.K. at three-thirty this morning.*"

"A ladder? You said she had to go out a window?"

He shook his head. "Why? When the house has doors? Besides, a ladder would break the vines in *two* places, and only where it touched, not in one straight line."

I was still not impressed. "A bag?"

Again he shook his head. "She left hers, remember? And, anyway, if a bag were thrown out of that window it might hit and break the forsythia. But the bush is out from the base of the house a good foot and a half. That would mean it would fall clear of the house. The vines wouldn't be broken."

"Suppose it were lowered?"

He threw up his hands. "My God, Sherry, for a girl who hates detecting, you think of everything."[10]

Both Kit and Sherry are good judges of character. They form their separate impressions from different perspectives. Clues for Kit are visual, and charming line drawings are sprinkled throughout the text. Sherry picks up her clues through conversation and when they compare notes, each fills in detail for the other and they jointly arrive at a solution to the crime.

WITH AN EYE FOR DETAIL, these visual artists often, quite literally, draw conclusions. Whether using one's talent as a cover, a means of travel to exotic places, or to secure a professional position, the artist/detective relies on vision to provide and interpret clues less apparent to the untrained eye.

Although Barney Gantt is written about in the "Murder Between the Pages" chapter as a newspaper reporter, he is also a photographer and has worked as a photojournalist. Lucy Ramsdale is a former magazine illustrator, and now, in her retirement, paints charming scenes which she exhibits in her hometown gallery.

Other books featuring the visual arts:

Margery Allingham, *Death of a Ghost*, 1934; *The Beckoning Lady*, 1955
Sarah Caudwell, *Thus Was Adonis Murdered*, 1981
Carolyn Coker, *The Other David*, 1984
Dorothy Salisbury Davis, *Scarlet Night*, 1980
E. X. Giroux, *A Death for Adonis*, 1984; *A Death for a Darling*, 1985

Patricia Highsmith, *Ripley Under Ground*, 1970
Elizabeth Lemarchand, *Change for the Worse*, 1980
Dorothy L. Sayers, *The Five Red Herrings*, 1931
June Thomson, *Portrait of Lilith*, 1982

PRIVATE EYES

PROFESSIONAL DETECTIVES

*T*he individual who pursues a career as a professional private investigator has got to be asking for trouble. The work can be violent and physically dangerous. At times, cases even lead to murder.

Checking on spouses suspected of straying, and other potentially embarrassing situations is an unpleasant way to make a living. Private eyes are paid for being curious, voyeuristic, and discreet. It's a nasty sort of job. There are, however, some rewarding tasks. Restoring lost property to its rightful owner, reuniting loved ones, and exonerating the innocent are some of the bright spots of this profession.

The professional detective is the client's champion and can serve as a liaison between the private citizen and the information sequestered by agencies and organizations. Inquiries made by a private detective may tend to be less obtrusive than those of the police. The confidentiality which is guaranteed those who employ the services of the professional sleuth, can often give rise to antagonism between the forces of law and order and the private eye. The private investigator is not hampered by the strictures imposed by bureaucracy and often has more latitude than the police in conducting an investigation. Sometimes they get underfoot and actually obstruct justice. At other times, though, their assistance is welcomed.

HERCULE POIROT
1920-1975   46 books   English
Agatha Christie

One of the best known investigators in crime and mystery fiction is M. Hercule Poirot, dapper detective extraordinaire who burst on the sleuthing scene in 1920. The retired Belgian policeman with the egg-shaped head and the distinctive moustaches is introduced in Agatha Christie's first mystery novel. Forced to flee his homeland as a result of the German invasion, Poirot finds he is a refugee in the wartime English countryside. His friend Captain Hastings secures the assistance of the little Belgian in *The Mysterious Affair at Styles* and M. Poirot's second investigative career is launched.

Poirot's conceits and eccentricities are as well documented as his successful solutions of crimes. His moustaches are always waxed and twirled into precise points. The creases in his trouser legs are knife-edge sharp and his small patent leather shoes gleam. He shuns alcohol, preferring sweet *sirops* and hot chocolate. M. Poirot has a positive passion for precision. Readers often find him straightening crooked pictures and moving ornaments into more geometrically pleasing arrangements.

This detective is rather indifferent to physical clues in a case, preferring to leave the gathering and investigation of footprints, fingerprints, and scraps of fabric to the police. Poirot relies instead on method and observation and, of course, the workings of his famous little gray cells.

> Poirot's gaze took on an admiring quality. "You have been of a marvelous promptness," he observed. "How exactly did you go to work, if I may ask?"
>
> "Certainly," said the inspector. "To begin with—method. That's what I always say—method!"
>
> "Ah!" cried the other. "That, too, is my watchword. Method, order and the little grey cells."
>
> "The cells?" said the inspector, staring.
>
> "The little grey cells of the brain," explained the Belgian.
>
> "Of course; well, we all use them, I suppose."
>
> "In a greater or lesser degree," murmured Poirot.[1]

From his introduction in 1920 through thirty-three full-length novels and numerous short stories, Poirot changes very little and his age can only be guessed at—our calculations grant him the great age of 136 at the time of his death. Throughout the series, Poirot emanates great dignity and force of character, even from the grave in his last appearance in *Curtain*, 1975.

Christie's career spanned fifty-six years, produced close to one hundred mystery books and five major series characters. She is, without a doubt, one of the most prolific and certainly the best known of all women authors in this metier. Need we say more? The lady obviously speaks for herself.

FLEMING STONE
1909-1942   61 books   American
PENNINGTON WISE
1918-1923   8 books   American
Carolyn Wells

Although he has appeared in sixty-one novels and is referred to as The Great Man by those with and for whom he has worked, Fleming Stone is not among today's well-known fictional private detectives. A quiet, bookish New Yorker, Stone is usually called in near the eleventh hour.

> "As I said, somebody killed him. I'm going to find out who. No, I don't propose to do any detective work myself, I don't know how. But I'm going to get somebody who does know how. And, understand, McGee, this is no reflection on you or your work. You have done well. You have worked hard and faithfully and with a good degree of efficiency. But you haven't hit upon the right tack, somehow. And I know you are willing to admit there are others in your profession who by reason of talent or experience or both stand above you. So, I'm going to employ one of these to solve the mystery of Vane's death and ferret out the slayer..."
>
> "Stone, I suppose," said McGee, laconically.
>
> "Who's Stone?" Thorndike asked.
>
> "Fleming Stone. He's the biggest private detective in the country," McGee returned.[2]

When Stone arrives on the scene, he ties all of the clues, which have baffled other investigators, together and presents the solution to the crime to all concerned in the case.

Another of Carolyn Wells' characters, Pennington Wise, operates in a similar fashion, also arriving on the scene late in the story. Described as a psychic investigator, Penny is assisted by an elfin creature named Zizi who boldly gathers information and evidence while Wise cerebrates.

The characters in this series are more devices than personalities. Wells applied these devices to a formula which served to showcase her ingenious plots and detailed the moral climate of the times as well. Wells was a prolific writer, authoring over 170 books in a variety of fields. Well known for her crime and mystery fiction, her work, *The Technique of the Mystery Story* (1913), according to Haycraft in *Murder for Pleasure* (1941), "still occupies top position among the 'how-to-do-it' manuals in America." Given the popularity of these books when they first appeared, we can't understand why they haven't been reprinted. Today, any interest in Stone and Wise forces readers to search far and wide for available titles.

PETER CLANCY
1919-1966   60 books   American
Lee Thayer

Red-haired man-about-town, private detective Peter Clancy was given a long and successful career by his creator, Lee Thayer. Although Clancy does not court publicity, he is well known to both the socially prominent and to members of the forces of law and order wherever he goes. At home on both coasts of the United States, in Europe and the Orient, Clancy is well paid for his discreet services, never lacks for clients, and is highly respected.

"Cord been dragged out by the roots, Clancy," he cried. "Now what do you make of that?"

"Something to think about," Peter replied. "Hello!"

As he stepped back from his close examination of the body, his eye caught the brilliant points of fiery light reflected from the tiny beads that lay along the heavy, dark rug. Dawes had been waiting for this. In fact he had found it difficult from the start to refrain from calling Clancy's attention to his discovery. It was nothing less than supreme confidence in his friend's powers that enabled him to hold in and let Clancy show Macpherson that he, Clancy, never missed a trick. Now that the point had been made Sergeant Dawes saw no reason for modesty.[3]

Personal integrity is a major element in all of the Peter Clancy novels. Potentially compromising evidence is frequently suppressed by someone early on the scene of the crime in order to prevent an innocent party from becoming embroiled in the ensuing murder investigation. Inevitably, the perpetrator of the murder is given the opportunity to take the honorable way out. The world is often a better place without the initial victim, and so, justice is served all around. Clearly, Thayer's early books are reflections of the era in which they were written and she, like Christie and Wells, remains true to that style.

The doyenne of this genre must be Lee Thayer. Her last Peter Clancy novel, *Dusty Death*, published in 1966 and written when she was ninety-two years old, nicely concludes the series. Though Thayer considered herself an artist rather than a writer, it is probable that she is best remembered for her books.

These entertaining novels are difficult to find today and are often inflated to collector's prices due to their scarcity. Given the popularity of his contemporaries, perhaps it is time to reintroduce Clancy to a new generation of readers.

MAUD SILVER
1928-1961   32 books   English
Patricia Wentworth (Dora Amy Elles Dillon Turnbull)

First introduced in 1928, Maud Silver is already well established as a discreet private inquiry agent as the series opens. Small, nondescript, and elderly, Miss Silver is a quiet paragon of respectability and morality. She prims her lips when distasteful subjects arise and coughs delicately before venturing to disagree. She seeks the truth above all and insists upon complete frankness and honesty from all her clients often quoting Tennyson to make her point, "Trust me all in all or not at all."[4]

As a professional private detective, Miss Silver is certainly doing what is traditionally considered a man's job. While she is not averse to occasionally following a suspect, she relies on logic and method to efficiently clear up her cases. Miss Silver is not intimidated by danger, though she does disdain violence. Her ever-present knitting needles would make a formidable weapon; however, to the best of our knowledge, they have never been used as such.

Maud Silver's detective career spans thirty years and follows her retirement from the schoolroom where she had long served as a very capable governess. Her manner often gives clients and suspects alike the sensation that they have returned to the nursery to find either ultimate authority or complete security.

He was in process of surprising himself. After some twenty minutes' conversation with this curiously dowdy little person, in the course of which she had neither said nor done anything at all remarkable, he was experiencing the strangest sense of relief. He could remember nothing like it since his nursery days. Old Nanna, the tyrant and mainstay of that dim early time before his parents died—there was something about Miss Silver that revived these memories. The old-fashioned decorum, the authority which has no need of self-assertion because it is unquestioned—it was these things that he discerned, and upon which he found himself disposed to lean. Miss Silver's shrewd, kind glance—perfectly kind, piercingly shrewd—took him back to things he had forgotten. 'Not the least manner of good your standing there and telling me a lie, Master Mark, I won't have it for one thing, and it won't do you no good for another.'[5]

Though the first Maud Silver was published in 1928, nine years elapsed before the second book in the series was released. Miss Silver's popularity grew throughout the 1940's. Patricia Wentworth's successful formula consists of a well-crafted puzzle with all the clues presented to the reader as the story unfolds. The innocent are protected, the criminals punished, and romance flourishes.

TOMMY and TUPPENCE BERESFORD
1922-1973   5 books   English
Agatha Christie

Tommy and Tuppence Beresford appear in only five mysteries by Agatha Christie. Though few in number, they span many years. Tommy and Tuppence have known each other from childhood. When the series begins, the Great War has just ended. Both are out of work and have no money. Over tea and buns at Lyons, they create the Young Adventurers, Ltd., and write an ad for the newspaper.

> Two young adventurers for hire. Willing to do anything, go anywhere. Pay must be good.[6]

The ad never gets placed but Tommy and Tuppence are nevertheless caught up in their first joint adventure in international espionage. At the successful conclusion of the case, they agree to marry. The second book finds them ensconced as proprietors of Blunt's Brilliant Detectives and their sleuthing continues.

Christie created these lighthearted characters for enjoyment—her own as much as her readers. Each story is a parody of the style of some fictional detective—even Christie's own Hercule Poirot. Tommy and Tuppence do some straight murder detecting though most of their cases involve exposing spies and counterspies and saving vital pieces of paper in the service of the Crown.

PAT and JEAN ABBOTT
1941-1965   26 books   American
Frances Crane

Pat and Jean Abbott are a detective duo introduced in the early 1940's. Pat is a well-established, tough private investigator in San Francisco, where he's considered the city's best detective. As his method consists mainly of guesswork one wonders at the competence of the city's other detectives. In the first novel, he meets Jean at her Turquoise Shop in New Mexico, and they marry at the end of the third book.

Many of their cases happen while the pair are on vacation and they are widely traveled. When Pat isn't looking for clues, he's looking for Jean who usually manages to get locked in a room and/or knocked on the head.

> I was tucking the edges of the towel around the bloody evidence when, without a sound on the heavy carpet outside, somebody turned the key in the door of the dressing room. I jumped up and tried the doorknob. I was locked in.
> A shovel slid into the fireplace. A heap of glowing coals was put on the carpet outside my locked door. Papers were crumpled and piled upon the coals. To hasten flames, a lighter clicked. As smoke began pouring under the dressing room door, I heard the hall door close softly.[7]

Each of the twenty-six books in the series uses a color in the title. Jean narrates these adventures which are of the had-I-but-known school with a dash of romance thrown in for good measure.

GALE GALLAGHER
1947-1949   2 books   American
Gale Gallagher (Margaret Scott and Will Oursler)

Gale Gallagher narrates her own stories, and, as the head of the Acme Investigating Bureau, explains her job this way.

> We trace persons who run out on hotel bills, flighty wives who traipse off with the milkman, husbands who duck financial responsibility.[8]

By definition, she does not court danger and seldom encounters violence in the course of her usual investigations. She is intelligent, uses her mind in her work, and acquits herself well when faced with peril. There are only two books in this well-written and entertaining series. We wish there were more.

CORDELIA GRAY
1972-1982   2 books   English
P. D. James

When Cordelia Gray was introduced in 1972 by P. D. James, new female private investigators were in short supply. In her first case, at the age of twenty-two, this young Englishwoman becomes —by default as much as by death—sole proprietor of Pryde's Detective Agency. Most of the important events in her life have occurred more by accident than by design. Her job and eventual partnership with Bernie Pryde had, in fact, come about in this fashion.

Cordelia was educated in a convent school because of an erroneous religious notation next to her name on a roster of foster children. Prepared for university by the sisters, her plans were set aside when her father, a minor and unsuccessful revolutionary, decided he needed her services for The Cause. For four years, Cordelia, her father, and the comrades roamed around Europe, fomenting various politically inspired intrigues. After her father's death, Cordelia returned to England.

Cordelia's unique background is important to who she is and to what she does. Bernie recognized her potential and elevated her from temporary secretary to full partner two months before his suicide. He knew that not only was she clever and intelligent but that she was capable of drawing upon her past experience to assist her in her new profession.

> Sometimes it helped to play the part of a vulnerable and naive young girl eager for information—this was a role in which Bernie had frequently sought to cast her—but she sensed that Sergeant Maskell would respond better to an unflirtatious competence. She wanted to appear efficient, but not too efficient. And her secrets must remain her own; she was here to get information, not to give it.[9]

In the second book—sadly, the last to date—Pryde's Detective Agency has developed a reputation for finding lost pets. While not entirely satisfied with the direction her work has taken, Cordelia is good at it and it pays the rent. Of course, she does get involved in a more adventuresome case and at the end of the story is relieved to get back to lost animals.

Cordelia doesn't bemoan what the Fates have handed her.

> She was on her own and that, when she came to think about it, was no different from how essentially it had always been. Ironically, the realization brought her comfort and a return of hope.[10]

Unlike novels in which the detective is pure device, the two books featuring Cordelia Gray depend upon this character's personality for their appeal. P. D. James, Cordelia's creator, has drawn a likable and believable portrait of a young woman eminently suited to private investigation. James has not motivated this character with false illusions nor unmet expectations. Instead, she has given readers a whole person—pragmatic, resourceful, and very human. We look forward to more of Cordelia.

SHARON MCCONE
1977-1985   7 books   American
Marcia Muller

> Don smiled, leaning back against a pillow. "Full of questions, aren't you?"
> "It's my stock in trade. Somehow, I've always known the right questions to ask. And people open up to me. I'm a

complete stranger, but they'll still tell me things they wouldn't
tell their best friend."

"You have an open face. You look like you won't judge
people." Don's eyes moved over my face, in the same
appreciative but inoffensive way they'd appraised my body
when he first saw me. I smiled back and lay down, my head
on a pillow, feeling warm and finally relaxed. The wine
had made me drowsy and a little disconnected from my
surroundings.

"I've always asked too many questions," I said, aware I was
almost repeating myself. "My mother used to get mad at me.
'Why, why, why?' she used to say. '*Why* are you always asking why?' "[11]

With a fairly average—for California—middle-class upbringing,
Sharon McCone graduated from the University of California,
Berkeley, with a degree in sociology. Unable to find a job in her field,
she went back into security work—which she had done part-time
while a student—and was trained as a detective. Now, she is the staff
private eye for the All Souls Legal Cooperative in San Francisco. In
typical, laid back, California style, the Co-op provides people with
low cost legal counseling and pays correspondingly low salaries to
its partners. To make up for the low pay, several of the attorneys,
including Sharon's good friend and boss, Hank Zahn, live in the old
Victorian house which serves as the office as well. Sharon doesn't
live there herself and actually spends more time in the field than in
her small office, but it serves as a center for her messages and the
inevitable monthly bills.

Sharon takes her job seriously and applies a high standard of professionalism to the work she does. One of the reasons that she is good
as an investigator is that she has an innate respect for the people she
has to deal with as well as enough objectivity to sort out the good
guys from the bad ones. In return, she demands respect for herself
and her profession but does not wear a chip on her shoulder in
defense of a less than traditionally feminine choice of work. In the
first book, *Edwin of the Iron Shoes*, Sharon meets Lieutenant Greg
Marcus, a homicide detective with the San Francisco police. Their
relationship is marked by constant bickering and many of the issues
of disagreement between them center around Sharon's work as a P.I.
The relationship ends at the end of *Ask the Cards a Question*.

Some of Sharon's investigations begin with murder. Others begin
as something else but turn to murder as the case progresses. She relies
on her skill in drawing people out for most of her information and
is good at assessing the answers she receives. Occasionally she needs

to run some risks in obtaining clues or evidence. In these situations, not all of her decisions are wise and Sharon finds herself in jeopardy. In *Double*, written jointly by Muller and Bill Pronzini, she has been shot, stranded on the desert at midday with no water, and is at the mercy of a murderer who has already killed twice. The Nameless Detective—Pronzini's own series character—a man with whom she is working on the case, arrives in the nick of time to save her.

This character has evolved through the seven books in which she appears. Any risks she takes seem to be a bit more calculated and she is using her intellect more than her gun to resolve sticky situations. Her relations with the police have improved and she is less antagonistic with officers of the law than she was in the early books. Perhaps Don Del Boccio, a disc jockey with whom she has become romantically involved, can be given some of the credit for these changes, as he gives her the respect she requires and a great deal of latitude to be who she is and to do what she does.

Most of Sharon's work takes place in and around the city of San Francisco. Author Marcia Muller is a S.F. Bay Area resident herself and provides wonderful descriptions of places all up and down the Peninsula. In *Games to Keep the Dark Away*, Sharon travels south to the small fishing community of Salmon Bay in search of a missing woman. Even though Salmon Bay itself is a fictional location, San Jose, Salinas, King City, and Highway 101 are real, and well sketched, if briefly, by Muller.

ANNA LEE
1980-1987   5 books   English
Liza Cody

In *Stalker*, Liza Cody's character, Englishwoman Anna Lee,

> was very annoyed with herself. It had been stupid to break in, but it was cretinous to get caught. She was fairly sure that the fat boy wouldn't talk but she couldn't be certain and she hated to have her fate in someone else's hands. Most of all, her pride was wounded. It was bad enough to act unprofessionally but being witnessed was infinitely worse.[12]

This ineptitude seems characteristic for Ms. Lee who works as an investigator for Brierly Security in London. In her first book, Anna is hospitalized as the result of a severe beating, and in another story, is kidnapped and locked in a small, cold, and dark room. Anna is dexterous and can fix almost anything. She might be better suited as a garage mechanic than a private eye.

V. I. WARSHAWSKI
1982-1987   4 books   American
Sara Paretsky

Chicago is not a gentle place to live. Its mean streets are about the meanest in the entire country. The mob still holds a great deal of power in the city—a holdover from the twenties and the prohibition era—and racial tension is manifested by the young members of Puerto Rican, Chicano, and black street gangs. Unions are strong in the Windy City and their burly representatives can be found at the docks and rail yards.

V. I. Warshawski is both tough and capable. She runs, has a black belt in Karate, and is a law school grad. She is self-supporting and autonomous.

"It makes an enormous difference. I'm the only person I take orders from, not a hierarchy of officers, aldermen, and commissioners."[13]

In every novel in which she appears, this lone-wolf operator is challenged and meets danger head-on, in full combat stance. Warshawksi's speciality is financial investigations, but all of her chronicled cases involve murder. Inevitably, she treads on some toes and, in a couple of her investigations, is actually asked to withdraw. As tenacious as she is tough, Warshawski can't let go until she has reached a conclusion which satisfies her. Along the way, V. I.'s actions also upset the lives of those only peripherally involved. Beatings, madness, and suicide are not unknown outcomes of her detecting.

While V. I. brings intelligence and competence to her job and maintains cool detachment throughout the series, this facade barely masks underlying feelings of anger and bitterness. Daughter of a Polish cop, V. I. still has connections with the Chicago police. Bobby Mallory, her late father's closest friend, frequently encounters her in the midst of a case and invariably tells her that she should be happily married and making babies instead of pursuing this dangerous career. Every time he throws down this gauntlet, V. I. reacts to the challenge with counter provocation.

With her family, as with the police force, V. I.'s antagonism runs high. In *Deadlock*, readers are introduced to some of the members of the Warshawski family at the funeral of her cousin Boom Boom, a former hockey star. In *Killing Orders*, the other side of the family is presented through her Aunt Rosa and Cousin Albert. Both sides make a point of wondering when she plans to settle down and raise a family. V. I.'s responses to these queries are predictable. These two books give readers information about her background and upbringing and pose some interesting explanations of this detective's abrasive nature.

Paretsky has done a good job with aspects of this series. Chicago comes alive under her pen. Riding with Warshawski, one can see the buildings, thoroughfares, and intersections clearly. The heat, the cold, the presence of the lake, and the people who inhabit this major metropolis are very true to life. The plots are tight and the stories capture readers from the first page and hold them to the last. Unfortunately, Warshawski, with her anger and her aggressive pugnacity, is one of the least attractive heroes we've recently encountered. She may have a sense of justice but it seems self-serving at best. She'd as soon shoot some of her suspects as question them and will not hesitate to practice the tricks of street fighting on anyone foolish enough to surprise her.

These readers think that the world really does not need any more stereotypical, hard-boiled private eyes. The mean streets aren't going to get any nicer unless those who have elected themselves private guardians rise above the dregs of humanity. In these books, those qualities such as tenderness, empathy, and nurturing are often set aside in favor of a *macha bravada* we find detrimental and counterproductive not only in the cause of feminism but humanism as well.

KINSEY MILLHONE
1982-1987   4 books   American
Sue Grafton

Kinsey Millhone likes small, cramped spaces, is not particularly domestic, and would be content to live out of her car. The '68 beige VW is well prepared for it. Files, law books, boxes, and a case of motor oil adorn the inside. On appropriate occasions, the back seat has surrendered pantyhose and black spike heels. Her efficient apartment in Santa Teresa is a converted one-car garage, about fifteen square feet, properly apportioned into bedroom, kitchen, living room, and laundry facility. Even her office is small, occupying a corner of the California Fidelity Insurance Company.

Kinsey is thirty-two and twice divorced. When she was twenty, she attended the police academy and on graduation joined the Santa Teresa Police Department. She found that there were too many restrictions to the job, and continually having to prove that she was tough was frustrating for the independent and self-reliant person she had become. After an internship as an investigator for the California Fidelity Insurance Company, she began a business of her own, bringing to it the tools of the trade as well as the procedure of police work.

> In any event, I was going to have to check it out item by item. I felt as if I were on an assembly line, inspecting reality with a jeweler's loupe. There's no place in a P.I.'s life for impatience, faintheartedness, or sloppiness. I understand the same qualifications apply for housewives.
>
> Most of my investigations proceed just like this. Endless notes, endless sources checked and rechecked, pursuing leads that sometimes go no place. Usually, I start in the same place, plodding along methodically, never knowing at first what might be significant. It's all detail; facts accumulated painstakingly.[14]

In *A is for Alibi*, the first book in the series, Millhone is hired by Nikki Fife, recently released from prison and out on parole. Nikki maintains that she is innocent of the murder of her philandering husband, Laurence, and wants Kinsey to locate the real killer. Though the case is eight years old and success is less than predictable, it is still intriguing and Kinsey takes the job. Quite a few people wanted the shrewd and despicable, but irresistible, Laurence dead, and Kinsey thoroughly retraces the steps which lead to his demise.

In *B is for Burglar*, two weeks after she winds up the smoldering Fife case, Kinsey is hired by the expensive and slightly crazy Beverly Danziger to find her sister, Elaine. Kinsey travels from Santa Teresa to Boca Raton, Florida, to search for the missing heiress and is assisted by two wonderfully feisty little old ladies, Tillie Ahlberg and Julia Ochsner. These amateur sleuths provide helpful long-distance clues for finding Elaine and the identity of the mysterious, hissing woman.

C is for Corpse, opens with Kinsey working out at the gym, and recuperating from the ravages of her second case. She meets Bobby Callahan, a badly injured and frightened young man, who thinks that someone is trying to kill him and asks Kinsey to help him. Though bits and pieces of Bobby's memory have been wiped out from a deadly car crash, he feels that he still carries information vital to his enemy. The young man proves to be correct and the investigation shifts to one of murder.

Delightfully warm and colorful characters recur in Kinsey's life. Henry Pitts, her sexy eighty-one-year-old landlord, is a former baker. He still creates delicacies for neighbors and friends, occasionally caters small affairs but currently earns a living devising impossibly complex crossword puzzles. Rosie, who is somewhere in her sixties, runs the neighborhood bar just a half block from Kinsey's apartment. It is a familiar stop for Kinsey, for dinner or for meeting clients or suspects. Rosie runs the bar, does the imaginative cooking flavored with a Hungarian touch, and deals with Life. Her rust-colored hair and distinctive eyebrows add a certain unnecessary flair to her appearance.

Grafton plans on giving readers the entire alphabet's worth of Kinsey Millhone mysteries. We applaud the idea because we have enjoyed watching Kinsey develop from an aggressive investigator who is simply competent and tough to an individual more at ease with her charge. While she doesn't give much away about who she really is, she is straightforward in her dealings with people and is respected and even liked by those she meets in the course of an investigation. The plots are for the most part believable, though Grafton exceeds several limits as the third book draws to its conclusion. At the rate the series has progressed to date, we predict that this character will continue to provide readers with pleasant surprises.

THE PRIVATE DETECTIVE, champion of the client, is ideally suited to investigate murder cases. With confidentiality insured, clients are inclined to divulge more personal information to the private eye than to the police. Any way one looks at it, much of the work deals with the more sordid aspects of humanity.

Perhaps the unsavory nature of the work causes some private investigators to allow their licenses to lapse—Michael Spraggue is one of these former P.I.'s. Or, like Conan Flagg, they keep their cards current although somewhat secret. Still others admit to the profession as the source of their livelihood while preferring other, less lucrative pursuits. Simon Brade, for example, is a noted expert on rare porcelain. Strictly speaking, these characters belong in this chapter. Out of deference for their feelings, however, we have elected to discuss them elsewhere.

Private investigators appear with some regularity in many mystery novels—so many, in fact, that we do not list other books in which they may be found.

STRANGE BEDFELLOWS IN BRASS BEDS

MILITARY AND GOVERNMENT SERVICE

G overnment service takes many forms. Whether politician or spy, individuals working in these fields have their country's best interest as their ultimate goal. While some actively choose a life of service, others find themselves in situations not of their choosing but which give them an opportunity to serve. Discretion and duplicity are a spy's stock in trade. Politicians embrace the former though the best deplore the latter. Those in political life need a measure of visibility and must be accessible to their constituents. All of their actions are overt, in theory at least. The spy relies on cover—appearing to be one thing while in reality being very much another. Some characters possess such effective cover that it becomes the way in which they are perceived by the world. So successful is their disguise, that they are written about elsewhere in these pages.

Secrecy seems to be an essential part of both war and peace. The practitioners of the arts of espionage and intelligence gathering we have selected for this chapter come to their professions by a variety of routes. Some of the stories are more traditional murder mysteries while others are essentially spy novels with bodies littering the landscape.

TOMMY HAMBLEDON
1940-1963   26 books   English
Manning Coles (Adelaide F. O. Manning and Cyril Henry Coles)

The first book in this series opens at the inquest into the death of the hero of the story. At the end of the book, Hambledon—the series' featured character—is missing, presumed drowned. This unlikely beginning launched a successful series which ran from 1940 on into the 1960's. *Drink to Yesterday* was an immediate international success and has been in constant print since its release. Authors Manning and Coles must have decided to capitalize on their initial success, as Tommy Hambledon was pulled from the cold waters of the North Sea and revived for the second book which came out in the same year (1940).

Thomas Elphinstone Hambledon is a classic spy. Brave, resourceful, and inventive, he looks on what he does as a job much like any other and does not view himself as heroic. At the same time, Hambledon is fully aware of the hazards attached to his particular line of work, the subtle as well as the obvious. His caution to his young assistant is realistic and compassionate.

"Has it occurred to you that you are a subject of interest to German Intelligence already? You could not easily return to England now unless they send you. You will be tailed wherever you go in Holland. They would know if you crossed to England."

A queer little thrill ran through Bill Saunders and his eyes brightened. This was Life. Tommy Hambledon watched him ruefully.

"Yes, it's got you now, and it will never let you go. When once the job has taken hold you'll find that nothing else in life has any kick in it, and apart from the job you're dead. Neither the fields of home nor the arts of peace nor the love of women will suffice—"[1]

Cyril Coles was himself a British Intelligence officer and served behind enemy lines in WWI. Fantastic as some of the plots may be, there is an attention to detail and overall tidiness which makes them plausible. Experience and familiarity are critical ingredients in the earlier novels. Hambledon is a believable and sympathetic character whose greatest security is his high visibility. His senses of humor and the absurd also provide him with excellent protection.

"...He has some papers in his little brown bag, and we are going to get them."

"How?"

"Goodness knows, it all depends on circumstances. I don't know anything about him, whether he's a big man or a little one, whether he'll have an escort or not—they don't as a rule, but these papers seem to be something special—whether he'll travel in a carriage with other people or in a first-class in lonely majesty, or, as they say, what."

"Then you haven't got any plan?"

"Of course not, how can I? Do get out of your head these ideas about elaborate plans which are so popular in fiction. You know. At 8.44½ precisely you will walk past the automatic weighing-machine on the down platform, and a man in a pale-blue Homburg hat will pass you and murmur either "Catfish", "Plaice" or "Cod", or "Salmon." "Catfish" means the courier is a large savage man armed to the teeth who never sleeps, with an escort of eight of the Prussian Guard so alert that they take it in turns to breathe. That's to let you know it's going to be a little difficult. "Plaice" means that he will have a girl friend with him, so look out for squalls. That's rather a good one, pass the beer. "Cod" means that, though he travels alone, he is a dangerous homicidal maniac who is quite sane till anybody touches his luggage, when a violent complex is suddenly released and he is possessed with a passion for peritoneotomy—"[2]

In spite of Hambledon's kindness, sympathy, and humor, he can be ruthless and kills without qualm or regret. His adaptability enables him to act counter to the breeding of English gentlemen of his generation. Fluent in many languages, Hambledon appreciates the variety of qualities offered by other cultures and applies that appreciation to his disguised persona. He is a tenacious and dangerous foe.

Over the years, critics have agreed unanimously that the first two books featuring Hambledon are the finest. As the series progresses, stories become more formula tinged. While they are still enjoyable, they lack the impact and psychological insights of the earliest works. Tommy didn't manage the transition from active, wartime espionage to the high-tech style required by the Cold War very well. Being somewhere in his seventies at the end of the series may have slowed him down a little. Hambledon's logical successor is James Bond. Readers are encouraged to sample the adventures of this adept forerunner.

GRACE LATHAM and JOHN PRIMROSE, COLONEL
1937-1953   15 books   American
Leslie Ford (Zenith Jones Brown)

As this series opens, Colonel John Primrose, 92nd Engineers, U.S. Army (retired), and his redoubtable sergeant, Phineas T. Buck, detect on their own. Three years later, in the second book, Mrs. Grace Latham, a widow with two nearly grown sons, is introduced and the two form an informal detecting team carefully chaperoned by Sergeant Buck.

The colonel and Grace both reside on P Street, Georgetown, D.C. The stories, however, take place in a variety of locations from Washington, D.C., to Yellowstone, Reno, San Francisco, and Honolulu. The colonel is still associated with the government and works closely with the police. Romance and star-crossed lovers are featured and Grace inevitably hides or destroys a clue she thinks might implicate one or another of the ill-fated pair. The colonel always seems to know what Grace has done and why and carries on with the case, regardless.

Colonel Primrose got up and walked across the room. I could see him visibly taking a deep breath. He came back.

"Do you know, Mrs. Latham," he said deliberately, "at times you are the most charming and delightful woman I've ever known. And at others you're so maddening that it's only great self-control that keeps me from wringing your lovely neck."

"I'm sorry," I said.

"And some day I'm going to. Listen, my dear. The only reason I'm concerned with this at all is because of you."

I was genuinely surprised at that.

"Because I don't want anybody loose with a lot of cyanide of potassium any place where you are. The temptation to use it might be just too strong."

He didn't smile when he said that either.[3]

The years between the two World Wars, especially those immediately preceding WWII, were fertile ones for crime and mystery fiction. Leslie Ford has captured some of the essence of those times in this fifteen-book series. While the plots are not the most unique and the stories' progress is rather predictable, we can not help liking the taciturn colonel, and the practical, if flighty, Grace. In their respective worlds of government and society, each is respected and admired. These are well-drawn characters, well suited to one another and to the practice of detecting.

SAM HOOK
1942-1946   3 books   American
Hildegarde Tolman Teilhet

We have only been able to find one Sam Hook book. It is the third in a series of three, written between 1942 and 1946, and is fascinating—though not because the series character is outstanding. Hook makes very brief appearances at the beginning and end of the story which is carried by Gordon Allgrove—a satellite character by our standards.

Hook is an old China hand. A large, rather rumpled man, he works for U.S. Intelligence, keeping an eye on things in post WWII, pre-revolutionary China. Knowing that Allgrove is on his way to northern China to re-establish his family rug factory in Chungwei, Kansu Province, Hook asks the China-born Gordon to pay attention to what's happening in the area.

> "Mr. Allgrove," said Mr. Hook, "I read your mother's book where she claims the Red Chinese evolved away from Communism and have become more or less agrarian socialists. Mr. Allgrove, maybe it's because I got the Republican habit of thinking something's wrong if the other party takes it up, but I can't help being a mite suspicious about the Nationalists, now the Russians have taken 'em up here in China. Suppose the Russians have cut loose from those three million or so Chinese Reds to support the three hundred million controlled by the Nationalist Government, even if our smart fellers in Washington don't quite believe it? Suppose the Russians've learned the Chinese Communists aren't red-hots any more, just as your mother claims they aren't? The Russians don't like fighting people if they can help it. They like joining up with people and persuading 'em. Mr. Allgrove, I figure if I was a Russian I'd rather try to join up with three hundred million people and persuade *them* than stick to three million miserable Chinese Reds who've quit being practicing Communists." He nodded his head.
>
> "Right now we're handing over war material and equipment and money to the Nationalists. We're not asking anything in return, because our smart fellers figure the Nationalists are going to unify China and keep it out of the hands of the Reds.

What's going to happen if the Russians are telling the truth? What if they aren't over on the Chinese Red side at all, but are sleeping in the same bed with the Nationalists and us? Maybe our smart fellers can't see the light for the trees—with the trees being that trifling little bunch of Chinese Reds who aren't even Reds any more and are practically defeated. About the only difference between the Russians and us is we believe we got the best machinery in the world and go out and sell it and the Russians believe they got the best government, and they like to go out and sell that. I don't blame 'em. It's natural for anybody to do, when he has something he believes is the best. But I don't consider our people'd much like to find, in five or ten years, that the Chinese National Government had taken all the machinery we could give 'em and at the same time had been persuaded by the Russians into Communism. No sir, somebody might wonder why we hadn't tried to sell our product in government, too, instead of being so almighty smart we couldn't believe the Russians had played a fair game and told us—*told* us,'' said Mr. Hook, his voice rising a little, ''beforehand they were going after the big customer, the three hundred million who hadn't yet tried out Communism and had time to change away from it!''

''... You might find Russian agents working with the Kansu Reds to get 'em to revolt. If you did I'd appreciate knowing about it, because that would bust my theory.''[4]

This low-key intelligence agent obviously has a grasp of the political situation in China at the time. This book, written in 1946, is full of historical bits which not only read well forty years later but are remarkably accurate in a geopolitical sense as well. We count this as a real find and look forward to locating the other two books in the series.

Teilhet's other series character is Baron Von Kaz. The three books featuring the Baron were published under Darwin Teilhet's name but were jointly penned by the husband/wife team.

BEN SAFFORD
1968-1983   8 books   American
R. B. Dominic (Martha Henissart and Mary Jane Latsis)

Though he is an agent of the American government, Ben Safford is not a spy.

Newburg, Ohio, which Ben had represented for nearly sixteen years, was a horse of a different color. Spectacular trips to distant places cut no ice in Newburg, unless these trips were taken in uniform. Safford, in Marine garb, had visited a satisfactory number of Pacific islands some years ago. Furthermore Newburg did not go in for fancy tailoring. Which was fortunate, since Ben Safford had a gift for making even new suits look rumpled.

No, what Newburg wanted and got from its congressman was close attention to its needs and desires. And despite outsiders, who kept voting Newburg the typical Midwest town and a rare piece of Americana, these needs went far beyond the price of soybeans. There were the factories out past Lincolnwood, worried about Japanese steel imports, union contracts and corporation taxes. There was Ed Daly, Democratic Committeeman, who worried about postmasterships and Federal Highway Programs. There was Newburg College, worried about AEC grants and the draft, as well as Newburg Savings and Loan, worried about the interest rate. And there were 34,765 men, women and children, worried about: a son at Fort Bragg, a job in the Veterans' Administration, a stray Social Security check, a disallowed tax deduction, a GPO publication or a new gun law.[5]

This Ohio Democrat is well chosen by his constituents to represent them. Even though he spends much of his time in Washington, D.C., Ben's feet are firmly planted on his home soil surrounded by just plain amazing folks.

His sister, Janet Lundgren, resides in Newburg and holds down the family homestead where Ben maintains bachelor quarters. Her husband Fred owns the large Ford dealership in town. Janet belongs to countless women's organizations and is devoted to good and charitable works. Ben relies on her and other members of the family network to provide all the local information he needs to keep his political fences mended.

Congressional committee work is often what gets Ben involved in murder investigations. He and his colleagues assist and support one another through a more formal, though hardly less intimate, network than the one at home. Val Oakes (Republican, South Dakota), Elsie Hollenbach (Democrat, California), and Tony Martinelli (Democrat, Rhode Island) appear in every novel and serve on many of the same committees as Congressman Safford.

Whether looking into charges of bribery on Capitol Hill or uncovering Medicaid fraud in his hometown, Safford goes directly to the heart of the issue and looks for the motive. He understands power; its uses and abuses. When murder occurs, as it inevitably does, he uses that understanding to sort out the players and unravel the clues to the murderer's identity.

> "Everyone knew how Mr. Gellert and Mr. Isham were going to vote, didn't they?" she asked innocently.
> This question needed no elaboration. Gellert and Isham had been voting against every conceivable form of federal regulation for over twenty years. Bribing them to do so would have been a waste of good money.[6]

R. B. Dominic is the joint pseudonym of Martha Henissart and Mary Jane Latsis. Writing as Emma Lathen, they have also created investment banker John Putnam Thatcher. The political arena is easily as fascinating as the world of high finance. J. P. Thatcher is the quintessential banker/sleuth and wears gray flannel as a mantle of quiet power. Rumpled Ben, on the other hand, embraces the homey, care-for-one's-neighbors attitude which inspires confidence and a steady term of office.

Dominic gives us a look at institutions, government, and military agencies through the close-up lens of a body designed to dictate the consequences of commerce, trade, and all legislation which effects the fabric of life for those who live in this country.

MRS. EMILY POLLIFAX
1966-1985 7 books American
Dorothy Gilman

The title of the first book in this series is *The Unexpected Mrs. Pollifax*, and it is accurate. This small, feminine, white-haired woman somewhere in her sixties is unlikely to be recognized as an agent for a secret service. Needing just this sort of individual for a simple courier job from Mexico City, OSS-trained Carstairs of the CIA is delighted to find the perfect person waiting for him in an interview room.

A widow for eight years whose grown children and grandchildren live far away, Emily has found herself feeling unused and without a purpose. Unwilling to sink into a geriatric morass, she concludes that it is time do what she's always longed to do: become a spy. Armed with an introduction from her congressman, Mrs. P. arrives at CIA headquarters in Langley, Virginia, where she volunteers her services and—not incidentally—her life in this capacity. Mistaken by Carstairs for agent Miss Webster, he offers Mrs. Pollifax the job which she readily accepts. Emily passes a quick, top-priority security check and is given her first assignment.

The unexpectedness of this character continues throughout the seven books in this series. Her characteristics include a charming mixture of eccentricity and pragmatism. Possessing no official credentials in any field, Emily knows that all she has learned through living is of value. She is willing to offer her services in a marketplace where such skills are not normally acknowledged, much less, compensated. A strong positive outlook aids Mrs. P. in getting a great deal of joy out of all aspects of life. A lively curiosity about people, places, and other cultures makes her an excellent traveler. Her sheltered life in 4-A of the Hemlock Apartments in New Brunswick, New Jersey, provides a certain informed naivete which is essential to her cover.

This is no flighty tourist plunked down in a contrived situation and saved by fluke or heroics. Emily Pollifax is competent, self-reliant, and reliable. When the chips are down and she is confronted with great danger, she assesses potential consequences and her own capabilities with practical realism and faces whatever is to come with equanimity.

> Mrs. Pollifax wanted to tell him that of course it bothered her. She had enjoyed herself very much in Mexico City and she had enjoyed being a secret agent and now she would like very much to be flying home to New Brunswick, New Jersey, to bandage her torn wrists and soak her bruises in a hot tub. There was, after all, a distinct difference between nearly deciding to step from the roof of an apartment house and in having such a decision wrested from her by men who appeared to be quite brutal. She did not want to die in a strange country and she did not labor under any illusions about Mr. Carstairs or her country coming to her rescue. If life was like a body of water, she had asked that she be allowed to walk again in its shallows; instead she had been abruptly seized by strong currents and pushed into deep water. It was a lonely situation, but Mrs. Pollifax was well acquainted with loneliness and it did not frighten her. What did frighten her was the thought of losing her dignity. The limits of her endurance had never been tested, and she had never met with cruelty before. If her life had to end soon she only hoped that it could end with dignity.[7]

Dorothy Gilman has created a character who embodies much of what we feel is true liberated womanhood. Mrs. Pollifax works comfortably in concert with members of different generations, nationalities, and gender. She does not compete. She gives respect to people and their talents and earns respect in return. Robust, vital, sincere, and loving, Emily humanizes her confederates and most of her opposition. The apparent simplicity of the stories is deceptive. Gilman's lighthearted and humorous treatment can veil the fact that there are major concepts addressed and philosophical truths stated.

DAVINA GRAHAM
1980-1983   4 books   English
Evelyn Anthony (Evelyn Ward-Thomas)

London and Moscow are the main venues of these novels of international intrigue and romance. The Cold War continues for members of the British Secret Intelligence Service and their Russian counterparts in the KGB. Politics, ideology, espionage, and counter-espionage add up to a hypergolic situation for these global superpowers.

Sir James White, head of SIS and longtime friend of the Graham family, has made Davina his assistant. In the first book of the series, she is assigned to "mind" a KGB agent who has defected from Russia. Her task is to extract every piece of information from the memory of this highly placed opponent turned ally. Sir James has chosen Davina for the job out of respect for her abilities which include patience and intuition as well as competence.

Sir James' choice is well founded. Davina is competent. Throughout this four-book series, she demonstrates this quality along with bravery and resourcefulness to the point that, at the end of the third novel, she has been selected by Sir James as his successor.

> "Tell me," she said suddenly. "Knowing how I felt about you, Chief, why did you recommend me for this job?"
>
> He put his head on one side, regarding her with the twinkle and the empty smile. "Because you're by far the cleverest of all the candidates," he said. "And I believe in that old cliche about the female being deadlier than the male."[8]

The qualities which make a successful spy do not necessarily make a successful human being. There is little joy in Davina's life and most of the motivation for her excellent espionage work arises from a strong desire for revenge—not only against the opposition but against her colleagues and her family, as well.

Davina's primary rival is her charming and beautiful younger sister, Charlie. Set up at an early age by this expert manipulator, Davina has become a classic victim. Events in both her personal and professional lives contribute to Davina's need for vengeance and help to develop the sense of ruthlessness which serves her so well in her work.

> "She made an odd remark about having no friends," Charlie said. "Only Peter Harrington used to take her round to the pub, till he handed her over to the KGB. She's very bitter, darling, and she can't hide it. She wouldn't listen to the idea of taking on the top job. She spoke about that very sourly too. She didn't think you'd fancy sending other people out to take the risks— that's what she said."
>
> "She's always had a chip on her shoulder," John Kidson remarked. "About you, about her parents, about herself—then Sasanov. She hates the Chief; she says she hasn't a friend in the office after working there for fifteen years. What the bloody hell's the matter with her? Doesn't she ever think it might be some of her fault?"
>
> "I don't think Colin helps," she said suddenly. "He's very chippy too, you know. All these Army specialist people have the same attitude, a sort of contempt for everyone outside their little world. I think they sit together criticizing and carping about Sir James and the office—undoubtedly you and I come in for a fair bit. I can just imagine Davy going back and saying how extravagant I am. I don't think she's after that job, darling. I don't disagree that she's probably working on something; she's very devious, always has been, but I don't think she's a serious rival to you. She's too full of grievance to be credible."[9]

The members of Davina's family and all of the men with whom she becomes emotionally involved are as crucial to the development of each of the stories and to the whole series as are her colleagues and counterparts. On the surface, these people lead comfortable, rather complacent, lives; however, the world in which they live does not give them much satisfaction. Threats to security and comfort do not only come from foreign agencies. There is little love, no trust, and not much honor among the people who are supposed to be on the same side. One wonders what they are defending and how, with so little respect for one another, anything meaningful can be accomplished.

The pace of these novels is slow, at times even tedious, and there are inconsistencies which get in the way of the action. Davina and the other main characters are predictable as is much of the drama, which, for these readers, dulls the edge of suspense. While each story is complete, the four-book series is tightly linked with a tantalizing clue to the next adventure given by Miss Anthony at the end of each novel.

EDMUND BROWN
1966-1971 4 books English
Joyce Porter

Edmund Brown became a spy simply because he was fluent in the Russian language. Sir Maurice Drom, head of the Special Overseas Directorate, hired Brown for one job and now finds himself permanently burdened with this paragon of ineptitude because of the colossal debt incurred by Brown on his maiden assignment.

Somewhere in his thirties and slightly overweight, Brown is nondescript enough to look like the ideal spy. Here the resemblance ends. Orders mean little to Edmund. He is more likely to act on his own misguided initiative than to follow the carefully laid plans of his superiors. Ever ready to improvise, Brown charges off in the wrong direction every time and succeeds in confusing his own side as well as the opposition. He considers himself a ladies' man, but in one story his seduction plans backfire and Brown finds himself captured and held as a love slave by an emaciated nineteen-year-old nymphomaniac. Throughout all of Edmund's misadventures, his ego remains intact making it virtually impossible for him to fade into the woodwork as an effective espionage agent.

Brown views life and his fellows with a bright, jaundiced eye. He, in return, is held in low esteem by his superiors, colleagues, and the minions of S. O. D.

"What I don't understand, Brown," he said unpleasantly, "is why you always manage to get out with a whole skin."

"Oh, I guess I was just born lucky," I said. Gazing at the water dripping down the walls of my cell. "When are you going to get me out of here?"

"Get you *out*? You don't know when you're well off, that's your trouble. Don't you realize just how much upset you've caused? The French are threatening to break off diplomatic relations, the Russians won't lend us their pictures for the French Impressionist exhibition, the Americans are going to have a Congressional inquiry and the Icelandic delegation is going to lay a complaint before the United Nations! And I hope you're satisfied! I just don't understand how you got yourself into this mess. You were sent on a perfectly simple, straightforward job and you've turned it into an international nightmare. If you'd reported in regularly as you were instructed to, none of this need happen."

"We didn't realize how serious it was," I explained, "until it was too late."

Sir Maurice shuddered. "We! That's another thing. Collaborating with a Russian! How could you? You've made the S. O. D. the laughing stock of the entire civilized espionage world. The humiliation of it! I don't know how we're ever going to live it down, I really don't!"

"We did stop a nuclear war," I pointed out.

"Ends rarely justify the means, Brown, and I doubt whether they do in this case. There are rules for these things, you know, rules which are not to be lightly disregarded by inexperienced junior operatives. If only you had kept me informed."[10]

To say that Joyce Porter writes tongue-in-cheek novels is a gross understatement. In Edmund Brown, she has created the perfectly wrong person for the job and has populated the four novels in which he appears with scathing caricatures of people from all walks of life. Her unmistakable style is carried out in two other series featuring the Honorable Constance Ethel Morrison-Burke and Inspector Wilfred Dover.

MURDER, MAYHEM, AND NATIONAL SECURITY are closely related. The foregoing characters attest to that, as all, in one way or another, find themselves in situations involving all three of these elements. Some are more graceful than others and some even regret their involvement and whatever steps must be taken to keep the peace and preserve their nation's sovereignty. Although styles and motivations vary among these characters, the cases in which they become entangled all make for interesting, even edge-of-your-seat reading.

Other books featuring spies and government officials include:

Margery Allingham, the series featuring Albert Campion
Linda Barnes, *Dead Heat*, 1984
Agatha Christie, *The Secret Adversary*, 1922; *Postern of Fate*, 1973, and others

Dorothy Dunnett, the series featuring Johnson Johnson
Helen McCloy, the series featuring Dr. Basil Willing
Craig Rice, *But the Doctor Died*, 1967
June Thomson, *The Long Revenge*, 1974

THEY PICK UP THE PIECES AND HOLD DOWN THE FORT

WIVES AND OTHER SIGNIFICANT OTHERS

Detecting can be an arduous business. When on the trail of wrongdoers, a sleuth may need to work round the clock and be in at least three places at once. Food and sustenance may be far from the mind of these men and women. The creature comforts are essential to the vigor, well-being, and safety of those dedicated to detection, and, in one way or another, the following characters meet these needs or can cause them to be met in the care and feeding of these special souls.

Not only domestic details are seen to by these paragons. More direct forms of assistance are often rendered as well. Where would Lord Peter be without Bunter's photographic skills? How could John Thatcher ever get out of the office if not for Miss Corsa's evasive talents? Back to the basics though, Antony Maitland might be doomed to starvation were it not for Jenny's casseroles.

On occasion, an assistant will be featured in a book within the series starring another. Laura Menzies moves out from under Dame Beatrice's wing on several occasions. In the second book in the Dr. Hillis Owen series, Miss Pomeroy, his competent office nurse, launches forth on her own investigation. Robert Forsythe's secretary, confidante, and foster mother, Miss "Sandy" Sanderson, is asked by the police to get to the bottom of an unexplained village crime. For the most part, however, these assistants assist and where would their "masters" be without them?

SPOUSES

Spouses can be of great aid and comfort to their husbands and wives. Some are actively involved in detection with their mates. They gather clues and data and interview individuals connected with the crime at hand.

"If you go, I go," said Emmy.

"A charming and gallant sentiment," said her husband, "but we'll see how things work out. You might be more of a nuisance than a help."

"Thank you very much."

"Well, darling, be sensible. You'd be useless in a fight and you're not armed."

"Neither are you."

"I am, as a matter of fact. Inspector van der Valk was kind enough to provide me with a gun as carried by the Dutch police."

"Well, if I'm not going to be any use..."

"But you are. You will be our channel of communication."

"What do you mean?"

"My face is too well known," said Henry. "Yours isn't. Trapp knows you, of course, but for the moment we have to assume that he's on our side. Madeleine La Rue only saw the back of your head on a crowded terrace, and none of the other characters in this drama has ever met you. I shall lie low, while you do the chatting with the local shopkeepers and so on and establish yourself as a harmless vacationer. In fact, now that I come to think of it, I shall develop influenza."[1]

At times, illuminated by a sudden insight, these sleuthing sleuths' spouses go off on their own to find the one piece of evidence needed to clinch the case. Others have their own occupations and are rarely seen outside the family home. Their job is to provide whatever solace is necessary for their tired and sometimes troubled spouse. Even though they remain in their own domain, they may serve as sounding boards and, from their own point of view, can provide information useful in the solution of the case. Finally, there are those who are true equals in the partnership of detecting as much as in the partnership of marriage. While their spouse is listed as the primary character of the series, there would often be nothing to detect were it not for the keen observation of these independent thinkers.

The following list gives the name of the spouse and the author of the series in which he/she appears:

Clara Gamadge	Elizabeth Daly
Helen Shandy	Charlotte MacLeod
Muriel Gantt	John Stephen Strange
Jane Pollard	Elizabeth Lemarchand
Harriet Vane	Dorothy L. Sayers
Emmy Tibbett	Patricia Moyes
Jenny Maitland	Sara Woods
Troy Alleyn	Ngaio Marsh
Robin Price	Anne Morice

BUTLERS

Butlers are a rare species. They are only found among the upper classes and nowadays—the servant problem being what it is—they are hard to find at all. Originally the butler was in charge of the bottled goods in a household. Over time, these worthies' duties expanded until they encompassed charge of most of the domestic arrangements in a family's life. A butler's tenure can span generations and he often provides continuity where little of a familial sort exists.

The door to Ardry End was opened by the butler, Ruthven. To say that Ruthven was of the old school was to put it very mildly. Plant speculated that every other manservant in England might have gone to school to Ruthven. Melrose could remember him from the time he was a tiny tot; Ruthven could be anywhere between fifty and a hundred—he had always looked the same to Melrose.

Plant had inherited Ruthven along with the portraits and stocks and Morris wallpapers, and during the course of their relationship, the master has done only one thing to upset the butler. Melrose had given up his title several years ago, after a few sessions in the House of Lords. It had nearly brought Ruthven to his bed. The news had been handed the butler one morning at breakfast, casually, like someone giving back the plate for more kippers: *Oh, incidentally, Ruthven, it won't be "my lord" any longer.* And Ruthven had stood there, carved out of rock, his expression magnificently unchanged. *I thought it inappropriate, you know, holding down a job, at the same time having that awkward title.* Ruthven had merely bowed and held out the silver dish of buttered eggs circumscribed by plump sausages. *And, anyway I never have fancied taking my seat in the House of Lords. What a bloody bore that would be.* As a sausage went *plop* on the plate, Ruthven begged to excuse himself, saying he felt a bit unwell.[2]

There are those who come to this honored position via other avenues. Myron Bunter was with Lord Peter in the Great War and actually saved Wimsey's life. Maggersfontein Lugg was a successful burglar until his expanding girth made it difficult for him to ply his chosen trade. These gentlemen's gentlemen serve above and beyond the call of household duty as do others who appear on the following list.

Myron Bunter	Dorothy L. Sayers
Maggersfontein Lugg	Margery Allingham
Ruthven	Martha Grimes
Theodore	Elizabeth Daly
Wiggar	Lee Thayer
Pierce	Linda Barnes
Gibbs	Sara Woods

HOUSEKEEPERS

Housekeepers are of a different stripe. Their profession is as old as that of the butler, though there is less status conferred on one holding the title of keeper of the house. Not much escapes their eye, and, for the most part, their duties are carried out unobtrusively. There are exceptions, however. Some housekeepers feel it an integral part of their responsibilities to keep up a running commentary on everything. They complain at the extra burden their employer's detecting adds to their already full work load, cajole overwrought sleuths into eating and sleeping, and even threaten to quit due to overwork or under appreciation.

It was past seven when Martin came up the back steps of the rectory with Bascomb trotting behind him, and he had just put his hand on the knob when Mrs. Beekman opened the door.

"You made quite a day of it," she said severely. "The mayor wants you to call. Hattie wants you to call. Clyde Hunnicut has been phoning every half hour to see if your remains have been brought in by any passing motorist. Dr. Campbell wants to speak to you, and Felix Harshaw would like your attention."

"Anything to eat?"

"Cold beans and wilted lettuce." Mrs. Beekman opened the oven, letting out a good odor of pot roast. "I'm tired keeping it warm. The carrots are shriveled. The gravy's boiled down. Did you find out who murdered Dean?"[3]

Whatever their style, they are invaluable to those fortunate enough to have their support—staunch or otherwise.

Mrs. Beekman	Margaret Scherf
Mrs. Howard	Clarissa Watson
Sister Joyce	Monica Quill
Phyllis	Leela Cutter

SECRETARIES

Secretaries keep the appointment books, write the letters, answer the phones, and guard the door to their employer's inner sanctum. Some even make the coffee without complaint. Skill is paramount in the secretarial trade and an efficient secretary is prized above rubies.

> He closed the door behind him. His seething subordinates, he knew, could be left to his secretary. Miss Corsa's splendid indifference to human passion left her capable of suggesting to these two warriors that they prepare reports on the *casus belli*. Any woman who can tell a soul in torment to send a memorandum is worth her weight in gold. Thatcher only hoped that last Christmas' present, a marvel of leathercraft by Gucci, conveyed how much he valued Miss Corsa. He would never know. Miss Corsa was also splendidly uncommunicative.[4]

Not all secretaries are female. In fact, the gentle sex was barred from the office until after the turn of the century. When they were allowed through the doors of business and commerce, they brought an added dimension to bear. Gender notwithstanding, the secretary is indispensable as much for intuition as for adroitness on both sides of the desk.

Miss Rosa Corsa	Emma Lathen
Albert	Agatha Christie
Miss Sanderson	E. X. Giroux
Fiona Clingmore	Martha Grimes
Miss Felicity Lemon	Agatha Christie
The Flowering Cherry	Antonia Fraser
Miss Dobie	M. K. Wren
Laura Menzies	Gladys Mitchell
Holly Chase	Leslie Grant-Adamson
Alan Kruzick	Julie Smith
Miss Climpson	Dorothy L. Sayers
Charity	Margaret Millar

ASSISTANTS

The term *assistant* fits a broad category. Help from these other significant others can be rendered professionally, familially, or simply by association. Not all of these characters have the official title of assistant: in fact, aunt, uncle, and various military designations are ways in which some these characters are primarily known. Some aren't even human. The aid these individuals render is as diverse as their nomenclature. Some assist grudgingly though most are willing accomplices.

"I can give you fifteen minutes at the absolute most," Aunt Mary said sternly some four hours later, when he'd finally bulled his way past Pierce and two fierce secretaries.

Today her bright red shawl livened up a conservative well-cut gray suit. Her bedroom had been converted for the day into its office mode; the peach-colored alcove containing the peach-satin-covered bed was curtained off. The click of computer keyboards, the muffled beat of footsteps, the clang of telephones punctuated her conversation. She stared meaningfully at her chunky gold watch.

"You want me to begin when the second hand hits the twelve?" he inquired.

"Darling," she said, indicating a desk filled with overflowing with papers, flickering computer terminal, a bank of telephones flashing angry red lights, "the market is in a bit of an uproar—"

"How long would it take you to lift fingerprints off a wine glass?"

She considered the question, eyes narrowed, pointed chin tilted to one side. "Crystal?"

"Yeah."

"Whose?"

"Oh, forget it," Spraggue said easily. "You probably don't have the time."

"I hope you do indeed possess a mysterious glass with unknown fingerprints on it. Otherwise I shall brain you in the hallway with a hatstand and the police will never pin it on me."

"Don't worry. I've got it. Where's your fingerprinting paraphernalia?"

She padded across the room and rang the bell on Davison Spraggue's mahogany desk. "I haven't the faintest. It's been ages since I've even thought about it. Soon the man from Sotheby's will be after me to auction it off as an antique, not that I would ever part with anything that provoked such pleasant memories. But Pierce will know."[5]

All of the following provide the primary character with support and readers with enjoyment and diversion.

Captain Hastings	Agatha Christie
Miss Pomeroy	Anna Mary Wells
Sergeant Buck	Leslie Ford
Zizi	Carolyn Wells
Carstairs	Dorothy Gilman
Janet Lundgren	R. B. Dominic
Sister Kimberly	Monica Quill
Benjamin Pinch	Edith Piñero Green
Maggie Rome	Lilian Jackson Braun
Aunt Mary Spraggue	Linda Barnes
The Dolly	Dorothy Dunnett
The Merlino Sisters	Pauline Glen Winslow
Cousin Toby	Anne Morice
Aunt Lydie Wentworth	Clarissa Watson
Wiggins	Gwen Bristow and Bruce Manning
John Smythe	Elizabeth Peters
Koko the cat	Lilian Jackson Braun
Phoebe Dameroux	Orania Papazoglou
Niece Julia	Leela Cutter
Uncle Nick, Meg Hamilton, and Roger Farrell	Sara Woods
The yellow Rolls Royce, Bill Parsons	Anthony Gilbert
Professor Tamar and members of The Nursery	Sarah Caudwell
Lady Alleyn, Troy and Ricky, Nigel Bathurst	Ngaio Marsh
Mr. and Mrs. Schwartz, Mickey and Rob Burns	Julie Smith
Geoff Bushnell	Nancy Pickard
Martha Hallard	Josephine Tey

Almost every detective has another soul with whom to share chores and deliberations. In some series, there is no one particular person but rather a succession of confidantes and partners to pick up the pieces and hold down the fort.

UNEXPECTED DETECTIVES

_A_ lthough some of the characters described in other chapters may be unexpected as detectives, they have professions which define at least a part of their personality and performance. Those described here are harder to pin down in general, being little old ladies with no specific calling in life, Jacks-and-Jills-of-all-trades with a multiplicity of careers, or retired persons at loose ends. Their very ambiguity and uncertainty seem to make them ideal observers of human nature. Readers are invited to discover what makes these detectives not only unexpected but decidedly out-of-the-ordinary as well.

Few readers of mystery are unfamiliar with this archetypal little old lady. Great age and ordinariness blending to drab are the elements which qualify Miss Jane Marple for unexpectedness as a detective. Long a resident of Saint Mary Mead, Miss Marple has had ample time to observe the all too human behavior of her neighbors, and has in her memory store a vast repertoire of recombinant reactions to any situation.

Catty and a little nasty in the first book, *The Murder at the Vicarage*, Jane mellows to a more pussylike amiability as the series progresses. Sweet, without being saccharine, she is a wonderful houseguest, especially when murder pays an unannounced call. Trailed about by balls of knitting wool for the inevitable small garments necessary to her many nieces' and nephews' offspring, Miss Marple contemplates the world and crime with each stitch she makes.

On one hand, it is easy to talk about Jane Marple in terms of the archetype. Almost the standard issue LOL (Little Old Lady), she sits and knits and chats with her friends and acquaintances. From that perspective, it could be said that any LOL could do what Jane does. Then we come to the other hand. Though all of her information comes from her village and her knowledge of it, Jane Marple is not limited by her geography. She makes Saint Mary Mead the metaphor for the world. Beyond that, she has a sense for malice and true evil. She is not taken in by either guile or stupidity and has an almost extrasensory perception for the truth even when it is *not* told by any of those involved. Through it all, Miss Marple remains untouched by what she knows and sees. Her faith in humanity remains undimmed.

In her next to last adventure, Miss Marple is called upon from the grave, so to speak, by one who knows one of her identities.

"Our code word, my dear lady, is Nemesis. I don't think you will have forgotten in what place and in what circumstances you first spoke that word to me. In the course of my business activities over what is now quite a long life, I have learnt one thing about a man whom I wish to employ. He has to have flair. A flair for the particular job I want him to do. It is not knowledge, it is not experience. The only word that describes it is *flair*. A natural gift for doing a certain thing.

　　You, my dear, if I may call you that, have a natural *flair* for justice, and that has led to your having a natural *flair* for crime. I want you to investigate a certain crime. I have ordered a certain sum to be placed so that if you accept this request and as a result of your investigation this crime is probably elucidated, the money will become yours absolutely."[1]

Miss Marple does rise to the occasion and lives up to the appellation, Nemesis. She is improbable and unexpected in the guise of the Greek goddess of retributive justice.

Miss Marple and Hercule Poirot are Agatha Christie's most well-known series characters. She did, however, devise another unexpected detective—one who appeared in only one book of short stories. Mr. Parker Pyne, retired after thirty-five years of compiling statistics in a government office, has taken up a new profession. His advertisement in the personal column of the morning paper reads:

PERSONAL

―――――――

ARE YOU HAPPY? IF NOT, CONSULT MR. PARKER PYNE,
17 Richmond Street.[2]

Mr. Pyne deals in his clients' hearts' desires. Like a physician, he first notes the symptoms, makes a diagnosis, and then prescribes. For some it is a dash of danger to counter a dull and uninspired life. For others, a gram of romance to rekindle flames long banked. For still others, a dose of their own medicine is what's called for.

His extensive and close association with statistics has given P.P. practice in quantifying the human experience. He declares that unhappiness can be classified under five main heads. No more, no less. With this information, he directs his clients onto paths designed to provide what each thinks they need. Mr. Pyne has failures. These failures are qualified though, and arise out of dishonesty—either the client's dishonesty with himself or with P.P.

The stories are short, sweet, and very to the point. Honesty is at the core of not only Parker Pyne's work but at all of Christie's other characters and tales as well. We recommend these adventures into the realms of personal gratification versus personal satisfaction. The truth will out.

RACHEL and JENNIFER MURDOCK
1939-1956   13 books   American
D. B. Olsen (Dolores Hitchens)

Because we were familiar with other characters created by D. B. Olsen, we were delighted to find a series by her featuring two little old ladies. They appear in books in which cats are mentioned in all the titles. Our hopes were justified, then dashed, as we were only able to find one of the books, the last.

The Misses, Rachel and Jennifer Murdock, are spinster sisters who live in Los Angeles. Jennifer, the elder, is the more reserved and proper of the two, maintaining a straight-laced demeanor in the face of lapsed manners and murder. Rachel, two years younger, is almost a madcap by comparison. Unfettered by the bounds of convention which seem to restrict her sister, she plunges into mystery and stirs things up among the suspects until the solution becomes obvious. Rachel enjoys life with gusto and is not above seeking a thrill or two for sheer pleasure. Jennifer follows along reluctantly, and the discovery that she is enjoying herself sends her into paroxysms of rectitude.

In *Death Walks on Cat Feet*, Rachel and Jennifer become involved in a mystery when they witness a woman being catapulted through the plate glass window of a pet store. Concerned for the woman's safety, Rachel goes to her aid. Amid the loose birds and fish out of water, Rachel gets her first inkling of foul play. Ruth Rand explains that she is the aunt of a young woman, Lila, who has been missing for three years and that the man who threw her through the window is Lila's husband. Convinced that he has had a hand in her niece's disappearance, Ruth seeks Rachel's assistance. The story progresses from the canyons behind Los Angeles to a racetrack. The sisters meet a wide variety of characters: the twin owners of the pet store, an ex-jockey, a racetrack tout, and the title character, Tom Boy, the missing woman's cat.

Rachel and Jennifer discover the body of one of the pet store owners in Lila's canyon cabin. When the police arrive, Rachel's reputation has obviously preceded her.

> At this moment a detective came to interview them. He had raised a shade in the kitchen window, giving a better light in the patio. He introduced himself as Lieutenant Shaw. He was young, tall, well built, handsome. In spite of her disdain for what she called "man-chasers," Jennifer was noticeably calmed down by his appearance. She even fluffed her hair a little.

He began, looking at Miss Rachel: "I believe you know Lieutenant Mayhew, don't you?"

She wondered in what sulfurous terms Mayhew had described her meddling in what he considered his business. "Quite well, though I haven't seen much of him and his wife these past months. They've bought a chicken farm near Ventura, haven't they?"

"I believe so." He seemed to be sizing her up cautiously. "You had something to do with a case of his, I think."

"That was some time past."

He nodded. He offered cigarettes politely before lighting one for himself. "You're working now as a private detective?"

"I would like to," Miss Rachel admitted, "but my sister feels that to go into it professionally would cause a scandal. As it is, you might say that because of undeserved notoriety, occasionally I get a chance to advise people in trouble."[3]

Behind the disguise of advanced years and snowy white hair lurks a sharp wit and dauntless spirit. Miss Rachel is not intimidated by much of anything, least of all her sister. She pursues and manipulates relentlessly and makes an entertaining and surprising detective.

Writing as D. B. Olsen, Hitchens created another series featuring Lieutenant Stephen Mayhew. He appears in two titles on his own and joins the Murdock sisters in five books before disappearing into the wilds of Ventura, we presume. Professor Pennyfeather, another of Olsen/Hitchens' creations, appears in a series which runs concurrent with the Murdocks'. Although the professor is described in another chapter, his mild, bookish manner and fragile appearance qualify him as an unexpected detective. Under her own name, Dolores Hitchens, she wrote two books featuring Jim Sader and, together with her husband Bert, created two more short series.

This prolific author has created some of the more delightful period pieces we've read. The stories are well plotted and the characters only require a modest suspension of disbelief on the reader's part. We were charmed by the one Murdock sisters book we found and hope to find more of this light, humorous series soon.

ABBIE HARRIS
1944-1954   8 books   American
Amber Dean

A lakeside community in upstate New York is the setting for this series featuring Abbie Harris.

> My name is Alberta Harris, age early forty, widow, and I live with my older sister, Margaret, in the old farmhouse in the cove at Ogg Lake that was named for my grandfather. The cove, not the lake. Both Maggie and I are widows and shouldn't use the name Harris. We don't, legally. But that is another story. Once there had been four of us Harris girls, and the "Harris sisters" is the name we have gone by since high-school days. That was before the last war.
>
> Thirty years ago my father broke up the old farm into lots and sold them off to city folks who wished to rusticate in the summer. He turned around and sold the lumber out of his woods to the same folks and, to top it off, contracted to build the cottages. All in all, he made a small fortune.
>
> Maggie and I have a very nice life, if an uneventful one. We retired from teaching when Papa died and have the leisure to do a spot of traveling in the winter and a bit of interfering with our neighbor cottagers in the summer. We are never bored.[4]

Maggie stays at home, cooking, washing, and hearth tending or makes runs to Old Village, the area's shopping district for groceries and other supplies for life's needs. Abbie is less domesticated. Maggie will do the wash every Monday, rain or shine. Abbie would put it off until the sun came out. Murder helps alleviate boredom for Abbie. One of the sisters' close friends is Dr. Fitzgerald Custom, medical examiner and coroner for Ogg Lake and its surrounds. Through his kind offices, Abbie is no stranger to death.

The cottage next door to the Harris sisters is summer home for the Johnson family. Mommie lives up to her name by being thoroughly involved with her offspring. Her husband Max was in intelligence during WWII and, in post war years, works for the U.S. Customs in New York City. At the lake he is a Jack-of-all-trades. Notes in all of the books we possess state that with the exception of the Johnson family, all characters are fictional. Max is described in one as being very, very real.

The stories themselves are little gems. In less than two hundred pages, Amber Dean manages to convey not only a well-plotted mystery but concise character sketches and odd information about disparate subjects such as Indian lore, archaeology, ancient Roman history, or cock fighting in the Finger Lake region of the state. As the series began in 1944, it comes as no surprise that WWII and its effects on people figure in many of the stories.

Amber Dean was not a prolific mystery writer; she has only seventeen titles to her credit. She is one of the genre's lesser lights, too, which seems strange as her work is certainly equal to that of many of her more well-known contemporaries. The books that we have found are all first editions and we can honestly say that the collector's prices demanded are almost well worth it.

LUCY RAMSDALE
1971-1977   4 books   American
Hildegarde Dolson

Introduced in *To Spite Her Face*, widow, Lucy Ramsdale, and James McDougal, retired inspector of Criminal Investigation, Connecticut State Police, become an interesting detecting duo over the course of the four books in which they appear. The inspector frequently comments on the fact that Lucy's mind is logical and her thinking clear. Her unexpectedness in detecting comes from her age, appearance, and station in life.

In her late sixties, Lucy is still a beautiful woman with fine skin over good bones. She dresses well and her choice of clothing becomes her petite frame. A cherished wife for over forty years, she misses her late husband's flattery and cajolery as much as his physical presence. Lucy extracts those offerings from all who know her, however, and if not courted with sweet words, good manners, and high praise, can turn petulant and downright vituperative. One does not want to get on Lucy's down side.

McDougal is a tall, lean man who wears an air of uncertainty about him in the first book. Deserted by his wife and recently retired, McDougal is a new arrival to the town of Wingate. While he looks for a possible permanent home, he lives in a one-room efficiency apartment which is conducive to neither of his personal pleasures—good food and gardening. At the end of their first foray into detecting together, Lucy makes a somewhat roundabout offer to McDougal, one which is equally circuitously accepted.

"Would you like me to send Trooper O'Shea back for a week or two, till you get over being edgy?" He had reason to believe that, from now on, not even a sudden avalanche would deflect Trooper O'Shea from his appointed duty.

A trooper wasn't at all what Lucy had had in mind; she came near making a nasty face. As it was, she said, "Good God, no! He's not my idea of protection."

"You didn't give him much chance."

Lucy turned a deaf mind. "I've decided I'll either have to get a big dog—maybe a police dog—or a tenant for Hal's studio."

The tightness eased in McDougal's face. He reached for the silver coffeepot and poured himself a fresh cupful, as if he felt very much at home. "A dog wouldn't be much help in the garden. He might even dig up your best bulbs."

"At least he'd keep the rabbits at bay. But he wouldn't pay me two hundred a month rent, either."

"That's a ridiculously low rent for that studio. You ought to charge at least three hundred."

"I'll split the difference. How about two hundred and fifty? And naturally I'd expect the tenant to do some weeding and planting."

The inspector said naturally. He decided he'd thin out the iris in August and transplant some of the bronze ones beside the studio...

"And to serve as a guinea pig," Lucy went on.

That brought her listener bolt upright. "For what?" he asked, with more than a modicum of hostility.

"For my cooking," Lucy said demurely. "I'm always trying new dishes."

"In that case," the inspector said, "you can forget about the dog."[5]

McDougal's uncertainty diminishes and, when the second book ends, he banters easily with his landlady, Lucy, from his hospital bed where he is recovering from a gunshot wound received while rescuing her.

Lucy may be good at detecting. She does reach the conclusion but often doesn't know that it is one. She can identify the hows and whys but is not as good at naming the who. Lucy does not want to admit that the people she knows are capable of killing and this naivete compels her into risky situations. Near the end of each story, she finds herself alone with and threatened by the murderer who makes a full confession and fills in any gaps in Lucy's prevailing theory. Her personal connection with McDougal is her greatest protection. Lucy sometimes withholds evidence or information, either out of petulance or the honest belief that so-and-so couldn't possibly have done that. McDougal's professional expertise puts him square in the picture and he arrives to save Lucy from the murderer, if not from herself.

The characters surrounding Lucy and the inspector are interesting and well drawn by the author. Nick Terrizi, now a policeman, has never quite been forgiven by Lucy for deserting her garden for the force. The young officer admires McDougal and is instrumental in getting the inspector and Lucy to bury their respective hatchets and cooperate with one another. Nick's fiancée, Angie, also appears in most of the stories. In *A Dying Fall*, the couple's engagement party is almost canceled when Nick is forced to arrest Angie's Uncle Mario as a prime murder suspect. One of the focal points in all of the stories is the Second Run Thrift Shop where Lucy and her circle gather to make money for charity and to keep abreast of all the gossip. New characters are introduced in each story and most of them find their way into the shop to become a part of the action.

A published author since 1938, Hildegarde Dolson didn't begin writing mysteries until after she married Richard Lockridge in 1965. All four of the Ramsdale books are dedicated to him, the first, *To Spite Her Face*, as her "accomplice in crime and unrelated matters." Dolson died in 1981, four years after the last Lucy Ramsdale was published. We're sad that there can be no more of this delightful, though often exasperating, unexpected detective.

MRS. POTTER
1982-1985   3 books   American
Virginia Rich

Ruminating on the stories featuring Eugenia Potter, created by Virginia Rich in the early 1980's, we found ourselves visibly affected by the author's writing style which overflows with color, history, lore, lessons in good manners, and tips on The Correct Way To Do Anything. Recipes abound in this recidivist recitation, and if, after finishing one of these tales, readers don't rush right out to their kitchens to whip up a batch of Bo Heidecker's Tennessee Mountain Stickies or Giselle's Acadian Plogues (Ployes), we want to know why! And if Mrs. Potter ever comes up with the recipe for Raccoon Tail Flambe, we'll be sure to try it and serve it as a birthday treat for one of Susan's two, or Victoria's three, children; each who knows just where to find the crunchy peanut butter and small wheat crackers in either of our kitchens.

Mrs. Potter is a wealthy widow in her sixties. Home is a ranch in Arizona, but she is not there in any of the three books in the series. Instead, she is back in her childhood home for her yearly visit to Harrington, Iowa, in *The Cooking School Murders*; at the summerhouse she and her husband Lew owned for ten years in Northcutt's Harbor, Maine, for *The Baked Bean Supper Murders*; and on Nantucket Island visiting her old college roommate in *The Nantucket Diet Murders*. Well heeled, well traveled, and loved by all and sundry who have gotten to know Genia over the years, her first and longest abiding love is cooking and the associations each recipe conjures in her memories. Each story reads as though it were dictated by Julia Child to M.F.K. Fischer. Mrs. Potter has used her years well in collecting and noting (on her ever-present, yellow legal pads) more domestic detail and housewifery hints than Fannie Farmer ever dreamed of.

Murder happens soon after Mrs. Potter arrives on the scene; in the first book, three people are dispatched by page two. Nosy and knowledgeable about her friends and their long-standing traits and habits, her detection is nevertheless both unexpected and ineffective. In spite of her yellow-padded musings and jottings, she is always surprised when she unmasks the killer and the denouement inevitably comes about at Genia's own peril.

Judgment must be suspended even higher than usual when reading these books. Improbability tends more toward the fantastic and plotting is disguised by a welter of irrelevant information on Everything Under The Sun. The plots themselves do hold water, however. Readers are as surprised as Mrs. P. to discover whodunit but may not even care, having been exhausted by all of the esoteric minutia. Genia herself seems to be a pleasant person—we'd love to be invited to dinner at her house or attend one of her parties. If Rich could have only cut down on the inessentials and stuck to developing the characters she created, these stories could have sparkle.

MISS MELINDA PINK
1973-1984   10 books   English
Gwen Moffatt

As with the Mrs. Potter stories, those featuring Miss Melinda Pink are cluttered with irrelevancies. However, no amount of uncluttering here can, in our opinion, give these stories sparkle. Miss Pink, a mountaineer, travels to beautiful locations which are bogged and darkened by the worst dregs of humanity. No amount of clean air or gorgeous scenery can offset the depraved, amoral, and even sociopathic nature of the people gathered there. Whether in the Scots Highlands, or the American southwest, Miss Pink finds those who easily take the law into their own hands and administer justice which is not only rough, but raw.

The one redeeming quality of these books is the featured character herself. Melinda Pink is an English justice of the peace and a writer, though we never see her on the bench or at the typewriter, as her ventures into murder all occur while she is traveling. Knowledgeable about human nature and forgiving of its honest stupidity, Miss Pink is relentless in pursuit of those who do evil unconscionably. Advanced in years, with a weight problem and arthritic twinges in her joints, Miss Pink nevertheless continues the challenging sport of mountain climbing. Presumably she avoids the toughest pitches and may have hung up her pitons, but, since mountaineering is mainly a matter of good judgment, good balance, and endurance, she should still be able to hold her own.

In spite of the finer qualities of Miss Pink, the stories are convoluted beyond belief and populated with the most unsavory of characters. Secrecy with intent to deceive, personal gain, and a total disregard for morality are characteristics of almost everyone Miss Pink encounters in the pubs and on the pitches. The striking settings are hung about with glowering clouds and fantastic shadows. Clean, clear air is tainted with a miasma. In *Last Chance Country*, Miss Pink goes to the high Arizona desert as a visitor to Sweetwater Ranch. The idyllic ranch is located in a valley ringed with towering mountains. There, millionaire owner Nielsen has created a protected stronghold for wildlife and guests alike. The nearest town is Molten, half ghost town, half last resort for the six remaining residents. In Molten, Miss Pink befriends two young prostitutes hiding out from some unnamed threat. Several days after their meeting, both girls are found burned to death in their car, on their way out of town. Four murders later, the case is concluded but we were so confused by the many explanations of how, why, and who, that we're not at all sure we understood the end.

Author Moffatt is no stranger to adventure. A mountain guide for over twenty years, she is familiar with technique and uses mountaineering jargon successfully in her scenes on rock faces and chimneys. Her sense of the ambiance of a place is true and many of her descriptions are highly evocative. Like rotten rock, these places and their inhabitants are flawed and at the mercies of not only the lack of internal integrity but the elements as well.

MRS. CHARLES
1976-1984   7 books   English
Mignon Warner

Over the years, Madame Adele Herrmann has acquired a reputation of renown as a clairvoyant. Semiretired for nearly a decade, Madame Herrmann lives in The Bungalow just outside the Village of Little Giddings where she is known to her neighbors as Mrs. Edwina Charles. As the series opens, Mrs. Charles has come to the attention of Detective Chief Superintendent David Sayer (retired) in connection with both an old murder case and a newer one. Suspected of both murders to the end of the story, Mrs. Charles solves the mysteries, clears her own name, and impresses the former detective with her surprisingly canny knowledge and its unorthodox presentation. The Tarot is her medium.

Edwina is an enigma. An attractive woman of middle years, she is known by several names, each legitimately granted by birth or through one of her three marriages—all disasters, each more spectacular than the last. She is comfortable as a chameleon. Living at the outer edge of the village, she and her half brother, Cyril Forbes, are viewed with mistrust and, at times, alarm. They live quietly and respectably, though some of Cyril's behavior is viewed as exceptionally eccentric as he waits for The Coming at The Designated Spot. It is mainly their neighbors' speculation which has created the aura of mystery around them. Mrs. Charles and Cyril remain silent, neither denying nor verifying others' suspicions. Only those who are able—if only for a moment—to look at things the way Edwina does, see her as more than a fortune-teller or possessor of guilty knowledge.

> Mrs. Charles responded with a grave smile and he was instantly struck with the disquieting thought that her deep blue eyes were capable of seeing a good deal more than he for one would like to believe was humanly possible. It was something he couldn't recall ever having noticed about her before, and with a fleeting twinge of regret he found himself wondering if this hadn't somehow been a very grave error on his part.[6]

The series builds upon itself. Characters introduced in the first book come into successive stories. New characters often refer to former aspects of Mrs. Charles' life and fill in the portrait of this most private person. Earlier phases of Adele Herrmann's life and career actually quicken by the way in which they are woven into the narrative. It is all done artfully and with great grace. There is nothing clumsy nor overt about this woman or her actions. She answers questions put to her honestly, and yet, has the ability to not respond at all, even by expression. As readers gain more insight into this person, her motives, and methods, they discover that still more is to be known about the illusory Mrs. Charles and those with whom she is in contact: victim, suspect, detective, innocent bystander...

Life imitates art imitates life is magic. It's all there. Rearrange it as you please. Make of it what you will. The truth is nothing more, nor less than the truth, and it can be known. Author Mignon Warner is a committed practitioner of illusion. She assists her husband in the art of magic apparatus, design, and implementation and is a student of things arcane. Her books featuring the clairvoyant can be read as stand-alone stories. We recommend beginning at the beginning and reading chronologically for the full flavor of character and series.

JULIE HAYES
1976-1987   4 books   American
Dorothy Salisbury Davis

A successful writer of mystery novels and short stories since 1949, Davis has been honing her craft to the point of the origin of Julie Hayes, her most recent series character. Readers first see Julie as an uncertain and confused young woman, married to a prosperous man fifteen years her senior. Author Davis manages, in the first twenty pages of *A Death in the Life*, to imbue Julie, Geoffrey, and other recurring characters with personal history and traits which follow them through the next three books. That the characters grow so much in dimension throughout the series and the fact that this growth seems to follow some pattern so naturally, leads us to believe that all the groundwork done by Davis is paying off in spades.

Set in contemporary New York City the series investigates not only murder but life as it is lived on many levels. Looking for something with which to occupy her time and give some sort of definition to her life, Julie rents a storefront on Forty-fourth Street, formerly occupied by a fortune-teller. A deck of Tarot cards and a crystal ball found in a theatrical supply shop confirm her first occupation, and she becomes Friend Julie, Reader and Advisor.

> The West Forties had been a kind of home away from home for Julie. In the two years she had tried to make it as an actress, much of her life centered around the Actors Forum which was

headquartered in a desanctified church. She thought she might stop by there after visiting Mr. Kanakas and see what was on the bulletin board. Or who. Some of her best friends were actors. And some were ordinary people who still lived in the neighborhood where they had grown up. They walked dogs, shopped at the market stalls on Ninth Avenue, and raised plants on the window sills. You could see these people in the daytime, even on Eighth Avenue, with their shopping carts and prayer beads. The older women almost all wore hats. If they came out at all at night, they got lost among the shady traffic, the highs and lows on drugs and alcohol, the whores and pimps, the "porn" shills and their customers. Julie had never been afraid there, night or day, though a lot of people told her that she should be. But then there were not many places where she was afraid.[7]

The death of a friend whose body is found in a hooker's apartment compels Julie into detecting. She works parallel to the police and, in the course of her investigations, encounters Sweets Romano, an underworld impresario. Sweets and Julie strike a rapport and he gives her a vital new perspective on the case. At the successful conclusion of it, Julie and Geoffrey take off for Paris. The second novel, *Scarlet Night*, takes place immediately after their return. There is no murder in the second book, rather a series of twists and turns involving greed, illegal arms sales, and smuggled national treasures. Julie and Sweets team up for the perfect sting operation—one which is less than strictly legal but which does not compound the felonies already committed.

Lullaby of Murder gives us a much more confident Julie. No longer needing the services of her analyst, she has been working for a year as legperson for gossip columnist Tony Alexander. Julie is good at ferreting out the details upon which hang the success of the column and has developed her own writing skills. Tony's murder and those suspected of killing him open her eyes still more to the sordid side of life and increase her awareness of her protection from it. The ending is a cliff-hanger and effectively sets the reader up for the fourth book.

Davis bends time. She gives us a close, chronological tale and makes us wait for installments. From the moment we opened each long-awaited book, our judgment was suspended and we were caught in the web Davis skillfully weaves. Elements of the web are by themselves fascinating. There is the anchor. The good solid characterization built in at the beginning of the series. There are the support strands. Little vignettes of central and ancillary characters throughout. Readers may not dismiss any of these informative bits though most are irrelevant to the central puzzle. Then there are the trigger lines, "A Ha" moments for both detective and reader, where the solution is set up and then tweaked into a plausible and unexpected ending.

BILL OWEN
1905-1925   8 books   English
Baroness Orczy

Bill Owen, the Old Man in the Corner, is one of the very first armchair detectives. Sitting at a marble-topped table in the corner of the Norfolk branch of the A.B.C. Teashops, Owen ties and unties complicated knots as he elucidates supposedly insoluble crimes to young Polly Burton, reporter for the *Evening Standard*. Early in their relationship, he propounds the theory that there are no mysteries against intelligence.

> Polly thought to herself that she had never seen anyone so pale, so thin, with such funny light-coloured hair, brushed very smoothly across the top of a very obviously bald crown. He looked so timid and nervous as he fidgeted incessantly with a piece of string; his long, lean, and trembling fingers tying and untying it into knots of wonderful and complicated proportions.
>
> Having carefully studied every detail of the quaint personality Polly felt more amiable.
>
> "And yet," she remarked kindly but authoritatively, "this article, in an otherwise well-informed journal, will tell you that, even that within the last year, no fewer than six crimes have completely baffled the police, and the perpetrators of them are still at large."
>
> "Pardon me," he said gently, "I never for a moment ventured to suggest that there were no mysteries to the *police*; I merely remarked that there were none where intelligence was brought to bear upon the investigation of crime."[8]

Readers never meet Bill Owen outside the teashop, but he attends court hearings and trials and makes photographic forays around the city, gathering pictures to illustrate his deductions. These ventures seem to be for his pleasure alone as he needs no aids for his conclusions. These conclusions are based on his knowledge of human nature alone and further support his contention that intelligence is all that is required to solve any mystery.

The Old Man in the Corner enjoys solving crimes of robbery and murder which have the police confounded. He feels no compunction to serve justice further, however, as he never takes his solutions far away from the table where he and Polly sit—certainly not to the officers of the law. No one seeing this unlikely couple huddled together in their teashop corner would guess that the rather nondescript gentleman could be described as a master sleuth.

Baroness Orczy was a prolific writer. Her first novel (nonmystery) was published in 1899. The original Bill Owen stories appeared in *The Royal Magazine* between 1901 and 1904. There is some confusion about the order in which the short stories were collected for publication. *The Case of Miss Elliott*, published in 1905, may be either the second or third collection. *The Old Man in the Corner*, published in 1909, probably combines the first and third but may be the first and second. The fourth collection, *Unraveled Knots*, appeared in print in 1925. Less successful than the earlier stories featuring this unlikely detective, it is thought to be an attempt on the author's part to recapture that early popularity. Given the surprise ending of *The Old Man in the Corner*, we find its lack of acclaim understandable.

Baroness Orczy's most famous work is *The Scarlet Pimpernel*. It was originally written as a book and was rejected by several publishers. Redrafted into a play, it became an immediate success and the book was issued in 1905. It is still in print today. The Baroness created several other series characters featured in short stories. Lady Molly of Scotland Yard appeared in a collection of stories in 1910. Patrick Mulligan, an Irish lawyer, is featured in the collection entitled *The Skin o' My Tooth*; secret agent Fernand is found in *The Man in Grey*; and the collection centered around M. Hector Ratichon, an unscrupulous volunteer policeman, is titled *Castles in the Air*.

There is an outlaw quality to most of the Baroness' featured characters. The Scarlet Pimpernel, Sir Percy, flaunts authority and delights in perplexing law and order during the French Revolution. The Robin Hood morality at work there is missing in the Bill Owen stories. The Old Man detects for his own pleasure and is conceited, in the extreme, about his abilities. The stories still read well today. The language is less stilted than that found in Anna Katharine Green's work and the logic is well founded. Polly is a forerunner of today's liberated woman without being the least bit militant. She is an apt pupil for Bill, and her part in the surprise at the end of *The Old Man in the Corner* stories is a credit to her attentive observations under his tutelage.

EVAN PINKERTON
1930–1950   14 books   English
David Frome (Zenith Jones Brown)

The small gray man in the inevitable brown bowler has the look of a perpetually startled rabbit. Anyone seeing him in the company of J. Humphrey Bull, of Scotland Yard, would assume that the inspector had collared a minor criminal in the act of committing some minor crime. They would be incorrect, however, as Mr. Evan Pinkerton is a well-loved friend and trusted comrade of the inspector's.

> For all that, meek and watery-eyed as he looked, grey and rabbity, Mr. Pinkerton had nevertheless two large purple patches in the drab frayed greatcoat, so to speak, of his soul. For years his life had been like an old bone, gnawed at in the first place by a pack of parsimonious aunts in a little Welsh village; tossed about then by an outrageous parcel of masters and boys when he was an underfed, underpaid undermaster; and finally buried in a pot-boy and scullery-maid existence by his vinegary-cheeked wife in her boarding house in Golders Green. Then Crime, in the person of his wife's lodger Inspector J. Humphrey Bull of the C.I. Department of New Scotland Yard had found him and dug him up—mouldy and not much to look at, but with his marrow still preserved intact. And Crime on the one hand, in Inspector Bull's large, tawny, stolid person, and the cinema on the other, had become what life chiefly was to him. Perhaps not so much purple patches as twin beacons of lovely light on a lonely windless sea on a barren unfriendly coast.[9]

The advent of the inspector's presence in Mr. Pinkerton's life marked a turning point for the little man. His fortunes continued to rise as his wife's unexpected death left him not only free from her dominance but a wealthy man as well. The penurious Mrs. Evans had left an estate of £75,000, which, in the absence of a will, went directly to her spouse. Despite these changes, Evan Pinkerton does not blossom. His wife may no longer be a physical presence, and his aunts may be long in their graves, but their years of influence overshadow the man and cloak his actions and emotions like a pall.

Springing from some deep, genetic reservoir within Mr. Pinkerton is a fey nature, characteristic of the Welsh. This sensitivity propels him into situations where murder is contemplated and carried out. It also gives him a slight edge in ferreting out the evildoer. His lack of self-esteem and his desire to see love requited often place him in danger, however, and the inspector is forced to save his skin time after time. Sir Charles Debenham, assistant commissioner of New Scotland Yard, sees Pinkerton as a rather dubious asset and simultaneously congratulates the little man, while regretting the care required to insure his continued well-being.

American author Zenith Jones Brown has created a very English series. In *The Black Envelope: Mr. Pinkerton Again!*, the British seaside resort of Brighton, especially the Pavilion, a royal pleasure palace, is so well described that readers familiar with the place are instantly transported there. We were surprised to find that, under the pseudonym of Leslie Ford, she also created the very American series featuring Colonel John Primrose and Grace Latham. There are similarities in the style in which both series are written. These similarities can be seen in the author's attention to location and setting and the juxtaposition of primary characters. Both Grace and Evan have a penchant for withholding vital evidence in the mistaken belief that they are protecting innocence. Both blunder over bodies and find themselves alone and in isolation with the murderer. The inspector and the colonel embody both authority and strength. Each respects his unofficial partner's cooperation but neither is dismayed to take the hero's position at the end and provide the saving grace.

The Pinkerton plots are convoluted and hard to follow. The final explanation of means, motive, and opportunity is often so confusing that even if the reader has figured it all out, doubts arise. There is a lot of boilerplate around Mr. Pinkerton's early life in all of the books which may be helpful for readers unfamiliar with the entire series. In spite of the drawbacks, these are charming stories—well told and representative of the era in which they were penned.

ASEY MAYO
1931-1951   24 books   American
Phoebe Atwood Taylor

Cape Cod resident Asey Mayo is the epitome of Yankee virtue. A sailor on the last of the wind ships, he also served as mate and cook on a variety of vessels during his seafaring years. A master mechanic, Asey left the sea for the lure of more landlocked high speed. Working for Colonel Porter, he first built carriages, then, as the automobile captured imaginations, designed and built the first Porter race car, known as the Century. She broke records at Daytona Beach and established the Porter Automotive Works as a force with which to be reckoned on the road. Hardworking and thrifty, Asey has been well paid for his labors over the years but prefers a modest life-style. Down to earth, independent, and infused with common sense he has always been relied upon by all and sundry. When murder enters the picture, it is no surprise that he is called in—as the Codfish Sherlock.

As the series opens, Asey is round-about sixty, though it is hard to guess at his age. He could be anywhere from thirty-five to seventy. Not only is this man laconic, he never even uses more syllables than abs'lut neces'ry. In *The Cape Cod Mystery*, Bill Porter, son of the old colonel, is suspected of murdering author Dale Sanborn. Over the years, Asey has gotten into the habit of getting various Porter family members out of hot water and it seems the only way to get Bill out of jail is to discover who really killed Sanborn. Aided by Miss Prue (aka Snoodles), her niece Betsey, and two of their houseguests, Asey proceeds to send telegrams off to all compass points, bribes and rewards various citizens of Wellfleet, and drives at his usual race driver's speed all over the Cape. The actual perpetrator confesses but Asey has figured out the hows and whys beforehand and offers opportunity for the noble solution. Bill marries Betsey and joins the family business in Detroit. From time to time, he or his older brother Jimmy sends Asey a new Porter roadster to test and to enjoy.

Each story can be read separately but the whole series, in order, will give readers the tang of the Cape and a sense of the interconnectedness of its inhabitants. Cousin Syl is a small man with a walrus mustache. He may look like a lightweight but more than carries his share of the load of any investigation Asey leads. Syl's wife Jennie keeps house for Asey and provides the necessary admonishments about warm clothing and rubbers in the heat of the chase. Dr. Cummings, medical examiner for the area, is something of a curmudgeon. Knowledgeable and curious, he goads and presses Asey to tell him what's going on throughout the cases. We find various women serving as Watson to Asey's Sherlock. Sometimes they are of an age and at others, quite young. In all cases, they are adventuresome, intelligent, and practical. In conversation with one, he explains a part of his method.

"Are you very sure," Kay asked, "that it's not a madman on the loose? There've been cases sort of like this. I've read about them."

"When everything else fails," Asey said, "you lay it to a maniac. But just the same, I tie this up with the things Sara an' Weston worried about. There's a plan somewhere. I can't tell where or what it is, or lay my hands on much of it, but it's there. We got odds an' ends an' corners, but nothin' to tell the shape of the thing. I wish to heaven this man'd make a move. He'd be a fathead to, because all he's got to do is sit tight an' say nothin', an' he's all set. But Mary Randall was killed for a purpose, prob'ly to keep her from tellin' somethin'. There is a plan here, I'm sure. I been hopin' if we sat back, some more of it would filter out."[10]

Asey's engineering mind and mechanical ability give him a practical approach to problem solving. Generally a man of action, he will, from time to time, just sit a spell and think things out.

There is a formula to this series. Asey's assistant is always female. There is a wealth of motive, opportunity, and conflicting information among those involved and a gathering of participants at the denouement. Asey is a fast worker and usually concludes his investigations in less than a week. The humor is of the driest sort though some of the antics of the Yankee eccentrics can cause the dunes to resound with echoing belly laughs.

Phoebe Atwood Taylor wrote only mysteries. Her other series character, Leonidas Witherall, is a retired professor, finder of rare books for collectors, and author of blood-and-thunder thrillers. Several books from the Asey Mayo series have been reprinted in the last few years. Those featuring Leonidas are difficult to find. We are charmed by this author's work.

THE GRUB-AND-STAKERS
1981-1985   2 books   Canadian
Alisa Craig (Charlotte MacLeod)

Like all Craig novels, these two books combine murder with high humor. The action takes place in Lobelia Falls, Ontario, and involves members of the Grub-and-Stake Gardening and Roving Club who divide their time between growing things and shooting things with bow and arrows. Dittany Henbit is the individual upon whom the action depends. In *The Grub-and-Stakers Move a Mountain*, she has her own secretarial service. Arethusa Monk, writer of regency romance novels, is one of her clients.

Besides Dittany and Arethusa, other members of this august organization—founded by Winona Pitcher around the turn of the century—include: Minerva Oakes, grandaughter of the foundress, Therese Boulanger, Samantha Burberry, Hazel Munson, and Zilla Trott. The Grub-and-Stakers are a force with which to be reckoned. Their arch enemy is Andrew McNaster, a devil of development and a constant threat to the natural beauty and simple ambiance of Lobelia Falls. Murder on the Enchanted Mountain, loose livestock, and a mysterious black van are elements of the first story. Andy McNasty is trying to despoil the primeval splendor of the mountain by building a house smack on top in defiance of a sacred trust established by the Hunneker brothers a century earlier. Villain he may be, but McNasty is not the perpetrator of murder. Newly deputized Osbert Monk, nephew of Arethusa, and Dittany aid Sergeant MacVicar in bringing the correct culprit to his rightful desserts. At the end of the first book, Osbert and Dittany are betrothed and discuss the respective merits of raisin hermits and large molasses cookies with crinkles around the edges and sugar on top, and how best to spend all the money Osbert makes writing Westerns under the pseudonym of Lex Laramie.

In *The Grub-and-Stakers Quilt a Bee*, Dittany is Mrs. Osbert Monk and the town has received a bequest from the murder victim in the first book, John Architrave. The bequest is in the form of the Architrave family home which is given to Lobelia Falls as a museum to be named for John's wife, Aralia Polyphema Architrave. Peregrine Fairfield, the newly hired curator is found dead on the ground outside the museum by Minerva Oakes and the (now) widow, Evangeline Fairfield. It appears that Mr. Fairfield has fallen from one of the attic windows, but in looking over the scene, Dittany, Osbert, and Sergeant MacVicar come across some inconsistencies.

> "Then would you care to speculate, eh, on how the flaming heck Mr. Fairfield could have managed to fall out by accident?"
>
> "I have speculated, Dittany. I have also remarked the absence of smudges, stains, or deposits of bird droppings on his garments despite the fact that yon aforementioned ledges have visibly served as roosting places for our feathered friends for, lo, these many decades. I have concluded that it would have taken a degree of ingenuity, agility, and persistence most remarkable in an elderly man of sedentary habit and scholarly inclination for Mr. Fairfield to have accomplished such a feat."

"But he is dead," said Osbert, who believed in facing facts even when he had to invent them himself.

"He is indeed defunct, Deputy Monk. I have seldom," Sergeant MacVicar amplified, "seen anybody deader, at least not on such short notice. There was a fracture of the occiput as well as of the cervical vertebrae."

"Meaning he landed smack on his head, bashed in his skull, and broke his neck, eh?"[11]

Craig does have a penchant for small, closed communities with a fixed and predictable populace. In nine years, she has written eighteen books unequally divided into four separate series, two under her own name, Charlotte MacLeod. Sarah Kelling and Max Bittersohn are the stars of one series, located on the proper side of Beacon Hill, Boston. Professor Peter Shandy and his wife Helen (née Marsh) are featured in another. They live and work in Balaclava Junction. As Craig, she has also penned the series featuring Madoc Rhys of the Royal Canadian Mounted Police. All of this author's characters have degrees of unexpectedness to their detecting, but the Grub-and-Stakers are the acme of this designation.

Craig/MacLeod is one of the genre's most consistent creators. Her style is easily recognized and she provides readers with great escapes. The mystery aspects of all this author's works are excellent. Readers may guess who but the why is elusive and well hidden in convoluted plots and challenging nomenclature. Wedding bells and other signs of happy endings are hallmarks of all of her series. Characters are likable and their eccentricities gently enhance each story in a memorable fashion. All of the books are humorous but most have a lighter touch than this one, which tends toward tedium as it progresses. MacLeod fans unfamiliar with her writing as Craig are encouraged to sample these wares.

VEJAY HASKELL
1984-1986   3 books   American
Susan Dunlap

Russian River meter reader Vejay Haskell lives in the small riverside community of Henderson. The population of the area is varied and scattered. Environmentalists, fisherfolk, innkeepers, hippies, and tourists meet and mingle, then retreat to their respective places along the great and usually slow-moving river as it makes its stately way to the sea. Power and the measurement of its consumption is what Vejay deals with. Her quest for the knowledge that the PG&E meters contain takes this intrepid soul up hill and down dale and causes her to be confronted by an occasional hostile hill dweller or large, unfriendly dog.

As in most small communities, acceptance by the locals is important for newcomers. Members of the large Fortimiglio family pervade the district and appear regularly in the series. Papa Carlo, a struggling salmon fisherman in an overfished sea, is aided by his son Chris. Matriarch, Rosa, Carlo's wife, makes the best ravioli in town and sweeps Vejay into the bosom of their family. The outcome of Vejay's first foray into detection substantially alters Rosa's cordiality and Vejay becomes, for a while at least, a pariah. Sheriff Wescott, of the Guerneville Sheriff's Department, finds himself attracted to Vejay but is also dismayed with her involvement in amateur detecting.

> There had been a time last summer when he had invited me for a drink at the bar in town, half to warn me to stay out of his case and half, perhaps, for more personal reasons. Then he had called me Vejay. For those few minutes while we sat drinking our beers, we had talked like a man and a woman, choosing each word, trying to be agreeable, but still just teasing enough to keep things rolling along to a more intimate connection. The potential had been there. I had seen it in the nervous way he fingered his mustache; I'd heard it in my own voice. And then the murder—what he viewed as an accident, and I saw as a murder—took over. The attraction between us was transformed into antipathy. His few moments of openness had made him resent what he viewed as my betrayal all the more. And when the investigation was over, the intensity of our meetings settled back not into promise but rather a brittle distrust. I had seen him around town, on duty, since then. We had been cautious, polite. It had always been "Miss Haskell."[12]

Vejay does find herself in hazardous situations on occasion. *An Equal Opportunity Death*, places her in a building where she is threatened by both the rising flood waters of the Russian River and a murderer. In *The Last Annual Slugfest*, she must choose between facing a burly guard—capable of bone-crushing brutality—and the turbulent sea at storm tide. Life is very different for Vejay than it was as a San Francisco advertising executive. Clearly, however, she is equal to the challenges of both.

Susan Dunlap has two series running concurrently. Her other character, Jill Smith, is a Berkeley policewoman. Officer Smith is our hands-down favorite but we do admire the independence and self-confidence exhibited by both series characters. Dunlap is a Bay Area resident herself, knows the territory, and writes about it well. We anticipate, with pleasure, more good books from this talented author.

JAKE SAMSON and ROSIE VICENTE
1983-1987   4 books   American
Shelley Singer

Wisecracking poker player Jake Samson is a Jack-of-many-trades. Rookie cop in Mayor Daly's Chicago in the sixties, Jake moved to California after the violence of the 1968 Democratic Convention. He smoked dope, dropped acid, plumbed, carpented, and dealt all along the Pacific coast. Married and divorced, Jake drifted down from Humboldt County to the East San Francisco Bay Area. As the series opens, he is now an Oakland homeowner and landlord with a small trust income. He rents the cottage on his property to carpenter Rosie Vicente and her companion, Alice B. Toklas, a standard poodle.

Over the years, Jake's friends—knowing of his police training—have asked for his help in solving their personal problems. Poker buddy Artie Perrine has called on Jake for assistance in the past and, in exchange for Jake's services, provides cover when necessary.

> I had my usual cover. A couple of years before, my old friend and poker buddy Artie Perrine, an editor at *Probe* magazine in San Francisco, had agreed to give me a letter of ID as a "freelance writer" on assignment. In exchange, I agreed to give him anything in the way of story material I might come up with while on a case. Chloe, who had gotten me involved in this one, was also an editor at *Probe*. Anyone who didn't believe the worn, yellowing, undated letter could just call the magazine for verification.
>
> I have considered getting a P.I. license. It's hard to explain why I haven't been able to bring myself to do it. I guess I just don't like government very much and don't want it looking over my shoulder. Maybe it's genetic memory—a long history of fending off Slavic despots, Turkish soldiers, and Tatar hordes. I'd rather keep a low profile, thanks just the same.[13]

Rosie helps him from time to time. Beyond their landlord/tenant relationship, they are occasional business partners. Their detecting methods vary. Sometimes Jake operates out of his house, and at others, he and/or Rosie move closer to the scene of the crime for better views of the situation and the possible suspects. Strong, independent, and capable, Rosie gets in and out of hazardous situations on her own and doesn't depend on Jake's manly talents for rescue. In fact, Rosie actually rescues Jake at least once. The two have an easygoing relationship as equals and there is constant evidence of respect and admiration between them.

The title of each of the books is a poker term. All are apt, though card games usually take place off the page. The best in our opinion is the newest, *Spit in the Ocean*, which, when combined with the theme of the book, makes a statement all its own. Singer has created a modern series, with modern characters who choose to keep their options as open as possible while being responsible to a personal code of honor. Intelligent, sharp, and streetwise, Jake and Rosie serve justice ultimately and always play their cards close to their chests.

A CONCATENATION OF FATE has put these individuals in the way of murder and those who commit it. With no professional compulsion to see justice done, each nevertheless takes matters through to their conclusion. No single personal compulsion for resolution can be applied across the board for these sleuths. They just do what they do unexpectedly well and keep us highly entertained in the process.

Some unexpected detectives are actually four-footed. Koko, the feline companion of newspaperman Jim Qwilleran, is a fine example of a sleuthing cat. D. C. Randall is the star of one of the series by the Gordons. Walt Disney made a movie out of the first book, *That Darn Cat*, in the sixties. Gala, Veterinarian Gordon Christy's doberman, is a murder witness in *The Doberman Wore Black* and an assistant in the subsequent book. The cat Bastet, constant companion of young Ramses Emerson, aids and abets Amelia and Radcliffe in their detecting, not to mention her full-time occupation of protecting her juvenile master. These creatures' antics are not only amusing but surprisingly perceptive. Animals may possess no more physical senses than humans but some are more highly developed than those of the Homo sapien. They are less likely to become confused by conflicting information of testimony. They know what they know and it is a wise master who heeds his pet's imprecations.

Little old ladies are always unexpected as detectives. Mrs. Emily Pollifax is actually described as such in the title of the first book in which she is featured. However, her involvement in international espionage elevates her to a more visible position than her unexpectedness could be expected to do. Like Jane Marple, Maud Silver is prim and proper. She has the air of the schoolroom about her and looks about as unlikely a detective as possible. Detect she does, however, and professionally to boot. Because these two have exceeded any limits age may have placed on their spirits and abilities, they appear elsewhere.

Unexpectedness is all around and because of its omnipresence no other titles are given.

MASTER LIST

There are as many ways to organize a reference work as there are authors of both reference books and mystery fiction. Many mystery fans are inveterate list makers and we are no exception. We have untidy minds, yet we crave order. To overcome our penchant for clutter and achieve our desired end, we have created the MASTER LIST, truly the foundation of this work. This section is alphabetically organized by autonym, listing the series characters created by each author, titles featuring each character, and each book's year of publication. Pseudonyms used by these authors in creating other series are cross-referenced to the autonym. For readers familiar with the character's name only, please see APPENDIX III: SERIES CHARACTER TO AUTHOR. Authors on the MASTER LIST include women, men writing under a female pseudonym, and writing teams: women, men and women, and married couples as well. When a writing team consists of two women, the autonym entry is given in alphabetical order, e.g.:

A: Ashton, Winifred w/Helen Simpson

The second name appears in its own alphabetical sequence and is cross-referenced to the autonym entry, e.g.:

JN: Simpson, Helen
Please see: Ashton, Winifred w/Helen Simpson

When a writing team consists of a woman and a man, the autonym entry appears alphabetically by the woman's last name, e.g.:

A: Abrahams, Doris Caroline w/Simon Jasha Skidelsky

The name of the male member of the mixed writing team appears in its alphabetical sequence and is cross-referenced to the autonym entry.

When the writing team is a married couple, the autonym entry appears under their common last name. The name of the male member of a married team appears in its own alphabetical sequence and is cross-referenced to the autonym entry.

Pseudonyms used by writing teams are treated the same as the names of single authors.

In the jacket blurb on the cover of the 1948 Penguin edition of

Death and Mary Dazill, author Mary Fitt said, "It is, I think, the writer of fiction who is of interest to the public, not the person of whom the writer is a part."[1] We agree and because biographical information on these authors is available through other sources, none is given here.

KEY TO MASTER LIST

A = Autonym
P = Pseudonym
JN = Joint name
SC = Series character
SS = Short story
Year = Year published
apa = also published as

A: Abrahams, Doris Caroline w/Simon Jasha Skidelsky
P: Brahms, Caryl and S. J. Simon
 SC: Adam Quill, Insp.

  1937 A Bullet in the Ballet
  1938 Casino for Sale
     apa Murder à la Stroganoff
  1940 Envoy on Excursion

 SC: Ballet Stroganoff

  1937 A Bullet in the Ballet
  1938 Casino for Sale
     apa Murder à la Stroganoff
  1945 Six Curtains for Stroganova
     apa Six Curtains for Natasha
  1975 Stroganoff at the Ballet

A: Adamson, M. J.
 SC: Balthazar Marten

  1987 Not Till a Hot January
  1987 A February Face
  1987 Remember March

P: Aird, Catherine
 Please see: McIntosh, Kinn Hamilton

A: Allan, Joan
 SC: Valerie Lambert

  1979 Who's Next?
  1979 Who Killed Me?
  1979 Who's on First?

A: Allingham (Carter), Margery
 SC: Albert Campion (see pg. 83)

  1929 The Crime at Black Dudley
     apa The Black Dudley Murder

Allingham (Carter), Margery (cont.)

	1930	Mystery Mile
	1931	Police at the Funeral
	1931	Look to the Lady
		apa The Gyrth Chalice Mystery
	1933	Sweet Danger
		apa Kingdom of Death
		apa The Fear Sign
	1934	Death of a Ghost
	1936	Flowers for the Judge
		apa Legacy in Blood
SS	1937	Mr. Campion: Criminologist
	1937	The Case of the Late Pig
	1937	Dancers in Mourning
		apa Who Killed Chloe?
	1938	The Fashion in Shrouds
SS	1939	Mr. Campion and Others
	1941	Traitor's Purse
		apa The Sabotage Murder Mystery
	1945	Coroner's Pidgin
		apa Pearls Before Swine
SS	1947	The Case Book of Mr. Campion
	1948	More Work for the Undertaker
	1952	Tiger in the Smoke
	1955	The Beckoning Lady
		apa The Estate of the Beckoning Lady
	1958	Hide My Eyes
		apa Tether's End
		apa Ten Were Missing
	1962	The China Governess
	1963	The Mysterious Mr. Campion
	1965	The Mind Readers
	1965	Mr. Campion's Lady
	1968	Cargo of Eagles
SS	1969	The Allingham Case-Book
SS	1973	The Allingham Minibus

A: Anthony, Elizabeth
SC: Pauline Lyons

	1979	Ballet of Fear
	1979	Ballet of Death

P: Anthony, Evelyn
  Please see: Ward-Thomas, Evelyn Bridget Patricia
  Stephens

P: Antill, Elizabeth
  Please see: Middleton, Elizabeth

P: Aresbys, The
  Please see: Bamberger, Helen w/Raymond

A: Arliss, Joen
  SC: Kate Graham

  1979   The Shark Bait Affair
  1980   The Lady Killer Affair

A: Armstrong, Charlotte
  SC: MacDougal Duff

  1942   Lay On, Mac Duff!
  1943   The Case of the Weird Sisters
  1945   The Innocent Flower
         apa Death Filled the Glass

P: Arnold, Margot
  Please see: Cook, Petronelle Marguerite Mary

A: Ashbrook, H(arriette) (C.)
  SC: Philip "Spike" Tracy

  1930   The Murder of Cecily Thane
  1931   The Murder of Steven Kester
  1933   The Murder of Sigurd Sharon
  1935   A Most Immoral Murder
  1937   Murder Makes Murder
  1940   Murder Comes Back
  1941   The Purple Onion Mystery
         apa Murder on Friday

 P: Shane, Susannah
   SC: Christopher Saxe

   1942   Lady in Danger
   1943   Lady in a Million

Ashbrook, H(arriette) (C.) (cont.)

    1944   The Baby in the Ash Can
    1946   Diamonds in the Dumplings

P: Ashe, Mary Ann
    Please see: Brand (Lewis), (Mary) Christianna (Milne)

A: Ashton, Winifred w/Helen Simpson
P: Dane, Clemence and Helen Simpson
    SC: Sir John Saumarez (see pg. 103)

    1928   Enter Sir John
    1932   Re-Enter Sir John

A: Atkins, Meg (Margaret) (Elizabeth)
    SC: Henry Beaumont, Insp.

    1975   By the North Door
    1976   Samain

A: Austin, Anne
    SC: James F. "Bonnie" Dundee

    1930   The Avenging Parrot
    1930   Murder Backstairs
    1931   Murder at Bridge
    1932   One Drop of Blood
    1939   Murdered But Not Dead

B

A: Babson, Marian
  SC: Douglas Perkins

  1971   Cover-Up Story
  1972   Murder on Show
  1984   A Fool for Murder?

A: Backhouse, (Enid) Elizabeth
  SC: Christopher Marsden, Insp.

  1957   Death Came Uninvited
  1961   The Night Has Eyes

  SC: Prentis, Insp.

  1960   The Web of Shadows
  1963   Death Climbs a Hill

A: Backus, Jean Louise
P: Montross, David
  SC: Remsen

  1962   Traitor's Wife
  1963   Troika
         apa Who is Elissa Sheldon?
  1965   Fellow-Traveler

P: Bailey, Hilea
  Please see: Marting, Ruth Lenore

A: Balfour, Eva w/Beryl Hearnden
P: Balfour, Hearnden
  SC: Jack Strickland, Insp.

  1927   The Paper Chase
         apa A Gentleman from Texas
  1928   The Enterprising Burglar
  1931   Anything Might Happen
         apa Murder and the Red-Haired Girl

P: Balfour, Hearnden
  Please see: Balfour, Eva w/Beryl Hearnden

A: Ball, Doris Bell
P: Bell, Josephine
   SC: Amy Tupper

   1979   Wolf! Wolf!
   1980   A Question of Inheritance

   SC: Claude Warrington-Reeve

   1959   Easy Prey
   1960   A Well-Known Face
   1963   A Flat Tyre in Fulham
          apa Fiasco in Fulham
          apa Room for a Body

   SC: Dr. David Wintringham   (see pg. 115)

   1937   Murder in Hospital
   1937   Death on the Borough Council
   1938   Fall over Cliff
   1939   From Natural Causes
   1939   Death at Half-Term
          apa Curtain Call for a Corpse
   1940   All is Vanity
   1942   Trouble at Wrekin Farm
   1944   Death at the Medical Board
   1949   Death in Clairvoyance
   1950   The Summer School Mystery
   1953   Bones in the Barrow
   1954   Fires at Fairlawn
   1956   The China Roundabout
          apa Murder on the Merry-Go-Round
   1958   The Seeing Eye

   SC: Dr. Henry Frost   (see pg. 115)

   1964   The Upfold Witch
   1966   Death on the Reserve

   SC: Steven Mitchell, Insp.

   1937   Murder in Hospital
   1938   The Port of London Murders
   1938   Fall Over Cliff

Ball, Doris Bell (cont.)

1939	Death at Half-Term
	apa Curtain Call for a Corpse
1949	Death in Clairvoyance
1950	The Summer School Mystery
1953	Bones in the Barrow
1956	The China Roundabout
	apa Murder on the Merry-Go-Round
1958	The Seeing Eye
1959	Easy Prey
1960	A Well-Known Face
1963	A Flat Tyre in Fulham
	apa Fiasco in Fulham
	apa Room for a Body
1964	The Upfold Witch

A: Bamberger, Helen w/Raymond
P: Aresbys, The
   SC: Parrish Darby

1927	Who Killed Coralie?
1929	The Mark of the Dead

JN: Bamberger, Raymond
   Please see: Bamberger, Helen w/Raymond

A: Bamburg, Lilian
   SC: Septimus March

1926	Beads of Silence
1927	Rays of Darkness

P: Barber, Willetta Ann and R. F. Schabelitz
   Please see: Barber, Willetta Ann w/Rudolph Fredrick
     Schabelitz

A: Barber, Willetta Ann w/Rudolph Fredrick Schabelitz
P: Barber, Willetta Ann and R. F. Schabelitz
   SC: Christopher Storm   (see pg. 200)

1940	Murder Draws A Line
1941	Pencil Points to Murder
1942	Murder Enters the Picture

Barber, Willetta Ann w/Rudolph Fredrick Schabelitz
(cont.)

	1942	Drawn Conclusion
	1945	The Noose is Drawn
	1947	Drawback to Murder
	1949	The Deed is Drawn

P: Barbette, Jay
Please see: Spicer, Betty Coe w/Bart

A: Barker, Elsa
SC: Dexter Drake

	1928	The Cobra Candlestick
SS	1929	The C.I.D. of Dexter Drake
	1930	The Redman Cave Murder

P: Barling, Charles
Please see: Barling, Muriel Vere M.

A: Barling, Muriel Vere M.
P: Barling, Charles
SC: Henderson, Insp.

	1968	Accessory to Murder
	1968	Death of a Shrew

P: Barrington, Pamela
SC: George Marshall, Insp.

	1951	The Rest is Silence
	1953	Account Rendered
	1959	Night of Violence
	1960	By Some Person Unknown
	1963	Motive for Murder
	1963	Afternoon of Violence
	1964	Appointment With Death
	1965	Time to Kill
	1966	Cage Without Bars
	1967	A Game of Murder
	1967	Confession of Murder
	1967	Slow Poison

Barling, Muriel Vere M. (cont.)

SC: George Travers, Insp.

1952   The Mortimer Story
1953   Among Those Present
1961   The Gentle Killer

A: **Barnes, Linda (Appelblatt)**
SC: Michael Spraggue   (see pg. 101)

1982   Blood Will Have Blood
1983   Bitter Finish
1984   Dead Heat
1986   Cities of the Dead

A: **Barnett, Glyn**
SC: Gramport, Insp.

1935   The Call-Box Murder
1936   Murder on Monday
1937   I Know Mrs. Lang
1946   Find the Lady

P: **Barrington, Pamela**
Please see: Barling, Muriel Vere M.

P: **Baskerville, Beatrice and Elliot Monk**
Please see: Baskerville, Beatrice
w/Elliot Monk

A: **Baskerville, Beatrice w/Elliot Monk**
P: Baskerville, Beatrice and Elliot Monk
SC: Briconi

1922   By Whose Hand?
1931   The St. Cloud Affair

A: **Bayne, Isabella**
SC: Benedict Breeze

1952   Death and Benedict
1956   Cruel as the Grave

P: Beck, K. K.
Please see: Marris, Kathrine

P: Bell, Josephine
Please see: Ball, Doris Bell

A: Bennett, Dorothy
SC: Dennis Devore

1935   Murder Unleashed
1942   Come and Be Killed

A: Bennett, Margot
SC: John Davies

1945   Time to Change Hats
1946   Away Went the Little Fish

A: Bentley, Phyllis (Eleanor)
SC: Miss Marian Phipps

SS   1953   The Way Round
SS   1954   A Telegram for Miss Phipps
SS   1954   The Tuesday and Friday Thefts
SS   1954   The Spirit of the Place
SS   1954   The Crooked Figures
SS   1954   Chain of Witnesses
SS   1954   Conversations at an Inn
SS   1955   The Significant Letter
SS   1955   The Incongruous Letter
SS   1961   Author in Search of a Character
SS   1962   Miss Phipps Improvises
SS   1962   Message in a Bottle
SS   1963   The Man on the Back Seat
SS   1963   Miss Phipps Jousts With the Press
SS   1963   Miss Phipps Discovers America
SS   1965   Miss Phipps Considers the Cat
SS   1967   Miss Phipps and the Invisible
             Murderer
SS   1967   Miss Phipps Goes to the Hairdresser
SS   1969   Miss Phipps and the Nest of Illusion
SS   1969   The Secret
SS   1971   Miss Phipps is Too Modest
SS   1973   A Midsummer Night's Crime

Bentley, Phyllis (Eleanor) (cont.)

SS   1975   Miss Phipps Meets a Dog
SS   1976   Miss Phipps Exercises Her Metier

P: Berne, Karin
        Please see: Bernell, Sue w/Michaela Karni

A: Bernell, Sue w/Michaela Karni
P: Berne, Karin
        SC: Ellie Gordon   (see pg. 151)

        1985   Bare Acquaintances
        1985   Shock Value
        1986   False Impressions

A: Beynon, Jane
P: Lewis, Lange
        SC: Richard Tuck, Lt.   (see pg. 24)

        1942   Murder Among Friends
                    apa Death Among Friends
        1943   Juliet Dies Twice
        1943   Meat for Murder
        1945   The Birthday Murder
        1952   The Passionate Victims

A: Bidwell, Margaret
        SC: Mr. Hodson

        1939   Death on the Agenda
        1940   Death and His Brother

A: Black, E(lizabeth) Best
        SC: Peter Strangely

        1933   The Ravenelle Riddle
        1934   The Crime of the Chromium Bowl

A: Blackmon, Anita
        SC: Adelaide Adams

        1937   Murder à la Richelieu
                    apa The Hotel Richelieu Murders

Blackmon, Anita (cont.)

  1938   There is No Return
         apa The Riddle of the Dead Cats

A: Blair, Dorothy w/Evelyn Page
P: Scarlett, Roger
  SC: Kane, Insp.

  1930   The Back Bay Murders
  1930   The Beacon Hill Murders
  1931   Cat's Paw
  1932   Murder Among the Angells
  1933   In the First Degree

A: Blair, Marcia
  SC: Tory Baxter

  1978   The Final Lie
  1978   The Final Pose
  1978   The Final Ring
  1979   The Final Target
  1979   The Final Appointment
  1979   The Final Guest
  1979   The Final Fear
  1980   Finale

A: Blanc, Suzanne
  SC: Menendez, Insp.

  1961   The Green Stone
  1964   The Yellow Villa
  1967   The Rose Window

A: Bodington, Nancy Hermione Courlander
P: Smith, Shelley
  SC: Jacob Chaos

  1942   Background for Murder
  1947   He Died of Murder!

P: Bond, Evelyn
  Please see: Hershman, Morris

P: Bonett, John and Emery
Please see: Coulson, Felicity Winifred Carter
w/John H. A.

A: Boniface, Marjorie
SC: Hiram Odom, Sheriff

1940   Murder as an Ornament
1942   Venom in Eden
1946   Wings of Death

P: Bonnamy, Francis
Please see: Walz, Audrey Boyers

A: Bonner, Geraldine
SC: Molly Morgenthau

1915   The Girl at Central
1916   The Black Eagle Mystery

A: Borthwick, J. S.
SC: Sarah Deane and Dr. Alex McKenzie

1982   The Case of the Hook-Billed
         Kites
1986   The Down East Murders
1987   The Student Body

A: Bowden, Jean
P: Curry, Avon
SC: Jerome Aylwin

1960   Derry Down Death
1961   Dying High

A: Bowen-Judd, Sara Hutton
P: Burton, Anne
SC: Richard Trenton   (see pg. 132)

1980   Where There's a Will
1980   The Dear Departed
1982   Worse Than a Crime

Bowen-Judd, Sara Hutton (cont.)

P: Challis, Mary
    SC: Jeremy Locke

    1980   Burden of Proof
    1980   Crimes Past
    1981   A Very Good Hater
    1981   The Ghost of an Idea

P: Leek, Margaret
    SC: Stephen Marryat   (see pg. 132)

    1980   We Must Have a Trial
    1980   The Healthy Grave

P: Woods, Sara
    SC: Antony Maitland   (see page 141)

    1962   Bloody Instructions
    1962   Malice Domestic
    1963   The Taste of Fears
            apa The Third Encounter
    1963   Error of the Moon
    1964   Trusted Like the Fox
    1964   This Little Measure
    1965   The Windy Side of the Law
    1965   Though I Know She Lies
    1966   Let's Choose Executors
    1966   Enter Certain Murderers
    1967   The Case is Altered
    1967   And Shame the Devil
    1968   Past Praying For
    1968   Knives Have Edges
    1969   Tarry and Be Hanged
    1970   An Improbable Fiction
    1971   The Knavish Crows
    1971   Serpent's Tooth
    1972   They Love Not Poison
    1973   Enter the Corpse
    1973   Yet She Must Die
    1974   Done to Death
    1975   A Show of Violence

Bowen-Judd, Sara Hutton (cont.)

1975	My Life is Done
1977	A Thief or Two
1977	The Law's Delay
1978	Exit Murderer
1979	Proceed to Judgement
1979	This Fatal Writ
1980	Weep for Her
1980	They Stay for Death
1981	Cry Guilty
1981	Dearest Enemy
1982	Most Grievous Murder
1982	Villains by Necessity
1982	Enter a Gentlewoman
1983	The Lie Direct
1983	Call Back Yesterday
1983	Where Should He Die?
1984	Murder's Out of Tune
1984	Defy the Devil
1984	The Bloody Book of Law
1985	Most Deadly Hate
1985	Put Out the Light
1985	An Obscure Grave
1985	Away With Them to Prison
1986	Nor Live So Long
1987	Naked Villainy

A: Bowers, Dorothy (Violet)
SC: Pardoe, Insp.

1938	Postscript to Poison
1939	Shadows Before
1940	A Deed Without a Name
1941	Fear for Miss Betony
	apa Fear and Miss Betony

A: Boyd, Eunice Mays
SC: F. Millard Smyth

1943	Murder Breaks Trail
1944	Doom in the Midnight Sun
1945	Murder Wears Mukluks

A: Braddon, M(ary) E(lizabeth)
SC: Valentine Hawkehurst

1867   Birds of Prey
1868   Charlotte's Inheritance

P: Brahms, Caryl and S. J. Simon
Please see: Abrahams, Doris Caroline
w/Simon Jasha Skidelsky

A: Brand (Lewis), (Mary) Christianna (Milne)
SC: Charlesworth, Insp.

1941   Death in High Heels
1948   Death of Jezebel
1952   London Particular
       apa Fog of Doubt
1979   The Rose in Darkness

SC: Cockrill, Insp.   (see pg. 51)

1941   Heads You Lose
1944   Green for Danger
1946   The Crooked Wreath
       apa Suddenly at His Residence
1948   Death of Jezebel
1952   London Particular
       apa Fog of Doubt
1955   Tour de Force
1957   The Three-Cornered Halo
SS 1968   What Dread Hand?

P: Ashe, Mary Ann
SC: Chucky, Insp.

1950   Cat and Mouse
1977   A Ring of Roses

A: Brandes, Rhoda
P: Ramsay, Diana
SC: Meredith, Lt.

1972   A Little Murder Music

Brandes, Rhoda (cont.)

    1973   Deadly Discretion
    1974   No Cause to Kill

A: Braun, Lilian Jackson
    SC: Jim Qwilleran   (see pg. 165)

    1966   The Cat Who Could Read Backwards
    1967   The Cat Who Ate Danish Modern
    1968   The Cat Who Turned On and Off
    1986   The Cat Who Saw Red
    1987   The Cat Who Played Brahms
    1987   The Cat Who Played Post Office

A: Brawner, Helen w/Francis Van Wyck Mason
P: Coffin, Geoffrey
    SC: Scott Stuart, Insp.

    1935   Murder in the Senate
    1936   The Forgotten Fleet Mystery

P: Bridge, Ann
    Please see: O'Malley, Lady Mary Dolling

P: Bristow, Gwen and Bruce Manning
    Please see: Bristow, Gwen w/Bruce Manning

A: Bristow, Gwen w/Bruce Manning
P: Bristow, Gwen and Bruce Manning
    SC: Wade   (see pg. 166)

    1931   The Gutenberg Murders
    1932   The Mardi Gras Murders

A: Brochet, Jean Alexandre
P: Bruce, Jean
    SC: Hubert Bonisseur de la Bath

    1963   Deep Freeze
    1964   Double Take
    1964   Short Wave
    1965   Flash Point

Brochet, Jean Alexandre (cont.)

1965	Live Wire
	apa The Last Quarter Hour
1965	Photo Finish
1965	Pole Reaction
1965	Soft Sell
1965	Shock Tactics
1967	Cold Spell
1967	Dead Silence
1967	High Treason
1967	Hot Line
	apa Trouble in Tokyo
1967	Top Secret
1968	Strip Tease

A: Brown, Morna Doris McTavert
P: Ferrars, E. X.
  SC: Andrew Basnett

1983	Something Wicked
1984	The Root of All Evil
1985	The Crime and The Crystal
1987	The Other Devil's Name

  SC: Toby Dyke

1940	Give a Corpse a Bad Name
1940	Remove the Bodies
	apa Rehearsals for Murder
1941	Death in Botanist's Bay
	apa Murder of a Suicide
1942	Don't Monkey with Murder
	apa The Shape of a Stain
1942	Your Neck in a Noose
	apa Neck in a Noose

  SC: Virginia Freer

1978	Last Will and Testament
1980	Frog in the Throat
1986	I Met Murder

A: Brown, Zenith Jones
P: Ford, Leslie
    SC: Grace Latham and John Primrose, Col.   (see pg. 223)

1937	Ill Met by Moonlight
1937	The Simple Way of Poison
1938	Three Bright Pebbles
1939	Reno Rendezvous
	apa Mr. Cromwell is Dead
1939	False to Any Man
	apa Snow-White Murder
1940	Old Lover's Ghost
1941	The Murder of the Fifth Columnist
	apa The Capital Crime
1942	Murder in the O.P.M.
	apa The Priority Murder
1943	Siren in the Night
1944	All for the Love of a Lady
	apa Crack of Dawn
1945	The Philadelphia Murder Story
1946	Honolulu Story
	apa Honolulu Murder Story
	apa Honolulu Murders
1947	The Woman in Black
1948	The Devil's Stronghold
1953	Washington Whispers Murder
	apa The Lying Jade

SC: John Primrose, Col.   (see pg. 223)

1934	The Strangled Witness

SC: Joseph Kelly, Lt.

1932	Murder in Maryland
1933	The Clue of the Judas Tree

P: Frome, David
    SC: Evan Pinkerton   (see pg. 264)

1930	The Hammersmith Murders
1931	Two Against Scotland Yard
	apa The By-Pass Murder

Brown, Zenith Jones (cont.)

	1932	The Man From Scotland Yard
		apa Mr. Simpson Finds a Body
	1933	The Eel Pie Murders
		apa The Eel Pie Mystery
	1934	Mr. Pinkerton Goes to Scotland Yard
		apa Arsenic in Richmond
	1934	Mr. Pinkerton Finds a Body
		apa The Body in the Turl
	1935	Mr. Pinkerton Grows a Beard
		apa The Body in Bedford Square
	1936	Mr. Pinkerton Has the Clue
SS	1936	Mr. Pinkerton is Present
	1937	The Black Envelope: Mr. Pinkerton Again
		apa The Guilt is Plain
	1939	Mr. Pinkerton at the Old Angel
		apa Mr. Pinkerton and the Old Angel
	1939	Mr. Pinkerton: Passage For One
SS	1940	Mr. Pinkerton Lends a Hand
	1950	Homicide House: Mr. Pinkerton Returns
		apa Murder on the Square

SC: Gregory Lewis, Major

1929	The Murder of an Old Man
1931	The Strange Death of Martin Green
	apa The Murder on the Sixth Hole

P: Bruce, Jean
Please see: Brochet, Jean Alexandre

A: Bryce, Mrs. Charles
SC: Mr. Gimblet

1914	Mrs. Vanderstein's Jewels
1915	The Ashiel Mystery

A: Buchanan, Betty Joan
P: Shepherd, Joan
SC: Jolivet, Insp.

1953	The Girl on the Left Bank
1956	Tender is the Knife

A: Buchanan, Eileen-Marie
P: Curzon, Clare
   SC: Mike Yeadings, Supt. and Angus Mott, Sgt.

    1983   I Give You Five Days
    1984   Masks and Faces

P: Petrie, Rhona
   SC: Dr. Nassim Pride

    1967   Foreign Bodies
    1969   Despatch of a Dove

   SC: Marcus MacLurg, Insp.

    1963   Death in Deakins Wood
    1964   Murder by Precedent
    1965   Running Deep
    1966   Dead Loss
    1968   MacLurg goes West

A: Budlong, Ware Torrey
P: Crosby, Lee
   SC: Eric Hazard

    1938   Terror by Night
    1941   Too Many Doors
           apa Doors to Death

A: Burger, Rosaylmer
P: Wallace, C. H.
   SC: Steve Ramsay

    1965   Crashlanding in the Congo
    1966   Highflight to Hell
    1966   Tailwind to Danger
    1967   E.T.A. for Death

A: Burger, Rosaylmer w/Julia Perceval
P: Paull, Jessica
   SC: Tracy Larrimore and Mike Thompson

    1968   Destination: Terror

Burger, Rosaylmer w/Julia Perceval (cont.)

 1968 Passport to Danger
 1969 Rendezvous With Death

A: **Burnham, Helen**
 SC: One Week Wimble

 1931 The Murder of Lalla Lee
 1932 The Telltale Telegram

A: **Burrows, Julie**
 SC: Bowman, Supt.

 1970 No Need for Violence
 1973 Like an Evening Gone

P: **Burton, Anne**
 Please see: Bowen-Judd, Sara Hutton

A: **Butler, Gwendoline**
 SC: John Coffin, Insp.

 1957 Dead in a Row
 1958 The Dull Head
 1958 The Murdering Kind
 1960 Death Lives Next Door
    apa Dine and Be Dead
 1961 Make Me a Murderer
 1962 Coffin in Oxford
 1963 Coffin Waiting
 1963 Coffin for Baby
 1964 Coffin in Malta
 1966 A Nameless Coffin
 1968 Coffin Following
 1969 Coffin's Dark Number
 1970 A Coffin From the Past
 1973 A Coffin for Pandora
    apa Olivia
 1974 A Coffin for the Canary
    apa Sarsen Place
 1986 A Coffin on the Water

Butler, Gwendoline (cont.)

P: Melville, Jennie
    SC: Charmian Daniels, WPC   (see pg. 54)

    1962   Come Home and Be Killed
    1963   Burning is a Substitute for Loving
    1964   Murderers' Houses
    1965   There Lies Your Love
    1966   Nell Alone
    1967   A Different Kind of Summer
    1970   A New Kind of Killer, An Old Kind of Death
           apa A New Kind of Killer
    1981   Murder Has a Pretty Face

A: Butterworth, Michael
P: Kemp, Sarah
    SC: Dr. Tina May

    1984   No Escape
    1986   The Lure of Sweet Death
    1987   What Dread Hand

A: Byfield, Barbara Ninde
    SC: Father Simon Bede and Helen Bullock
    (see pp. 90, 197)

    1976   Forever Wilt Thou Die
    1977   A Harder Thing Than Triumph
    1979   A Parcel of Their Fortunes

P: Byfield, Barbara Ninde and Frank L. Tedeschi
    Please see: Byfield, Barbara Ninde w/Frank L. Tedeschi

A: Byfield, Barbara Ninde w/Frank L. Tedeschi
P: Byfield, Barbara Ninde and Frank L. Tedeschi
    SC: Father Simon Bede and Helen Bullock

    1975   Solemn High Murder

C

A: Cameron, Evelyn
   SC: Jack Thompson, Sheriff

   1939   Dead Man's Shoes
   1940   Malice Domestic

A: Campbell, Alice
   SC: Headcorn, Insp.

   1937   Death Framed in Silver
   1940   They Hunted a Fox
   1941   No Murder of Mine
           apa The Borrowed Cottage
   1946   The Cockroach Sings
           apa With Bated Breath
   1948   The Bloodstained Toy

   SC: Tommy Rostetter

   1931   The Click of the Gate
   1934   Desire to Kill
   1938   Flying Blind
   1948   The Bloodstained Toy

A: Campbell, Harriette (Russell)
   SC: Simon Brade   (see pg. 189)

   1936   The String Glove Mystery
   1937   The Porcelain Fish Mystery
           apa The Porcelain Fish
   1938   The Moor Fires Mystery
   1940   Three Names for Murder
   1941   Murder Set to Music
   1943   Magic Makes Murder
   1946   Crime in Crystal

P: Candy, Edward
   Please see: Neville, Barbara Alison

P: Cannan, Joanna
   Please see: Pullein-Thompson, Joanna M. C.

A: Carlon, Patricia
SC: Jefferson Shields

1970   Death By Demonstration
1970   The Souvenir

A: Carlson, P(atricia) M.
SC: Maggie Ryan

1985   Audition for Murder
1985   Murder is Academic
1986   Murder is Pathological
1987   Murder Unrenovated

P: Carnac, Carol
Please see: Rivett, Edith Caroline

P: Castle, Jayne
Please see: Krentz, Jayne

P: Caudwell, Sarah
Please see: Cockburn, Sarah

P: Challis, Mary
Please see: Bowen-Judd, Sara Hutton

A: Chanslor, (Marjorie) Torrey
SC: Lutie and Amanda Beagle

1940   Our First Murder
1941   Our Second Murder

A: Chetwynd, Bridget
SC: Petunia Best and Max Frend

1951   Death Has Ten Thousand Doors
1952   Rubies, Emeralds and Diamonds

A: Child, Nellise
SC: Jeremiah Irish

1933   Murder Comes Home
1934   The Diamond Ransom Murders

P: Chipperfield, Robert O.
Please see: Ostrander, Isabel

A: Christie, Agatha
SC: Battle, Supt.

	1925	The Secret of Chimneys
	1929	The Seven Dials Mystery
	1936	Cards on the Table
	1939	Murder is Easy
		apa Easy to Kill
	1944	Towards Zero

SC: Harley Quin

SS	1930	The Mysterious Mr. Quin
SS	1950	Three Blind Mice
		apa The Mousetrap

SC: Hercule Poirot   (see pg. 205)

	1920	The Mysterious Affair at Styles
	1923	Murder on the Links
SS	1924	Poirot Investigates
	1926	The Murder of Roger Ackroyd
	1927	The Big Four
	1928	The Mystery of the Blue Train
	1932	Peril at End House
	1933	Lord Edgware Dies
		apa Thirteen at Dinner
	1934	Murder on the Orient Express
		apa Murder in the Calais Coach
	1934	Murder in Three Acts
		apa Three-Act Tragedy
	1935	Death in the Air
		apa Death in the Clouds
	1936	The ABC Murders
	1936	Cards on the Table
	1936	Murder in Mesopotamia
	1937	Dumb Witness
		apa Poirot Loses a Client
	1937	Death on the Nile

Christie, Agatha (cont.)

SS	1937	Murder in the Mews
		apa Dead Man's Mirror and Other Stories
	1938	Appointment with Death
	1938	Hercule Poirot's Christmas
		apa Murder for Christmas
		apa A Holiday for Murder
	1940	Sad Cypress
	1940	One, Two, Buckle My Shoe
		apa An Overdose of Death
		apa The Patriotic Murders
	1941	Evil Under the Sun
	1942	Murder in Retrospect
		apa Five Little Pigs
SS	1943	Problem at Pollensa Bay and Christmas Adventure
SS	1943	Poirot On Holiday
SS	1943	Poirot and the Regatta Mystery
SS	1944	The Veiled Lady and the Mystery of the Baghdad Chest
	1946	The Hollow
		apa Murder After Hours
SS	1946	Poirot Knows the Murderer
SS	1946	Poirot Lends a Hand
SS	1947	The Labours of Hercules
	1948	Taken at the Flood
		apa There is a Tide
SS	1950	Three Blind Mice
		apa The Mousetrap
	1952	Mrs. McGinty's Dead
		apa Blood Will Tell
	1953	After the Funeral
		apa Murder at the Gallop
		apa Funerals are Fatal
	1955	Hickory Dickory Death
		apa Hickory Dickory Dock
	1956	Dead Man's Folly
	1959	Cat Among the Pigeons
SS	1960	The Adventure of the Christmas Pudding
SS	1961	Double Sin and Other Stories
	1963	The Clocks
	1966	Third Girl
	1969	Hallowe'en Party

Christie, Agatha (cont.)

	1972	Elephants Can Remember
SS	1974	Poirot's Early Cases
		apa Hercule Poirot's Early Cases
	1975	Curtain

SC: Jane Marple   (see pg. 249)

	1930	The Murder at the Vicarage
SS	1932	The Thirteen Problems
		apa The Tuesday Club Murders
SS	1940	The Mystery of the Blue Geranium and Other Tuesday Club Murders
	1942	The Body in the Library
	1942	The Moving Finger
	1950	A Murder is Announced
SS	1950	Three Blind Mice
		apa The Mousetrap
	1952	They Do It With Mirrors
		apa Murder With Mirrors
	1953	A Pocket Full of Rye
	1957	4.50 from Paddington
		apa Murder, She Said
		apa What Mrs. McGillicuddy Saw!
SS	1960	The Adventure of the Christmas Pudding
SS	1961	Double Sin and Other Stories
	1962	The Mirror Crack'd from Side to Side
		apa The Mirror Crack'd
	1964	A Caribbean Mystery
	1965	At Bertram's Hotel
SS	1966	Thirteen Clues for Miss Marple
	1971	Nemesis
SS	1979	Sleeping Murder
SS	1979	Miss Marple's Final Case and Two Other Stories

SC: Parker Pyne   (see pg. 249)

| SS | 1934 | Parker Pyne Investigates |
| | | *apa* Mr. Parker Pyne: Detective |

SC: Race, Col.

| | 1924 | The Man in the Brown Suit |

Christie, Agatha (cont.)

1936	Cards on the Table
1937	Death on the Nile
1945	Remembered Death
	apa Sparkling Cyanide

SC: Tommy and Tuppence Beresford   (see pg. 209)

	1922	The Secret Adversary
SS	1929	Partners in Crime
		apa The Sunningdale Mystery
	1941	N or M?
	1968	By the Pricking of My Thumbs
	1973	Postern of Fate

A: Christopher, Laura Kim
SC: Bosco of the Yard, Insp.

1974	Insp. Bosco and the Cat Burglar
1976	Insp. Bosco Spots the Crime
1977	Insp. Bosco and Lady Indiana

P: Clandon, Henrietta
Please see: Vahey, John G. H.

A: Clarke, Anna
SC: Paula Glenning

1985	Last Judgment
1986	Cabin 3033
1986	The Mystery Lady
1987	Last Seen in London

JN: Clements, Colin
Please see: Ryerson, Florence w/Colin Clements

A: Clements, E(ileen) H(elen)
SC: Alister Woodhead

1939	Let Him Die
1943	Cherry Harvest
1945	Berry Green
1949	Weathercock

Clements, E(ileen) H(elen) (cont.)

1955   Chair-Lift
1955   Discord in the Air
1956   The Other Island
1957   Back in Daylight
1958   Uncommon Cold
1959   High Tension
1960   Honey for the Marshal
1961   A Note of Enchantment
1963   Let or Hindrance

A: Cockburn, Sarah
P: Caudwell, Sarah
    SC: Julia Larwood   (see pg. 145)

1981   Thus Was Adonis Murdered
1984   The Shortest Way to Hades

A: Cody, Liza
    SC: Anna Lee   (see pg. 214)

1980   Dupe
1982   Bad Company
1985   Stalker
1985   Head Case
1987   Under Contract

P: Coffin, Geoffrey
    Please see: Brawner, Helen w/Francis Van Wyck Mason

A: Cohen, Anthea
    SC: Nurse Carmichael

1984   Angel Without Mercy
1984   Angel of Vengeance
1985   Angel of Death
1985   Guardian Angel

A: Cohen, Susan Handler
P: St. Clair, Elizabeth
    SC: Marilyn Ambers

1978   Murder in the Act

Cohen, Susan Handler (cont.)

    1979   The Sandcastle Murders
    1980   Trek or Treat

A: Coker, Carolyn
   SC: Andrea Perkins

    1984   The Other David
    1986   The Vines of Ferrara
    1987   The Hand of the Lion

A: Colburn, Laura
   SC: Carol Gates

    1979   Death Through the Mill
    1979   Death in a Small World
    1979   Death of a Prima Donna

JN: Cole, George Douglas Howard
   Please see: Cole, Margaret Isabel Postgate
     w/George Douglas Howard

P: Cole, Margaret and G. D. H.
   Please see: Cole, Margaret Isabel Postgate
     w/George Douglas Howard

A: Cole, Margaret Isabel Postgate
    w/George Douglas Howard
P: Cole, Margaret and G. D. H.
   SC: Everard Blatchington

    1926   The Blatchington Tangle
    1930   Burglars in Bucks
          apa The Berkshire Mystery
    1934   Death in the Quarry
    1935   Scandal at School
          apa The Sleeping Death

   SC: Henry Wilson, Supt.

    1923   The Brooklyn Murders
    1925   Death of a Millionaire

Cole, Margaret Isabel Postgate
w/George Douglas Howard (cont.)

	1926	The Blatchington Tangle
SS	1928	Superintendent Wilson's Holiday
	1928	The Man From the River
	1929	Poison in the Garden Suburb
		apa Poison in a Garden Suburb
	1930	Burglars in Bucks
		apa The Berkshire Mystery
	1930	Corpse in Canonicals
		apa The Corpse in the Constable's Garden
	1931	The Great Southern Mystery
		apa The Walking Corpse
	1931	Dead Man's Watch
	1933	End of an Ancient Mariner
	1934	Death in the Quarry
	1935	Dr. Tancred Begins; or, The Pendexter Saga, First Canto
	1935	Big Business Murder
	1936	Last Will and Testament; or, The Pendexter Saga, Second (and last) Canto
	1936	The Brothers Sackville
	1937	The Missing Aunt
	1938	Off With Her Head!
	1939	Greek Tragedy
	1939	Double Blackmail
	1940	The Murder at the Munition Works
	1940	Counterpoint Murder
SS	1940	Wilson and Some Others
	1941	Knife in the Dark
	1942	Toper's End

SC: Mrs. Elizabeth Warrender

SS	1938	Mrs. Warrender's Profession
	1941	Knife in the Dark

JN: Coles, Cyril Henry
Please see: Manning, Adelaide Frances Oke
w/Cyril Henry Coles

P: Coles, Manning
Please see: Manning, Adelaide Frances Oke
w/Cyril Henry Coles

A: Collins, Michelle
SC: Megan Marshall

1979 Murder at Willow Run
1980 Premiere at Willow Run

A: Colter, Eli(zabeth)
SC: Pat Campbell

1946 The Gull Cove Murders
1947 Cheer for the Dead

A: Colver, Anne
P: Harris, Colver
SC: Timothy Fowler

1933 Hide and Go Seek
1936 Going to St. Ives
1938 Murder in Amber
apa Murder by Proxy

A: Cook, Petronelle Marguerite Mary
P: Arnold, Margot
SC: Dr. Penelope Spring
and Sir Tobias Glendower   (see pg. 5)

1979 Exit Actors, Dying
1980 The Cape Cod Caper
1980 Zadok's Treasure
1982 Death on the Dragon's Tongue
1982 Lament for a Lady Laird
1982 Death of a Voodoo Doll
1983 Affairs of State

A: Cooper, (Evelyn) Barbara
SC: Gibbon, Insp.

1964 Target for Malice
1966 Drown Him Deep

A: Cores, Lucy (Michaela)
    SC: Andrew Torrent, Capt.

    1943   Painted for the Kill
    1944   Corpse de Ballet

A: Corne, M(olly)
    SC: Mac McIntyre

    1938   Death at a Masquerade
            apa Death is No Lady
    1938   Death at the Manor
            apa Death Hides a Mask
    1939   A Magnet for Murder
            apa Jealousy Pulls the Trigger

JN: Corrington, John William
    Please see: Corrington, Joyce H. w/John William

P: Corrington, Joyce H. and John William
    Please see: Corrington, Joyce H. w/John William

A: Corrington, Joyce H. w/John William
P: Corrington, Joyce H. and John William
    SC: Rat Trapp, Capt.

    1986   So Small a Carnival
    1987   A Project Named Desire

A: Coulson, Felicity Winifred Carter
** w/John H. A.**
P: Bonett, John and Emery
    SC: Mandrake, Prof. (see pg. 12)

    1949   Dead Lion
    1951   A Banner for Pegasus
            apa Not in the Script
    1959   No Grave for a Lady

    SC: Salvador Borges, Insp.

    1964   Better Dead
            apa Better Off Dead
    1966   The Private Face of Murder

Coulson, Felicity Winifred Carter w/John H. A. (cont.)

    1967   This Side Murder
               apa Murder on the Costa Brava
    1970   The Sound of Murder
    1972   No Time to Kill
    1984   Perish the Thought

JN: Coulson, John H. A.
    Please see: Coulson, Felicity Winifred Carter
    w/John H. A.

A: Cowdroy, Joan
    SC: Gorham, Chief Insp.

    1936   Framed Evidence
    1944   Murder Out of Court

    SC: Li Moh

    1931   Watch Mr. Moh
               apa The Flying Dagger Murder
    1933   Murder of Lydia
    1934   Disappearance
    1936   Murder Unsuspected
    1938   Death Has No Tongue
    1940   Merry-Go-Round

P: Craig, Alisa
    Please see: MacLeod, Charlotte

A: Craig, Georgiana Ann Randolph
P: Lee, Gypsy Rose
    SC: Gypsy Rose Lee

    1941   The G-String Murders
               apa The Strip-Tease Murders
               apa Lady of Burlesque
    1942   Mother Finds a Body

P: Rice, Craig
    SC: Bingo Riggs and Handsome Kusak

    1942   The Sunday Pigeon Murders

Craig, Georgiana Ann Randolph (cont.)

1943	The Thursday Turkey Murders
1958	The April Robin Murders

SC: John J. Malone and The Justuses
   (see pg. 148)

	1939	Eight Faces at Three
		apa Death at Three
	1940	The Corpse Steps Out
	1940	The Wrong Murder
	1941	Trial By Fury
	1941	The Right Murder
	1942	The Big Midget Murders
	1943	Having Wonderful Crime
	1945	The Lucky Stiff
	1948	The Fourth Postman
	1957	Knocked for a Loop
		apa The Double Frame
	1957	My Kingdom for a Hearse
SS	1958	The Name is Malone
SS	1963	People vs. Withers and Malone
	1967	But the Doctor Died

P: Venning, Michael
   SC: Melville Fairr

1942	The Man Who Slept All Day
1943	Murder Through the Looking Glass
1944	Jethro Hammer

A: **Crane, Frances**
   SC: Pat and Jean Abbott   (see pg. 210)

1941	The Turquoise Shop
1942	The Golden Box
1942	The Yellow Violet
1943	The Pink Umbrella
	apa The Pink Umbrella Murder
1943	The Applegreen Cat
1944	The Amethyst Spectacles
1945	The Indigo Necklace
	apa The Indigo Necklace Murders

Crane, Frances (cont.)

1946	The Shocking Pink Hat
1946	The Cinnamon Murder
1947	Murder on the Purple Water
1948	Black Cypress
1949	The Flying Red Horse
1950	The Daffodil Blonde
1951	Murder in Blue Street
	apa Death in the Blue Hour
1951	The Polkadot Murder
1953	Murder in Bright Red
1953	13 White Tulips
1954	The Coral Princess Murders
1955	Death in Lilac Time
1956	The Ultraviolet Widow
1956	Horror on the Ruby X
1958	The Man in Gray
	apa The Gray Stranger
1958	The Buttercup Case
1960	Death-Wish Green
1962	The Amber Eyes
1965	Body Beneath a Mandarin Tree

A: Cranston, Claudia
SC: Clarice Claremont

1934	The Murder on Fifth Avenue
1935	Murder Maritime

P: Crosby Lee
Please see: Budlong, Ware Torrey

P: Cross, Amanda
Please see: Heilbrun, Carolyn G.

A: Crossley, Maude
SC: Guy Bannister

1925	The Forbidden Hour
1931	Crookery Inn

P: Curry, Avon
Please see: Bowden, Jean

A: Curtiss, E(lizabeth) M.
  SC: Dr. Nathaniel Bunce

  1937   Nine Doctors and a Madman
  1939   Dead Dogs Bite

P: Curzon, Clare
  Please see: Buchanan, Eileen-Marie

A: Cushing, E. Louise
  SC: MacKay, Insp.

  1954   Murder Without Regret
  1956   Blood on My Rug
  1957   The Unexpected Corpse

A: Cutter, Leela
  SC: Lettie Winterbottom   (see pg. 176)

  1981   Murder After Teatime
  1983   Who Stole Stonehenge?
  1985   Death of the Party

D

A: Daiger, K(atherine) S.
SC: Everett Anderson, Insp.

1931 Fourth Degree
1934 Murder on Ghost Tree Island

A: Daly, Elizabeth (Theresa)
SC: Henry Gamadge (see pg. 190)

1940 Deadly Nightshade
1940 Unexpected Night
1941 Murders in Volume 2
1942 The House Without the Door
1943 Nothing Can Rescue Me
1943 Evidence of Things Seen
1944 Arrow Pointing Nowhere
     apa Murder Listens In
1944 The Book of the Dead
1945 Any Shape or Form
1946 Somewhere in the House
1946 The Wrong Way Down
     apa Shroud For a Lady
1947 Night Walk
1948 The Book of the Lion
1949 And Dangerous to Know
1950 Death and Letters
1951 The Book of the Crime

P: Dane, Clemence and Helen Simpson
Please see: Ashton, Winifred w/Helen Simpson

A: Darby, Ruth
SC: Peter and Janet Barron

1939 Death Boards the Lazy Lady
1940 Death Conducts a Tour
1941 If This Be Murder
1942 Beauty Sleep
1943 Murder With Orange Blossoms

P: Davey, Jocelyn
Please see: Raphael, Chaim

JN: Davis, Burton
   Please see: Davis, Clare w/Burton

A: Davis, Clare w/Burton
P: Saunders, Lawrence
   SC: Wylie King and Nels Lundberg

   1931   The Columnist Murder
   1933   The Devil's Den

A: Davis, Dorothy Salisbury
   SC: Jasper Tully

   1957   Death of an Old Sinner
   1958   A Gentleman Called

   SC: Julie Hayes   (see pg. 260)

   1976   A Death in the Life
   1980   Scarlet Night
   1984   Lullaby of Murder
   1987   The Habit of Fear

   SC: Mrs. Norris

   1957   Death of an Old Sinner
   1958   A Gentleman Called
   1959   Old Sinners Never Die

A: Davis, Julia
P: Draco, F.
   SC: Lord and Lady Tintagel   (see pg. 81)

   1951   The Devil's Church
   1952   Cruise with Death

A: Davis, Lavinia R(iker)
   SC: Nora Hughes and Larry Blaine

   1945   Evidence Unseen
   1947   Taste of Vengeance

A: de la Torre (Bueno) (McCue), Lillian
    SC: Dr. Sam: Johnson

    1946   Dr. Sam: Johnson, Detector
    1960   The Detections of Dr. Sam: Johnson
    1984   The Return of Dr. Sam: Johnson, Detector
    1985   The Exploits of Dr. Sam: Johnson, Detector

A: Dean (Getzin), Amber
    SC: Abbie Harris   (see pg. 253)

    1944   Dead Man's Float
    1945   Chanticleer's Muffled Crow
    1946   Wrap It Up
    1946   Call Me Pandora
             apa The Blonde is Dead
    1948   No Traveller Returns
    1949   Snipe Hunt
    1951   August Incident
    1954   The Devil Threw Dice

A: Dean, Elizabeth
    SC: Emma Marsh and Hank Fairbanks

    1939   Murder is a Collector's Item
    1940   Murder is a Serious Business
    1944   Murder a Mile High

A: Dennison, Dulcie Winifred
P: Gray, Dulcie
    SC: Cardiff, Insp.

    1960   Epitaph for a Dead Actor
    1968   Died in the Red

A: Denniston, Elinore
P: Foley, Rae
    SC: Hiram Potter   (see pg. 77)

    1955   Death and Mr. Potter
             apa The Peacock is a Bird of Prey

Denniston, Elinore (cont.)

1956	The Last Gamble
1957	Run for Your Life
1958	Where is Nancy Bostwick?
	apa Where is Mary Bostwick?
1959	Dangerous to Me
1961	It's Murder, Mr. Potter
	apa Curtain Call
1962	Repent at Leisure
	apa The Deadly Noose
1963	Back Door to Death
	apa Nightmare Honeymoon
1964	Fatal Lady
1965	Call it Accident
1970	A Calculated Risk

SC: John Harland

1949	The Girl from Nowhere
1950	The Hundredth Door
1951	An Ape in Velvet

A: Dentinger, Jane
SC: Jocelyn O'Roarke   (see pg. 100)

1983	Murder on Cue
1984	First Hit of the Season

A: Disney, Doris Miles
SC: David Madden

1956	Unappointed Rounds
	apa The Post Office Case
1958	Black Mail
1961	Mrs. Meeker's Money

SC: Jeff DiMarco

1946	Dark Road
	apa Dead Stop
1949	Family Skeleton
1951	Straw Man
	apa The Case of the Straw Man

Disney, Doris Miles (cont.)

    1955   Trick or Treat
             apa The Halloween Murder
    1957   Method in Madness
             apa Quiet Violence
             apa Too Innocent to Kill
    1959   Did She Fall or Was She Pushed?
    1962   Find the Woman
    1971   The Chandler Policy

    SC: Jim O'Neill

    1943   A Compound for Death
    1945   Murder on a Tangent
    1947   Appointment at Nine
    1950   Fire at Will
    1954   The Last Straw
             apa Driven to Kill

A: Dolson, Hildegarde
    SC: Lucy Ramsdale   (see pg. 254)

    1971   To Spite Her Face
    1973   A Dying Fall
    1975   Please Omit Funeral
    1977   Beauty Sleep

P: Dominic, R. B.
    Please see: Henissart, Martha w/Mary Jane Latsis

P: Draco, F.
    Please see: Davis, Julia

A: Dreher, Sarah
    SC: Stoner McTavish

    1985   Stoner McTavish
    1986   Something Shady

A: DuBois, Theodora M.
    SC: Anne and Jeffrey McNeill (see pg. 117)

    1936   Armed With a New Terror

DuBois, Theodora M. (cont.)

1938   Death Wears a White Coat
1939   Death Dines Out
1939   Death Tears a Comic Strip
1940   Death Comes to Tea
1941   The McNeills Chase a Ghost
1941   Death is Late to Lunch
1942   The Body Goes Round and Round
1943   The Wild Duck Murders
1944   The Case of the Perfumed Mouse
1945   Death Sails in a High Wind
1946   Murder Strikes an Atomic Unit
1947   The Footsteps
1948   The Devil and Destiny
1948   The Face of Hate
1949   It's Raining Violence
     apa Money, Murder and the McNeills
1951   Fowl Play
1952   The Cavalier's Corpse
1954   Seeing Red

A: Duke, Madelaine
SC: Dr. Norah North

1975   Death of a Holy Murderer
1976   Death at the Wedding
1978   Death of a Dandie Dinmont

A: Dunlap, Susan
SC: Jill Smith, Det.   (see pg. 32)

1984   Karma
1984   As a Favor
1985   Not Exactly a Brahmin
1987   Too Close to the Edge
1987   A Dinner to Die For

SC: Vejay Haskell   (see pg. 269)

1984   An Equal Opportunity Death
1985   The Bohemian Connection
1986   The Last Annual Slugfest

A: Dunnett, Dorothy (Halliday)
SC: Johnson Johnson   (see pg. 199)

1968	Dolly and the Singing Bird
	apa The Photogenic Soprano
1970	Dolly and the Cookie Bird
	apa Murder in the Round
1971	Dolly and the Doctor Bird
	apa Match for a Murderer
1973	Dolly and the Starry Bird
	apa Murder in Focus
1976	Dolly and the Nanny Bird
1984	Dolly and the Bird of Paradise

A: Durham, Mary
SC: York, Insp.

1945	Hate is My Livery
1945	Why Pick on Pickles?
1946	Keeps Death His Court
1947	Crime Insoluble
1948	Murder by Multiplication

E

A: Eades, M(aude) L.
SC: Winston Barrows

1925   The Crown Swindle
1932   The Torrington Square Mystery

A: Eberhart, Mignon (Good)
SC: Sarah Keate   (see pg. 114)

1942   Wolf in Man's Clothing
1954   Man Missing

SC: Sarah Keate and Lance O'Leary   (see pg. 114)

1929   The Patient in Room 18
1930   The Mystery of Hunting's End
1930   While the Patient Slept
1931   From this Dark Stairway
1932   Murder by an Aristocrat
       apa Murder of My Patient

SC: Susan Dare   (see pg. 168)

SS   1934   The Cases of Susan Dare

JN: Edington, Arlo Channing
Please see: Edington, Carmen Ballen w/Arlo Channing

A: Edington, Carmen Ballen w/Arlo Channing
P: Edingtons, The
SC: Smith, Capt.

1929   The Studio Murder Mystery
1930   The House of the Vanishing Goblets
       apa Murder to Music
1931   The Monk's Hood Murders

P: Edingtons, The
Please see: Edington, Carmen Ballen w/Arlo Channing

A: Edmiston, Helen Jean Mary
P: Robertson, Helen
    SC: Lathom Dynes, Insp.

    1956   Venice of the Black Sea
    1957   The Crystal-Gazers
    1960   The Chinese Goose
           apa Swan Song

P: Egan, Lesley
    Please see: Linington, Elizabeth

A: Eiker, Mathilde
P: Evermay, March
    SC: Glover, Insp.

    1938   They Talked of Poison
    1940   This Death Was Murder

A: Ellery, Jan
    SC: Adrienne Bishop

    1979   The Last Set
    1980   High Strung

P: Erskine, Margaret
    Please see: Williams, Margaret Wetherby

JN: Eustace, Robert
    Please see: Meade (Smith), Elizabeth Thomasina
      w/Robert Eustace

A: Evans, Julie Rendel
P: Hobson, Polly
    SC: Basil, Insp.

    1964   Murder Won't Out
    1968   Titty's Dead
           apa A Terrible Thing Has Happened to
              Miss Dupont
    1970   The Three Graces

P: Evermay, March
  Please see: Eiker, Mathilde

A: Eyles, (M.) Leonora (P.)
  SC: Dr. Joan Marvin

  1936   Death of a Dog
  1936   They Wanted Him Dead!

F

A: Farrer, Katherine
   SC: Richard Ringwood, Insp.

   1952   The Missing Link
   1954   The Cretan Counterfeit
   1957   Gownsman's Gallows

A: Feagles, Anita Macrae
P: Macrae, Travis
   SC: Jim and Kate Harris

   1960   Death in View
   1961   Twenty Per Cent
          apa Multiple Murder

A: Fearon, Diana
   SC: Arabella Frant

   1959   Death Before Breakfast
   1960   Murder-On-Thames

A: Fenisong, Ruth
   SC: Gridley Nelson, Capt.

   1942   Murder Needs a Face
   1942   Murder Needs a Name
   1943   Murder Runs a Fever
   1943   The Butler Died in Brooklyn
   1950   Grim Rehearsal
   1951   Dead Yesterday
   1952   Deadlock
   1953   The Wench is Dead
   1954   Miscast for Murder
          apa Too Lovely to Live
   1956   Bite the Hand
          apa The Blackmailer
   1958   Death of the Party
   1960   But Not Forgotten
          apa Sinister Assignment
   1962   Dead Weight

P: Ferrars, E. X.
Please see: Brown, Morna Doris McTavert

A: Fetta, Emma Lou
SC: Lyle Curtis and Susan Yates

1939   Murder in Style
1940   Murder on the Face of It

JN: Fickling, Forrest
Please see: Fickling, Gloria w/Forrest

P: Fickling, G. G.
Please see: Fickling, Gloria w/Forrest

A: Fickling, Gloria w/Forrest
P: Fickling, G. G.
SC: Erik March

1962   Naughty But Dead
1963   The Case of the Radioactive Redhead
1964   The Crazy Mixed-Up Nude
1971   Stiff as a Broad

SC: Honey West

1957   This Girl for Hire
1958   Girl on the Loose
1958   A Gun for Honey
1959   Honey in the Flesh
1959   Girl on the Prowl
1960   Dig a Dead Doll
1960   Kiss for a Killer
1961   Blood and Honey
1964   Bombshell
1971   Honey on Her Tail
1971   Stiff as a Broad

A: Field, Katherine
SC: Ross Paterson, Det. Insp.

1941   Disappearance of a Niece
1942   The Two-Five to Mardon

Field, Katherine (cont.)

    1944   Murder to Follow

A: Field, Moira
    SC: Flower, Det. Insp.

    1950   Foreign Body
    1951   Gunpowder Treason and Plot

P: Fielding, A. E.
    Please see: Fielding, Dorothy

A: Fielding, Dorothy
P: Fielding, A. E.
    SC: Pointer, Insp.

    1924   The Eames-Erskine Case
    1925   The Charteris Mystery
    1926   The Footsteps that Stopped
    1927   The Clifford Affair
           apa The Clifford Mystery
    1928   The Cluny Problem
    1928   The Net Around Joan Ingilby
    1929   The Mysterious Partner
    1929   Murder at the Nook
    1930   The Craig Poisoning Mystery
    1930   The Wedding-Chest Mystery
    1931   The Upfold Farm Mystery
    1932   Death of John Tait
    1932   The Westwood Mystery
    1933   The Tall House Mystery
    1934   The Cautley Conundrum
           apa The Cautley Mystery
    1934   The Paper-Chase
           apa The Paper-Chase Mystery
    1935   The Case of the Missing Diary
    1935   Tragedy at Beechcroft
    1936   The Case of the Two Pearl Necklaces
    1936   Mystery at the Rectory
    1937   Black Cats are Lucky
    1937   Scarecrow
    1944   Pointer to Crime

A: Filgate, C. Macartney
SC: Charlotte Eliot

1979   Bravo Charlie
       apa Runway to Death
1979   Delta November

P: Fitt, Mary
Please see: Freeman, Kathleen

A: Fleming, Joan (Margaret)
SC: Nuri Iskirlak

1962   When I Grow Rich
1965   Nothing is the Number When You Die

A: Flower, Pat(ricia)
SC: Swinton, Insp.

1958   Wax Flowers for Gloria
1959   Goodbye, Sweet William
1960   A Wreath of Water-Lilies
1961   One Rose Less
1962   Hell for Heather
1963   Term of Terror
1966   Fiends of the Family

P: Foley, Rae
Please see: Denniston, Elinore

A: Foote-Smith, Elizabeth
SC: Will Woodfield

1976   A Gentle Albatross
1977   Never Say Die

A: Forbes, DeLoris
P: Wells, Tobias
SC: Knute Severson   (see pg. 25)

1966   A Matter of Love and Death
1967   Dead By the Light of the Moon
1967   What Should You Know of Dying?
1968   Murder Most Fouled Up

Forbes, DeLoris (cont.)

1969	The Young Can Die Protesting
1969	Die Quickly, Dear Mother
1970	Dinky Died
1971	The Foo Dog
	apa The Lotus Affair
1971	What to Do Until the Undertaker Comes
1972	A Die in the Country
1972	How to Kill a Man
1973	Brenda's Murder
1974	Have Mercy Upon Us
1975	Hark, Hark, the Watchdogs Bark
1977	A Creature Was Stirring

P: Ford, Leslie
Please see: Brown, Zenith Jones

P: Fox, David
Please see: Ostrander, Isabel

A: Fraser, Anthea
SC: David Webb, Chief Insp.

1986	A Necessary End
1986	A Shroud for Delilah
1987	Pretty Maids All in a Row

A: Fraser, Antonia
SC: Jemima Shore   (see pg. 105)

	1977	Quiet as a Nun
	1978	The Wild Island
	1981	A Splash of Red
	1982	Cool Repentance
SS	1983	Jemima Shore Investigates
	1985	Oxford Blood
SS	1986	Jemima Shore's First Cases and Other Stories

A: Freeman, Kathleen
P: Fitt, Mary
SC: Mallett, Supt. Insp.   (see pg. 53)

1938	Sky-Rocket

Freeman, Kathleen (cont.)

	1938	Expected Death
	1939	Death at Dancing Stones
	1940	Death Starts a Rumor
	1941	Death on Heron's Mere
		apa Death Finds a Target
	1941	Death and Mary Dazill
		apa Aftermath of Murder
	1942	Requiem for Robert
	1944	Clues to Christabel
	1946	Death and the Pleasant Voices
	1947	A Fine and Private Place
	1948	Death and the Bright Day
	1949	The Banquet Ceases
	1951	An Ill Wind
	1952	Death and the Shortest Day
	1954	Love From Elizabeth
SS	1954	The Man Who Shot Birds and Other Tales
	1956	Sweet Poison
	1959	Mizmaze

A: Freeman, Lucy
SC: Dr. William Ames   (see pg. 124)

1971	The Dream
1973	The Psychiatrist Says Murder
1975	The Case on Cloud Nine

P: Frome, David
Please see: Brown, Zenith Jones

A: Frost, Barbara
SC: Marka de Lancey

1949	The Corpse Said No
1951	The Corpse Died Twice
1955	Innocent Bystander

G

A: Gaines, Audrey
  SC: Chauncey O'Day

  1939   The Old Must Die
  1940   While the Wind Howled
  1942   The Voodoo Goat

  SC: Jeff Strange

  1946   Omit Flowers, Please
  1952   No Crime Like the Present

P: Gaite, Francis
  Please see: Manning, Adelaide Frances Oke
    w/Cyril Henry Coles

P: Gallagher, Gale
  Please see: Scott, Margaret w/William Charles Oursler

A: Gallison, Kate
  SC: Nick Magaracz

  1986   Unbalanced Accounts
  1987   The Death Tape

A: Gardiner, Dorothy
  SC: Moss Magill, Sheriff   (see pg. 66)

  1956   What Crime Is It?
         apa The Case of the Hula Clock
  1958   The Seventh Mourner
  1963   Lion in Wait
         apa Lion? or Murder?

  SC: Mr. Watson

  1933   The Transatlantic Ghost
  1934   A Drink for Mr. Cherry
         apa Mr. Watson Intervenes

A: Gavin, Catherine
   SC: Jacques Brunel

   1976   Traitor's Gate
   1978   None Dare Call It Treason

P: Gayle, Newton
   Please see: Marin, Muna Lee
      w/Maurice C. Guiness

P: Gilbert, Anthony
   Please see: Malleson, Lucy Beatrice

A: Gill, Elizabeth
   SC: Benevenuto Brown

   1931   Strange Holiday
             apa The Crime Coast
   1932   What Dread Hand?
   1933   Crime de Luxe

A: Gilman, Dorothy
   SC: Mrs. Emily Pollifax   (see pg. 227)

   1966   The Unexpected Mrs. Pollifax
             apa Mrs. Pollifax, Spy
   1970   The Amazing Mrs. Pollifax
   1971   The Elusive Mrs. Pollifax
   1973   A Palm for Mrs. Pollifax
   1977   Mrs. Pollifax on Safari
   1984   Mrs. Pollifax on the China Station
   1985   Mrs. Pollifax and the Hong Kong
             Buddha

A: Gilruth, Susan
   SC: Hugh Gordon, Insp. and Liane Crawford

   1951   Sweet Revenge
   1952   Death in Ambush
   1954   Postscript to Penelope
   1956   A Corpse for Charybdis
   1957   To This Favor
   1961   Drown Her Remembrance
   1963   The Snake is Living Yet

P: Giroux, E. X.
Please see: Shannon, Doris

A: Glidden, M(inna) W.
SC: Carey Brent

1937   Death Strikes Home
1937   The Long Island Murders

JN: Gordon, Gordon
Please see: Gordon, Mildred w/Gordon

A: Gordon, Mildred w/Gordon
P: Gordons, The
SC: D. C. Randall (a cat)

1963   Undercover Cat
       apa That Darn Cat
1966   Undercover Cat Prowls Again
1974   Catnapped: The Further Adventures of
          Undercover Cat

SC: Gail and Mitch Mitchell   (see pg. 149)

1969   Night Before the Wedding
1979   Night After the Wedding

SC: John Ripley

1950   FBI Story
1953   Case File: FBI
1957   Captive
1961   Operation Terror
       apa Experiment in Terror
1973   The Informant

P: Gordons, The
Please see: Gordon, Mildred w/Gordon

A: Goulart, Ron
P: Kains, Josephine
SC: Terry Spring

1978   The Devil Mask Mystery

Goulart, Ron (cont.)

1978	The Curse of the Golden Skull
1979	The Whispering Cat Mystery
1979	The Green Lama Mystery
1979	The Witch's Tower Mystery
1980	The Laughing Dragon Mystery

A: Goyder, Margot w/Anne N. G. Joske
P: Neville, Margot
  SC: Grogan, Insp.

1943	Lena Hates Men
	apa Murder in Rockwater
1946	Murder and Gardenias
1948	Murder in a Blue Moon
1949	Murder of a Nymph
1951	Murder Before Marriage
1952	The Seagull Said Murder
1953	Murder of the Well-Beloved
1954	Murder and Poor Jenny
1956	Murder of Olympia
1957	Murder to Welcome Her
1958	The Flame of Murder
1959	Sweet Night for Murder
1960	Confession of Murder
1961	Murder Beyond the Pale
1962	Drop Dead
1963	Come See Me Die
1964	My Bad Boy
1965	Ladies in the Dark
1966	Head on the Sill

A: Grafton, Sue
  SC: Kinsey Millhone   (see pg. 216)

1982	"A" is for Alibi
1985	"B" is for Burglar
1986	"C" is for Corpse
1987	"D" is for Deadbeat

A: Graham, (M.) Winifred (M.)
   SC: Miss Woolfe

   1930   A Wolf of the Evenings
   1930   The Last Laugh
   1931   Wolf-Net

A: Granbeck, Marilyn w/Arthur Moore
P: Hamilton, Adam
   SC: Barrington Hewes-Bradford

   1974   The Zaharan Pursuit
   1974   The Yashar Pursuit
   1974   The Xander Pursuit
   1975   The Wyss Pursuit

A: Grant-Adamson, Leslie
   SC: Rain Morgan   (see pg. 175)

   1985   Death on Widow's Walk
   1986   The Face of Death

P: Gray, Dulcie
   Please see: Dennison, Dulcie Winifred

A: Grayland, (Valerie) Merle (Spanner)
   SC: Hoani Mata

   1962   The Dead Men of Eden
   1963   Night of the Reaper
   1964   The Grave-Digger's Apprentice
   1965   Jest of Darkness

A: Green, Anna Katherine
   SC: Amelia Butterworth and Ebenezer Gryce
      (see pp. 77, 19)

   1897   That Affair Next Door
   1898   Lost Man's Lane: A Second Episode in the Life of
             Amelia Butterworth
   1900   The Circular Study

Green, Anna Katherine (cont.)

    1901   One of My Sons
    1911   Initials Only
    1917   The Mystery of the Hasty Arrow

    SC: Caleb Sweetwater

    1899   Agatha Webb
    1900   The Circular Study
    1906   The Woman in the Alcove
    1910   The House of the Whispering Pines
    1911   Initials Only
    1917   The Mystery of the Hasty Arrow

    SC: Ebenezer Gryce   (see pg. 19)

    1878   The Leavenworth Case: A Lawyer's
           Story
    1880   A Strange Disappearance
    1883   Hand and Ring
    1888   Behind Closed Doors
    1890   A Matter of Millions
SS 1895   The Doctor, His Wife and the Clock
    1897   That Affair Next Door
    1898   Lost Man's Lane: A Second Episode in the
           Life of Amelia Butterworth
    1900   The Circular Study
    1901   One of My Sons
    1911   Initials Only
    1917   The Mystery of the Hasty Arrow

    SC: Violet Strange

SS 1915   The Golden Slipper and Other Problems for
           Violet Strange

A: Green, Edith Piñero
    SC: Dearborn V. Pinch   (see pg. 76)

    1977   Rotten Apples
    1979   Sneaks
    1982   Perfect Fools

P: Green, Glint
Please see: Peterson, Margaret Ann

A: Gresham, Elizabeth
P: Grey, Robin
SC: Jenny Gilette and Hunter Lewis

1945   Puzzle in Porcelain
1947   Puzzle in Pewter
1972   Puzzle in Paisley
1973   Puzzle in Parquet
1973   Puzzle in Patchwork
1973   Puzzle in Parchment

P: Grey, Robin
Please see: Gresham, Elizabeth

A: Grimes, Martha
SC: Richard Jury, Det. Chief Insp.   (see pp. 45, 80)

1981   The Man With A Load of Mischief
1982   The Old Fox Deceiv'd
1983   The Anodyne Necklace
1984   Jerusalem Inn
1984   The Dirty Duck
1985   The Deer Leap
1985   Help the Poor Struggler
1986   I Am the Only Running Footman
1987   The Five Bells and Bladebone

A: Grove, Marjorie
SC: Maxine Reynolds   (see pg. 174)

1978   You'll Die When You Hear This
1978   You'll Die Tomorrow
1978   You'll Die Laughing
1979   You'll Die Darling
1979   You'll Die Today
1979   You'll Die Yesterday
1979   You'll Die Tonight

JN: Guiness, Maurice C.
Please see: Marin, Muna Lee w/Maurice C. Guiness

H

A: **Haddad, C(arolyn) (A.)**
SC: David Haham

1976   Bloody September
1978   Operation Apricot

A: **Hagen, Miriam-Ann**
SC: Hortense Clinton

1947   Plant Me Now
1949   Dig Me Later
1951   Murder—But Natch

P: **Hale, Christopher**
Please see: Stevens, Frances M. R.

P: **Hambledon, Phyllis**
Please see: MacVean, Phyllis

P: **Hamilton, Adam**
Please see: Granbeck, Marilyn w/Arthur Moore

A: **Hamilton, Elaine**
SC: Reynolds, Insp.

1930   Some Unknown Hand
       apa The Westminster Mystery
1931   Murder in the Fog
1932   The Green Death
1932   The Chelsea Mystery
1934   Peril at Midnight
1935   Tragedy in the Dark
1936   The Casino Mystery
1937   Murder Before Tuesday

A: **Hamilton, Henrietta**
SC: Sally and Johnny Heldar

1956   The Two Hundred Ghost
1957   Death at One Below
1959   Answer in the Negative
1959   At Night to Die

A: Hamilton, Nan
    SC: Isamu "Sam Irish" Ohara

    1984   Killer's Rights
    1986   The Shape of Fear

A: Hanshew, Hazel Phillips
    SC: Hamilton Cleek

    1931   The Riddle of the Winged Death
    1932   Murder in the Hotel

P: Hanshew, Mary and Thomas
    SC: Hamilton Cleek

    1920   The Frozen Flame
             apa The Riddle of the Frozen Flame
    1921   The Riddle of the Mysterious Light
    1922   The House of Discord
             apa The Riddle of the Spinning Wheel
    1924   The Amber Junk
             apa The Riddle of the Amber Ship
    1925   The House of the Seven Keys

A: Hanshew, Hazel Phillips w/Mary
P: Hanshew, Thomas
    SC: Hamilton Cleek

    1915   The Riddle of the Night
    1918   The Riddle of the Purple Emperor

JN: Hanshew, Mary
    Please see: Hanshew, Hazel Phillips w/Mary

P: Hanshew, Mary and Thomas
    Please see: Hanshew, Hazel Phillips

P: Hanshew, Thomas
    Please see: Hanshew, Hazel Phillips w/Mary

A: Hanson, Virginia
    SC: Adam Drew and Katherine Cornish

    1938   Death Walks the Post

Hanson, Virginia (cont.)

> 1939   Casual Slaughters
> 1942   Mystery for Mary

A:. Hardwick, Mollie
SC: Doran Fairweather and
Rodney Chelmarsh

> 1986   Malice Domestic
> 1987   Parson's Pleasure

P: Harris, Colver
Please see: Colver, Anne

A: Hart, Carolyn G.
SC: Annie Laurance

> 1987   Death on Demand
> 1987   Design for Murder

A: Haymon, S. T.
SC: Benjamin Jurnet, Det. Insp.

> 1980   Death and the Pregnant Virgin
> 1982   Ritual Murder
> 1984   A Stately Homicide
> 1987   Death of a God

A: Haynes, Annie
SC: Furnival, Insp.

> 1923   The Abbey Court Murder
> 1926   The House in Charlton Crescent
> 1927   The Crow's Inn Tragedy

SC: Stoddart, Insp.

> 1929   Who Killed Charmian Karslake?
> 1929   The Crime at Tattenham Corner
> 1930   The Crystal Beads Murder

A: Head, (Joanna) Lee
SC: Lexey Jane Pelazoni

1976   The Terrarium
1977   The Crystal Clear Case

JN: Hearnden, Beryl
Please see: Balfour, Eva w/Beryl Hearnden

A: Heberden, M(ary) V(iolet)
SC: Desmond Shannon

1939   Death on the Door Mat
1940   Fugitive From Murder
1940   Subscription to Murder
1941   Aces, Eights and Murder
1941   The Lobster Pick Murder
1942   Murder Follows Desmond Shannon
1942   Murder Makes a Racket
1943   Murder Goes Astray
1944   Murder of a Stuffed Man
1945   Vicious Pattern
1947   Drinks on the Victim
1947   They Can't All Be Guilty
1948   The Case of the Eight Brothers
1950   Exit This Way
       apa You'll Fry Tomorrow
1950   That's the Spirit
       apa Ghost's Can't Kill
1952   Tragic Target
1953   Murder Unlimited

SC: Rick Vanner

1946   Murder Cancels All Debts
1949   Engaged to Murder
1951   The Sleeping Witness

P: Leonard, Charles L.
SC: Paul Kilgerrin

1942   The Stolen Squadron

Heberden, M(ary) V(iolet) (cont.)

1942	Deadline for Destruction
1943	The Fanatic of Fez
	apa Assignment to Death
1944	The Secret of the Spa
1945	Expert in Murder
1946	Pursuit in Peru
1947	Search for a Scientist
1948	The Fourth Funeral
1949	Sinister Shelter
1950	Secrets for Sale
1951	Treachery in Trieste

A: Heilbrun, Carolyn G.
P: Cross, Amanda
   SC: Kate Fansler   (see pg. 11)

1964	In the Last Analysis
1967	The James Joyce Murder
1970	Poetic Justice
1971	The Theban Mysteries
1976	The Question of Max
1978	Death in a Tenured Position
	apa Death in the Faculty
1984	Sweet Death, Kind Death
1986	No Word from Winifred

A: Hely (Younger), Elizabeth
   SC: Antoine Cirret

1959	Dominant Third
	apa I'll Be Judge, I'll Be Jury
1960	A Mark of Displeasure

A: Henissart, Martha w/Mary Jane Latsis
P: Dominic, R. B.
   SC: Ben Safford   (see pg. 225)

1968	Murder, Sunny Side Up
1969	Murder in High Place
1971	There is No Justice
	apa Murder Out of Court

Henissart, Martha w/Mary Jane Latsis (cont.)

1974	Epitaph for a Lobbyist
1976	Murder Out of Commission
1980	The Attending Physician
1983	Unexpected Developments
1983	A Flaw in the System

P: Lathen, Emma
   SC: John Putnam Thatcher   (see pg. 131)

1961	Banking on Death
1963	A Place for Murder
1964	Accounting for Murder
1966	Death Shall Overcome
1966	Murder Makes the Wheels Go Round
1967	Murder Against the Grain
1968	Come To Dust
1968	A Stitch in Time
1969	Murder to Go
1969	When in Greece
1970	Pick Up Sticks
1971	The Longer the Thread
1971	Ashes to Ashes
1972	Murder Without Icing
1974	Sweet and Low
1975	By Hook or By Crook
1978	Double, Double, Oil and Trouble
1981	Going for the Gold
1983	Green Grow the Dollars

A: **Hershman, Morris**
P: Bond, Evelyn
   SC: Ira Yedder

1971	Doomway
1972	Dark Sonata
1972	The Devil's Footprints
1972	The Girl from Nowhere

P: **Hervey, Evelyn**
   Please see: Keating, H(enry) R(eymond) F(itzwalter)

A: Hess, Joan
   SC: Claire Malloy

   1986   Murder at the Murder at the
              Mimosa Inn
   1986   Strangled Prose
   1987   Dear Miss Demeanor

A: Heyer, Georgette
   SC: Hannasyde, Supt. and Hemingway, Sgt.
   (see pg. 38)

   1935   Death in the Stocks
              apa Merely Murder
   1936   Behold, Here's Poison
   1937   They Found Him Dead
   1938   A Blunt Instrument
   1939   No Wind of Blame
   1941   Envious Casca
   1951   Duplicate Death
   1953   Detection Unlimited

A: Highsmith, Patricia
   SC: Tom Ripley

   1955   The Talented Mr. Ripley
   1970   Ripley Under Ground
   1974   Ripley's Game
   1980   The Boy Who Followed Ripley
   1985   The Mysterious Mr. Ripley

A: Hill, Katharine
   SC: Lorna Donahue

   1944   Dear Dead Mother-in-Law
   1945   Case for Equity

JN: Hitchens, (Hu)Bert
   Please see: Hitchens, Dolores (Birk) w/(Hu)Bert

P: Hitchens, Bert and Dolores
   Please see: Hitchens, Dolores (Birk) w/(Hu)Bert

A: Hitchens, Dolores (Birk)
SC: Jim Sader

1955   Sleep With Strangers
1960   Sleep With Slander

P: Olsen, D. B.
SC: A. Pennyfeather, Prof.   (see pg. 13)

1945   Bring the Bride a Shroud
1947   Gallows for the Groom
1948   Devious Design
1950   Something About Midnight
1951   Love Me in Death
1952   Enrollment Cancelled
         apa Dead Babes in the Wood

SC: Rachel and Jennifer Murdock   (see pg. 251)

1939   The Cat Saw Murder
1942   The Alarm of the Black Cat
1943   Catspaw for Murder
1943   Cat's Claw
1944   The Cat Wears a Noose
1945   Cat's Don't Smile
1946   Cat's Don't Need Coffins
1948   Cat's Have Tall Shadows
1949   The Cat Wears A Mask
1950   Death Wears Cat's Eyes
1951   The Cat and the Capricorn
1953   The Cat Walk
1956   Death Walks on Cat Feet

SC: Stephen Mayhew, Lt.

1938   The Clue in the Clay
1939   The Cat Saw Murder
1940   The Ticking Heart
1943   Cat's Claw
1943   Catspaw for Murder
1944   The Cat Wears a Noose
1946   Cat's Don't Need Coffins

A: Hitchens, Dolores (Birk) w/(Hu)Bert
P: Hitchens, Bert and Dolores
    SC: Collins and McKechnie

      1955   F.O.B. Murder
      1959   The Man Who Followed
                  Women

    SC: John Farrel

      1957   End of the Line
      1963   The Grudge

P: Hobson, Polly
    Please see: Evans, Julie Rendel

A: Hocking, (Mona) (Naomi) Anne (Messer)
    SC: William Austen, Insp.

      1939   Old Mrs. Fitzgerald
              apa Deadly is the Evil Tongue
      1940   The Wicked Flee
      1941   Miss Milverton
              apa Poison is a Bitter Brew
      1942   One Shall Be Taken
      1943   Nile Green
      1943   Death Loves a Shining Mark
              apa All My Pretty Chickens
      1943   Six Green Bottles
      1945   The Vultures Gather
      1946   Death at the Wedding
      1947   Prussian Blue
              apa The Finishing Touch
      1949   At "The Cedars"
      1950   The Best Laid Plans
      1950   Death Disturbs Mr. Jefferson
      1951   Mediterranean Murder
              apa Killing Kin
      1953   Death Among the Tulips
      1953   The Evil that Men Do
      1954   And No One Wept
      1955   A Reason for Murder
      1955   Poison in Paradise

Hocking, (Mona) (Naomi) Anne (Messer) (cont.)

1956	Murder at Mid-Day
1957	The Simple Way of Poison
1957	Relative Murder
1958	Epitaph for a Nurse
	apa A Victim Must Be Found
1959	Poisoned Chalice
1959	To Cease Upon the Midnight
1960	The Thin-Spun Thread
1961	Candidates for Murder
1962	He Had to Die
1968	Murder Cries Out

A: Hodges, Doris Marjorie
P: Hunt, Charlotte
   SC: Dr. Paul Holton

1967	The Gilded Sarcophagus
1968	The Cup of Thanatos
1970	The Lotus Vellum
1972	The Thirteenth Treasure
1974	A Touch of Myrrh
1975	Chambered Tomb

P: Holden, Genevieve
   Please see: Pou, Genevieve Long

A: Holding, Elisabeth Sanxay
   SC: Levy, Lt.

1940	Who's Afraid?
1947	The Blank Wall
1951	Too Many Bottles
	apa The Party Was the Pay-Off
1953	Widow's Mite

A: Holland, Isabelle
   SC: Rev. Claire Aldington

1985	Flight of the Archangel
1985	A Death at St. Anselm's
1986	A Lover Scorned

A: Holley, Helen
SC: Tessie Venable

1946   Blood on the Beach
1947   Dead Run

A: Hood, Margaret Page
SC: Gil Donan

1954   The Silent Women
1956   The Scarlet Thread
1957   In the Dark Night
       apa The Murders on Fox Island
1959   The Bell on Lonely
1961   Drown the Wind

A: Hughes, Dorothy B(elle)
SC: Tobin, Insp.   (see pg. 22)

1940   The So Blue Marble
1940   The Cross-Eyed Bear
       apa The Cross-Eyed Bear Murders
1942   The Fallen Sparrow

A: Hultman, Helen Joan
SC: Tim Asher

1929   Find the Woman
1931   Death at Windward Hill

P: Hunt, Charlotte
Please see: Hodges, Doris Marjorie

A: Hurt, Freda (Mary) (E.)
SC: Herbert Broom, Insp.

1960   Death By Bequest
1961   Sweet Death
1962   Acquainted With Murder
1963   Death and the Bridegroom
1964   Cold and Unhonoured
1966   A Cause for Malice

A: Huxley, Elspeth
    SC: Paul Vachell, Supt.

    1937   Murder at Government House
    1938   Murder on Safari
    1939   Death of an Aryan
          apa The African Poison Murders

I, J

A: Ingate, Mary
SC: Ann Hales

1974 The Sound of the Weir
apa Remembrance of Miranda
1977 This Water Laps Gently

P: Ironside, John
Please see: Tait, Euphemia Margaret

A: Irwin, Inez H.
SC: Patrick O'Brien

1935 Murder Masquerade
apa Murder in Fancy Dress
1936 The Poison Cross Mystery
1938 A Body Rolled Downstairs
1941 Many Murders
1946 The Woman Swore Revenge

A: James, P(hyllis) D(orothy)
SC: Adam Dalgliesh, Supt.   (see pg. 43)

1962 Cover Her Face
1963 A Mind to Murder
1967 Unnatural Causes
1971 Shroud for a Nightingale
1972 An Unsuitable Job for a Woman
1975 The Black Tower
1977 Death of an Expert Witness
1986 A Taste For Death

SC: Cordelia Gray   (see pg. 211)

1972 An Unsuitable Job for a Woman
1982 The Skull Beneath the Skin

A: Johns, Veronica P(arker)
    SC: Agatha Welch

      1940   Hush, Gabriel!
      1941   Shady Doings

    SC: Webster Flagg

      1953   Murder By the Day
      1958   Servant's Problem

A: Johnston, Madeleine
    SC: Noah Bradshaw

      1938   Death Casts a Lure
      1938   Comets Have Long Tails

A: Jones, Jennifer
    SC: Daisy Jane Mott

      1937   Murder-on-Hudson
      1939   Dirge for a Dog
      1939   Murder al Fresco

JN: Joske, Anne N. G.
    Please see: Goyder, Margot w/Anne N. G. Joske

K

P: Kains, Josephine
Please see: Goulart, Ron

A: Kallen, Lucille
SC: C. B. Greenfield (see pg. 163)

1979   Introducing C. B. Greenfield
1980   C. B. Greenfield: The Tanglewood Murder
1982   C. B. Greenfield: No Lady in the House
1984   C. B. Greenfield: The Piano Bird
1986   C. B. Greenfield: A Little Madness

JN: Karni, Michaela
Please see: Bernell, Sue w/Michaela Karni

A: Keate, E(dith) M(urray)
SC: Margetson, Sgt.

1930   The Wild-Cat Scheme
1931   The Jackanapes Jacket
1936   Demon of the Air
1937   Demon Again

A: Keating, H(enry) R(eymond) F(itzwalter)
P: Hervey, Evelyn
SC: Miss Harriet Unwin

1983   The Governess
1986   Into the Valley of Death

A: Kellerman, Faye
SC: Rina Lazarus

1986   Ritual Bath
1987   Sacred and Profane

A: Kelly, Mary
SC: Brett Nightingale, Insp.

1956   A Cold Coming
1957   Dead Man's Riddle
1958   The Christmas Egg

Kelly, Mary (cont.)

    SC: Nicholson

    1961   The Spoilt Kill
    1962   Due to a Death
            apa The Dead of Summer

A: Kelly, Susan
    SC: Liz Connors   (see pg. 177)

    1985   The Gemini Man
    1986   The Summertime Soldiers

A: Kelsey, Vera
    SC: Diego, Lt.

    1941   The Owl Sang Three Times
    1943   Satan Has Six Fingers

P: Kemp, Sarah
    Please see: Butterworth, Michael

A: Kenney, Susan
    SC: Roz Howard

    1983   Garden of Malice
    1985   Graves in Academe

A: Kilpatrick, Florence
    SC: Elizabeth

    1946   Elizabeth the Sleuth
    1949   Elizabeth Finds the Body

A: Knight, Kathleen Moore
    SC: Elisha Macomber

    1935   Death Blew Out the Match
    1936   The Wheel that Turned
            apa Murder Greets Jean Holton
    1936   The Clue of the Poor Man's
            Shilling
            apa The Poor Man's Shilling

Knight, Kathleen Moore (cont.)

1937	Seven Were Veiled
	apa Death Wears a Bridal Veil
	apa Seven Were Suspect
1938	Acts of Black Night
1938	The Tainted Token
	apa The Case of the Tainted Token
1940	Death Came Dancing
1946	The Trouble at Turkey Hill
1947	Footbridge to Death
1948	Bait for Murder
1949	The Bass Derby Murder
1952	Death Goes to A Reunion
1952	Valse Macabre
1953	Three of Diamonds
1953	Akin to Murder
1959	Beauty is a Beast

SC: Margot Blair

1940	Rendezvous With the Past
1941	Exit a Star
1942	Terror By Twilight
1944	Design in Diamonds

A: Krentz, Jayne
P: Castle, Jayne
   SC: Guinevere Jones

1986	The Desperate Game
1986	The Chilling Deception
1987	The Sinister Touch

P: Kruger, Paul
   Please see: Sebenthal, Roberta E.

L

A: Labus, Martha Haake
P: McCormick, Claire
    SC: John Waltz

    1982   Resume for Murder
    1983   The Club Paradis Murders

P: Laing, Patrick
    Please see: Long, Amelia Reynolds

JN: Lambert, Dudley
    Please see: Lambert, Rosa w/Dudley

P: Lambert, Rosa and Dudley
    Please see: Lambert, Rosa w/Dudley

A: Lambert, Rosa w/Dudley
P: Lambert, Rosa and Dudley
    SC: Glyn Morgan

    1928   Monsieur Faux-Pas
            apa Death Goes to Brussels
    1930   The Mediterranean Murder
    1935   The Mystery of the Golden Wings
    1938   Crime in Quarantine

A: Lane, (Margaret) Gret
    SC: Hook, Insp.

    1937   Three Died that Night
    1938   The Red Mirror Mystery

    SC: John Barrin

    1930   The Curlew Coombe Mystery
    1932   The Hotel Cremona Mystery
    1933   The Unknown Enemy
    1939   Death Visits the Summer-House
    1940   Death in Mermaid Lane
    1942   Death Prowls the Cove
    1943   The Guest With the Scythe

Lane, (Margaret) Gret (cont.)

SC: Kate Marsh

1930   The Curlew Coombe Mystery
1931   The Lantern House Affair
1932   The Hotel Cremona Mystery
1933   The Unknown Enemy
1939   Death Visits the Summer-House
1940   Death in Mermaid Lane
1942   Death Prowls the Cove
1943   The Guest With the Scythe

P: Lang, Maria
Please see: Lange, Dagmar

A: Lange, Dagmar
P: Lang, Maria
SC: Christer Wick

1966   A Wreath for the Bride
1967   Death Awaits Thee
1967   No More Murders

P: Langley, Lee
Please see: Langley, Sarah

A: Langley, Sarah
P: Langley, Lee
SC: Christopher Jensen, Lt.

1964   Osiris Died in Autumn
       apa Twilight of Death
1968   Dead Center

A: Langton, Jane
SC: Homer Kelly

1964   The Transcendental Murder
       apa The Minuteman Murder
1975   Dark Nantucket Noon
1978   The Memorial Hall Murder
1982   Natural Enemy

Langton, Jane (cont.)

    1984   Emily Dickinson is Dead
    1986   Good and Dead

P: Lathen, Emma
    Please see: Henissart, Martha w/Mary Jane Latsis

JN: Latsis, Mary Lane
    Please see: Henissart, Martha w/Mary Jane Latsis

A: Law, Janice
    SC: Anna Peters

    1976   The Big Payoff
    1977   Gemini Trip
    1978   Under Orion
    1980   The Shadow of the Palms
    1981   Death Under Par

A: Lawrence, Hilda (Hildegarde) (Kronemiller)
    SC: Mark East

    1944   Blood Upon the Snow
    1945   A Time to Die
    1947   Death of a Doll

A: Lawrence, Margery
    SC: Miles Pennoyer

SS   1945   Number Seven Queer Street
SS   1959   Master of Shadows

P: Lee, Gypsy Rose
    Please see: Craig, Georgiana Ann Randolph

A: Lee, Jennette
    SC: Millicent Newberry

    1917   The Green Jacket
    1922   The Mysterious Office
    1925   Dead Right

A: Lee, Norma
  SC: Norma "Nicky" Lee

  1953   The Beautiful Gunner
  1953   Lover—Say It With Mink!
  1954   Another Woman's Man
  1954   The Broadway Jungle

P: Leek, Margaret
  Please see: Bowen-Judd, Sara Hutton

A: Lemarchand, Elizabeth
  SC: Tom Pollard, Insp.   (see pg. 42)

  1967   Death of an Old Girl
  1968   The Affacombe Affair
  1969   Alibi for a Corpse
  1971   Death on Doomsday
  1972   Cyanide With Compliments
  1973   Let or Hindrance
         apa No Vacation From Murder
  1974   Buried in the Past
  1976   Step in the Dark
  1977   Unhappy Returns
  1978   Suddenly While Gardening
  1980   Change for the Worse
  1981   Nothing to Do With the Case
  1982   Troubled Waters
  1984   Light Through Glass
  1984   The Wheel Turns
  1986   Who Goes Home?

P: Leonard, Charles L.
  Please see: Heberden, M(ary) V(iolet)

A: Leslie, Jean
  SC: Peter Ponsonby

  1945   One Cried Murder
  1946   Two Faced Murder
  1947   Three-Cornered Murder

P: Lewis, Lange
Please see: Beynon, Jane

A: Lilly, Jean
SC: Bruce Perkins

1929   False Face
1934   Death in B-Minor
1940   Death Thumbs a Ride

A: Lincoln, Natalie S.
SC: Ferguson, Det.

1920   The Red Seal
1921   The Unseen Ear

SC: Mitchell, Insp.

1916   I Spy
1917   The Nameless Man
1918   The Three Strings
1918   The Moving Finger
1922   The Cat's Paw
1923   The Meredith Mystery
1925   The Missing Initial
1926   The Blue Car Mystery
1927   P.P.C.
1927   The Dancing Silhouette

A: Linington, Elizabeth
SC: Ivor Maddox, Sgt.

1964   Greenmask!
1964   No Evil Angel
1966   Date With Death
1967   Something Wrong
1968   Policeman's Lot
1971   Practice to Deceive
1973   Crime By Chance
1977   Perchance of Death
1979   No Villain Need Be

Linington, Elizabeth (cont.)

    1980   Consequence of Crime
    1982   Skeletons in the Closet
    1986   Strange Felony

P: Egan, Lesley
    SC: Jesse Falkenstein

    1961   A Case for Appeal
    1962   Against the Evidence
    1965   My Name is Death
    1966   Some Avenger, Rise!
    1968   A Serious Investigation
    1970   In the Death of a Man
    1972   Paper Chase
    1977   The Blind Search
    1978   Look Back on Death
    1980   Motive in Shadow
    1981   The Miser
    1983   Little Boy Lost
    1985   Wine of Life

    SC: Vic Varallo

    1961   A Case for Appeal
    1962   The Borrowed Alibi
    1963   Run to Evil
    1965   Detective's Due
    1967   The Nameless Ones
    1969   The Wine of Violence
    1971   Malicious Mischief
    1976   Scenes of Crime
    1978   A Dream Apart
    1979   The Hunter and the Hunted
    1980   A Choice of Crimes
    1982   Random Death
    1984   Crime for Christmas

P: Shannon, Dell
    SC: Luis Mendoza, Lt. (see pg. 26)

    1960   Case Pending
    1961   The Ace of Spades

Linington, Elizabeth (cont.)

	1962	Extra Kill
	1962	Knave of Hearts
	1963	Double Bluff
	1963	Death of a Busybody
	1964	Root of All Evil
	1964	Mark of Murder
	1965	The Death-Bringers
	1965	Death by Inches
	1966	Coffin Corner
	1966	With a Vengeance
	1967	Rain With Violence
	1967	Chance to Kill
	1968	Kill With Kindness
	1969	Schooled to Kill
	1969	Crime on Their Hands
	1970	Unexpected Death
	1971	The Ringer
	1971	Whim to Kill
	1972	With Intent to Kill
	1972	Murder With Love
	1973	Spring of Violence
	1973	No Holiday for Crime
	1974	Crime File
	1975	Deuces Wild
	1976	Streets of Death
	1977	Appearances of Death
	1978	Cold Trail
	1979	Felony at Random
	1980	Felony File
	1981	Murder Most Strange
	1982	The Motive on Record
	1983	Exploits of Death
	1984	Destiny of Death
	1985	Chaos of Crime
	1986	Blood Count
SS	1987	Murder By the Tale

A: Livingston, Nancy
SC: G. D. H. Pringle

	1985	The Trouble at Aquitaine
	1987	Fatality at Bath and Wells

A: Locke, G(ladys) E(dson)
  SC: Burton, Insp.

  1922　The Red Cavalier
  1923　The Scarlet Macaw
  1924　The Purple Mist
  1925　The House on the Downs

  SC: Mercedes Quero

  1914　The Affair at Portstead Manor
  1922　The Red Cavalier

P: Lockridge, Frances and Richard
  Please see: Lockridge, Frances w/Richard

A: Lockridge, Frances w/Richard
P: Lockridge, Frances and Richard
  SC: Bernard Simmons

  1962　And Left for Dead
  1964　The Devious Ones
      apa Four Hours to Fear

  SC: Merton Heimrich, Insp.

  1946　Death of a Tall Man
  1947　Think of Death
  1948　I Want to Go Home
  1949　Spin Your Web, Lady!
  1950　Foggy, Foggy Death
  1951　A Client is Cancelled
  1952　Death By Association
      apa Trial By Terror
  1953　Stand Up and Die
  1954　Death and the Gentle Bull
      apa Killer in the Straw
  1955　Burnt Offering
  1956　Let Dead Enough Alone
  1957　Practise to Deceive
  1958　Accent on Murder
  1960　Show Red for Danger
  1961　With One Stone
      apa No Dignity in Death

Lockridge, Frances w/Richard (cont.)

1962 First Come, First Kill
1963 The Distant Clue

SC: Nathan Shapiro

1956 The Faceless Adversary
     apa The Case of the Murdered Redhead
1957 The Tangled Cord
1959 Murder and Blueberry Pie
     apa Call it Coincidence
1961 The Drill is Death

SC: Pam and Jerry North

1940 The Norths Meet Murder
     apa Mr. & Mrs. North Meet Murder
1941 Murder out of Turn
1941 A Pinch of Poison
1942 Hanged for a Sheep
1942 Death on the Aisle
1943 Death Takes a Bow
1944 Killing the Goose
1945 Payoff for the Banker
1946 Death of a Tall Man
1946 Murder Within Murder
1947 Untidy Murder
1948 Murder is Served
1949 The Dishonest Murderer
1950 Murder in a Hurry
1951 Murder Comes First
1952 Dead as a Dinosaur
1953 Death Has a Small Voice
1953 Curtain for a Jester
1954 A Key to Death
1955 Death of an Angel
     apa Mr. & Mrs. North and the Poisoned Playboy
1956 Voyage into Violence
1958 The Long Skeleton
1959 Murder is Suggested
1960 The Judge is Reversed
1961 Murder Has its Points
1963 Murder By the Book

Lockridge, Frances w/Richard (cont.)

SC: Paul Lane

1962   Night of Shadows
1964   Quest for the Bogeyman

JN: Lockridge, Richard
Please see: Lockridge, Frances w/Richard

A: Long, Amelia Reynolds
SC: "Peter" Piper

1940   The Corpse at the Quill Club
1941   Four Feet in the Grave
1942   Murder Goes South
1942   Murder By Scripture
1945   Death Looks Down
1948   It's Death, My Darling!

SC: Edward Trelawny

1939   The Shakespeare Murders
1940   Invitation to Death
        apa The Carter Kidnapping Case
1940   Murder Times Three
1943   The Triple Cross Murders
1944   Symphony in Murder
1945   Death Looks Down

SC: Steve Carter

1943   Murder to Type
1943   Death Wears a Scarab
1944   Death Has a Will
1944   Murder By Treason
1945   Once Acquitted
1947   Murder By Magic
1950   The House With Green Shutters

P: Laing, Patrick
SC: Patrick Laing

1945   Stone Dead

Long, Amelia Reynolds (cont.)

    1945   If I Should Murder
    1946   Murder from the Mind
    1949   A Brief Case of Murder
    1951   The Lady is Dead
    1957   The Shadow of Murder

P: Reynolds, Adrian
    SC: Dennis Barrie, Prof.

    1947   Formula for Murder
    1950   The Leprechaun Murders
    1952   The Round Table Murders

P: Lorac, E. C. R.
    Please see: Rivett, Edith Caroline

P: Lynch, Lawrence
    Please see: Van Deventer, Emma M.

P: Lynch, Miriam
    Please see: Wallace, Mary

A: Lyon, (Mabel) Dana
    SC: Hilda Trenton

    1950   The Tentacles
    1963   Spin the Web Tight

M

A: Mace, Merlda
   SC: Christine Andersen

   1943   Headlong for Murder
   1945   Blondes Don't Cry

P: MacGowan, Alice and Perry Newberry
   Please see: MacGowan, Alice w/Perry Newberry

A: MacGowan, Alice w/Perry Newberry
P: MacGowan, Alice and Perry Newberry
   SC: Jerry Boyne

   1922   The Million Dollar Suitcase
   1924   The Mystery Woman
   1925   Shaken Down
   1926   The Seventh Passenger
   1927   Who is this Man?

A: MacKintosh, Elizabeth
P: Tey, Josephine
   SC: Alan Grant, Insp.   (see pg. 49)

   1929   The Man in the Queue
          apa Killer in the Crowd
   1936   A Shilling for Candles
   1948   The Franchise Affair
   1950   To Love and Be Wise
   1951   The Daughter of Time
   1952   The Singing Sands

A: MacKintosh, May
   SC: Laurie Grant and Stewart Noble

   1972   Appointment in Andalusia
   1973   A King and Two Queens
          apa Assignment in Andorra
   1974   The Sicilian Affair
          apa Dark Paradise

A: MacLeod, Charlotte
SC: Peter Shandy, Prof.   (see pg. 6)

1978   Rest You Merry
1979   The Luck Runs Out
1982   Wrack and Rune
1983   Something the Cat Dragged In
1985   The Curse of the Giant Hogweed
1987   The Corpse in Oozak's Pond

SC: Sarah Kelling and Max Bittersohn   (see pp. 75, 187)

1979   The Family Vault
1980   The Withdrawing Room
1981   The Palace Guard
1983   The Bilbao Looking Glass
1984   The Convivial Codfish
1985   The Plain Old Man
1987   The Recycled Citizen

P: Craig, Alisa
SC: Madoc Rhys, Insp.   (see pg. 65)

1980   A Pint of Murder
1981   Murder Goes Mumming
1986   A Dismal Thing to Do

SC: The Grub-and-Stakers   (see pg. 267)

1981   The Grub-and-Stakers Move a Mountain
1985   The Grub-and-Stakers Quilt a Bee

P: Macrae, Travis
Please see: Feagles, Anita Macrae

A: MacVean, Phyllis
P: Hambledon, Phyllis
SC: "Tubby" Hall, Insp.

1958   Keys for the Criminal
1959   Murder and Miss Ming

P: MacVeigh, Sue
  Please see: Nearing, Elizabeth C.

A: Malim, Barbara
  SC: Simon Chard

  1937   Murder on Holiday
  1939   Seven Looked On

A: Malleson, Lucy Beatrice
P: Gilbert, Anthony
  SC: Arthur G. Crook   (see pg. 146)

  1936   Murder By Experts
  1937   Murder Has No Tongue
  1937   The Man Who Wasn't There
  1938   Treason in My Breast
  1939   The Bell of Death
  1939   The Clock in the Hatbox
  1940   Dear Dead Woman
          apa Death Takes a Redhead
          apa Mystery House
  1941   The Vanishing Corpse
          apa She Vanished in the Dawn
  1941   The Woman in Red
          apa The Mystery of the Woman in Red
  1942   Something Nasty in the Woodshed
          apa Mystery in the Woodshed
  1942   The Case of the Tea-Cosy's Aunt
          apa Death in the Blackout
  1943   The Mouse Who Wouldn't Play Ball
          apa 30 Days to Live
  1944   A Spy for Mr. Crook
  1944   The Scarlet Button
          apa Murder is Cheap
  1945   The Black Stage
          apa Murder Cheats the Bride
  1945   Don't Open the Door
          apa Death Lifts the Latch
  1946   The Spinster's Secret
          apa By Hook or By Crook
  1947   Death in the Wrong Room
  1947   Die in the Dark
          apa The Missing Widow

Malleson, Lucy Beatrice (cont.)

1948	Lift Up the Lid
	apa The Innocent Bottle
1949	Death Knocks Three Times
1950	Murder Comes Home
1950	A Nice Cup of Tea
	apa The Wrong Body
1951	Lady Killer
1952	Miss Pinnegar Disappears
	apa A Case for Mr. Crook
1953	Footsteps Behind Me
	apa Black Death
	apa Dark Death
1954	Snake in the Grass
	apa Death Won't Wait
1955	A Question of Murder
	apa Is She Dead Too?
1956	Riddle of a Lady
1956	And Death Came Too
1957	Give Death a Name
1958	Death Against the Clock
1959	Third Crime Lucky
	apa Prelude To Murder
1959	Death Takes a Wife
	apa Death Casts a Long Shadow
1960	Out for the Kill
1961	She Shall Die
	apa After the Verdict
1961	Uncertain Death
1962	No Dust in the Attic
1963	Ring for a Noose
1964	The Fingerprint
1964	Knock, Knock, Who's There?
	apa The Voice
1965	Passenger to Nowhere
1966	The Looking Glass Murder
1967	The Visitor
1968	Night Encounter
	apa Murder Anonymous
1969	Missing From Her Home
1970	Death Wears a Mask
	apa Mr. Crook Lifts the Mask
1971	Tenant for the Tomb

Malleson, Lucy Beatrice (cont.)

    1972   Murder's a Waiting Game
    1974   A Nice Little Killing

    SC: M. Dupuy

    1934   The Man in the Button Boots
    1936   Courtier to Death
           apa The Dover Train Mystery

    SC: Scott Egerton

    1927   The Tragedy at Freyne
    1928   The Murder of Mrs. Davenport
    1929   Death at Four Corners
    1929   The Mystery of the Open Window
    1930   The Night of the Fog
    1932   The Long Shadow
    1932   The Body on the Beam
    1933   The Musical Comedy Crime
    1934   An Old Lady Dies
    1935   The Man Who Was Too Clever

A: **Mann, Jessica**
    SC: Thea Crawford

    1973   The Only Security
           apa Troublecross
    1975   Captive Audience

A: **Manning, Adelaide Frances Oke w/Cyril Henry Coles**
P: Coles, Manning
    SC: Tommy Hambledon   (see pg. 221)

    1940   Drink to Yesterday
    1940   Pray Silence
           apa A Toast to Tomorrow
    1941   They Tell No Tales
    1943   Without Lawful Authority
    1945   Green Hazard
    1946   The Fifth Man
    1947   Let the Tiger Die

**Manning, Adelaide Frances Oke
w/Cyril Henry Coles** (cont.)

1947	A Brother for Hugh
	apa With Intent to Deceive
1948	Among Those Absent
1949	Diamonds to Amsterdam
1949	Not Negotiable
1950	Dangerous By Nature
1951	Now or Never
1952	Night Train to Paris
1952	Alias Uncle Hugo
	apa Operation Manhunt
1953	A Knife for the Juggler
	apa The Vengeance Man
1954	Not for Export
	apa The Mystery of the Stolen Plans
	apa All that Glitters
1955	The Man in the Green Hat
1956	Birdwatcher's Quarry
	apa The Three Beans
1956	The Basle Express
1957	Death of an Ambassador
1958	No Entry
1960	Crime in Concrete
	apa Concrete Crime
1960	Nothing to Declare
1961	Search for a Sultan
1963	House at Pluck's Gutter

P: Gaite, Francis
   SC: Charles and James Latimer

1954	Brief Candles
1956	Happy Returns
	apa A Family Matter
1958	Come and Go

JN: Manning, Bruce
   Please see: Bristow, Gwen w/Bruce Manning

P: Mannon, M. M.
   Please see: Mannon, Martha w/Mary Ellen Mannon

A: Mannon, Martha w/Mary Ellen Mannon
P: Mannon, M. M.
    SC: George White, Sheriff

    1942   Here Lies Blood
    1944   Murder on the Program

JN: Mannon, Mary Ellen
    Please see: Mannon, Martha w/Mary Ellen Mannon

A: Mantell, Laurie
    SC: Steve Arrow, Sgt.

    1978   Murder in Fancy Dress
    1980   Murder and Chips
    1980   A Murder or Three

A: Marin, Muna Lee w/Maurice C. Guiness
P: Gayle, Newton
    SC: James Greer

    1935   The Sentry-Box Murder
           apa Murder in the Haunted
               Sentry-Box
    1935   Death Follows a Formula
    1936   Murder at 28:10
    1937   Death in the Glass
    1938   Sinister Crag

A: Marlett, Melba
    SC: Sarah O'Brien

    1941   Death Has a Thousand Doors
    1943   Another Day Toward Dying
           apa Witness in Peril

A: Maron, Margaret
    SC: Sigrid Harald, Det.

    1982   One Coffee With
    1984   Death of a Butterfly
    1985   Death in Blue Folders
    1987   The Right Jack

A: Marris, Kathrine
P: Beck, K. K.
  SC: Iris Cooper and Jack Clancy

  1984   Death in a Deck Chair
  1986   Murder in a Mummy Case

A: Marsh, (Edith) Ngaio
  SC: Roderick Alleyn, Insp.   (see pp. 47, 195)

  1934   A Man Lay Dead
  1935   Enter a Murderer
  1935   The Nursing Home Murder
  1936   Death in Ecstasy
  1937   Vintage Murder
  1938   Artists in Crime
  1938   Death in a White Tie
  1939   Overture to Death
  1940   Death of a Peer
         apa Surfeit of Lampreys
  1940   Death at the Bar
  1941   Death and the Dancing Footman
  1943   Colour Scheme
  1945   Died in the Wool
  1947   Final Curtain
  1949   Swing, Brother, Swing
         apa A Wreath for Rivera
  1951   Opening Night
         apa Night at the Vulcan
  1953   Spinsters in Jeopardy
         apa The Bride of Death
  1955   Scales of Justice
  1956   Death of a Fool
         apa Off With His Head
  1958   Singing in the Shrouds
  1959   False Scent
  1962   Hand in Glove
  1963   Dead Water
  1966   Killer Dolphin
         apa Death at the Dolphin
  1968   Clutch of Constables
  1970   When in Rome
  1972   Tied Up in Tinsel

Marsh, (Edith) Ngaio (cont.)

    1974   Black as He's Painted
    1977   Last Ditch
    1978   Grave Mistake
    1980   Photo-Finish
    1982   Light Thickens

A: Marting, Ruth Lenore
P: Bailey, Hilea
    SC: Hilea Bailey and Hilary D. Bailey III

    1939   What Night Will Bring
    1940   Give Thanks to Death
    1941   The Smiling Corpse
    1946   Breathe No More, My Lady

JN: Mason, Francis Van Wyck
    Please see: Brawner, Helen
        w/Francis Van Wyck Mason

A: Mason, Sara Elizabeth
    SC: Bill Davies, Sheriff

    1943   Murder Rents a Room
    1945   The Crimson Feather

A: Matschat, Cecile Hulse
    SC: Andrea Reid (Ramsay) and David Ramsay

    1941   Murder at the Okefenokee
    1943   Murder at the Black Crook

A: Mavity, Nancy Barr
    SC: Peter Piper   (see pg. 167)

    1929   The Body on the Floor
    1929   The Tule Marsh Murder
    1930   The Other Bullet
    1930   The Case of the Missing Sandals
    1932   The Man Who Didn't Mind
           Hanging
          apa He Didn't Mind Hanging

P: Maxwell, A. E.
    Please see: Maxwell, Ann w/Evan

A: Maxwell, Ann w/Evan
P: Maxwell, A. E.
    SC: Fiddler

    1985   Just Another Day in Paradise
    1986   The Frog and the Scorpion
    1987   Gatsby's Vineyard

JN: Maxwell, Evan
    Please see: Maxwell, Ann w/Evan

A: McChesney, Mary F.
P: Rayter, Joe
    SC: Johnny Powers

    1954   The Victim was Important
    1955   Asking for Trouble

A: McCloy, Helen
    SC: Dr. Basil Willing   (see pg. 122)

    1938   Dance of Death
            apa Design for Dying
    1940   The Man in the Moonlight
    1941   The Deadly Truth
    1942   Cue for Murder
    1942   Who's Calling?
    1943   The Goblin Market
    1945   The One That Got Away
    1950   Through a Glass Darkly
    1951   Alias Basil Willing
    1955   The Long Body
    1956   Two-Thirds of a Ghost
    1968   Mr. Splitfoot
    1980   Burn This

    SC: Miguel Urizar

    1943   The Goblin Market
    1948   She Walks Alone
            apa Wish You Were Dead

A: McConnell, Vicki
  SC: Nyla Wade

    1982   Mrs. Porter's Letter
    1984   The Burntown Widows

P: McCormick, Claire
  Please see: Labus, Martha Haake

A: McCrumb, Sharyn
  SC: Elizabeth MacPherson

    1984   Sick of Shadows
    1985   Lovely In Her Bones
    1986   Highland Laddie Gone

A: McCully, (Ethel) Walbridge
  SC: D. A. Carey Galbreath

    1942   Death Rides Tandem
    1943   Doctors Beware!

A: McGerr, Patricia
  SC: Selena Mead

    1964   Is There a Traitor in the House?
    1970   Legacy of Danger

A: McInerny, Ralph
P: Quill, Monica
  SC: Sister Mary Teresa Dempsey   (see pg. 92)

    1981   Not A Blessed Thing!
    1982   Let Us Prey
    1984   And Then There Was Nun
    1985   Nun of the Above
    1986   Sine Qua Nun

A: McIntosh, Kinn Hamilton
P: Aird, Catherine
  SC: C. D. Sloan, Insp.   (see pg. 57)

    1966   The Religious Body
    1968   Henrietta Who?

McIntosh, Kinn Hamilton (cont.)

1969	The Complete Steel
	apa The Stately Home Murder
1970	A Late Phoenix
1973	His Burial Too
1975	Slight Mourning
1977	Parting Breath
1979	Some Die Eloquent
1980	Passing Strange
1982	Last Respects
1984	Harm's Way
1987	A Dead Liberty

A: McKenna, Marthe
  SC: Clive Granville

1937	Lancer Spy
1941	The Spy in Khaki

**A: Meade (Smith), Elizabeth Thomasina
  w/Robert Eustace**
P: Meade, L. T.
  SC: Madame Koluchy

SS   1900   The Brotherhood of the Seven Kings

  SC: Madame Sara

SS   1903   The Sorceress of the Strand

P: Meade, L. T.
  Please see: Meade (Smith), Elizabeth Thomasina
    w/Robert Eustace

A: Meek, M(argaret) R(eid) D(uncan)
  SC: Lennox Kemp

1985	Hang The Consequences
1985	The Split Second
1987	In Remembrance of Rose

P: Melville, Jennie
  Please see: Butler, Gwendoline

A: Meredith, D(oris) R.
   SC: Charles Matthews, Sheriff

   1984   The Sheriff and the Panhandle Murders
   1985   The Sheriff and the Branding Iron
            Murders
   1987   The Sheriff and the Folsom Man
            Murders

A: Merrick, Mollie
   SC: Red Hanlon

   1936   Upper Case
   1938   Mysterious Mr. Frame

A: Mertz, Barbara L. G.
P: Peters, Elizabeth
   SC: Amelia Peabody and Radcliffe Emerson
      (see pg. 9)

   1975   Crocodile on the Sandbank
   1981   The Curse of the Pharoahs
   1985   The Mummy Case
   1986   Lion in the Valley

   SC: Jacqueline Kirby   (see pg. 7)

   1972   The Seventh Sinner
   1974   The Murders of Richard III
   1984   Die for Love

   SC: Vicky Bliss   (see pg. 184)

   1973   Borrower of the Night
   1978   Street of the Five Moons
   1983   Silhouette in Scarlet
   1987   Trojan Gold

A: Middleton, Elizabeth
P: Antill, Elizabeth
   SC: Simon Ashton, Insp.

   1950   Murder in Mid-Atlantic
   1952   Death on the Barrier Reef

A: Millar, Margaret
SC: Dr. Paul Prye

1941   The Invisible Worm
1942   The Devil Loves Me
1942   The Weak-Eyed Bat

SC: Sands, Insp.

1942   The Devil Loves Me
1943   Wall of Eyes
1945   The Iron Gates
       apa Taste of Fears

SC: Tom Aragon (see pg. 152)

1976   Ask for Me Tomorrow
1979   The Murder of Miranda
1982   Mermaid

A: Milne, Shirley
SC: Steytler, Det. Sgt.

1962   Stiff Silk
1963   The Hammer of Justice
1964   False Witness

A: Mitchell, Gladys
SC: Dame Beatrice Adela Lestrange Bradley
  (see pg. 120)

1929   Speedy Death
1929   The Mystery of a Butcher's Shop
1930   The Longer Bodies
1932   The Saltmarsh Murders
1933   Ask a Policeman
1934   Death at the Opera
       apa Death in the Wet
1935   The Devil at Saxon Wall
1936   Dead Man's Morris
1937   Come Away, Death
1938   St. Peter's Finger
1939   Printer's Error
1940   Brazen Tongue

Mitchell, Gladys (cont.)

1941	When Last I Died
1941	Hangman's Curfew
1942	Laurels are Poison
1943	Sunset over Soho
1943	The Worsted Viper
1944	My Father Sleeps
1945	The Rising of the Moon
1946	Here Comes a Chopper
1947	Death and the Maiden
1948	The Dancing Druids
1949	Tom Brown's Body
1950	Groaning Spinney
1951	The Devil's Elbow
1952	The Echoing Strangers
1953	Merlin's Furlong
1954	Faintley Speaking
1955	Watson's Choice
1956	Twelve Horses and the Hangman's Noose
1957	The Twenty-Third Man
1958	Spotted Hemlock
1959	The Man Who Grew Tomatoes
1960	Say it With Flowers
1961	The Nodding Canaries
1962	My Bones Will Keep
1963	Adders on the Heath
1964	Death of a Delft Blue
1965	Pageant of Murder
1966	The Croaking Raven
1967	Skeleton Island
1968	Three Quick and Five Dead
1969	Dance to Your Daddy
1970	Gory Dew
1971	Lament for Leto
1972	A Hearse on May-Day
1973	The Murder of Busy Lizzie
1974	Winking at the Brim
1974	A Javelin for Jonah
1975	Convent on Styx
1976	Late, Late in the Evening
1977	Noonday and Night
1977	Fault in the Structure
1978	Wraiths and Changelings

Mitchell, Gladys (cont.)

1978   Mingled with Venom
1979   The Mudflats of the Dead
1979   Nest of Vipers
1980   The Whispering Knights
1980   Uncoffin'd Clay
1981   The Death Cap Dancers
1982   Here Lies Gloria Mundy
1982   Lovers Make Moan
1982   Death of a Burrowing Mole
1983   Cold, Lone and Still
1983   The Green Stone Griffins
1984   No Winding Sheet
1984   The Crozier Pharoahs
1984   Crime on the Coast and No Flowers
    By Request

P: Torrie, Malcolm
 SC: Timothy Herring

1966   Heavy as Lead
1967   Late and Cold
1968   Your Secret Friend
1969   Churchyard Salad
1970   Shades of Darkness
1971   Bismarck Herrings

A: **Moffat, Gwen**
 SC: Melinda Pink   (see pg. 257)

1973   Lady With a Cool Eye
1975   Miss Pink at the Edge of the World
1976   A Short Time to Live
1976   Over the Sea to Death
1978   Persons Unknown
1982   Die Like a Dog
1982   The Buckskin Girl
1982   Miss Pink's Mistake
1983   Last Chance Country
1984   Grizzly Trail

JN: **Monk, Elliot**
 Please see: Baskerville, Beatrice w/Elliot Monk

A: Montgomery, Ione
    SC: Christopher Gibson

    1940   The Golden Dress
    1941   Death Won a Prize

P: Montross, David
    Please see: Backus, Jean Louise

A: Moody, Susan
    SC: Penny Wanawake

    1981   Penny Wise
    1984   Penny Black
    1984   Penny Dreadful
    1985   Penny Post
    1986   Penny Royal

JN: Moore, Arthur
    Please see: Granbeck, Marilyn w/Arthur Moore

A: Moore, Barbara
    SC: Dr. Gordon Christy   (see pg. 118)

    1983   The Doberman Wore Black
    1985   The Wolf Whispered Death

P: Morice, Anne
    Please see: Shaw, Felicity

A: Morris, Jean
P: O'Hara, Kenneth
    SC: Dr. Alun Barry

    1958   A View to Death
    1960   Sleeping Dogs Lying

A: Moyes, Patricia
    SC: Henry Tibbett, Insp.   (see pg. 41)

    1959   Dead Men Don't Ski
    1961   The Sunken Sailor
             apa Down Among the Dead Men
    1962   Death of the Agenda

Moyes, Patricia (cont.)

1963	Murder à la Mode
1964	Falling Star
1965	Johnny Under Ground
1967	Murder Fantastical
1968	Death and the Dutch Uncle
1970	Who Saw Her Die?
	apa Many Deadly Returns
1971	Season of Snows and Sins
1973	The Curious Affair of the Third Dog
1975	Black Widower
1977	To Kill a Coconut
	apa The Coconut Killings
1978	Who is Simon Warwick?
1980	Angel Death
1983	A Six Letter Word for Death
1985	Night Ferry to Death
1987	Many Deadly Returns

A: Muir, D(orothy) Erskine
SC: Woods, Insp.

1933	In Muffled Night
1934	Five to Five

A: Muller, Marcia
SC: Elena Oliverez   (see pg. 185)

1983	The Tree of Death
1985	The Legend of the Slain Soldiers

SC: Sharon McCone   (see pg. 212)

1977	Edwin of the Iron Shoes
1982	Ask the Cards a Question
1983	The Cheshire Cat's Eye
1984	Leave a Message for Willie
1984	Games to Keep the Dark Away
1985	There's Nothing to be Afraid of

P: Muller, Marcia and Bill Pronzini
Please see: Muller, Marcia w/Bill Pronzini

A: Muller, Marcia w/Bill Pronzini
P: Muller, Marcia and Bill Pronzini
    SC: Elena Oliverez

    1986   Beyond the Grave

    SC: Sharon McCone

    1984   Double

A: Myers, Isabel Briggs
    SC: Peter Jerningham

    1930   Murder Yet to Come
    1934   Give Me Death

N

A: Nabb, Magdalen
SC: Guarnaccia, Marshal   (see pg. 70)

1981   Death of an Englishman
1982   Death of a Dutchman
1983   Death in Springtime
1985   Death in Autumn
1987   The Marshal and the Murderer

A: Nash, Anne
SC: Mark Tudor

1943   Said With Flowers
1944   Death By Design

A: Nearing, Elizabeth C.
P: MacVeigh, Sue
SC: Captain Andy and Sue MacVeigh

1939   Murder Under Construction
1939   Grand Central Murder
1940   Streamlined Murder
1941   The Corpse and the Three Ex-Husbands

A: Neville, Barbara Alison
P: Candy, Edward
SC: Burnivel, Insp.   (see pg. 39)

1953   Which Doctor
1954   Bones of Contention
1971   Words for Murder Perhaps

P: Neville, Margot
Please see: Goyder, Margot w/Anne N. G. Joske

JN: Newberry, Perry
Please see: MacGowan, Alice
w/Perry Newberry

A: Nicholson, Margaret B.
P: Yorke, Margaret
   SC: Patrick Grant

    1970   Dead in the Morning
    1972   Silent Witness
    1973   Grave Matters
    1974   Mortal Remains
    1976   Cast for Death

A: Nielsen, Helen
   SC: Simon Drake

    1951   Gold Coast Nocturne
           apa Dead on the Level
           apa Murder by Proxy
    1966   After Midnight
    1967   A Killer in the Street
    1969   Darkest Hour
    1973   The Severed Key
    1976   The Brink of Murder

A: Nisot, Elizabeth
   SC: Payran, Commissaire

    1935   Twelve to Dine
    1936   Hazardous Holiday
    1938   False Witness
    1939   Unnatural Deeds

A: Nolan, Jeannette Covert
   SC: Lace White

    1943   Final Appearance
    1945   "I Can't Die Here"
    1955   Sudden Squall
    1956   A Fearful Way to Die

O

A: O'Callaghan, Maxine
SC: Delilah West

1981   Death is Forever
1982   Run From the Nightmare
1987   Hit and Run

A: O'Donnell, Lillian (Udvardy)
SC: Mici Anhalt

1977   Aftershock
1979   Falling Star
1980   Wicked Designs

SC: Norah Mulcahaney, Det. Sgt.   (see pg. 30)

1972   The Phone Calls
1973   Don't Wear Your Wedding Ring
1974   Dial 577 R-A-P-E
1975   The Baby Merchants
1976   Leisure Dying
1979   No Business Being a Cop
1981   The Children's Zoo
1983   Cop Without a Shield
1984   Ladykiller
1985   Casual Affairs
1986   Shadow in Red
1987   The Other Side of the Door

P: O'Hara, Kenneth
Please see: Morris, Jean

A: O'Malley, Lady Mary Dolling
P: Bridge, Ann
SC: Julia Probyn   (see pg. 169)

1956   The Lighthearted Quest
1958   The Portuguese Escape
1960   The Numbered Account
1962   Julia Involved

O'Malley, Lady Mary Dolling (cont.)

    1962   The Tightening Screw
    1963   The Dangerous Islands
    1965   Emergency in the Pyrenees
    1966   The Episode at Toledo
    1969   The Malady in Madeira
    1973   Julia in Ireland

A: O'Marie, Sister Carol Anne
    SC: Sister Mary Helen   (see pg. 93)

    1984   A Novena For Murder
    1986   Advent of Dying

A: Oellrichs, Inez H.
    SC: Matt Winters

    1939   The Kettel Mill Mystery
    1939   The Man Who Didn't Answer
    1940   Murder Comes at Night
    1945   And Die She Did
    1947   Murder Helps
    1949   Death of a White Witch
    1964   Death in a Chilly Corner

A: Offord, Lenore Glen
    SC: Bill and Coco Hastings

    1938   Murder on Russian Hill
           apa Murder Before Breakfast
    1942   Clues to Burn

    SC: Todd McKinnon

    1943   Skeleton Key
    1944   The Glass Mask
    1949   The Smiling Tiger
    1959   Walking Shadow

P: Olsen, D. B.
    Please see: Hitchens, Dolores (Birk)

A: Orczy, Baroness (Emmuska) [Emma Magdalena Rosalia Maria Josefa Barbara, Baroness Orczy]
SC: Bill Owen, The Old Man in the Corner   (see pg. 262)

SS	1905	The Case of Miss Elliott
SS	1909	The Old Man in the Corner
		apa The Man in the Corner
SS	1923	The Old Man in the Corner Unravels the Mystery of the Khaki Tunic
SS	1924	The Old Man in the Corner Unravels the Mystery of the Pearl Necklace
SS	1924	The Old Man in the Corner Unravels the Mystery of the Russian Prince, and of Dog's Tooth Cliff
SS	1925	The Old Man in the Corner Unravels the Mystery of the White Carnation and the Montmartre Hat
SS	1925	The Old Man in the Corner Unravels the Mystery of the Fulton Gardens Mystery, and the Moorland Tragedy
SS	1925	Unravelled Knots

SC: Fernand

SS	1918	The Man in Grey

SC: Lady Molly

SS	1910	Lady Molly of Scotland Yard

SC: M. Hector Ratichon

SS	1921	Castles in the Air

SC: Patrick Mulligan

SS	1928	Skin o' My Tooth

A: Ostrander, Isabel
SC: Timothy McCarty

1917	The Clue in the Air
1919	The Twenty-Six Clues
1920	How Many Cards?

Ostrander, Isabel (cont.)

    1922   McCarty, Incog.
    1923   Annihilation

P: Chipperfield, Robert O.
    SC: Barry O'Dell

    1920   Unseen Hands
    1921   The Man in the Jury Box

P: Fox, David
    SC: The Shadowers, Inc.

    1920   The Man Who Convicted Himself
    1922   Ethel Opens the Door
    1923   The Doom Dealer
    1924   The Handwriting on the Wall

JN: Oursler, William Charles
    Please see: Scott, Margaret w/William Charles Oursler

P, Q

P: Page, Emma
Please see: Tirbutt, Honoria

JN: Page, Evelyn
Please see: Blair, Dorothy w/Evelyn Page

A: Palmer, Madelyn
P: Peters, Geoffrey
SC: Trevor Nicholls, Insp.

1964   The Claw of a Cat
1964   The Eye of a Serpent
1965   The Whirl of a Bird
1966   The Twist of a Stick
1967   The Flick of a Fin
1967   The Mark of a Buoy
1968   The Chill of a Corpse

A: Papazoglou, Orania
SC: Patience C. McKenna   (see pg. 71)

1984   Sweet, Savage Death
1985   Wicked, Loving Murder
1986   Death's Savage Passion

A: Paretsky, Sara
SC: V. I. Warshawski   (see pg. 215)

1982   Indemnity Only
1984   Deadlock
1986   Killing Orders
1987   Bitter Medicine

A: Pargeter, Edith Mary
P: Peters, Ellis
SC: Brother Cadfael   (see pg. 89)

1977   A Morbid Taste for Bones: A Medieval Whodunit
1979   One Corpse Too Many
1980   Monk's-Hood
1981   Saint Peter's Fair
1981   The Leper of St. Giles

Pargeter, Edith Mary (cont.)

1982	The Virgin in the Ice
1983	The Devil's Novice
1983	The Sanctuary Sparrow
1984	Dead Man's Ransom
1984	The Pilgrim of Hate
1985	An Excellent Mystery
1986	The Raven in the Foregate
1987	The Rose Rent

SC: George Felse, Insp. and Family

1951	Fallen into the Pit
1960	The Will and the Deed
	apa Where There's a Will
1961	Death and the Joyful Woman
1964	Flight of a Witch
1965	A Nice Derangement of Epitaphs
	apa Who Lies Here?
1966	The Piper on the Mountain
1967	Black is the Colour of My True Love's Heart
1968	The Grass-Widow's Tale
1969	Mourning Raga
1969	The House of Green Turf
1970	The Knocker on Death's Door
1972	Death to the Landlords!
1973	City of Gold and Shadows
1979	Rainbow's End

A: **Parker, Maude**
SC: Jim Little

1951	Which Mrs. Torr?
1952	The Intriguer
	apa Blood Will Tell
1955	Murder in Jackson Hole
	apa Final Crossroads

A: **Patterson, (Isabella) Innis**
SC: Sebald Craft

1930	The Eppworth Case
1931	The Standish Gaunt Case

A: Paul, Barbara
SC: Enrico Caruso and Geraldine Farrar

1984   A Cadenza for Caruso
1985   Prima Donna at Large
1987   Chorus of Detectives

P: Paull, Jessica
Please see: Burger, Rosaylmer w/Julia Perceval

A: Payes, Rachel
SC: Forsythia Brown

1960   Forsythia Finds Murder
1964   Memoirs of Murder

A: Pearson, Ann
SC: Maggie Courtney

1979   Murder By Degrees
1979   A Stitch in Time
1980   Cat Got Your Tongue?

JN: Perceval, Julia
Please see: Burger, Rosaylmer w/Julia Perceval

A: Perdue, Virginia
SC: Eleanor Burke

1941   The Case of the Grieving Monkey
1942   The Case of the Foster Father

A: Perry, Anne
SC: Thomas Pitt, Insp. and Charlotte Ellison (Pitt)
(see pp. 34, 78)

1979   The Cater Street Hangman
1980   Callander Square
1981   Paragon Walk
1981   Resurrection Row
1983   Rutland Place
1984   Bluegate Fields
1985   Death in the Devil's Acre
1987   Cardington Crescent

P: Peters, Elizabeth
  Please see: Mertz, Barbara L. G.

P: Peters, Ellis
  Please see: Pargeter, Edith Mary

P: Peters, Geoffrey
  Please see: Palmer, Madelyn

A: Peterson, Margaret Ann
P: Green, Glint
  SC: Wield, Insp.

> 1931   Strands of Red...Hair!
> 1932   Devil Spider
> 1933   Poison Death
> 1933   Beauty—A Snare

P: Petrie, Rhona
  Please see: Buchanan, Eileen-Marie

A: Phillips, Stella
  SC: Matthew Furnival, Insp.

> 1967   Down to Death
> 1968   The Hidden Wrath
> 1969   Death in Arcady
> 1970   Death Makes the Scene
> 1971   Death in Sheep's Clothing

A: Pickard, Nancy
  SC: Jennifer Cain   (see pg. 135)

> 1984   Generous Death
> 1985   Say No To Murder
> 1986   No Body
> 1987   Marriage is Murder

A: Pirkis, C(atharine) L(ouisa)
  SC: Loveday Brooke, Lady Detective

> SS   1894   The Experiences of Loveday Brooke,
>   Lady Detective

A: Plain, Josephine
SC: Colin Anstruther

1934 The Secret of the Sandbanks
1935 The Secret of the Snows
1936 The Pazenger Problem

A: Plum, Mary
SC: John Smith

1930 The Killing of Judge McFarlane
1931 Dead Man's Secret
1932 Murder at the Hunting Club
1933 Murder at the World's Fair
      apa The Broken Vase Mystery

A: Popkin, Zelda
SC: Mary Carner

1938 Death Wears a White Gardenia
1940 Murder in the Mist
1940 Time Off for Murder
1941 Dead Man's Gift
1942 No Crime for a Lady

A: Porter, Joyce
SC: Constance Morrison-Burke   (see pg. 80)

1970 Rather a Common Sort of Crime
1972 A Meddler and Her Murderer
1975 The Package Included Murder
1977 Who the Heck is Sylvia?
1979 The Cart Before the Crime

SC: Edmund Brown   (see pg. 231)

1966 Sour Cream With Everything
1967 The Chinks in the Curtain
1969 Neither a Candle Nor a Pitchfork
1971 Only With a Bargepole

SC: Wilfred Dover, Insp.   (see pg. 40)

1964 Dover One

Porter, Joyce (cont.)

	1965	Dover Two
	1965	Dover Three
	1967	Dover and the Unkindest Cut of All
SS	1968	Dover and the Sense of Justice
	1968	Dover Goes to Pott
SS	1969	Dover Pulls a Rabbit
SS	1970	Dover Fails to Make His Mark
	1970	Dover Strikes Again
SS	1971	A Terrible Drag for Dover
SS	1972	Dover and the Dark Lady
	1973	It's Murder With Dover
SS	1975	Dover Tangles With High Finance
	1976	Dover and the Claret Tappers
SS	1977	Dover Does Some Spadework
SS	1977	When Dover Got Knotted
SS	1978	Dover Without Perks
SS	1978	Dover Doesn't Dilly-Dally
	1978	Dead Easy for Dover
SS	1978	Dover Goes to School
	1980	Dover Beats the Band

A: Pou, Genevieve Long
P: Holden, Genevieve
    SC: Al White, Lt.

1953	Killer Loose!
1954	Sound an Alarm
1956	The Velvet Target
1958	Something's Happened to Kate

A: Powers, Elizabeth
    SC: Viera Kolarova

1981	All That Glitters
1984	On Account of Murder

P: Prichard, K. and V.
    Please see: Prichard, Katherine w/Vernon

A: Prichard, Katherine w/Vernon
P: Prichard, K. and V.
SC: Don Q

SS   1904   The Chronicles of Don Q
SS   1906   The New Chronicles of Don Q
apa Don Q in the Sierra
1909   Don Q's Love Story

JN: Prichard, Vernon
Please see: Prichard, Katherine
w/Vernon

JN: Pronzini, Bill
Please see: Muller, Marcia w/Bill Pronzini

A: Pullein-Thompson, Joanna M. C.
P: Cannan, Joanna
SC: Guy Northeast, Insp.

1939   They Rang Up the Police
1940   Death at the Dog

SC: Ronald Price, Insp.

1950   Murder Included
apa Poisonous Relations
apa The Taste of Murder
1952   Body in the Beck
1955   Long Shadows
1958   And Be A Villain
1962   All is Discovered

A: Pullein-Thompson, Josephine
SC: James Flecker, Insp.

1959   Gin and Murder
1960   They Died in the Spring
1963   Murder Strikes Pink

JN: Punnett, Ivor
Please see: Punnett, Margaret w/Ivor

A: Punnett, Margaret w/Ivor
P: Simons, Roger
    SC: Fadiman Wace, Insp.

    1959   The Houseboat Killings
    1960   A Frame for Murder
    1960   Murder Joins the Chorus
    1961   Arrangement for Murder
    1961   Gamble With Death
    1962   The Killing Chase
    1963   Silver and Death
    1964   Bullet for a Beast
    1965   Dead Reckoning
    1966   The Veil of Death
    1967   Taxed to Death
    1968   Death on Display
    1969   Murder First Class
    1970   Reel of Death
    1973   Picture of Death
    1974   Murder By Design

A: Quick, Dorothy
    SC: Peter Donnegan, Lt.

    1947   The Fifth Dagger
    1959   The Doctor Looks at Murder

P: Quill, Monica
    Please see: McInerny, Ralph

A: Quinn, E(leanora) Baker
    SC: James Strange

    1936   One Man's Muddle
    1940   Death is a Restless Sleeper

R

P: Radford, E. and M.
  Please see: Radford, Mona w/Edwin

JN: Radford, Edwin
  Please see: Radford, Mona w/Edwin

A: Radford, Mona w/Edwin
P: Radford, E. and M.
  SC: Dr. Manson

1944	Inspector Manson's Success
1944	Murder Jigsaw
1945	Crime Pays No Dividends
1946	Murder Isn't Cricket
1947	It's Murder to Live
1947	Who Killed Dick Whittington?
1949	John Kyleing Died
1950	The Heel of Achilles
1956	Look in at Murder
1957	Death on the Broads
1959	Death of a Frightened Editor
1960	Murder on My Conscience
1960	Death at the Chateau Noir
1961	Death's Inheritance
1962	From Information Received
1962	Death Takes the Wheel
1963	Murder of Three Ghosts
1963	A Cosy Little Murder
1964	The Hungry Killer
1965	Mask of Murder
1965	Murder Magnified
1966	Death of a "Gentleman"
1967	No Reason for Murder
1967	The Middlefold Murders
1967	Jones's Little Murders
1968	Trunk Call to Murder
1968	The Safety First Murders
1969	Death of a Peculiar Rabbit
1969	Two Ways to Murder
1969	Death of an Ancient Saxon
1970	Murder is Ruby Red
1970	Murder Speaks

Radford, Mona w/Edwin (cont.)

    1971   Dead Water
    1971   The Greedy Killers
    1972   Death Has Two Faces

P: **Radley, Sheila**
    Please see: Robinson, Sheila (Mary)

P: **Ramsay, Diana**
    Please see: Brandes, Rhoda

A: **Raphael, Chaim**
P: Davey, Jocelyn
    SC: Ambrose Usher

    1956   The Undoubted Dead
            apa A Capitol Offense
    1958   The Naked Villainy
    1960   A Touch of Stagefright
    1965   A Killing in Hats
    1976   A Treasury Alarm
    1982   Murder in Paradise

A: **Rath, Virginia Anne**
    SC: Michael Dundas

    1938   The Dark Cavalier
    1939   Murder With a Theme Song
    1940   Death of a Lucky Lady
    1941   Death Breaks the Ring
    1942   Epitaph for Lydia
    1942   Posted for Murder
    1947   A Shroud for Rowena
    1947   A Dirge for Her

    SC: Rocky Allan, Sheriff

    1935   Death at Dayton's Folly
    1936   Murder on the Day of Judgment
    1936   Ferryman, Take Him Across!
    1937   An Excellent Night for a Murder
    1937   The Anger of the Bells
    1939   Murder With a Theme Song

P: Rayter, Joe
Please see: McChesney, Mary F.

A: Rea, M(argaret) P(aine)
SC: Powledge, Lt.

1941   Compare These Dead!
1941   A Curtain for Crime
1943   Death of an Angel

A: Reilly, Helen
SC: Christopher McKee, Insp.   (see pg. 21)

1930   The Diamond Feather
1931   Murder in the Mews
1934   McKee of Centre Street
1934   The Line-Up
1936   Dead Man Control
1936   Mr. Smith's Hat
1939   Dead for a Ducat
1939   All Concerned Notified
1940   The Dead Can Tell
1940   Death Demands an Audience
1940   Murder in Shinbone Alley
1941   Three Women in Black
1941   Mourned on Sunday
1942   Name Your Poison
1944   The Opening Door
1945   Murder on Angler's Island
1946   The Silver Leopard
1947   The Farmhouse
1949   Staircase 4
1950   Murder at Arroways
1951   Lament for the Bride
1952   The Double Man
1953   The Velvet Hand
1954   Tell Her It's Murder
1955   Compartment K
          apa Murder Rides the Express
1956   The Canvas Dagger
1958   Ding, Dong, Bell
1959   Not Me, Inspector
1960   Follow Me

Reilly, Helen (cont.)

    1961   Certain Sleep
    1962   The Day She Died

A: Rendell, Ruth
    SC: Reg Wexford, Det. Chief Insp.
      (see pg. 64)

    1964   From Doon With Death
    1967   Wolf to the Slaughter
    1967   A New Lease of Death
           apa Sins of the Fathers
    1969   The Best Man to Die
    1970   A Guilty Thing Surprised
    1971   No More Dying Then
    1972   Murder Being Once Done
    1973   Some Lie and Some Die
    1975   Shake Hands Forever
    1978   A Sleeping Life
    1981   Death Notes
           apa Put On by Cunning
    1983   The Speaker of Mandarin
    1985   An Unkindness of Ravens

A: Renfroe, Martha Kay
P: Wren, M. K.
    SC: Conan Flagg   (see pg. 183)

    1973   Curiosity Didn't Kill the Cat
    1975   A Multitude of Sins
    1976   Oh, Bury Me Not
    1978   Nothing's Certain But Death
    1981   Seasons of Death
    1984   Wake up Darlin' Corey

A: Revell, Louisa
    SC: Julia Tyler

    1947   The Bus Station Murders
    1948   No Pockets in Shrouds
    1950   A Silver Spade
    1952   The Kindest Use a Knife
    1955   The Men With Three Eyes

Revell, Louisa (cont.)

    1957   See Rome and Die
    1960   A Party for the Shooting

P: Reynolds, Adrian
    Please see: Long, Amelia Reynolds

P: Rice, Craig
    Please see: Craig, Georgiana Ann Randolph

A: Rich, Virginia
    SC: Mrs. Potter   (see pg. 256)

    1982   The Cooking School Murders
    1983   The Baked Bean Supper Murders
    1985   The Nantucket Diet Murders

A: Rinehart, Mary Roberts
    SC: Nurse Hilda Adams (Miss Pinkerton)   (see pg. 112)

    1932   Miss Pinkerton
            apa The Double Alibi
    1933   Mary Roberts Rinehart's Crime Book
    1942   Haunted Lady

A: Rippon, Marion (Edith)
    SC: Maurice Ygrec, Insp.

    1969   The Hand of Solange
    1970   Behold, the Druid Weeps
    1974   The Ninth Tentacle
    1979   Lucien's Tomb

A: Rivett, Edith Caroline
P: Carnac, Carol
    SC: Julian Rivers, Insp.

    1945   A Double for Detection
    1946   The Striped Staircase
    1947   Clue Sinister
    1948   Over the Garden Wall
    1950   Upstairs, Downstairs
            apa Upstairs and Downstairs

Rivett, Edith Caroline (cont.)

    1950   Copy for Crime
    1951   It's Her Own Funeral
    1952   Crossed Skis
    1953   Murder As a Fine Art
    1953   A Policeman At the Door
    1954   Impact of Evidence
    1955   Rigging the Evidence
    1955   Murder Among Members
    1956   The Double Turn
           apa The Late Miss Trimming
    1958   Long Shadows
           apa Affair at Helen's Court

SC: Ryvet, Insp.

    1936   Triple Death
    1937   Murder At Mornington
    1937   The Missing Rope
    1939   The Case of the First-Class Carriage
    1939   When the Devil Was Sick
    1940   Death in the Diving Pool

P: Lorac, E. C. R.
    SC: Macdonald, Insp.   (see pg. 37)

    1931   The Murder on the Burrows
    1932   The Affair at Thor's Head
    1932   The Greenwell Mystery
    1933   The Case of Colonel Marchand
    1933   Death on the Oxford Road
    1934   Murder in St. John's Wood
    1934   Murder in Chelsea
    1935   The Organ Speaks
    1936   Post After Post-Mortem
    1936   Crime Counter Crime
    1936   A Pall for a Painter
    1937   Bats in the Belfry
    1937   These Names Make Clues
    1938   The Devil and the C.I.D.
    1938   Slippery Staircase
    1939   Black Beadle
    1939   John Brown's Body

Rivett, Edith Caroline (cont.)

1940	Tryst for a Tragedy
1940	Death at Dyke's Corner
1941	Case in the Clinic
1942	The Sixteenth Stair
1942	Rope's End Rogue's End
1943	Death Came Softly
1944	Fell Murder
1944	Checkmate to Murder
1945	Murder By Matchlight
1946	The Theft of the Iron Dogs
	apa Murderer's Mistake
1946	Fire in the Thatch
1947	Relative to Poison
1948	Part for a Poisoner
	apa Place for a Poisoner
1948	Death Before Dinner
	apa A Screen for Murder
1949	Still Waters
1949	Policemen in the Precinct
	apa And Then Put Out the Light
1950	Accident By Design
1951	Murder of a Martinet
	apa I Could Murder Her
1952	Murder in the Mill-Race
	apa Speak Justly of the Dead
1952	The Dog It Was That Died
1953	Crook O' Lune
	apa Shepherd's Crook
1954	Shroud of Darkness
1954	Let Well Alone
1955	Ask a Policeman
1956	Murder in Vienna
1957	Picture of Death
1957	Dangerous Domicile
1958	Death in Triplicate
	apa People Will Talk
1958	Murder on a Monument
1959	Dishonour Among Thieves
	apa The Last Escape

P: Robertson, Helen
Please see: Edmiston, Helen Jean Mary

A: Robinson, Sheila (Mary)
P: Radley, Sheila
SC: Douglas Quantrill, Insp.   (see pg. 61)

    1978   Death and the Maiden
                apa Death in the Morning
    1980   The Chief Inspector's Statement
                apa The Chief Inspector's Daughter
    1982   A Talent for Destruction
    1984   Blood on the Happy Highway
    1984   The Quiet Road to Death
    1986   Fate Worse Than Death

P: Roffman, Jan
    Please see: Summerton, Margaret

A: Roos, Audrey Kelley w/William
P: Roos, Kelley
SC: Haila and Jeff Troy   (see pg. 196)

    1940   Made Up to Kill
                apa Made Up for Murder
    1941   If the Shroud Fits
                apa Dangerous Blondes
    1942   The Frightened Stiff
    1944   Sailor, Take Warning!
    1945   There Was a Crooked Man
    1947   Ghost of a Chance
    1948   Murder in Any Language
    1949   Triple Threat
    1951   Beauty Marks the Spot
    1966   One False Move

P: Roos, Kelley
    Please see: Roos, Audrey Kelley w/William

JN: Roos, William
    Please see: Roos, Audrey Kelley w/William

A: Ross, Z(ola) H(elen) (Gridey)
SC: Beau Smith and Pogy Rogers

    1946   Three Down Vulnerable
    1948   One Corpse Missing

A: Roth, Holly
    SC: Kelly, Lt.

    1954   The Content Assignment
             apa The Shocking Secret
    1966   Button, Button

    SC: Medford, Insp.

    1957   Shadow of a Lady
    1962   Operation Doctors
             apa Too Many Doctors

A: Rowe, Anne
    SC: Barry, Insp.

    1944   Too Much Poison
             apa Cobra Venom
    1945   Up to the Hilt
    1946   Deadly Intent

    SC: Pettengill, Insp.

    1942   The Little Dog Barked
    1945   The Painted Monster

A: Russell, Charlotte Murray
    SC: Homer Fitzgerald

    1947   Lament for William
    1949   The Careless Mrs. Christian
    1950   Between Us and Evil
    1952   June, Moon and Murder

    SC: Jane Amanda Edwards

    1935   Murder at the Old Stone House
    1936   Death of an Eloquent Man
    1937   The Tiny Diamond
    1938   Night on the Pathway
             apa Night on the Devil's Pathway
    1939   The Clue of the Naked Eye
    1940   I Heard the Death Bell
    1942   The Message of the Mute Dog

Russell, Charlotte Murray (cont.)

    1945   No Time for Crime
    1946   The Bad Neighbor Murder
    1948   Ill Met in Mexico
    1949   Hand Me a Crime
    1951   Cook Up a Crime

A: Russell, E(nid)
    SC: Ben Louis

    1968   She Should Have Cried on Monday
    1971   Nice Enough to Murder

A: Rutland, Harriet
    SC: Mr. Winkley

    1938   Knock, Murderer, Knock!
    1940   Bleeding Hooks
           apa The Poison Fly Murder

A: Ryan, Jessica
    SC: Gregory Pavlov and O'Shaunnessey

    1945   The Man Who Asked Why
           apa The Clue of the Frightening Coin
    1947   Exit Harlequin

P: Ryerson, Florence and Colin Clements
Please see: Ryerson, Florence w/Colin Clements

A: Ryerson, Florence w/Colin Clements
P: Ryerson, Florence and Colin Clements
    SC: Jimmy Lane

    1930   Seven Suspects
    1931   Fear of Fear
    1933   Blind Man's Bluff
           apa Sleep No More
    1934   Shadows

S

A: Salter, Elizabeth
  SC: Michael Hornsley, Insp.

1957	Death in a Mist
1958	Will to Survive
1960	There Was a Witness
1962	The Voice of the Peacock
1965	Once Upon a Tombstone

A: Sanborn, Ruth Burr
  SC: Angeline Tredennick

1932	Murder By Jury
1935	Murder on the Aphrodite

A: Sarsfield, Maureen
  SC: Lane Parry, Insp.

1945	Green December Fills the Graveyard
1948	Dinner for None
	apa A Party for Lawty

P: Saunders, Lawrence
  Please see: Davis, Clare w/Burton

A: Sayers, Dorothy L.
  SC: Lord Peter Wimsey   (see pg. 82)

	1923	Whose Body?
	1926	Clouds of Witness
	1927	Unnatural Death
		apa The Dawson Pedigree
SS	1928	Lord Peter Views the Body
	1928	The Unpleasantness at the Bellona Club
	1930	Strong Poison
	1931	The Five Red Herrings
		apa Suspicious Characters
	1932	Have His Carcase
SS	1933	Hangman's Holiday
	1933	Murder Must Advertise
	1934	The Nine Tailors
	1935	Gaudy Night

Sayers, Dorothy L. (cont.)

	1937	Busman's Honeymoon
SS	1939	In the Teeth of the Evidence and Other Stories
SS	1958	A Treasury of Sayers Stories
SS	1972	Striding Folly
SS	1972	Lord Peter: A Collection of all the Lord Peter Stories

SC: Montague Egg   (see pg. 134)

| SS | 1933 | Hangman's Holiday |
| SS | 1939 | In the Teeth of the Evidence |

P: Scarlett, Roger
Please see: Blair, Dorothy w/Evelyn Page

JN: Schabelitz, Rudolph Fredrick
Please see: Barber, Willetta Ann w/Rudolph Fredrick Schabelitz

A: Scherf, Margaret (Louise)
SC: Dr. Grace Severance   (see pg. 111)

1968	The Banker's Bones
1971	The Beautiful Birthday Cake
1972	To Cache a Millionaire
1978	The Beaded Banana

SC: Emily and Henry Bryce   (see pg. 134)

1948	Always Murder A Friend
1949	The Gun in Daniel Webster's Bust
1951	The Green Plaid Pants
	apa The Corpse with One Shoe
1954	Glass on the Stairs
1963	The Diplomat and the Gold Piano
	apa Death and the Diplomat

SC: Rev. Martin Buell   (see pg. 94)

| 1949 | Gilbert's Last Toothache |
| | *apa* For the Love of Murder |

Scherf, Margaret (Louise) (cont.)

    1950   The Curious Custard Pie
              apa Divine and Deadly
    1952   The Elk and the Evidence
    1956   The Cautious Overshoes
    1959   Never Turn Your Back
    1965   The Corpse in the Flannel Nightgown

    SC: Ryan, Lt.

    1945   The Owl in the Cellar
    1948   Murder Makes Me Nervous

A: Schier, Norma
    SC: Kay Barth

    1978   Death on the Slopes
    1979   Murder By the Book
    1979   Death Goes Skiing
    1980   Demon of the Opera

A: Scott, Margaret w/William Charles Oursler
P: Gallagher, Gale
    SC: Gale Gallagher   (see pg. 211)

    1947   I Found Him Dead
    1949   Chord in Crimson

A: Scott, Marian Gallagher
P: Wolffe, Katherine
    SC: Courtney Brade, Capt.

    1942   The Attic Room
    1946   Death's Long Shadow

A: Sebenthal, Roberta E.
P: Kruger, Paul
    SC: Phil Kramer

    1966   Weep for Willow Green
    1967   Weave a Wicked Web
    1969   If the Shroud Fits

Sebenthal, Roberta E. (cont.)

    1972   The Cold Ones
    1972   The Bronze Claws

A: Seifert, Adele
    SC: Gregory Trent

    1939   Shadows Tonight
    1939   Deeds Ill Done
            apa Kill Your Own Snakes
    1942   3 Blind Mice

P: Shane, Susannah
    Please see: Ashbrook, H(arriette) (C.)

P: Shannon, Dell
    Please see: Linington, Elizabeth

A: Shannon, Doris
P: Giroux, E. X.
    SC: Robert Forsythe   (see pg. 143)

    1984   A Death for Adonis
    1985   A Death for a Darling
    1985   A Death for a Dancer
    1986   A Death for a Doctor
    1987   A Death for a Dilettante

A: Sharp, Marilyn (Augburn)
    SC: Richard Owen, Agent

    1979   Sunflower
    1984   Falseface

A: Shaw, Felicity
P: Morice, Anne
    SC: Tessa Crichton   (see pg. 104)

    1970   Death in the Grand Manor
    1971   Murder in Married Life
    1971   Death of a Gay Dog
    1972   Murder on French Leave

Shaw, Felicity (cont.)

1973	Death and the Dutiful Daughter
1974	Killing with Kindness
1974	Death of a Heavenly Twin
1975	Nursery Tea and Poison
1976	Death of a Wedding Guest
1977	Murder in Mimicry
1977	Scared to Death
1978	Murder by Proxy
1979	Murder in Outline
1980	Death in the Round
1981	The Men in Her Death
1982	Sleep of Death
1982	Hollow Vengeance
1984	Getting Away With Murder?
	apa Murder Post-Dated
1985	Dead on Cue
1987	Publish and Be Killed

P: Shepherd, Joan
Please see: Buchanan, Betty Joan

A: Sheridan, Juanita
SC: Lilly Wu and Janice Cameron

1949	The Chinese Chop
1951	The Kahuna Killer
1952	The Mamo Murders
	apa While the Coffin Waited
1953	The Waikiki Widow

A: Shore, Viola Brothers
SC: Colin Keats and Gwynn Leith

1930	The Beauty-Mask Murder
	apa The Beauty-Mask Mystery
1932	Murder on the Glass Floor

A: Shriber, Ione Sandburg
SC: Bill Grady, Lt.

1940	Head Over Heels in Murder

Shriber, Ione Sandburg (cont.)

    1940   The Dark Arbor
    1941   Family Affair
    1941   Murder Well Done
    1942   A Body for Bill
    1943   Invitation to Murder
    1944   Pattern for Murder
    1946   The Last Straw

A: Siegel, Doris
P: Wells, Susan
    SC: Anthony Ware

    1939   Murder is Not Enough
    1940   Footsteps in the Air
    1942   Death is My Name
    1947   The Witches' Pond

P: Siller, Van
    Please see: Van Siller, Hilda

A: Silverman, Marguerite R.
    SC: Christopher Adrian, Insp.

    1945   The Vet It Was That Died
    1948   Who Should Have Died?
    1951   9 Had No Vet

P: Simons, Roger
    Please see: Punnett, Margaret w/Ivor

A: Simpson, Dorothy
    SC: Luke Thanet, Det. Insp. (see pg. 59)

    1981   The Night She Died
    1982   Six Feet Under
    1983   Puppet For a Corpse
    1984   Close Her Eyes: An Inspector Thanet
              Mystery
    1985   Last Seen Alive
    1986   Dead on Arrival

JN: Simpson, Helen
  Please see: Ashton, Winifred w/Helen Simpson

A: Sinclair, Fiona
  SC: Paul Grainger, Insp.

  1960   Scandalize My Name
  1961   Dead of a Physician
         apa But the Patient Died
  1963   Meddle With the Mafia
  1964   Three Slips to a Noose
  1965   Most Unnatural Murder

A: Singer, Shelley
  SC: Jake Samson and Rosie Vicente   (see pg. 271)

  1983   Samson's Deal
  1984   Free Draw
  1986   Full House
  1987   Spit in the Ocean

P: Sjowall, Maj and Per Wahloo
  Please see: Sjowall, Maj w/Per Wahloo

A: Sjowall, Maj w/Per Wahloo
P: Sjowall, Maj and Per Wahloo
  SC: Martin Beck, Chief Insp.   (see pg. 68)

  1967   Roseanna
  1968   The Man on the Balcony
  1969   The Man Who Went up in Smoke
  1970   The Laughing Policeman
  1971   The Fire Engine that Disappeared
  1971   Murder at the Savoy
  1972   The Abominable Man
  1973   The Locked Room
  1975   Cop Killer
  1976   The Terrorists

JN: Skidelsky, Simon Jasha
  Please see: Abrahams, Doris Caroline w/Simon Jasha
    Skidelsky

A: Smith, Alison
 SC: Judd Springfield

 1984   Someone Else's Grave
 1987   Rising

A: Smith, Evelyn E.
 SC: Miss Susan Melville

 1986   Miss Melville Regrets
 1987   Miss Melville Returns

A: Smith, Julie
 SC: Paul McDonald

 1985   True-Life Adventures
 1987   Huckleberry Fiend

 SC: Rebecca Schwartz   (see pg. 157)

 1982   Death Turns a Trick
 1984   The Sourdough Wars
 1986   Tourist Trap

P: Smith, Shelley
 Please see: Bodington, Nancy Hermione
  Courlander

A: Spain, Nancy
 SC: Johnny DuVivien

 1946   Death Before Wicket
 1946   Poison in Play
 1948   Murder, Bless It!
 1949   Death Goes on Skis
 1949   Poison for Teacher

 SC: Miriam Birdseye

 1949   Death Goes on Skis
 1949   Poison for Teacher
 1950   R in the Month

Spain, Nancy (cont.)

    1950   Cinderella Goes to the Morgue
    1951   Not Wanted on Voyage
    1952   Out, Damned Tot!

JN: Spicer, Bart
    Please see: Spicer, Betty Coe w/Bart

A: Spicer, Betty Coe w/Bart
P: Barbette, Jay
    SC: Harry Butten

    1950   Final Copy
    1953   Dear Dead Days
            apa Death's Long Shadow
    1958   The Deadly Doll
    1960   Look Behind You

A: Sproul, Kathleen
    SC: Dick Wilson

    1932   The Birthday Murder
    1933   Death and the Professors
            apa Death Among the Professors
    1934   Murder Off Key
    1935   The Mystery of the Closed Car

P: St. Clair, Elizabeth
    Please see: Cohen, Susan Handler

A: St. Dennis, Madelon
    SC: Sydney Treherne

    1932   The Death Kiss
    1932   The Perfumed Lure

A: Stand, Marguerite
    SC: Bill Rice

    1964   Escape from Murder
    1965   Death Came With Darkness
    1966   Death Came With Flowers

Stand, Marguerite (cont.)

> 1966   Death Came With Diamonds
> 1966   Death Came in Lucerne
> 1968   Death Came to "Lighthouse
>   Steps"
> 1969   Death Came in the Studio
> 1970   Death Came Too Soon
>
> SC: Robins, Police Constable
>
> 1964   Murder in the Camp
> 1967   Diana is Dead

A: Stevens, Frances M. R.
P: Hale, Christopher
> SC: Bill French, Lt.

> 1935   Smoke Screen
> 1937   Stormy Night
> 1939   Murder on Display
> 1940   Witch Wood
> 1941   Dead of Winter
>   *apa* Going, Going, Gone
> 1942   Exit Screaming
> 1943   Murder in Tow
> 1943   Hangman's Tie
> 1945   Rumor Hath It
> 1945   Midsummer Nightmare
> 1948   Deadly Ditto
> 1949   He's Late This Morning

A: Stevenson, Florence
> SC: Kitty Telefair

> 1971   Where Satan Dwells
> 1971   The Witching Hour
> 1973   Mistress of Devil's Manor
> 1973   Altar of Evil
> 1974   The Sorcerer of the Castle
> 1975   The Silent Watcher

A: Stewart, Flora
    SC: Newsom, Insp.

    1966   Deadly Nightcap
    1967   Blood Relations

A: Stockwell, Gail
    SC: Kingsley Toplitt

    1937   Death By Invitation
    1938   The Embarrassed Murderer

A: Stone, Elizabet M.
    SC: Maggie Slone

    1946   Poison, Poker and Pistols
    1947   Murder at the Mardi Gras

A: Strahan, Kay Cleaver
    SC: Lynn MacDonald

    1928   The Desert Moon
                Mystery
    1929   Footprints
    1930   Death Traps
    1931   October House
    1932   The Meriweather Mystery
    1934   The Hobgoblin Murder
    1936   The Desert Lake
                Mystery

P: Strange, John Stephen
    Please see: Tillett, Dorothy Stockbridge

A: Stubbs, Jean
    SC: John Joseph Lintott, Insp.

    1973   Dear Laura
    1974   The Painted Face
    1976   The Golden Crucible

A: Summerton, Margaret
P: Roffman, Jan
   SC: Ratlin, Sgt.

    1965   A Penny for the Guy
          apa Mask of Words
    1965   The Hanging Woman

A: Swan, Phyllis
   SC: Anna J(agedinski)

    1979   Trigger Lady
    1979   Find Sherri!
    1979   You've Had It Girl
    1980   Death Inheritance

A: Symons, Beryl (Mary) (E.)
   SC: Henry Doight, Insp.

    1928   The Devine Court Mystery
    1929   The Leering House
    1932   The Opal Murder Case

   SC: Jane Carberry

    1940   Jane Carberry Investigates
    1940   Jane Carberry: Detective
    1941   Magnet for Murder
    1943   Jane Carberry and the Laughing Fountain
    1947   Jane Carberry's Weekend

T

A: Tait, Euphemia Margaret
P: Ironside, John
    SC: John Freeman, Det. Insp.

    1910   The Red Symbol
    1933   The Marten Mystery

A: Taylor, Elizabeth Atwood
    SC: Maggie Elliott

    1981   The Cable Car Murder
    1987   Murder at Vassar

A: Taylor, L(aurie) A(ylma)
    SC: J. J. Jamison

    1984   Deadly Objective
    1986   Only Half a Hoax

A: Taylor, Mary Ann
    SC: Emil Martin

    1980   Red is for Shrouds
    1980   Return to Murder

A: Taylor, Phoebe Atwood
    SC: Asey Mayo   (see pg. 265)

    1931   The Cape Cod Mystery
    1932   Death Lights a Candle
    1933   The Mystery of the Cape Cod Players
    1934   Sandbar Sinister
    1934   The Mystery of the Cape Cod Tavern
    1935   The Tinkling Symbol
    1935   Deathblow Hill
    1936   Out of Order
    1936   The Crimson Patch
    1937   Octagon House
    1937   Figure Away
    1938   Banbury Bog
    1938   The Annulet of Guilt
    1939   Spring Harrowing

Taylor, Phoebe Atwood (cont.)

1940	The Deadly Sunshade
1940	The Criminal C.O.D.
1941	The Perennial Boarder
1942	Three Plots for Asey Mayo
1942	The Six Iron Spiders
1943	Going, Going, Gone
1945	Proof of the Pudding
1946	The Asey Mayo Trio
1946	Punch With Care
1951	Diplomatic Corpse

P: Tilton, Alice
   SC: Leonidas Witherall

1937	Beginning With a Bash
1938	The Cut Direct
1939	Cold Steal
1940	The Left Leg
1941	The Hollow Chest
1943	File for Record
1944	Dead Ernest
1947	The Iron Clew
	apa The Iron Hand

JN: **Tedeschi, Frank L.**
   Please see: Byfield, Barbara Ninde
      w/Frank L. Tedeschi

P: **Teilhet, Darwin L.**
   Please see: Teilhet, Hildegarde Tolman

A: **Teilhet, Hildegarde Tolman**
   SC: Sam Hook   (see pg. 224)

1942	Hero By Proxy
1945	The Dougle Agent
1946	The Assassins

P: Teilhet, Darwin L.
   SC: Baron Von Kaz

1936	The Feather Cloak Murders

Teilhet, Hildegarde Tolman (cont.)

   1936   The Crimson Hair Murders
   1940   The Broken Face Murders

P: Tey, Josephine
Please see: MacKintosh, Elizabeth

A: Thayer, (Emma) (R.) Lee
SC: Peter Clancy   (see pg. 207)

   1919   The Mystery of the Thirteenth Floor
   1920   The Unlatched Door
   1921   That Affair at "The Cedars"
   1922   Q.E.D.
          apa The Puzzle
   1923   The Sinister Mark
   1924   The Key
   1926   Poison
   1927   Alias Dr. Ely
   1928   The Darkest Spot
   1929   Dead Men's Shoes
   1930   They Tell No Tales
   1931   Set a Thief
          apa To Catch a Thief
   1931   The Last Shot
   1932   The Glass Knife
   1932   The Scrimshaw Millions
   1933   Hell-Gate Tides
   1933   Counterfeit
          apa The Counterfeit Bill
   1934   The Second Bullet
          apa The Second Shot
   1935   Dead Storage
          apa The Death Weed
   1935   Sudden Death
          apa Red-Handed
   1936   Dead End Street, No Outlet
          apa Murder in the Mirror
   1936   Dark of the Moon
          apa Death in the Gorge
   1937   A Man's Enemies
          apa This Man's Doom
   1937   Last Trump

Thayer, (Emma) (R.) Lee (cont.)

1938	Ransom Racket
1938	That Strange Sylvester Affair
	apa The Strange Sylvester Affair
1939	Stark Murder
1939	Lightning Strikes Twice
1940	Guilty!
1940	X Marks the Spot
1941	Hallowe'en Homicide
1941	Persons Unknown
1942	Murder on Location
1942	Murder is Out
1943	Hanging's Too Good
1943	Accessory After the Fact
1944	Five Bullets
1944	A Plain Case of Murder
1945	Accident, Manslaughter or Murder?
1946	A Hair's Breadth
1946	The Jaws of Death
1947	Murder Stalks the Circle
1948	Pig in a Poke
	apa A Clue for Clancy
1948	Out, Brief Candle!
1949	Evil Root
1950	Too Long Endured
1950	Within the Vault
	apa Death Within the Vault
1951	Guilt Edged
	apa Guilt-Edged Murder
1951	Do Not Disturb
	apa Clancy's Secret Mission
1952	Blood on the Knight
1953	The Prisoner Pleads "Not Guilty"
1954	Dead Reckoning
	apa Murder on the Pacific
1954	No Holiday for Death
1955	Who Benefits?
	apa Fatal Alibi
1957	Guilt Is Where You Find It
1958	Still No Answer
	apa Web of Hate

Thayer, (Emma) (R.) Lee (cont.)

    1959   Two Ways to Die
    1960   Dead on Arrival
    1961   And One Cried Murder
    1966   Dusty Death
           apa Death Walks in Shadow

A: Thomson, June
    SC: Finch (Rudd), Insp.   (see pg. 56)

    1971   Not One of Us
    1973   Death Cap
    1974   The Long Revenge
    1977   Case Closed
    1977   A Question of Identity
    1979   Deadly Relations
           apa The Habit of Loving
    1980   Alibi in Time
    1981   Shadow of a Doubt
    1982   To Make a Killing
           apa Portrait of Lilith
    1985   Sound Evidence
    1986   The Dark Stream
    1987   No Flowers By Request

A: Thynne, Molly
    SC: Dr. Constantine

    1931   The Crime at the "Noah's Ark"
    1932   Murder in the Dentist Chair
    1933   He Dies and Makes No Sign

A: Tillett, Dorothy Stockbridge
P: Strange, John Stephen
    SC: Barney Gantt   (see pg. 172)

    1936   The Bell in the Fog
    1938   Rope Enough
           apa The Ballot Box Murders
    1938   Silent Witnesses
           apa The Corpse and the Lady

Tillet, Dorothy Stockbridge (cont.)

1940	A Picture of the Victim
1943	Look Your Last
1948	Make My Bed Soon
1952	Deadly Beloved
1976	The House on 9th Street

SC: George Honegger, Lt.

1941	Murder Gives A Lovely Light
1948	All Men Are Liars
	apa Come to Judgment
1961	Eye Witness
1976	The House on 9th Street

SC: Van Dusen Ormsberry

1928	The Man Who Killed Fortescue
1929	The Clue of the Second Murder
1931	Murder on the Ten-Yard Line
	apa Murder Game

P: Tilton, Alice
Please see: Taylor, Phoebe Atwood

A: Tirbutt, Honoria
P: Page, Emma
   SC: Kelsey, Chief Insp.   (see pg. 62)

1981	Every Second Thursday
1982	Last Walk Home
1984	Cold Light of Day
1986	Scent of Death
1987	Final Moments

A: Tone, Teona
SC: Kyra Keaton

1983	Lady on the Line
1985	Full Cry

P: Torrie, Malcolm
Please see: Mitchell, Gladys

A: Turnbull, Dora Amy Elles Dillon
P: Wentworth, Patricia
    SC: Ernest Lamb, Insp.

    1939   The Blind Side
    1940   Who Pays the Piper?
            apa Account Rendered
    1942   Pursuit of a Parcel

    SC: Maud Silver   (see pg. 208)

    1928   Grey Mask
    1937   The Case is Closed
    1939   Lonesome Road
    1941   In the Balance
            apa Danger Point
    1943   Miss Silver Deals With Death
            apa Miss Silver Intervenes
    1943   The Chinese Shawl
    1944   The Key
    1944   The Clock Strikes Twelve
    1945   She Came Back
            apa The Traveler Returns
    1946   Pilgrim's Rest
            apa Dark Threat
    1947   Wicked Uncle
            apa Spotlight
    1947   Latter End
    1948   Eternity Ring
    1948   The Case of William Smith
    1949   Miss Silver Comes to Stay
    1949   The Catherine Wheel
    1950   Through the Wall
    1950   The Brading Collection
    1951   The Ivory Dagger
    1951   The Watersplash
    1951   Anna, Where are You?
            apa Death at Deep End
    1952   Ladies' Bane
    1953   Out of the Past
    1953   Vanishing Point
    1954   The Benevent Treasure
    1954   The Silent Pool
    1955   Poison in the Pen

Turnbull, Dora Amy Elles Dillon (cont.)

    1955   The Listening Eye
    1956   The Fingerprint
    1956   The Gazebo
            apa The Summerhouse
    1958   The Alington Inheritance
    1961   The Girl in the Cellar

A: Turnbull, Margaret
SC: Juliet Jackson

    1926   Madame Judas
    1928   Rogues' March
    1932   The Return of Jenny Weaver
    1934   The Coast Road Murder

U, V

A: **Uhnak, Dorothy**
　　SC: Christie Opara, Det.　(see pg. 28)

　　1968　The Bait
　　1969　The Witness
　　1970　The Ledger

A: **Vahey, John G. H.**
P: Clandon, Henrietta
　　SC: Penny and Vincent Mercer

　　1935　Rope By Arrangement
　　1936　This Delicate Murder
　　1937　Power on the Scent
　　1938　Fog Off Weymouth

　　SC: William Power

　　1935　Rope By Arrangement
　　1936　This Delicate Murder
　　1936　Good By Stealth
　　1937　Power on the Scent

A: **Van Deventer, Emma M.**
P: Lynch, Lawrence
　　SC: Carl Masters

　　1894　Against Odds
　　1904　A Woman's Tragedy; or, the Detective's Task
　　1908　Man and Master

　　SC: Madeline Payne

　　1884　Madeline Payne, the Detective's Daughter
　　　　　apa The Detective's Daughter; or, Madeline
　　　　　　　Payne
　　1891　Moina; or, Against the Mighty
　　　　　apa Moina

Van Deventer, Emma M. (cont.)

SC: Neil Bathurst

1879　Shadowed By Three
1882　Diamond Coterie
1885　Out of the Labyrinth

SC: Van Vernet

1885　Dangerous Ground; or, the Rival Detectives
　　　apa The Rival Detectives; or, Dangerous Ground
1886　A Mountain Mystery; or, the Outlaws of the
　　　Rockies

A: **Van Siller, Hilda**
P: Siller, Van
　　SC: Allan Stewart

1965　A Complete Stranger
1966　The Mood of Murder
1967　The Biltmore Call

SC: Pete Rector

1943　Good Night, Ladies
1944　Under a Cloud

SC: Richard Massey

1943　Echo of a Bomb
1947　The Curtain Between
　　　apa Fatal Bride

A: **Van Urk, Virginia**
　　SC: Tom Craig

1951　Speaking of Murder
1958　Grounds for Murder

P: **Venning, Michael**
　　Please see: Craig, Georgiana Ann Randolph

A: Vincent, Lady Kitty
   SC: Gyp Kidnadze

   1924   "No. 3"
   1928   The Ruby Cup
   1934   An Untold Tale

W

JN: Wahloo, Per
Please see: Sjowall, Maj.
w/Per Wahloo

A: Walker, Ir(m)a (Ruth) (Roden)
SC: Steve Rhoden

1963   Someone's Stolen Nellie Grey
1964   The Man in the Driver's Seat
1980   Murder in 25 Words or Less

P: Wallace, C. H.
Please see: Burger, Rosaylmer

A: Wallace, Mary
P: Lynch, Miriam
SC: Nell Willard

1979   Time to Kill
1979   You'll Be the Death of Me

A: Wallis, Ruth (O.) Sawtell
SC: Eric Lund

1944   No Bones About It
1947   Cold Bed in the Clay
1950   Forget My Fate

P: Walter, A. and H.
Please see: Walter, Alexia w/Hubert

A: Walter, Alexia w/Hubert
P: Walter, A. and H.
SC: Sir Edgar Ewart

1928   The Patriot
1929   Betrayal

JN: Walter, Hubert
Please see: Walter, Alexia w/Hubert

A: Walz, Audrey Boyers
P: Bonnamy, Francis
　　SC: Peter Uteley Shane, Prof.

　　1931　Death By Appointment
　　1937　Death on a Dude Ranch
　　1943　Dead Reckoning
　　1944　A Rope of Sand
　　1945　The King is Dead on Queen Street
　　1947　Portrait of the Artist as a Dead Man
　　　　　apa Murder as a Fine Art
　　　　　apa Self-Portrait of Murder
　　1949　Blood and Thirsty
　　1951　The Man in the Mist

A: Ward-Thomas, Evelyn Bridget Patricia Stephens
P: Anthony, Evelyn
　　SC: Davina Graham　(see pg. 229)

　　1980　The Defector
　　1981　The Avenue of the Dead
　　1982　Albatross
　　1983　The Company of Saints

A: Warner, Mignon
　　SC: Mrs. Charles　(see pg. 259)

　　1976　A Nice Way to Die
　　　　　apa A Medium for Murder
　　1978　The Tarot Murders
　　1982　The Girl Who Was Clairvoyant
　　1982　Death in Time
　　1983　Devil's Knell
　　1984　Speak No Evil
　　1984　Illusion

A: Watson, Clarissa
　　SC: Persis Willum　(see pg. 198)

　　1977　The Fourth Stage of Gainsborough Brown
　　1980　The Bishop in the Back Seat
　　1985　Runaway

A: Wees, Frances Shelley
  SC: Michael Forrester

  1931   The Mystery of the Creeping Man
  1931   The Maestro Murders
       apa Detectives, Ltd.

A: Wells, Anna Mary
  SC: Dr. Hillis Owen and Miss Pomeroy   (see pg. 125)

  1942   A Talent for Murder
  1943   Murderer's Choice
  1948   Sin of Angels

A: Wells, Carolyn
  SC: Alan Ford

  1916   The Bride of a Moment
  1917   Faulkner's Folly

  SC: Fleming Stone   (see pg. 206)

  1909   The Clue
  1911   The Gold Bag
  1912   A Chain of Evidence
  1913   The Maxwell Mystery
  1914   Anybody But Anne
  1915   The White Alley
  1916   The Curved Blades
  1917   The Mark of Cain
  1918   Vicky Van
       apa The Elusive Vicky Van
  1919   The Diamond Pin
  1920   Raspberry Jam
  1921   The Mystery of the Sycamore
  1922   The Mystery Girl
  1923   Spooky Hollow
  1923   Feathers Left Around
  1924   Prillilgirl
  1924   The Furthest Fury
  1925   Anything But the Truth
  1925   The Daughter of the House
  1926   The Bronze Hand

Wells, Carolyn (cont.)

1926	The Red-Haired Girl
1927	Where's Emily
1927	All At Sea
1928	The Tannahill Tangle
1928	The Crime in the Crypt
1929	The Tapestry Room Murder
1929	Triple Murder
1930	The Ghost's High Noon
1930	The Doomed Five
1931	The Umbrella Murder
1931	Horror House
1932	The Roll-Top Desk Mystery
1932	Fuller's Earth
1933	The Broken O
1933	The Master Murderer
1933	The Clue of the Eyelash
1934	Eyes in the Wall
1934	The Visiting Villain
1934	In the Tiger's Cage
1935	For Goodness' Sake
1935	The Wooden Indian
1935	The Beautiful Derelict
1936	Money Musk
1936	Murder in the Bookshop
1936	The Huddle
1937	The Radio Studio Murder
1937	The Mystery of the Tarn
1938	The Killer
1938	The Missing Link
1938	Gilt-Edged Guilt
1939	Calling All Suspects
1939	Crime Tears On
1939	The Importance of Being Murdered
1940	Crime Incarnate
1940	Murder on Parade
1940	Murder Plus
1940	Devil's Work
1941	The Black Night Murders
1941	Murder at the Casino
1942	Who Killed Caldwell?
1942	Murder Will In

Wells, Carolyn (cont.)

SC: Kenneth Carlisle   (see pg. 102)

1929   Sleeping Dogs
1930   The Doorstep Murders
1931   The Skeleton at the Feast

SC: Lorimer Lane

1923   More Lives than One
1924   The Fourteenth Key

SC: Pennington Wise   (see pg. 206)

1918   The Room With the Tassels
1919   The Man Who Fell Through the Earth
1920   In the Onyx Lobby
1921   The Luminous Face
1921   The Come-Back
1922   The Vanishing of Betty Varian
1923   The Affair at Flower Acres
1923   Wheels Within Wheels

P: **Wells, Susan**
Please see: Siegel, Doris

P: **Wells, Tobias**
Please see: Forbes, DeLoris

A: **Wendell, Sarah**
SC: Dolly and The Old Buffer

1973   The Old Buffer's Tale
1979   Dolly and The Old Buffer Dig
          for Clews
1984   Dolly and The Old Buffer in Oxford

A: **Wender, Dorothea**
P: Wender, Theodora
SC: Glad Gold, Prof. and Chase, Police Chief

1985   Knight Must Fall
1986   Murder Gets a Degree

P: Wender, Theodora
Please see: Wender, Dorothea

P: Wentworth, Patricia
Please see: Turnbull, Dora Amy Elles Dillon

A: Weston, Carolyn
SC: Al Krug and Casey Kellog

1972	Poor, Poor Ophelia
1975	Susannah Screaming
1976	Rouse the Demon

A: Wheat, Carolyn
SC: Cass Jameson   (see pg. 154)

| 1983 | Dead Man's Thoughts |
| 1986 | Where Nobody Dies |

A: Whitaker, Beryl
SC: John Abbot

1967	The Chained Crocodile
1967	Of Mice and Murder
1967	A Matter of Blood
1968	The Man Who Wasn't There

A: White, Teri
SC: Blue Maguire and Spaceman Kowalski

| 1981 | Triangle |
| 1986 | Tightrope |

A: Williams, Margaret Wetherby
P: Erskine, Margaret
SC: Septimus Finch, Insp.   (see pg. 36)

1938	And Being Dead
	apa The Limping Man
	apa The Painted Mask
1947	The Whispering House
	apa The Voice of the House
1948	I Knew MacBean
	apa Caravan of Night

Williams, Margaret Wetherby (cont.)

1949	Give Up the Ghost
1950	The Disappearing Bridegroom
	apa The Silver Ladies
1952	Death of Our Dear One
	apa Don't Look Behind You
	apa Look Behind You, Lady
1953	Dead By Now
1955	Fatal Relations
	apa The Dead Don't Speak
	apa Old Mrs. Ommanney is Dead
1956	The Voice of Murder
1958	Sleep No More
1959	The House of the Enchantress
	apa A Graveyard Plot
1961	The Woman at Belguardo
1963	The House in Belmont Square
	apa No. 9 Belmont Square
1965	Take a Dark Journey
	apa The Family at Tammerton
1967	Case With Three Husbands
1968	The Ewe Lamb
1970	The Case of Mary Fielding
1971	The Brood of Folly
1973	Besides the Wench is Dead
1975	Harriet Farewell
1977	The House in Hook Street

A: Williamson, Audrey
SC: Richard York, Supt.

1979	Funeral March for Siegfried
1980	Death of a Theatre Filly

A: Wilson, Barbara
SC: Pam Nilsen

1984	Murder in the Collective
1986	Sisters of the Road

A: Wilson, G(ertrude) M(ary)
   SC: Lovick, Insp.

   1957   Bury That Poker
   1957   I Was Murdered
   1959   Shadows on the Landing
   1961   Witchwater
   1962   Roberta Died
   1963   Murder on Monday
   1964   Shot at Dawn
   1965   The Devil's Skull
   1967   Cake for Caroline
   1967   The Headless Man
   1968   Do Not Sleep
   1969   Death Is Buttercups
   1970   A Deal of Death Caps
   1971   The Bus Ran Late
   1972   She Kept On Dying

A: Wiltz, Chris
   SC: Neal Rafferty

   1981   The Killing Circle
   1987   A Diamond Before You Die

A: Winslow, Pauline Glen
   SC: Merlin Capricorn, Supt.   (see pg. 99)

   1975   Death of an Angel
   1976   The Brandenberg Hotel
   1977   The Witch Hill Murder
   1978   Coppergold
          apa Copper Gold
   1980   The Counsellor Heart
          apa Sister Death
   1981   The Rockefeller Gift

P: Wolffe, Katherine
   Please see: Scott, Marian Gallagher

P: Woods, Sara
   Please see: Bowen-Judd, Sara Hutton

A: Worsley-Gough, Barbara
SC: Aloysius Kelly

1954   Alibi Innings
1957   Lantern Hill

P: Wren, M. K.
Please see: Renfroe, Martha Kay

A: Wright, L(aurali) R.
SC: Cassandra Mitchell and Karl Alberg, Sgt.

1985   The Suspect
1986   Sleep While I Sing

Y, Z

A: Yarbro, Chelsea Quinn
SC: Charles Spotted Moon   (see pg. 155)

1976   Ogilvie, Tallant & Moon
1979   Music When Sweet Voices Die

A: Yates, Margaret Tayler
SC: Anne "Davvie" Davenport McLean

1937   The Hush-Hush Murders
1938   Death Sends a Cable
1941   Midway to Murder
1942   Murder By the Yard

P: Yorke, Margaret
Please see: Nicholson, Margaret B.

A: Zaremba, Eve
SC: Helen Keremos

1978   A Reason to Kill
1986   Work for a Million

APPENDIX I: SERIES CHARACTER CHRONOLOGY

This chronological listing is designed to assist readers in several ways. With this information, a series can be fixed in time. A favorite character can then be placed with her/his fictional counterparts. Often, writing style and vernacular reflect the era in which a book was written. Trends and character type also vary with different periods.

The first date of each entry marks the series character's first appearance in print. The second date shows when the last book in the series was published. The number of books in which each series character appears is next, followed by the series character's name in bold print. The author's name appears under the series character's.

Pub. Dates	Book Count	Character/ Author
1867–1868	2	**Valentine Hawkehurst** Braddon, M(ary) E(lizabeth)
1878–1917	12	**Ebenezer Gryce** Green, Anna Katharine
1879–1885	3	**Neil Bathurst** Lynch, Lawrence
1884–1891	2	**Madeline Payne** Lynch, Lawrence
1885–1886	2	**Van Vernet** Lynch, Lawrence
1894–1894	1	**Loveday Brooke, Lady Detective** Pirkis, C(atharine) L(ouisa)
1894–1908	3	**Carl Masters** Lynch, Lawrence
1897–1917	6	**Amelia Butterworth & Ebenezer Gryce** Green, Anna Katharine
1899–1917	6	**Caleb Sweetwater** Green, Anna Katharine
1900–1900	1	**Madame Koluchy** Meade, L. T.
1903–1903	1	**Madame Sara** Meade, L. T.
1904–1909	3	**Don Q** Prichard, K. and V.
1905–1925	8	**Bill Owen, The Old Man in the Corner** Orczy, Baroness (Emmuska)
1909–1942	61	**Fleming Stone** Wells, Carolyn
1910–1933	2	**John Freeman** Ironside, John
1910–1910	1	**Lady Molly** Orczy, Baroness (Emmuska)

1914–1922	2	**Mercedes Quero** Locke, G(ladys) E(dson)
1914–1915	2	**Mr. Gimblet** Bryce, Mrs. Charles
1915–1916	2	**Molly Morgenthau** Bonner, Geraldine
1915–1918	2	**Hamilton Cleek** Hanshew, Thomas
1915–1915	1	**Violet Strange** Green, Anna Katharine
1916–1917	2	**Alan Ford** Wells, Carolyn
1916–1927	10	**Mitchell** Lincoln, Natalie S.
1917–1923	5	**Timothy McCarty** Ostrander, Isabel
1917–1925	3	**Millicent Newberry** Lee, Jennette
1918–1918	1	**Fernand** Orczy, Baroness (Emmuska)
1918–1923	8	**Pennington Wise** Wells, Carolyn
1919–1966	60	**Peter Clancy** Thayer, (Emma) (R.) Lee
1920–1925	5	**Hamilton Cleek** Hanshew, Mary and Thomas
1920–1975	46	**Hercule Poirot** Christie, Agatha
1920–1921	2	**Ferguson** Lincoln, Natalie S.
1920–1921	2	**Barry O'Dell** Chipperfield, Robert O.
1920–1924	4	**The Shadowers, Inc.** Fox, David
1921–1921	1	**M. Hector Ratichon** Orczy, Baroness (Emmuska)

1922–1927	5	**Jerry Boyne** MacGowan, Alice and Perry Newberry
1922–1925	4	**Burton** Locke, G(ladys) E(dson)
1922–1931	2	**Briconi** Baskerville, Beatrice and Elliot Monk
1922–1973	5	**Tommy and Tuppence Beresford** Christie, Agatha
1923–1942	25	**Henry Wilson** Cole Margaret and G. D. H.
1923–1972	17	**Lord Peter Wimsey** Sayers, Dorothy L.
1923–1927	3	**Furnival** Haynes, Annie
1923–1924	2	**Lorimer Lane** Wells, Carolyn
1924–1934	3	**Gyp Kidnadze** Vincent, Lady Kitty
1924–1945	4	**Race** Christie, Agatha
1924–1944	23	**Pointer** Fielding, A. E.
1925–1944	5	**Battle** Christie, Agatha
1925–1931	2	**Guy Bannister** Crossley, Maude
1925–1932	2	**Winston Barrows** Eades, M(aude) L.
1926–1935	4	**Everard Blatchington** Cole, Margaret and G. D. H.
1926–1927	2	**Septimus March** Bamburg, Lilian
1926–1934	4	**Juliet Jackson** Turnbull, Margaret
1927–1935	10	**Scott Egerton** Gilbert, Anthony

1927–1931	3	**Jack Strickland** Balfour, Hearnden
1927–1929	2	**Parrish Darby** Aresbys, The
1928–1930	3	**Dexter Drake** Barker, Elsa
1928–1932	2	**Sir John Saumarez** Dane, Clemence and Helen Simpson
1928–1961	32	**Maud Silver** Wentworth, Patricia
1928–1936	7	**Lynn MacDonald** Strahan, Kay Cleaver
1928–1928	1	**Patrick Mulligan** Orczy, Baroness (Emmuska)
1928–1929	2	**Sir Edgar Ewart** Walter, A. and H.
1928–1938	4	**Glyn Morgan** Lambert, Rosa and Dudley
1928–1932	3	**Henry Doight** Symons, Beryl (Mary) (E.)
1928–1931	3	**Van Dusen Ormsberry** Strange, John Stephen
1929–1930	3	**Stoddart** Haynes, Annie
1929–1952	6	**Alan Grant** Tey, Josephine
1929–1931	2	**Tim Asher** Hultman, Helen Joan
1929–1973	26	**Albert Campion** Allingham (Carter), Margery
1929–1932	5	**Sarah Keate and Lance O'Leary** Eberhart, Mignon (Good)
1929–1931	3	**Smith** Edingtons, The

1929–1984	68	**Dame Beatrice Adela Lestrange Bradley** Mitchell, Gladys
1929–1931	2	**Gregory Lewis** Frome, David
1929–1931	3	**Kenneth Carlisle** Wells, Carolyn
1929–1940	3	**Bruce Perkins** Lilly, Jean
1929–1932	5	**Peter Piper** Mavity, Nancy Barr
1930–1941	7	**Philip "Spike" Tracy** Ashbrook, H(arriette) (C.)
1930–1979	19	**Jane Marple** Christie, Agatha
1930–1934	4	**Jimmy Lane** Ryerson, Florence and Colin Clements
1930–1943	7	**John Barrin** Lane, (Margaret) Gret
1930–1933	4	**John Smith** Plum, Mary
1930–1934	2	**Peter Jerningham** Myers, Isabel Briggs
1930–1933	5	**Kane** Scarlett, Roger
1930–1937	4	**Margetson** Keate, E(dith) M(urray)
1930–1943	8	**Kate Marsh** Lane, (Margaret) Gret
1930–1931	2	**Sebald Craft** Patterson, (Isabella) Innis
1930–1950	14	**Evan Pinkerton** Frome, David
1930–1950	2	**Harley Quin** Christie, Agatha

1930–1931	3	**Miss Woolfe** Graham, (M.) Winifred (M.)
1930–1939	5	**James F. "Bonnie" Dundee** Austin, Anne
1930–1937	8	**Reynolds** Hamilton, Elaine
1930–1932	2	**Colin Keats and Gwynn Leith** Shore, Viola Brothers
1930–1962	31	**Christopher McKee** Reilly, Helen
1931–1951	8	**Peter Uteley Shane** Bonnamy, Francis
1931–1933	3	**Dr. Constantine** Thynne, Molly
1931–1951	24	**Asey Mayo** Taylor, Phoebe Atwood
1931–1933	3	**Benvenuto Brown** Gill, Elizabeth
1931–1931	2	**Michael Forrester** Wees, Frances Shelley
1931–1932	2	**One Week Wimble** Burnham, Helen
1931–1932	2	**Hamilton Cleek** Hanshew, Hazel Phillips
1931–1959	47	**Macdonald** Lorac, E. C. R.
1931–1940	6	**Li Moh** Cowdroy, Joan
1931–1934	2	**Everett Anderson** Daiger, K(atherine) S.
1931–1933	2	**Wylie King and Nels Lundberg** Saunders, Lawrence
1931–1932	2	**Wade** Bristow, Gwen and Bruce Manning
1931–1948	4	**Tommy Rostetter** Campbell, Alice

1931–1933	4	**Wield** Green, Glint
1932–1932	2	**Sydney Treherne** St. Dennis, Madelon
1932–1935	4	**Dick Wilson** Sproul, Kathleen
1932–1933	2	**Joseph Kelly** Ford, Leslie
1932–1942	3	**Nurse Hilda Adams (Miss Pinkerton)** Rinehart, Mary Roberts
1932–1935	2	**Angeline Tredennick** Sanborn, Ruth Burr
1933–1934	2	**Peter Strangely** Black, E(lizabeth) Best
1933–1939	2	**Montague Egg** Sayers, Dorothy L.
1933–1938	3	**Timothy Fowler** Harris, Colver
1933–1934	2	**Jeremiah Irish** Child, Nellise
1933–1934	2	**Mr. Watson** Gardiner, Dorothy
1933–1934	2	**Woods** Muir, D(orothy) Erskine
1934–1934	1	**Parker Pyne** Christie, Agatha
1934–1936	2	**M. Dupuy** Gilbert, Anthony
1934–1935	2	**Clarice Claremont** Cranston, Claudia
1934–1934	1	**Susan Dare** Eberhart, Mignon (Good)
1934–1936	3	**Colin Anstruther** Plain, Josephine
1934–1982	32	**Roderick Alleyn** Marsh, (Edith) Ngaio

1934–1934	1	**John Primrose**	Ford, Leslie
1935–1953	8	**Hannasyde, Supt.** **and Hemingway, Sgt.**	Heyer, Georgette
1935–1938	4	**Penny and Vincent Mercer**	Clandon, Henrietta
1935–1946	5	**Patrick O'Brien**	Irwin, Inez H.
1935–1959	16	**Elisha Macomber**	Knight, Kathleen Moore
1935–1951	12	**Jane Amanda Edwards**	Russell, Charlotte M.
1935–1946	4	**Gramport**	Barnett, Glyn
1935–1939	6	**Rocky Allan**	Rath, Virginia Anne
1935–1936	2	**Scott Stuart**	Coffin, Geoffrey
1935–1939	4	**Payran**	Nisot, Elizabeth
1935–1938	5	**James Greer**	Gayle, Newton
1935–1949	12	**Bill French**	Hale, Christopher
1935–1942	2	**Dennis Devore**	Bennett, Dorothy
1935–1937	4	**William Power**	Clandon, Henrietta
1936–1944	2	**Gorham**	Cowdroy, Joan
1936–1940	6	**Ryvet**	Carnac, Carol
1936–1938	2	**Red Hanlon**	Merrick, Mollie

1936–1976	8	**Barney Gantt** Strange, John Stephen
1936–1974	50	**Arthur G. Crook** Gilbert, Anthony
1936–1954	19	**Anne and Jeffrey McNeill** DuBois, Theodora M.
1936–1940	2	**James Strange** Quinn, E(leanora) Baker
1936–1946	7	**Simon Brade** Campbell, Harriette (Russell)
1936–1936	2	**Dr. Joan Marvin** Eyles, (M.) Leonora (P.)
1936–1940	3	**Baron Von Kaz** Teilhet, Darwin L.
1937–1938	2	**Kingsley Toplitt** Stockwell, Gail
1937–1953	15	**Grace Latham and John Primrose** Ford, Leslie
1937–1958	14	**Dr. David Wintringham** Bell, Josephine
1937–1948	5	**Headcorn** Campbell, Alice
1937–1939	2	**Simon Chard** Malim, Barbara
1937–1947	8	**Leonidas Witherall** Tilton, Alice
1937–1939	3	**Daisy Jane Mott** Jones, Jennifer
1937–1939	3	**Paul Vachell** Huxley, Elspeth
1937–1937	2	**Carey Brent** Glidden, M(inna) W.
1937–1941	2	**Clive Granville** McKenna, Marthe
1937–1964	13	**Steven Mitchell** Bell, Josephine

1937–1940	3	**Adam Quill** Brahms, Caryl and S. J. Simon
1937–1975	4	**Ballet Stroganoff** Brahms, Caryl and S. J. Simon
1937–1942	4	**Anne "Davvie" Davenport McLean** Yates, Margaret Tayler
1937–1938	2	**Hook** Lane, (Margaret) Gret
1937–1939	2	**Dr. Nathaniel Bunce** Curtiss, E(lizabeth) M.
1937–1938	2	**Adelaide Adams** Blackmon, Anita
1938–1940	2	**Mr. Winkley** Rutland, Harriet
1938–1959	18	**Mallett** Fitt, Mary
1938–1942	3	**Adam Drew and Katherine Cornish** Hanson, Virginia
1938–1947	8	**Michael Dundas** Rath, Virginia Anne
1938–1940	2	**Glover** Evermay, March
1938–1980	13	**Dr. Basil Willing** McCloy, Helen
1938–1946	7	**Stephen Mayhew** Olsen, D. B.
1938–1939	3	**Mac McIntyre** Corne, M(olly)
1938–1942	5	**Mary Carner** Popkin, Zelda
1938–1941	2	**Mrs. Elizabeth Warrender** Cole, Margaret and G. D. H.
1938–1941	2	**Eric Hazard** Crosby, Lee
1938–1977	21	**Septimus Finch** Erskine, Margaret

1938–1942	2	**Bill and Coco Hastings** Offord, Lenore Glen
1938–1941	4	**Pardoe** Bowers, Dorothy (Violet)
1938–1938	2	**Noah Bradshaw** Johnston, Madeleine
1939–1944	3	**Emma Marsh and Hank Fairbanks** Dean, Elizabeth
1939–1945	6	**Edward Trelawny** Long, Amelia Reynolds
1939–1947	4	**Anthony Ware** Wells, Susan
1939–1942	3	**Ernest Lamb** Wentworth, Patricia
1939–1943	5	**Peter and Janet Barron** Darby, Ruth
1939–1940	2	**Lyle Curtis and Susan Yates** Fetta, Emma Lou
1939–1956	13	**Rachel and Jennifer Murdock** Olsen, D. B.
1939–1940	2	**Mr. Hodson** Bidwell, Margaret
1939–1964	7	**Matt Winters** Oellrichs, Inez H.
1939–1940	2	**Jack Thompson** Cameron, Evelyn
1939–1953	17	**Desmond Shannon** Heberden, M(ary) V(iolet)
1939–1942	3	**Chauncey O'Day** Gaines, Audrey
1939–1963	13	**Alister Woodhead** Clements, E(ileen) H(elen)
1939–1941	4	**Captain Andy and Sue MacVeigh** MacVeigh, Sue
1939–1940	2	**Guy Northeast** Cannan, Joanna

1939–1942	3	**Gregory Trent** Seifert, Adele
1939–1946	4	**Hilea Bailey and Hilary D. Bailey III** Bailey, Hilea
1939–1967	14	**John J. Malone and The Justuses** Rice, Craig
1939–1968	29	**William Austen** Hocking, (Mona) (Naomi) Anne (Messer)
1940–1966	10	**Haila and Jeff Troy** Roos, Kelley
1940–1941	2	**Lutie and Amanda Beagle** Chanslor, (Marjorie) Torrey
1940–1941	2	**Agatha Welch** Johns, Veronica P(arker)
1940–1946	3	**Hiram Odom** Boniface, Marjorie
1940–1951	16	**Henry Gamadge** Daly, Elizabeth (Theresa)
1940–1946	8	**Bill Grady** Shriber, Ione Sandburg
1940–1942	3	**Tobin** Hughes, Dorothy B(elle)
1940–1941	2	**Christopher Gibson** Montgomery, Ione
1940–1948	6	**"Peter" Piper** Long, Amelia Reynolds
1940–1947	5	**Jane Carberry** Symons, Beryl (Mary) (E.)
1940–1953	4	**Levy** Holding, Elisabeth Sanxay
1940–1944	4	**Margot Blair** Knight, Kathleen Moore
1940–1949	7	**Christopher Storm** Barber, Willetta Ann and R. F. Schabelitz
1940–1963	26	**Pam and Jerry North** Lockridge, Frances and Richard

1940–1942	5	**Toby Dyke** Ferrars, E. X.
1940–1963	26	**Tommy Hambledon** Coles, Manning
1941–1943	2	**Diego** Kelsey, Vera
1941–1944	3	**Ross Paterson** Field, Katherine
1941–1968	8	**Cockrill** Brand (Lewis), (Mary) Christianna (Milne)
1941–1965	26	**Pat and Jean Abbott** Crane, Frances
1941–1976	4	**George Honegger** Strange, John Stephen
1941–1943	2	**Andrea Reid (Ramsay) and David Ramsay** Matschat, Cecile Hulse
1941–1942	2	**Eleanora Burke** Perdue, Virginia
1941–1943	2	**Sarah O'Brien** Marlett, Melba
1941–1979	4	**Charlesworth** Brand (Lewis), (Mary) Christianna (Milne)
1941–1943	3	**Powledge** Rea, M(argaret) P(aine)
1941–1942	3	**Dr. Paul Prye** Millar, Margaret
1941–1942	2	**Gypsy Rose Lee** Lee, Gypsy Rose
1942–1962	13	**Gridley Nelson** Fenisong, Ruth
1942–1944	3	**Melville Fairr** Venning, Michael
1942–1947	2	**Jacob Chaos** Smith, Shelley

1942–1944	2	**George White** Mannon, M. M.
1942–1952	5	**Richard Tuck** Lewis, Lange
1942–1954	2	**Sarah Keate** Eberhart, Mignon (Good)
1942–1945	2	**Pettengill** Rowe, Anne
1942–1943	2	**D. A. Carey Galbreath** McCully, (Ethel) Walbridge
1942–1945	3	**Sands** Millar, Margaret
1942–1946	2	**Courtney Brade** Wolffe, Katherine
1942–1958	3	**Bingo Riggs and Handsome Kusak** Rice, Craig
1942–1945	3	**MacDougal Duff** Armstrong, Charlotte
1942–1948	3	**Dr. Hillis Owen and Miss Pomeroy** Wells, Anna Mary
1942–1946	3	**Sam Hook** Teilhet, Hildegarde Tolman
1942–1946	4	**Christopher Saxe** Shane, Susannah
1942–1951	11	**Paul Kilgerrin** Leonard, Charles L.
1943–1944	2	**Andrew Torrent** Cores, Lucy (Michaela)
1943–1945	2	**Christine Andersen** Mace, Merlda
1943–1945	2	**Bill Davies** Mason, Sara Elizabeth
1943–1966	19	**Grogan** Neville, Margot
1943–1945	3	**F. Millard Smyth** Boyd, Eunice Mays

1943–1954	5	**Jim O'Neill** Disney, Doris Miles
1943–1948	2	**Miguel Urizar** McCloy, Helen
1943–1947	2	**Richard Massey** Siller, Van
1943–1950	7	**Steve Carter** Long, Amelia Reynolds
1943–1944	2	**Mark Tudor** Nash, Anne
1943–1944	2	**Pete Rector** Siller, Van
1943–1956	4	**Lace White** Nolan, Jeannette Covert
1943–1959	4	**Todd McKinnon** Offord, Lenore Glen
1944–1954	8	**Abbie Harris** Dean (Getzin), Amber
1944–1950	3	**Eric Lund** Wallis, Ruth (O.) Sawtell
1944–1946	3	**Barry** Rowe, Anne
1944–1972	35	**Dr. Manson** Radford, E. and M.
1944–1945	2	**Lorna Donahue** Hill, Katharine
1944–1947	3	**Mark East** Lawrence, Hilda (Hildegarde) (Kronemiller)
1945–1947	3	**Peter Ponsonby** Leslie, Jean
1945–1957	6	**Patrick Laing** Laing, Patrick
1945–1948	2	**Ryan** Scherf, Margaret (Louise)
1945–1951	3	**Christopher Adrian** Silverman, Marguerite R.

1945–1947	2	**Nora Hughes and Larry Blaine** Davis, Lavinia R(iker)
1945–1959	2	**Miles Pennoyer** Lawrence, Margery
1945–1952	6	**A. Pennyfeather** Olsen, D. B.
1945–1947	2	**Gregory Pavlov and O'Shaunnessey** Ryan, Jessica
1945–1946	2	**John Davies** Bennett, Margot
1945–1958	15	**Julian Rivers** Carnac, Carol
1945–1948	2	**Lane Parry** Sarsfield, Maureen
1945–1973	6	**Jenny Gilette and Hunter Lewis** Grey, Robin
1945–1948	5	**York** Durham, Mary
1946–1951	3	**Rick Vanner** Heberden, M(ary) V(iolet)
1946–1947	2	**Maggie Slone** Stone, Elizabet M.
1946–1985	4	**Dr. Sam: Johnson** de la Torre (Bueno) (McCue), Lillian
1946–1947	2	**Pat Campbell** Colter, Eli(zabeth)
1946–1963	17	**Merton Heimrich** Lockridge, Frances and Richard
1946–1952	2	**Jeff Strange** Gaines, Audrey
1946–1948	2	**Beau Smith and Pogy Rogers** Ross, Z(ola) H(elen) (Gridey)
1946–1949	2	**Elizabeth** Kilpatrick, Florence
1946–1971	8	**Jeff DiMarco** Disney, Doris Miles

1946–1947	2	**Tessie Venable** Holley, Helen
1946–1949	5	**Johnny DuVivien** Spain, Nancy
1947–1951	3	**Hortense Clinton** Hagen, Miriam-Ann
1947–1952	4	**Homer Fitzgerald** Russell, Charlotte M.
1947–1952	3	**Dennis Barrie** Reynolds, Adrian
1947–1959	2	**Peter Donnegan** Quick, Dorothy
1947–1960	7	**Julia Tyler** Revell, Louisa
1947–1949	2	**Gale Gallagher** Gallagher, Gale
1948–1963	5	**Emily and Henry Bryce** Scherf, Margaret (Louise)
1949–1959	3	**Mandrake** Bonett, John and Emery
1949–1955	3	**Marka de Lancey** Frost, Barbara
1949–1952	6	**Miriam Birdseye** Spain, Nancy
1949–1953	4	**Lilly Wu and Janice Cameron** Sheridan, Juanita
1949–1965	6	**Rev. Martin Buell** Scherf, Margaret (Louise)
1949–1951	3	**John Harland** Foley, Rae
1950–1952	2	**Simon Ashton** Antill, Elizabeth
1950–1962	5	**Ronald Price** Cannan, Joanna
1950–1963	2	**Hilda Trenton** Lyon, (Mabel) Dana

1950–1977	2	**Chucky** Ashe, Mary Ann
1950–1960	4	**Harry Butten** Barbette, Jay
1950–1951	2	**Flower** Field, Moira
1950–1973	5	**John Ripley** Gordons, The
1951–1967	12	**George Marshall** Barrington, Pamela
1951–1952	2	**Petunia Best and Max Frend** Chetwynd, Bridget
1951–1952	2	**Lord and Lady Tintagel** Draco, F.
1951–1963	7	**Hugh Gordon, Insp.** **and Liane Crawford** Gilruth, Susan
1951–1955	3	**Jim Little** Parker, Maude
1951–1976	6	**Simon Drake** Nielsen, Helen
1951–1979	14	**George Felse, Insp.** **and Family** Peters, Ellis
1951–1958	2	**Tom Craig** Van Urk, Virginia
1952–1956	2	**Benedict Breeze** Bayne, Isabella
1952–1957	3	**Richard Ringwood** Farrer, Katharine
1952–1961	3	**George Travers** Barrington, Pamela
1953–1971	3	**Burnivel** Candy, Edward
1953–1956	2	**Jolivet** Shepherd, Joan

1953–1958	4	**Al White** Holden, Genevieve
1953–1954	4	**Norma "Nicky" Lee** Lee, Norma
1953–1976	24	**Miss Marian Phipps** Bentley, Phyllis (Eleanor)
1953–1958	2	**Webster Flagg** Johns, Veronica P(arker)
1954–1957	3	**MacKay** Cushing, E. Louise
1954–1958	3	**Charles and James Latimer** Gaite, Francis
1954–1955	2	**Johnny Powers** Rayter, Joe
1954–1957	2	**Aloysius Kelly** Worsley-Gough, Barbara
1954–1966	2	**Kelly** Roth, Holly
1954–1961	5	**Gil Donan** Hood, Margaret Page
1955–1960	2	**Jim Sader** Hitchens, Dolores (Birk)
1955–1959	2	**Collins and McKechnie** Hitchens, Bert and Dolores
1955–1970	11	**Hiram Potter** Foley, Rae
1955–1985	5	**Tom Ripley** Highsmith, Patricia
1956–1973	10	**Julia Probyn** Bridge, Ann
1956–1961	4	**Nathan Shapiro** Lockridge, Frances and Richard
1956–1963	3	**Moss Magill** Gardiner, Dorothy
1956–1959	4	**Sally and Johnny Heldar** Hamilton, Henrietta

1956–1961	3	**David Madden** Disney, Doris Miles
1956–1982	6	**Ambrose Usher** Davey, Jocelyn
1956–1958	3	**Brett Nightingale** Kelly, Mary
1956–1960	3	**Lathom Dynes** Robertson, Helen
1957–1962	2	**Medford** Roth, Holly
1957–1971	11	**Honey West** Fickling, G. G.
1957–1965	5	**Michael Hornsley** Salter, Elizabeth
1957–1959	3	**Mrs. Norris** Davis, Dorothy Salisbury
1957–1963	2	**John Farrel** Hitchens, Bert and Dolores
1957–1958	2	**Jasper Tully** Davis, Dorothy Salisbury
1957–1986	16	**John Coffin** Butler, Gwendoline
1957–1961	2	**Christopher Marsden** Backhouse, (Enid) Elizabeth
1957–1972	15	**Lovick** Wilson, G(ertrude) M(ary)
1958–1966	7	**Swinton** Flower, Pat(ricia)
1958–1959	2	**"Tubby" Hall** Hambledon, Phyllis
1958–1960	2	**Dr. Alun Barry** O'Hara, Kenneth
1959–1963	3	**Claude Warrington-Reeve** Bell, Josephine
1959–1974	16	**Fadiman Wace** Simons, Roger

1959–1987	18	**Henry Tibbett** Moyes, Patricia
1959–1960	2	**Antoine Cirret** Hely (Younger), Elizabeth
1959–1963	3	**James Flecker** Pullein-Thompson, Josephine
1959–1960	2	**Arabella Frant** Fearon, Diana
1960–1966	6	**Herbert Broom** Hurt, Freda (Mary) (E.)
1960–1968	2	**Cardiff** Gray, Dulcie
1960–1964	2	**Forsythia Brown** Payes, Rachel
1960–1961	2	**Jerome Aylwin** Curry, Avon
1960–1961	2	**Jim and Kate Harris** Macrae, Travis
1960–1987	38	**Luis Mendoza** Shannon, Dell
1960–1963	2	**Prentis** Backhouse, (Enid) Elizabeth
1960–1965	5	**Paul Grainger** Sinclair, Fiona
1961–1962	2	**Nicholson** Kelly, Mary
1961–1985	13	**Jesse Falkenstein** Egan, Lesley
1961–1982	19	**John Putnam Thatcher** Lathen, Emma
1961–1967	3	**Menendez** Blanc, Suzanne
1961–1984	13	**Vic Varallo** Egan, Lesley
1962–1971	4	**Erik March** Fickling, G. G.

1962–1965	3	**Remsen** Montross, David
1962–1964	3	**Steytler** Milne, Shirley
1962–1964	2	**Bernard Simmons** Lockridge, Frances and Richard
1962–1964	2	**Paul Lane** Lockridge, Frances and Richard
1962–1981	8	**Charmian Daniels** Melville, Jennie
1962–1987	48	**Antony Maitland** Woods, Sara
1962–1965	2	**Nuri Iskirlak** Fleming, Joan (Margaret)
1962–1965	4	**Hoani Mata** Grayland, (Valerie) Merle (Spanner)
1962–1986	8	**Adam Dalgliesh** James, P(hyllis) D(orothy)
1963–1968	5	**Marcus MacLurg** Petrie, Rhona
1963–1968	15	**Hubert Bonisseur de la Bath** Bruce, Jean
1963–1974	3	**D. C. Randall (a cat)** Gordons, The
1963–1980	3	**Steve Rhoden** Walker, Ir(ma) (Ruth) (Roden)
1964–1986	12	**Ivor Maddox** Linington, Elizabeth
1964–1970	2	**Selena Mead** McGerr, Patricia
1964–1970	8	**Bill Rice** Stand, Marguerite
1964–1967	2	**Robins** Stand, Marguerite
1964–1968	2	**Christopher Jensen** Langley, Lee

1964–1984	6	**Salvador Borges** Bonett, John and Emery
1964–1966	2	**Gibbon** Cooper, (Evelyn) Barbara
1964–1985	13	**Reg Wexford** Rendell, Ruth
1964–1970	3	**Basil** Hobson, Polly
1964–1966	2	**Dr. Henry Frost** Bell, Josephine
1964–1986	8	**Kate Fansler** Cross, Amanda
1964–1986	6	**Homer Kelly** Langton, Jane
1964–1968	7	**Trevor Nicholls** Peters, Geoffrey
1964–1980	21	**Wilfred Dover** Porter, Joyce
1965–1967	3	**Allan Stewart** Siller, Van
1965–1967	4	**Steve Ramsay** Wallace, C. H.
1965–1965	2	**Ratlin** Roffman, Jan
1966–1972	5	**Phil Kramer** Kruger, Paul
1966–1977	15	**Knute Severson** Wells, Tobias
1966–1967	3	**Christer Wick** Lang, Maria
1966–1987	12	**C. D. Sloan** Aird, Catherine
1966–1987	6	**Jim Qwilleran** Braun, Lilian Jackson
1966–1971	6	**Timothy Herring** Torrie, Malcolm

1966–1967	2	**Newsom** Stewart, Flora
1966–1971	4	**Edmund Brown** Porter, Joyce
1966–1985	7	**Mrs. Emily Pollifax** Gilman, Dorothy
1967–1976	10	**Martin Beck** Sjowall, Maj and Per Wahloo
1967–1971	5	**Matthew Furnival** Phillips, Stella
1967–1975	6	**Dr. Paul Holton** Hunt, Charlotte
1967–1968	4	**John Abbot** Whitaker, Beryl
1967–1969	2	**Dr. Nassim Pride** Petrie, Rhona
1967–1986	16	**Tom Pollard** Lemarchand, Elizabeth
1968–1968	2	**Henderson** Barling, Charles
1968–1978	4	**Dr. Grace Severance** Scherf, Margaret (Louise)
1968–1970	3	**Christie Opara** Uhnak, Dorothy
1968–1984	6	**Johnson Johnson** Dunnett, Dorothy (Halliday)
1968–1983	8	**Ben Safford** Dominic, R. B.
1968–1971	2	**Ben Louis** Russell, E(nid)
1968–1969	3	**Tracy Larrimore and Mike Thompson** Paull, Jessica
1969–1979	4	**Maurice Ygrec** Rippon, Marion (Edith)
1969–1979	2	**Gail and Mitch Mitchell** Gordons, The

1970–1976	5	**Patrick Grant** Yorke, Margaret	
1970–1987	20	**Tessa Crichton** Morice, Anne	
1970–1973	2	**Bowman** Burrows, Julie	
1970–1979	5	**Constance Morrison-Burke** Porter, Joyce	
1970–1970	2	**Jefferson Shields** Carlon, Patricia	
1971–1975	3	**Dr. William Ames** Freeman, Lucy	
1971–1984	3	**Douglas Perkins** Babson, Marian	
1971–1975	6	**Kitty Telefair** Stevenson, Florence	
1971–1987	12	**Finch (Rudd)** Thomson, June	
1971–1972	4	**Ira Yedder** Bond, Evelyn	
1971–1977	4	**Lucy Ramsdale** Dolson, Hildegarde	
1972–1982	2	**Cordelia Gray** James, P(hyllis) D(orothy)	
1972–1976	3	**Al Krug and Casey Kellog** Weston, Carolyn	
1972–1974	3	**Laurie Grant and Stewart Noble** MacKintosh, May	
1972–1984	3	**Jacqueline Kirby** Peters, Elizabeth	
1972–1974	3	**Meredith** Ramsay, Diana	
1972–1987	12	**Norah Mulcahaney** O'Donnell, Lillian (Udvardy)	
1973–1984	6	**Conan Flagg** Wren, M. K.	

1973–1975	2	**Thea Crawford** Mann, Jessica
1973–1976	3	**John Joseph Lintott** Stubbs, Jean
1973–1984	10	**Melinda Pink** Moffat, Gwen
1973–1984	3	**Dolly and The Old Buffer** Wendell, Sarah
1973–1987	4	**Vicky Bliss** Peters, Elizabeth
1974–1977	3	**Bosco of the Yard** Christopher, Laura Kim
1974–1975	4	**Barrington Hewes-Bradford** Hamilton, Adam
1974–1977	2	**Ann Hales** Ingate, Mary
1975–1986	4	**Amelia Peabody and Radcliffe Emerson** Peters, Elizabeth
1975–1979	4	**Father Simon Bede and Helen Bullock** Byfield, Barbara Ninde
1975–1978	3	**Dr. Norah North** Duke, Madelaine
1975–1976	2	**Henry Beaumont** Atkins, Meg (Margaret) (Elizabeth)
1975–1981	6	**Merlin Capricorn** Winslow, Pauline Glen
1976–1984	7	**Mrs. Charles** Warner, Mignon
1976–1978	2	**Jacques Brunel** Gavin, Catherine
1976–1977	2	**Lexey Jane Pelazoni** Head, (Joanna) Lee
1976–1978	2	**David Haham** Haddad, C(arolyn) (A.)

1976–1987	4	**Julie Hayes** Davis, Dorothy Salisbury
1976–1981	5	**Anna Peters** Law, Janice
1976–1979	2	**Charles Spotted Moon** Yarbro, Chelsea Quinn
1976–1977	2	**Will Woodfield** Foote-Smith, Elizabeth
1976–1982	3	**Tom Aragon** Millar, Margaret
1977–1985	7	**Sharon McCone** Muller, Marcia
1977–1987	13	**Brother Cadfael** Peters, Ellis
1977–1982	3	**Dearborn V. Pinch** Green, Edith Piñero
1977–1980	3	**Mici Anhalt** O'Donnell, Lillian (Udvardy)
1977–1986	7	**Jemima Shore** Fraser, Antonia
1977–1985	3	**Persis Willum** Watson, Clarissa
1978–1980	3	**Steve Arrow** Mantell, Laurie
1978–1980	6	**Terry Spring** Kains, Josephine
1978–1980	4	**Kay Barth** Schier, Norma
1978–1986	6	**Douglas Quantrill** Radley, Sheila
1978–1980	3	**Marilyn Ambers** St. Clair, Elizabeth
1978–1987	6	**Peter Shandy** MacLeod, Charlotte
1978–1979	7	**Maxine Reynolds** Grove, Marjorie

1978–1986	2	**Helen Keremos** Zaremba, Eve
1978–1986	3	**Virginia Freer** Ferrars, E. X.
1978–1980	8	**Tory Baxter** Blair, Marcia
1979–1979	2	**Pauline Lyons** Anthony, Elizabeth
1979–1979	3	**Carol Gates** Colburn, Laura
1979–1979	2	**Charlotte Elliot** Filgate, C. Macartney
1979–1980	2	**Richard York** Williamson, Audrey
1979–1980	2	**Amy Tupper** Bell, Josephine
1979–1987	7	**Sarah Kelling and Max Bittersohn** MacLeod, Charlotte
1979–1986	5	**C. B. Greenfield** Kallen, Lucille
1979–1980	2	**Kate Graham** Arliss, Joen
1979–1980	2	**Megan Marshall** Collins, Michelle
1979–1980	2	**Adrienne Bishop** Ellery, Jan
1979–1987	8	**Thomas Pitt, Insp. and Charlotte Ellison (Pitt)** Perry, Anne
1979–1984	2	**Richard Owen, Agent** Sharp, Marilyn (Augburn)
1979–1983	7	**Dr. Penelope Spring and Sir Tobias Glendower** Arnold, Margot
1979–1980	3	**Maggie Courtney** Pearson, Ann

1979–1980	4	**Anna J(agedinski)** Swan, Phyllis
1979–1979	2	**Nell Willard** Lynch, Miriam
1979–1979	3	**Valerie Lambert** Allan, Joan
1980–1983	4	**Davina Graham** Anthony, Evelyn
1980–1980	2	**Emil Martin** Taylor, Mary Ann
1980–1987	5	**Anna Lee** Cody, Liza
1980–1981	4	**Jeremy Locke** Challis, Mary
1980–1980	2	**Stephen Marryat** Leek, Margaret
1980–1982	3	**Richard Trenton** Burton, Anne
1980–1986	3	**Madoc Rhys** Craig, Alisa
1980–1987	4	**Benjamin Jurnet** Haymon, S. T.
1981–1987	5	**Guarnaccia** Nabb, Magdalen
1981–1986	2	**Blue Maguire and Spaceman Kowalski** White, Teri
1981–1987	9	**Richard Jury** Grimes, Martha
1981–1987	5	**Kelsey** Page, Emma
1981–1985	3	**Lettie Winterbottom** Cutter, Leela
1981–1986	5	**Penny Wanawake** Moody, Susan

1981–1986	5	**Sister Mary Teresa Dempsey** Quill, Monica
1981–1987	2	**Neal Rafferty** Wiltz, Chris
1981–1986	6	**Luke Thanet** Simpson, Dorothy
1981–1987	3	**Delilah West** O'Callaghan, Maxine
1981–1987	2	**Maggie Elliott** Taylor, Elizabeth Atwood
1981–1984	2	**Julia Larwood** Caudwell, Sarah
1981–1985	2	**The Grub-and-Stakers** Craig, Alisa
1981–1984	2	**Viera Kolarova** Powers, Elizabeth
1982–1987	4	**Kinsey Millhone** Grafton, Sue
1982–1986	4	**Michael Spraggue** Barnes, Linda (Appelblatt)
1982–1983	2	**John Waltz** McCormick, Claire
1982–1985	3	**Mrs. Potter** Rich, Virginia
1982–1984	2	**Nyla Wade** McConnell, Vicki
1982–1986	3	**Rebecca Schwartz** Smith, Julie
1982–1987	3	**Sarah Deane and Dr. Alex McKenzie** Borthwick, J. S.
1982–1987	4	**V. I. Warshawski** Paretsky, Sara
1983–1986	3	**Elena Oliverez** Muller, Marcia
1983–1986	2	**Cass Jameson** Wheat, Carolyn

1983–1987	4	**Andrew Basnett** Ferrars, E. X.
1983–1984	2	**Jocelyn O'Roarke** Dentinger, Jane
1983–1985	2	**Dr. Gordon Christy** Moore, Barbara
1983–1987	4	**Jake Samson and Rosie Vicente** Singer, Shelley
1983–1985	2	**Roz Howard** Kenney, Susan
1983–1984	2	**Mike Yeadings, Supt. and Angus Mott, Sgt.** Curzon, Clare
1983–1986	2	**Miss Harriet Unwin** Hervey, Evelyn
1983–1985	2	**Kyra Keaton** Tone, Teona
1984–1987	5	**Jill Smith** Dunlap, Susan
1984–1986	3	**Elizabeth MacPherson** McCrumb, Sharyn
1984–1987	5	**Robert Forsythe** Giroux, E. X.
1984–1986	2	**Isamu "Sam Irish" Ohara** Hamilton, Nan
1984–1987	3	**Dr. Tina May** Kemp, Sarah
1984–1987	4	**Sigrid Harald, Detective** Maron, Margaret
1984–1986	2	**Iris Cooper and Jack Clancy** Beck, K. K.
1984–1987	3	**Charles Matthews** Meredith, D(oris) R.
1984–1985	4	**Nurse Carmichael** Cohen, Anthea

1984–1986	2	**Pam Nilsen** Wilson, Barbara
1984–1987	4	**Jennifer Cain** Pickard, Nancy
1984–1987	2	**Judd Springfield** Smith, Alison
1984–1986	3	**Patience C. McKenna** Papazouglou, Orania
1984–1986	2	**Sister Mary Helen** O'Marie, Sister Carol Ann
1984–1987	3	**Enrico Caruso and Geraldine Farrar** Paul, Barbara
1984–1986	2	**J. J. Jamison** Taylor, L(aurie) A(ylma)
1984–1987	3	**Andrea Perkins** Coker, Carolyn
1984–1986	3	**Vejay Haskell** Dunlap, Susan
1985–1986	3	**Rev. Claire Aldington** Holland, Isabelle
1985–1987	2	**Paul McDonald** Smith, Julie
1985–1987	2	**G. D. H. Pringle** Livingston, Nancy
1985–1986	2	**Liz Connors** Kelly, Susan
1985–1987	3	**Fiddler** Maxwell, A. E.
1985–1986	3	**Ellie Gordon** Berne, Karin
1985–1987	4	**Maggie Ryan** Carlson, P(atricia) M.
1985–1986	2	**Stoner McTavish** Dreher, Sarah
1985–1986	2	**Rain Morgan** Grant-Adamson, Leslie

1985–1987	4	**Paula Glenning** Clarke, Anna
1985–1986	2	**Cassandra Mitchell and Karl Alberg** Wright, L(aurali) R.
1985–1986	2	**Glad Gold, Prof. and** **Chase, Police Chief** Wender, Theodora
1985–1987	3	**Lennox Kemp** Meek, M(argaret) R(eid) D(uncan)
1986–1987	2	**Doran Fairweather and Rodney** **Chelmarsh** Hardwick, Mollie
1986–1987	3	**Guinevere Jones** Castle, Jayne
1986–1987	2	**Nick Magaracz** Gallison, Kate
1986–1987	3	**David Webb** Fraser, Anthea
1986–1987	3	**Claire Malloy** Hess, Joan
1986–1987	2	**Rina Lazarus** Kellerman, Faye
1986–1987	2	**Rat Trapp** Corrington, Joyce H. and John William
1986–1987	2	**Miss Susan Melville** Smith, Evelyn E.
1987–1987	3	**Balthazar Marten** Adamson, M. J.
1987–1987	2	**Annie Laurance** Hart, Carolyn G.

APPENDIX II: PSEUDONYM TO AUTONYM

There are any number of reasons for an author to use a nom de plume. A new name often gives an undeveloped aspect of an author's personality a chance to flourish. Perhaps a man writes under a female pseudonym thinking that readers may be more sympathetic towards a certain character developed by a woman rather than a man. On the other hand, a woman might choose to send her work to a publisher under a male pseudonym to improve her chances of publication. Sometimes a publisher will suggest that a woman adopt a male pseudonym or publish under her first initials because the market seems more receptive to works by men. An established author might adopt a new style and would want the new work to be judged on its merit rather than her well-known name. Several authors in our MASTER LIST have created a new pseudonym for each new series character. An author whose books are well known in one field may want to separate this work from her crime and mystery fiction writing. Some team writers in the true sense of collaboration choose a single name under which their works appear. All in all, pseudonyms are useful monikers.

This section makes it possible for readers familiar with an author's pseudonym to discover the autonym and any other pseudonyms the author may have used. Readers may find that a favorite author's name is in fact a pseudonym. This list is compiled alphabetically by pseudonym (last name first). The autonym appears on the same line.

Pseudonym	Autonym
Aird, Catherine	McIntosh, Kinn Hamilton
Anthony, Evelyn	Ward-Thomas, Evelyn Bridget Patricia Stephens
Antill, Elizabeth	Middleton, Elizabeth
Aresbys, The	Bamberger, Helen w/Raymond
Arnold, Margot	Cook, Petronelle Marguerite Mary
Ashe, Mary Ann	Brand (Lewis), (Mary) Christianna (Milne)
Bailey, Hilea	Marting, Ruth Lenore
Balfour, Hearnden	Balfour, Eva w/Beryl Hearnden
Barber, Willetta Ann and R. F. Schabelitz	Barber, Willetta Ann w/Rudolph Fredrick Schabelitz
Barbette, Jay	Spicer, Betty Coe w/Bart
Barling, Charles	Barling, Muriel Vere M.
Barrington, Pamela	Barling, Muriel Vere M.
Baskerville, Beatrice and Elliot Monk	Baskerville, Beatrice w/Elliot Monk
Beck, K. K.	Marris, Kathrine
Bell, Josephine	Ball, Doris Bell
Berne, Karin	Bernell, Sue w/Michaela Karni
Bond, Evelyn	Hershman, Morris
Bonett, John and Emery	Coulson, Felicity Winifred Carter w/John H. A.
Bonnamy, Francis	Walz, Audrey Boyers
Brahms, Caryl and S. J. Simon	Abrahams, Doris Caroline w/Simon Jasha Skidelsky
Bridge, Ann	O'Malley, Lady Mary Dolling

Bristow, Gwen and Bruce Manning	Bristow, Gwen w/Bruce Manning
Bruce, Jean	Brochet, Jean Alexandre
Burton, Anne	Bowen-Judd, Sara Hutton
Byfield, Barbara Ninde and Frank L. Tedeschi	Byfield, Barbara Ninde w/Frank L. Tedeschi
Candy, Edward	Neville, Barbara Alison
Cannan, Joanna	Pullein-Thompson, Joanna M. C.
Carnac, Carol	Rivette, Edith Caroline
Castle, Jayne	Krentz, Jayne
Caudwell, Sarah	Cockburn, Sarah
Challis, Mary	Bowen-Judd, Sara Hutton
Chipperfield, Robert O.	Ostrander, Isabel
Clandon, Henrietta	Vahey, John G. H.
Coffin, Geoffrey	Brawner, Helen w/Francis Van Wyck Mason
Cole, Margaret and G. D. H.	Cole, Margaret Isabel Postgate w/George Douglas Howard
Coles, Manning	Manning, Adelaide Frances Oke w/Cyril Henry Coles
Corrington, Joyce H. and John William	Corrington, Joyce H. w/John William
Craig, Alisa	MacLeod, Charlotte
Crosby, Lee	Budlong, Ware Torrey
Cross, Amanda	Heilbrun, Carolyn G.
Curry, Avon	Bowden, Jean
Curzon, Clare	Buchanan, Eileen-Marie
Dane, Clemence and Helen Simpson	Ashton, Winifred w/Helen Simpson
Davey, Jocelyn	Raphael, Chaim
Dominic, R. B.	Henissart, Martha w/Mary Jane Latsis

Draco, F.	Davis, Julia
Edingtons, The	Edington, Carmen Ballen w/Arlo Channing
Egan, Lesley	Linington, Elizabeth
Erskine, Margaret	Williams, Margaret Wetherby
Evermay, March	Eiker, Mathilde
Ferrars, E. X.	Brown, Morna Doris McTavert
Fickling, G. G.	Fickling, Gloria w/Forrest
Fielding, A. E.	Fielding, Dorothy
Fitt, Mary	Freeman, Kathleen
Foley, Rae	Denniston, Elinore
Ford, Leslie	Brown, Zenith Jones
Fox, David	Ostrander, Isabel
Frome, David	Brown, Zenith Jones
Gaite, Francis	Manning, Adelaide Frances Oke w/Cyril Henry Coles
Gallagher, Gale	Scott, Margaret w/William Charles Oursler
Gayle, Newton	Marin, Muna Lee w/Maurice C. Guiness
Gilbert, Anthony	Malleson, Lucy Beatrice
Giroux, E. X.	Shannon, Doris
Gordons, The	Gordon, Mildred w/Gordon
Gray, Dulcie	Dennison, Dulcie Winifred
Green, Glint	Peterson, Margaret Ann
Grey, Robin	Gresham, Elizabeth
Hale, Christopher	Stevens, Frances M. R.
Hambledon, Phyllis	MacVean, Phyllis
Hamilton, Adam	Granbeck, Marilyn w/Arthur Moore
Hanshew, Mary and Thomas	Hanshew, Hazel Phillips

Hanshew, Thomas	Hanshew, Hazel Phillips w/Mary
Hanshew, Thomas	Hanshew, Mary
Harris, Colver	Colver, Anne
Hervey, Evelyn	Keating, H(enry) R(eymond) F(itzwalter)
Hitchens, Bert and Dolores	Hitchens, Dolores (Birk) w/(Hu)Bert
Hobson, Polly	Evans, Julie Rendel
Holden, Genevieve	Pou, Genevieve Long
Hunt, Charlotte	Hodges, Doris Marjorie
Ironside, John	Tait, Euphemia Margaret
Kains, Josephine	Goulart, Ron
Kemp, Sarah	Butterworth, Michael
Kruger, Paul	Sebenthal, Roberta E.
Laing, Patrick	Long, Amelia Reynolds
Lambert, Rosa and Dudley	Lambert, Rosa w/Dudley
Lang, Maria	Lange, Dagmar
Langley, Lee	Langley, Sarah
Lathen, Emma	Henissart, Martha w/Mary Jane Latsis
Lee, Gypsy Rose	Craig, Georgiana Ann Randolph
Leek, Margaret	Bowen-Judd, Sara Hutton
Leonard, Charles L.	Heberden, M(ary) V(iolet)
Lewis, Lange	Beynon, Jane
Lockridge, Frances and Richard	Lockridge, Frances w/Richard
Lorac, E. C. R.	Rivett, Edith Caroline
Lynch, Lawrence	Van Deventer, Emma M.
Lynch, Miriam	Wallace, Mary
MacGowan, Alice and Perry Newberry	MacGowan, Alice w/Perry Newberry

MacVeigh, Sue	Nearing, Elizabeth C.
Macrae, Travis	Feagles, Anita Macrae
Mannon, M. M.	Mannon, Martha w/Mary Ellen Mannon
Maxwell, A. E.	Maxwell, Ann w/Evan
McCormick, Claire	Labus, Martha Haake
Meade, L. T.	Meade (Smith), Elizabeth Thomasina w/Robert Eustace
Melville, Jennie	Butler, Gwendoline
Montross, David	Backus, Jean Louise
Morice, Anne	Shaw, Felicity
Muller, Marcia and Bill Pronzini	Muller, Marcia w/Bill Pronzini
Neville, Margot	Goyder, Margot w/Anne N. G. Joske
O'Hara, Kenneth	Morris, Jean
Olsen, D. B.	Hitchens, Dolores (Birk)
Page, Emma	Tirbutt, Honoria
Paull, Jessica	Burger, Rosaylmer w/Julie Perceval
Peters, Elizabeth	Mertz, Barbara L. G.
Peters, Ellis	Pargeter, Edith Mary
Peters, Geoffrey	Palmer, Madelyn
Petrie, Rhona	Buchanan, Eileen-Marie
Prichard, K. and V.	Prichard, Katherine w/Vernon
Quill, Monica	McInerny, Ralph
Radford, E. and M.	Radford, Mona w/Edwin
Radley, Sheila	Robinson, Sheila (Mary)
Ramsay, Diana	Brandes, Rhoda
Rayter, Joe	McChesney, Mary F.
Reynolds, Adrian	Long, Amelia Reynolds

Rice, Craig	Craig, Georgiana Ann Randolph
Robertson, Helen	Edmiston, Helen Jean Mary
Roffman, Jan	Summerton, Margaret
Roos, Kelley	Roos, Audrey Kelley w/William
Ryerson, Florence and Colin Clements	Ryerson, Florence w/Colin Clements
Saunders, Lawrence	Davis, Clare w/Burton
Scarlett, Roger	Blair, Dorothy w/Evelyn Page
Shane, Susannah	Ashbrook, H(arriette) (C.)
Shannon, Dell	Linington, Elizabeth
Shepherd, Joan	Buchanan, Betty Joan
Siller, Van	Van Siller, Hilda
Simons, Roger	Punnett, Margaret w/Ivor
Sjowall, Maj and Per Wahloo	Sjowall, Maj w/Per Wahloo
Smith, Shelley	Bodington, Nancy Hermione Courlander
St. Clair, Elizabeth	Cohen, Susan Handler
Strange, John Stephen	Tillett, Dorothy Stockbridge
Teilhet, Darwin L.	Teilhet, Hildegarde Tolman
Tey, Josephine	MacKintosh, Elizabeth
Tilton, Alice	Taylor, Phoebe Atwood
Torrie, Malcolm	Mitchell, Gladys
Venning, Michael	Craig, Georgiana Ann Randolph
Wallace, C. H.	Burger, Rosaylmer
Walter, A. and H.	Walter, Alexia w/Hubert
Wells, Susan	Siegel, Doris
Wells, Tobias	Forbes, DeLoris
Wender, Theodora	Wender, Dorothea

APPENDIX III: SERIES CHARACTER TO AUTHOR

The authors appearing in our MASTER LIST have created nearly six hundred series characters. This APPENDIX links the series character—arranged alphabetically by first name—to the writer. As some of these characters rise through the ranks of their profession, their titles change. For that reason, we have put professional designations—with the exception of physicians, the religious, and Ph.D.s—at the end of the character's name.

Readers may be familiar with a certain series character's name. By referring to this list, they can find the writer, then check the MASTER LIST to find all the titles of the books in which that character appears, as well as any other series characters created by the same author.

Character	Author
A. Pennyfeather, Prof.	Olsen, D. B.
Abbie Harris	Dean (Getzin), Amber
Adam Dalgliesh, Supt.	James, P(hyllis) D(orothy)
Adam Drew and Katherine Cornish	Hanson, Virginia
Adam Quill, Insp.	Brahms, Caryl and S. J. Simon
Adelaide Adams	Blackmon, Anita
Adrienne Bishop	Ellery, Jan
Agatha Welch	Johns, Veronica P(arker)
Al Krug and Casey Kellog	Weston, Carolyn
Al White, Lt.	Holden, Genevieve
Alan Ford	Wells, Carolyn
Alan Grant, Insp.	Tey, Josephine
Albert Campion	Allingham (Carter), Margery
Alister Woodhead	Clements, E(ileen) H(elen)
Allan Stewart	Siller, Van
Aloysius Kelly	Worsley-Gough, Barbara
Ambrose Usher	Davey, Jocelyn
Amelia Butterworth and Ebenezer Gryce	Green, Anna Katharine
Amelia Peabody and Radcliffe Emerson	Peters, Elizabeth
Amy Tupper	Bell, Josephine
Andrea Perkins	Coker, Carolyn
Andrea Reid (Ramsay) and David Ramsay	Matschat, Cecile Hulse
Andrew Basnett	Ferrars, E. X.
Andrew Torrent, Capt.	Cores, Lucy (Michaela)
Angeline Tredennick	Sanborn, Ruth Burr
Ann Hales	Ingate, Mary
Anna J(agedinski)	Swan, Phyllis

Anna Lee	Cody, Liza
Anna Peters	Law, Janice
Anne "Davvie" Davenport McLean	Yates, Margaret Tayler
Anne and Jeffrey McNeill	DuBois, Theodora M.
Annie Laurance	Hart, Carolyn G.
Anthony Ware	Wells, Susan
Antoine Cirret	Hely (Younger), Elizabeth
Antony Maitland	Woods, Sara
Arabella Frant	Fearon, Diana
Arthur G. Crook	Gilbert, Anthony
Asey Mayo	Taylor, Phoebe Atwood
Ballet Stroganoff	Brahms, Caryl and S. J. Simon
Balthazar Marten	Adamson, M. J.
Barney Gantt	Strange, John Stephen
Baron Von Kaz	Teilhet, Darwin L.
Barrington Hewes-Bradford	Hamilton, Adam
Barry, Insp.	Rowe, Anne
Barry O'Dell	Chipperfield, Robert O.
Basil, Insp.	Hobson, Polly
Battle, Supt.	Christie, Agatha
Beau Smith and Pogy Rogers	Ross, Z(ola) H(elen) (Gridey)
Ben Louis	Russell, E(nid)
Ben Safford	Dominic, R. B.
Benedict Breeze	Bayne, Isabella
Benjamin Jurnet, Det. Insp.	Haymon, S. T.
Benvenuto Brown	Gill, Elizabeth
Bernard Simmons	Lockridge, Frances and Richard
Bill and Coco Hastings	Offord, Lenore Glen
Bill Davies, Sheriff	Mason, Sara Elizabeth
Bill French, Lt.	Hale, Christopher

Charlotte Eliot	Filgate, C. Macartney
Charmian Daniels, WPC	Melville, Jennie
Chauncey O'Day	Gaines, Audrey
Christer Wick	Lang, Maria
Christie Opara, Det.	Uhnak, Dorothy
Christine Andersen	Mace, Merlda
Christopher Adrian, Insp.	Silverman, Marguerite R.
Christopher Gibson	Montgomery, Ione
Christopher Jensen, Lt.	Langley, Lee
Christopher Marsden, Insp.	Backhouse, (Enid) Elizabeth
Christopher McKee, Insp.	Reilly, Helen
Christopher Saxe	Shane, Susannah
Christopher Storm	Barber, Willetta Ann and R. F. Schabelitz
Chucky, Insp.	Ashe, Mary Anne
Claire Malloy	Hess, Joan
Clarice Claremont	Cranston, Claudia
Claude Warrington-Reeve	Bell, Josephine
Clive Granville	McKenna, Marthe
Cockrill, Insp.	Brand (Lewis), (Mary) Christianna (Milne)
Colin Anstruther	Plain, Josephine
Colin Keats and Gwynn Leith	Shore, Viola Brothers
Collins and McKechnie	Hitchens, Bert and Dolores
Conan Flagg	Wren, M. K.
Constance Morrison-Burke	Porter, Joyce
Cordelia Gray	James, P(hyllis) D(orothy)
Courtney Brade, Capt.	Wolffe, Katherine
D. A. Carey Galbreath	McCully, (Ethel) Walbridge
D. C. Randall (a cat)	Gordons, The
Daisy Jane Mott	Jones, Jennifer

Dame Beatrice Adela Lestrange Bradley	Mitchell, Gladys
David Haham	Haddad, C(arolyn) (A.)
David Madden	Disney, Doris Miles
David Webb, Chief Insp.	Fraser, Anthea
Davina Graham	Anthony, Evelyn
Dearborn V. Pinch	Green, Edith Piñero
Delilah West	O'Callaghan, Maxine
Dennis Barrie, Prof.	Reynolds, Adrian
Dennis Devore	Bennett, Dorothy
Desmond Shannon	Heberden, M(ary) V(iolet)
Dexter Drake	Barker, Elsa
Dick Wilson	Sproul, Kathleen
Diego, Lt.	Kelsey, Vera
Dolly and The Old Buffer	Wendell, Sarah
Don Q	Prichard, K. and V.
Doran Fairweather and Rodney Chelmarsh	Hardwick, Mollie
Douglas Perkins	Babson, Marian
Douglas Quantrill, Insp.	Radley, Sheila
Dr. Alun Barry	O'Hara, Kenneth
Dr. Basil Willing	McCloy, Helen
Dr. Constantine	Thynne, Molly
Dr. David Wintringham	Bell, Josephine
Dr. Gordon Christy	Moore, Barbara
Dr. Grace Severance	Scherf, Margaret (Louise)
Dr. Henry Frost	Bell, Josephine
Dr. Hillis Owen and Miss Pomeroy	Wells, Anna Mary
Dr. Joan Marvin	Eyles, (M.) Leonora (P.)
Dr. Manson	Radford, E. and M.
Dr. Nassim Pride	Petrie, Rhona
Dr. Nathaniel Bunce	Curtiss, E(lizabeth) M.

Dr. Norah North	Duke, Madelaine
Dr. Paul Holton	Hunt, Charlotte
Dr. Paul Prye	Millar, Margaret
Dr. Penelope Spring and Sir Tobias Glendower	Arnold, Margot
Dr. Sam: Johnson	de la Torre (Bueno) (McCue), Lillian
Dr. Tina May	Kemp, Sarah
Dr. William Ames	Freeman, Lucy
Ebenezer Gryce	Green, Anna Katharine
Edmund Brown	Porter, Joyce
Edward Trelawny	Long, Amelia Reynolds
Eleanora Burke	Perdue, Virginia
Elena Oliverez	Muller, Marcia
Elisha Macomber	Knight, Kathleen Moore
Elizabeth	Kilpatrick, Florence
Elizabeth MacPherson	McCrumb, Sharyn
Ellie Gordon	Berne, Karin
Emil Martin	Taylor, Mary Ann
Emily and Henry Bryce	Scherf, Margaret (Louise)
Emma Marsh and Hank Fairbanks	Dean, Elizabeth
Enrico Caruso and Geraldine Farrar	Paul, Barbara
Eric Hazard	Crosby, Lee
Eric Lund	Wallis, Ruth (O.) Sawtell
Erik March	Fickling, G. G.
Ernest Lamb, Insp.	Wentworth, Patricia
Evan Pinkerton	Frome, David
Everard Blatchington	Cole, Margaret and G. D. H.
Everett Anderson, Insp.	Daiger, K(atherine) S.
F. Millard Smyth	Boyd, Eunice Mays
Fadiman Wace, Insp.	Simons, Roger

Gridley Nelson, Capt.	Fenisong, Ruth
Grogan, Insp.	Neville, Margot
Guarnaccia, Marshal	Nabb, Magdalen
Guinevere Jones	Castle, Jayne
Guy Bannister	Crossley, Maude
Guy Northeast, Insp.	Cannan, Joanna
Gyp Kidnadze	Vincent, Lady Kitty
Gypsy Rose Lee	Lee, Gypsy Rose
Haila & Jeff Troy	Roos, Kelley
Hamilton Cleek	Hanshew, Hazel Phillips
Hamilton Cleek	Hanshew, Mary and Thomas
Hamilton Cleek	Hanshew, Thomas
Hannasyde, Supt. and Hemingway, Sgt.	Heyer, Georgette
Harley Quin	Christie, Agatha
Harry Butten	Barbette, Jay
Headcorn, Insp.	Campbell, Alice
Helen Keremos	Zaremba, Eve
Henderson, Insp.	Barling, Charles
Henry Beaumont, Insp.	Atkins, Meg (Margaret) (Elizabeth)
Henry Doight, Insp.	Symons, Beryl (Mary) (E.)
Henry Gamadge	Daly, Elizabeth (Theresa)
Henry Tibbett, Insp.	Moyes, Patricia
Henry Wilson, Supt.	Cole, Margaret and G. D. H.
Herbert Broom, Insp.	Hurt, Freda (Mary) (E.)
Hercule Poirot	Christie, Agatha
Hilda Trenton	Lyon, (Mabel) Dana
Hilea Bailey and Hilary D. Bailey III	Bailey, Hilea
Hiram Odom, Sheriff	Boniface, Marjorie
Hiram Potter	Foley, Rae

Hoani Mata	Grayland, (Valerie) Merle (Spanner)
Homer Fitzgerald	Russell, Charlotte M.
Homer Kelly	Langton, Jane
Honey West	Fickling, G. G.
Hook, Insp.	Lane, (Margaret) Gret
Hortense Clinton	Hagen, Miriam-Ann
Hubert Bonisseur de la Bath	Bruce, Jean
Hugh Gordon, Insp. and Liane Crawford	Gilruth, Susan
Ira Yedder	Bond, Evelyn
Iris Cooper and Jack Clancy	Beck, K. K.
Isamu "Sam Irish" Ohara	Hamilton, Nan
Ivor Maddox, Sgt.	Linington, Elizabeth
J. J. Jamison	Taylor, L(aurie) A(ylma)
Jack Strickland, Insp.	Balfour, Hearnden
Jack Thompson, Sheriff	Cameron, Evelyn
Jacob Chaos	Smith, Shelley
Jacqueline Kirby	Peters, Elizabeth
Jacques Brunel	Gavin, Catherine
Jake Samson and Rosie Vicente	Singer, Shelley
James F. "Bonnie" Dundee	Austin, Anne
James Flecker, Insp.	Pullein-Thompson, Josephine
James Greer	Gayle, Newton
James Strange	Quinn, E(leanora) Baker
Jane Amanda Edwards	Russell, Charlotte M.
Jane Carberry	Symons, Beryl (Mary) (E.)
Jane Marple	Christie, Agatha
Jasper Tully	Davis, Dorothy Salisbury
Jeff DiMarco	Disney, Doris Miles
Jeff Strange	Gaines, Audrey

Jefferson Shields	Carlon, Patricia
Jemima Shore	Fraser, Antonia
Jennifer Cain	Pickard, Nancy
Jenny Gilette and Hunter Lewis	Grey, Robin
Jeremiah Irish	Child, Nellise
Jeremy Locke	Challis, Mary
Jerome Aylwin	Curry, Avon
Jerry Boyne	MacGowan, Alice and Perry Newberry
Jesse Falkenstein	Egan, Lesley
Jill Smith, Det.	Dunlap, Susan
Jim and Kate Harris	Macrae, Travis
Jim Little	Parker, Maude
Jim O'Neill	Disney, Doris Miles
Jim Qwilleran	Braun, Lilian Jackson
Jim Sader	Hitchens, Dolores (Birk)
Jimmy Lane	Ryerson, Florence and Colin Clements
Jocelyn O'Roarke	Dentinger, Jane
John Abbot	Whitaker, Beryl
John Barrin	Lane, (Margaret) Gret
John Coffin, Insp.	Butler, Gwendoline
John Davies	Bennett, Margot
John Farrel	Hitchens, Bert and Dolores
John Freeman, Det. Insp.	Ironside, John
John Harland	Foley, Rae
John J. Malone and The Justuses	Rice, Craig
John Joseph Lintott, Insp.	Stubbs, Jean
John Primrose, Col.	Ford, Leslie
John Putnam Thatcher	Lathen, Emma
John Ripley	Gordons, The

Laurie Grant and Stewart Noble	MacKintosh, May
Lennox Kemp	Meek, M(argaret) R(eid) D(uncan)
Leonidas Witherall	Tilton, Alice
Lettie Winterbottom	Cutter, Leela
Levy, Lt.	Holding, Elisabeth Sanxay
Lexey Jane Pelazoni	Head, (Joanna) Lee
Li Moh	Cowdroy, Joan
Lilly Wu and Janice Cameron	Sheridan, Juanita
Liz Connors	Kelly, Susan
Lord and Lady Tintagel	Draco, F.
Lord Peter Wimsey	Sayers, Dorothy L.
Lorimer Lane	Wells, Carolyn
Lorna Donahue	Hill, Katharine
Loveday Brooke, Lady Detective	Pirkis, C(atharine) L(ouisa)
Lovick, Insp.	Wilson, G(ertrude) M(ary)
Lucy Ramsdale	Dolson, Hildegarde
Luis Mendoza, Lt.	Shannon, Dell
Luke Thanet, Det. Insp.	Simpson, Dorothy
Lutie and Amanda Beagle	Chanslor, (Marjorie) Torrey
Lyle Curtis and Susan Yates	Fetta, Emma Lou
Lynn MacDonald	Strahan, Kay Cleaver
M. Dupuy	Gilbert, Anthony
M. Hector Ratichon	Orczy, Baroness (Emmuska)
Mac McIntyre	Corne, M(olly)
MacDougal Duff	Armstrong, Charlotte
MacKay, Insp.	Cushing, E. Louise
Macdonald, Insp.	Lorac, E. C. R.
Madame Koluchy	Meade, L. T.
Madame Sara	Meade, L. T.

Madeline Payne	Lynch, Lawrence
Madoc Rhys, Insp.	Craig, Alisa
Maggie Courtney	Pearson, Ann
Maggie Elliott	Taylor, Elizabeth Atwood
Maggie Ryan	Carlson, P(atricia) M.
Maggie Slone	Stone, Elizabet M.
Mallett, Supt. Insp.	Fitt, Mary
Mandrake, Prof.	Bonett, John and Emery
Marcus MacLurg, Insp.	Petrie, Rhona
Margetson, Sgt.	Keate, E(dith) M(urray)
Margot Blair	Knight, Kathleen Moore
Marilyn Ambers	St. Clair, Elizabeth
Mark East	Lawrence, Hilda (Hildegarde) (Kronemiller)
Mark Tudor	Nash, Anne
Marka de Lancey	Frost, Barbara
Martin Beck, Chief Insp.	Sjowall, Maj and Per Wahloo
Mary Carner	Popkin, Zelda
Matt Winters	Oellrichs, Inez H.
Matthew Furnival, Insp.	Phillips, Stella
Maud Silver	Wentworth, Patricia
Maurice Ygrec, Insp.	Rippon, Marion (Edith)
Maxine Reynolds	Grove, Marjorie
Medford, Insp.	Roth, Holly
Megan Marshall	Collins, Michelle
Melinda Pink	Moffat, Gwen
Melville Fairr	Venning, Michael
Menendez, Insp.	Blanc, Suzanne
Mercedes Quero	Locke, G(ladys) E(dson)
Meredith, Lt.	Ramsay, Diana
Merlin Capricorn, Supt.	Winslow, Pauline Glen
Merton Heimrich, Insp.	Lockridge, Frances and Richard

Michael Dundas	Rath, Virginia Anne
Michael Forrester	Wees, Frances Shelley
Michael Hornsley, Insp.	Salter, Elizabeth
Michael Spraggue	Barnes, Linda (Appelblatt)
Mici Anhalt	O'Donnell, Lillian (Udvardy)
Miguel Urizar	McCloy, Helen
Mike Yeadings, Supt. and Angus Mott, Sgt.	Curzon, Clare
Miles Pennoyer	Lawrence, Margery
Millicent Newberry	Lee, Jennette
Miriam Birdseye	Spain, Nancy
Miss Harriet Unwin	Hervey, Evelyn
Miss Marian Phipps	Bentley, Phyllis (Eleanor)
Miss Susan Melville	Smith, Evelyn E.
Miss Woolfe	Graham (M.) Winifred (M.)
Mitchell, Insp.	Lincoln, Natalie S.
Molly Morgenthau	Bonner, Geraldine
Montague Egg	Sayers, Dorothy L.
Moss Magill, Sheriff	Gardiner, Dorothy
Mr. Gimblet	Bryce, Mrs. Charles
Mr. Hodson	Bidwell, Margaret
Mr. Watson	Gardiner, Dorothy
Mr. Winkley	Rutland, Harriet
Mrs. Charles	Warner, Mignon
Mrs. Elizabeth Warrender	Cole, Margaret and G. D. H.
Mrs. Emily Pollifax	Gilman, Dorothy
Mrs. Norris	Davis, Dorothy Salisbury
Mrs. Potter	Rich, Virginia
Nathan Shapiro	Lockridge, Frances and Richard
Neal Rafferty	Wiltz, Chris
Neil Bathurst	Lynch, Lawrence
Nell Willard	Lynch, Miriam

Pauline Lyons	Anthony, Elizabeth
Payran, Commissaire	Nisot, Elizabeth
Pennington Wise	Wells, Carolyn
Penny and Vincent Mercer	Clandon, Henrietta
Penny Wanawake	Moody, Susan
Persis Willum	Watson, Clarissa
Pete Rector	Siller, Van
Peter and Janet Barron	Darby, Ruth
Peter Clancy	Thayer, (Emma) (R.) Lee
Peter Donnegan, Lt.	Quick, Dorothy
Peter Jerningham	Myers, Isabel Briggs
"Peter" Piper	Long, Amelia Reynolds
Peter Piper	Mavity, Nancy Barr
Peter Ponsonby	Leslie, Jean
Peter Shandy, Prof.	MacLeod, Charlotte
Peter Strangely	Black, E(lizabeth) Best
Peter Uteley Shane, Prof.	Bonnamy, Francis
Pettengill, Insp.	Rowe, Anne
Petunia Best and Max Frend	Chetwynd, Bridget
Phil Kramer	Kruger, Paul
Philip "Spike" Tracy	Ashbrook, H(arriette) (C.)
Pointer, Insp.	Fielding, A. E.
Powledge, Lt.	Rea, M(argaret) P(aine)
Prentis, Insp.	Backhouse, (Enid) Elizabeth
Race, Col.	Christie, Agatha
Rachel and Jennifer Murdock	Olsen, D. B.
Rain Morgan	Grant-Adamson, Leslie
Rat Trapp, Capt.	Corrington, Joyce H. and John William
Ratlin, Sgt.	Roffman, Jan
Rebecca Schwartz	Smith, Julie
Red Hanlon	Merrick, Mollie

Reg Wexford, Det. Chief Insp.	Rendell, Ruth
Remsen	Montross, David
Rev. Claire Aldington	Holland, Isabelle
Rev. Martin Buell	Scherf, Margaret (Louise)
Reynolds, Insp.	Hamilton, Elaine
Richard Jury, Det. Chief Insp.	Grimes, Martha
Richard Massey	Siller, Van
Richard Owen, Agent	Sharp, Marilyn (Augburn)
Richard Ringwood, Insp.	Farrer, Katherine
Richard Trenton	Burton, Anne
Richard Tuck, Lt.	Lewis, Lange
Richard York, Supt.	Williamson, Audrey
Rick Vanner	Heberden, M(ary) V(iolet)
Rina Lazarus	Kellerman, Faye
Robert Forsythe	Giroux, E. X.
Robins, Police Constable	Stand, Marguerite
Rocky Allan, Sheriff	Rath, Virginia Anne
Roderick Alleyn, Insp.	Marsh, (Edith) Ngaio
Ronald Price, Insp.	Cannan, Joanna
Ross Paterson, Det. Insp.	Field, Katherine
Roz Howard	Kenney, Susan
Ryan, Lt.	Scherf, Margaret (Louise)
Ryvet, Insp.	Carnac, Carol
Sally and Johnny Heldar	Hamilton, Henrietta
Salvador Borges, Insp.	Bonett, John and Emery
Sam Hook	Teilhet, Hildegarde Tolman
Sands, Insp.	Millar, Margaret
Sarah Deane and Dr. Alex McKenzie	Borthwick, J. S.
Sarah Keate	Eberhart, Mignon (Good)

Sarah Keate and Lance O'Leary	Eberhart, Mignon (Good)
Sarah Kelling and Max Bittersohn	MacLeod, Charlotte
Sarah O'Brien	Marlett, Melba
Scott Egerton	Gilbert, Anthony
Scott Stuart, Insp.	Coffin, Geoffrey
Sebald Craft	Patterson, (Isabella) Innis
Selena Mead	McGerr, Patricia
Septimus Finch, Insp.	Erskine, Margaret
Septimus March	Bamburg, Lilian
Sharon McCone	Muller, Marcia
Sigrid Harold, Det.	Maron, Margaret
Simon Ashton, Insp.	Antill, Elizabeth
Simon Brade	Campbell, Harriette (Russell)
Simon Chard	Malim, Barbara
Simon Drake	Neilsen, Helen
Sir Edgar Ewart	Walter, A. and H.
Sir John Saumarez	Dane, Clemence and Helen Simpson
Smith, Capt.	Edingtons, The
Sister Mary Helen	O'Marie, Sister Carol Ann
Sister Mary Teresa Dempsey	Quill, Monica
Stephen Marryat	Leek, Margaret
Stephen Mayhew, Lt.	Olsen, D. B.
Steve Arrow, Sgt.	Mantell, Laurie
Steve Carter	Long, Amelia Reynolds
Steve Ramsay	Wallace, C. H.
Steve Rhoden	Walker, Ir(m)a (Ruth) (Roden)
Steven Mitchell, Insp.	Bell, Josephine
Steytler, Det. Sgt.	Milne, Shirley
Stoddart, Insp.	Haynes, Annie

Valentine Hawkehurst	Braddon, M(ary) E(lizabeth)
Valerie Lambert	Allan, Joan
Van Dusen Ormsberry	Strange, John Stephen
Van Vernet	Lynch, Lawrence
Vejay Haskell	Dunlap, Susan
Vic Varallo	Egan, Lesley
Vicky Bliss	Peters, Elizabeth
Viera Kolarova	Powers, Elizabeth
Violet Strange	Green, Anna Katharine
Virginia Freer	Ferrars, E. X.
Wade	Bristow, Gwen and Bruce Manning
Webster Flagg	Johns, Veronica P(arker)
Wield, Insp.	Green, Glint
Wilfred Dover, Insp.	Porter, Joyce
Will Woodfield	Foote-Smith, Elizabeth
William Austen, Insp.	Hocking, (Mona) (Naomi) Anne (Messer)
William Power	Clandon, Henrietta
Winston Barrows	Eades, M(aude) L.
Woods, Insp.	Muir, D(orothy) Erskine
Wylie King and Nels Lundberg	Saunders, Lawrence
York, Insp.	Durham, Mary

EPILOGUE

Because mystery reading is a subjective adventure and all readers' tastes differ, we have made a clear attempt at objectivity in the selection of characters we have presented and the type of story in which they appear. We didn't want to limit our own horizons by reading and writing about only what we thought we liked. However, when we have had strong feelings one way or another about a character or an aspect of their adventures, we haven't held back. Keeping the subjective nature of our topic in mind, we don't expect that our readers will agree with all our declarations. We trust though, that the panorama we have presented will provide them with horizon-expanding potentials.

One of the many things we have learned is that there are a variety of ways to read a series. One is to begin at the beginning and devour every title featuring the character, in chronological order, pausing only briefly to catch a breath between books. A feat not always as easy as it sounds. Readers may find, however, that though they enjoy a particular character, three or more books from some series, without pause, is ill-advised. Too much of a good thing is just too much. Another way, of course, is to read the books as they are found—whatever order that may be. Using our chapter designations, readers might enjoy selecting series featuring a particular type of detective. Using our chronology, readers may select books penned in the same particular era. Rereading can be a pleasure. Some characters almost require this approach. The first time around, one almost always concentrates on the murder central to the story. After getting to know a character or an author's style of writing, it is sometimes necessary to return to earlier books to find out just who this character is and what the author is saying about things other than the mystery. Other books are simply good old friends with whom it is pleasant to visit again and again. In reading series, any way or combination of ways or no particular way at all is fine. Have a good time.

As researchers, it is both gratifying and exciting to find a literary genre that is so quantifiable. It is even better to find one with a beginning, an ever-expanding middle, and seemingly no end. Classics have emerged. Some books penned in the early years of this century have never gone out of print. Others rode a long swell of popularity around the time of their initial appearance, then dropped onto the back shelves of obscurity. The market has forgotten them and new readers haven't discovered them. Perhaps it is time for some of those forgotten golden oldies to be reissued. Publishers, take note.

Because many of the earlier series are long out of print, finding them can be a challenge for readers. We are fortunate to live in an area blessed with a large number of used book stores. We regularly make the rounds and almost always find one or two titles for which we have been searching. The very best of these, in our opinion, is Elsewhere Books on the corner of 9th Avenue and Judah in San Francisco. Not only are the shelves loaded with treasures, the proprietor herself is a jewel. Amy Beasom is a fountain of knowledge on authors, characters, and plots and is always happy to chat with customers about their interests and hers. If she hasn't got the book you want in stock, she'll do what she can to obtain it. Thanks Amy. When traveling anywhere, we always look for these stores and have found that the smallest towns often have the best selections. Garage and estate sales are often good sources of older works. It takes a lot of time to go through whatever people are throwing out, but it can be a pleasant way to spend several weekend hours and you might meet some interesting people in the process. Goodwill, the Salvation Army, and other secondhand stores are potential sources. These places seldom categorize their books so you'll have to wade through everything else to get to the goodies. Your neighborhood library is also a surprisingly good source—especially if it is connected to an inter-library loan system. If so, your request is circulated to as many libraries as yours is linked to, and though it may take some time, the wait may be rewarded. Libraries and schools hold periodic book sales. Devoted scavengers watch for them and get there early. Finally, there are the specialized mystery bookstores. Some put out catalogues listing available out of print titles and some even search far and wide for what you want. Expect to pay dearly at these places.

Beyond the difficulty in simply finding these books is that collectors have discovered the monetary value of books within this genre and have sent prices through the roof. We have paid nine dollars for a paperback that originally sold for a quarter. One of the saddest results of this collecting mania is that many of the books are grabbed by individuals with no interest in what's between the covers of their prizes. The books just sit on shelves—well tended but unread and loved only for their growing dollar value. What's a poor reader to do?

While this will be the most comprehensive work of its kind to date, due to the nature of the information it contains, it cannot ever be complete, as new series are constantly being created. Readers and writers with essential details are invited to correspond with us and fill in our unintentional gaps and lapses. Few authors outside of the United States and the United Kingdom are included because little information on them is available in the United States. We look forward to meeting undiscovered authors and their characters and adding book titles to our list. It is our hope that others will take the information we have gathered and use it as a foundation stone for their own examinations of author, character, generation...the list goes on and on.

This information is yours now. Make of it what you will.

NOTES

PROLOGUE

1. Carolyn G. Heilbrun, *Towards a Recognition of Androgyny: Aspects of Male and Female in Literature* (New York: Harper, 1973), p. 10.

A BLOT IN THE COPYBOOK

1. Margot Arnold, *Exit Actors Dying* (New York: Playboy Paperbacks, 1979), p. 28.
2. Charlotte MacLeod, *Rest You Merry* (New York: Doubleday & Co., 1978), pp. 33–34.
3. Elizabeth Peters, *The Murders of Richard III* (New York: The Mysterious Press, 1986), p. 2.
4. Elizabeth Peters, *Die for Love* (New York: Congdon & Weed, 1984), pp. 6–7.
5. Elizabeth Peters, *Crocodile on the Sandbank* (New York: The Mysterious Press, 1984), p. 215.
6. Amanda Cross, *In the Last Analysis* (New York: Avon Books, 1964), p. 170.
7. John and Emery Bonett, *Dead Lion* (New York: Harper & Row, 1982), p. 36.
8. D. B. Olsen, *Something About Midnight* (New York: Pocket Books, 1951), pp. 176–177.

BEHIND THE BADGE
Major Metropolitan Forces

1. Anna Katharine Green, *The Leavenworth Case* (New York: Dover Publications, 1981), pp. 106–107. (First published 1878).
2. Helen Reilly, *Murder in the Mews* (New York: Macfadden Books, 1966), p. 5.
3. Dorothy B. Hughes, *The Fallen Sparrow* (New York: Golden Apple Publishers, 1984), p. 162.
4. Lange Lewis, *The Birthday Murder* (New York: Perennial Library, 1980), pp. 57–58.
5. Dell Shannon, *Case Pending* (New York: The Mysterious Press, 1984), p. 18.
6. Dorothy Uhnak, *The Ledger* (New York: Simon and Schuster, 1970), pp. 207–208.

BEHIND THE BADGE (cont.)

    7. Lillian O'Donnell, *Dial 577 R-A-P-E* (New York: G. P. Putnam's Sons, 1974), pp. 108–109.

    8. Susan Dunlap, *As a Favor* (New York: St. Martin's Press, 1984), p. 12.

    9. Anne Perry, *Bluegate Fields* (New York: Ballantine Books, 1986), p. 11.

Scotland Yard

    10. E. C. R. Lorac, *And Then Put Out the Light* (New York: Bantam Books, 1968), p. 86.

    11. Edward Candy, *Which Doctor* (New York: Ballantine Books, 1982), p. 130.

    12. Joyce Porter, *Dover Goes to Pott* (New York: Charles Scribner's Sons, 1968), pp. 14–15.

    13. Elizabeth Lemarchand, *Death of an Old Girl* (New York: Walker & Co., 1985), p. 80.

    14. P. D. James, *Cover Her Face* (New York: Popular Library, 1976), p. 79.

    15. Martha Grimes, *The Anodyne Necklace* (New York: Dell Publishing, 1984), p. 54.

    16. Ngaio Marsh, *Death in a White Tie* (New York: Jove Publications, 1980), p. 78.

    17. Josephine Tey, *The Man in the Queue* (New York: Washington Square Press, 1977), p. 11.

The Provincials

    18. *Webster's Seventh New Collegiate Dictionary* (Springfield, Mass.: G. and C. Merriam Co., 1965), p. 687.

    19. Christianna Brand, *Heads you Lose* (Harmondsworth: Penguin Books, 1950), pp. 34–35.

    20. Mary Fitt, *Death on Heron's Mere* (Harmondsworth: Penguin Books, 1948), p. 130.

    21. Jennie Melville, *A New Kind of Killer* (New York: David McKay Co., Ives Washburn, 1971), pp. 13–14.

    22. June Thomson, *The Long Revenge* (New York: Bantam Books, 1981), p. 85.

    23. Catherine Aird, *The Stately Home Murder* (New York: Bantam Books, 1981), p. 137.

    24. Catherine Aird, *Slight Mourning* (New York: Bantam Books, 1982), pp. 168–169.

    25. Dorothy Simpson, *The Night She Died* (New York: Bantam Books, 1985), pp. 5–6.

BEHIND THE BADGE (cont.)

26. Sheila Radley, *Death in the Morning* (New York: Dell Publishing, 1980), pp. 13–14.

27. Sheila Radley, *Blood on the Happy Highway* (New York: Penguin Books, 1984), p. 56.

28. Emma Page, *Scent of Death* (Garden City, N.Y.: Doubleday & Co., 1986), p. 99.

29. Ruth Rendell, *Wolf to the Slaughter* (New York: Ballantine Books, 1980), p. 15.

30. Alisa Craig, *A Pint of Murder* (New York: Bantam Books, 1981), p. 84.

31. Dorothy Gardiner, *The 7th Mourner* (New York: Popular Library, 1968), pp. 53–54.

Foreign

32. Maj Sjowall and Per Wahloo, *The Man on the Balcony* (New York: Bantam Books, 1969), p. 46.

33. Magdalen Nabb, *Death of an Englishman* (New York: Penguin Books, 1984), p. 9.

34. Ibid., p. 89.

THE BLOOD RUNS BLUE

1. *Webster's Seventh New Collegiate Dictionary* (Springfield, Mass.: G. and C. Merriam Co., 1965), p. 47.

2. Charlotte MacLeod, *The Withdrawing Room* (New York: Avon Books, 1981), pp. 9–10.

3. Edith Piñero Green, *Rotten Apples* (New York: E. P. Dutton, 1977), pp. 133–134.

4. Rae Foley, *Where is Mary Bostwick?* (New York: Dell Publishing, 1973), p. 85.

5. Rae Foley, *Repent at Leisure* (New York: Dell Publishing, 1975), p. 7.

6. Anna Katharine Green, *The Circular Study* (Garden City, N.Y.: Garden City Publishing Co., 1926), p. 63.

7. Ibid., p. 289.

8. Anne Perry, *Bluegate Fields* (New York: Ballantine Books, 1984), p. 109.

9. Joyce Porter, *Rather a Common Sort of Crime* (New York: McCall Publishing Co., 1970), p.71.

10. Ibid., p. 113.

11. Martha Grimes, *The Dirty Duck* (New York: Dell Publishing, 1984), p. 130.

THE BLOOD RUNS BLUE (cont.)

12. Martha Grimes, *The Man With a Load of Mischief* (New York: Dell Publishing, 1981), p. 31.

13. Dorothy L. Sayers, *Whose Body?* (New York: Avon Books, 1961), p. 39.

14. Margery Allingham, *The Estate of the Beckoning Lady* (New York: MacFadden Bartell Corp., 1966), p. 47.

CRIME AND THE CORPUS DIVINE

1. Ellis Peters, *A Morbid Taste for Bones* (London and Sydney: Futura Macdonald & Co., 1977), p. 187.

2. Barbara Ninde Byfield, *Solemn High Murder* (Garden City, N.Y.: Doubleday & Co., 1975), p. 17.

3. Monica Quill, *Sine Qua Nun* (New York: The Vanguard Press, 1986), pp. 74–75.

4. Sister Carol Ann O'Marie, *A Novena For Murder* (New York: Charles Scribner's Sons, 1984), p. 10.

5. Margaret Scherf, *Gilbert's Last Toothache* (Garden City, N.Y.: Doubleday & Co., 1949), p. 7.

CRIME ON CUE

1. Pauline Glen Winslow, *Copper Gold* (New York: Dell Publishing Co., 1981), p. 87.

2. Ibid., pp. 217–218.

3. Jane Dentinger, *First Hit of the Season* (Garden City, N.Y.: Doubleday & Co., 1984), p. 60.

4. Linda Barnes, *Blood Will Have Blood* (New York: Fawcett Crest Books, 1986), p. 8.

5. Carolyn Wells, *Sleeping Dogs* (Garden City, N.Y.: Doubleday, Doran and Co., 1926), p. 56–57.

6. Clemence Dane and Helen Simpson, *Enter Sir John* (New York: J. J. Little & Ives Co., 1928), p. 139–140.

7. Anne Morice, *Murder Post-dated* (New York: Bantam Books, 1986), p. 120.

8. Ibid., pp. 3–4.

9. Antonia Fraser, *Cool Repentance* (New York: W. W. Norton and Co., 1985), p. 163.

CURE IT OR KILL IT

1. Margaret Scherf, *The Banker's Bones* (New York: Popular Library, 1968), pp. 11–12.
2. Mary Roberts Rinehart, *Miss Pinkerton* (New York: Dell Publishing, 1964), p. 8.
3. Ibid., p. 105.
4. Mignon G. Eberhart, *While the Patient Slept* (New York: Macfadden Books, 1963), pp. 38–39.
5. Ibid., pp. 46–47.
6. Josephine Bell, *The Seeing Eye* (London: Hodder & Stoughton, 1958), pp. 21–22.
7. Josephine Bell, *The Upfold Witch* (New York: Ballantine Books, 1966), pp. 13–14.
8. Theodora M. DuBois, *The Face of Hate* (Garden City, N. Y.: Doubleday & Co., 1949), pp. 25–26.
9. Barbara Moore, *The Doberman Wore Black* (New York: Dell Publishing, 1984), pp. 164–165.
10. Gladys Mitchell, *Laurels are Poison* (Harmondsworth: Penguin Books, 1961), p. 9.
11. Gladys Mitchell, *The Saltmarsh Murders* (London: The Hogarth Press, 1984), pp. 45–46.
12. Helen McCloy, *Cue for Murder* (New York: Bantam Books, Inc., 1965), p. 2.
13. Helen McCloy, *The Long Body* (New York: Ace Books, 1955), p. 115.
14. Anna Mary Wells, *A Talent for Murder* (New York: Perennial Library, Harper & Row, 1981), pp. 51–52.

KILLINGS ON THE MARKET

1. Dorothy L. Sayers, *Hangman's Holiday* (Harmondsworth: Penguin Books, 1964), p. 127.
2. Emma Lathen, *Double, Double, Oil and Trouble* (New York: Pocket Books, 1980), p. 8.
3. Dorothy L. Sayers, *Hangman's Holiday* (Harmondsworth: Penguin Books, 1964), p. 162.
4. Margaret Scherf, *The Gun in Daniel Webster's Bust* (New York: The Detective Book Club, 1949), p. 65.
5. Nancy Pickard, *Generous Death* (New York: Avon Books, 1984), p. 14.
6. Ibid., p. 117.
7. Nancy Pickard, *Say No to Murder* (New York: Avon Books, 1985), p. 50.

LEGAL EAGLES

1. Sara Woods, *The Windy Side of the Law* (New York: Popular Library, Harper & Row, 1965), pp. 25–26.

2. E. X. Giroux, *A Death for Adonis* (New York: Ballantine Books, 1986), p. 5.

3. Ibid., p. 103.

4. Sarah Caudwell, *Thus Was Adonis Murdered* (New York: Penguin Books, 1985), p. 12.

5. Sarah Caudwell, *The Shortest Way to Hades* (New York: Penguin Books, 1986), p. 7.

6. Anthony Gilbert, *Dark Death* (New York: Pyramid Books, 1963), pp. 127–128.

7. Anthony Gilbert, *The Looking Glass Murder* (New York: Pyramid Books, 1968), p. 117.

8. Craig Rice, *But the Doctor Died* (New York: Lancer Books, 1967), pp. 11–12.

9. The Gordons, *Night Before the Wedding* (Roslyn, N.Y.: Walter J. Black, Detective Book Club, 1969), p. 13.

10. Karin Berne, *Shock Value* (New York: Popular Library, Warner Books, 1985), p. 13.

11. Margaret Millar, *The Murder of Miranda* (New York: Random House, 1979), pp. 44–45.

12. Carolyn Wheat, *Dead Man's Thoughts* (New York: St. Martin's Press, 1983), p. 12.

13. Ibid., p. 228.

14. Chelsea Quinn Yarbro, *Music When Sweet Voices Die* (New York: G. P. Putnam's Sons, 1979), pp. 214–215.

15. Julie Smith, *The Sourdough Wars* (New York: Walker & Co., 1984), p. 100.

MURDER BETWEEN THE PAGES

1. Lucille Kallen, *Introducing C. B. Greenfield* (New York: Ballantine Books, 1983), p. 2.

2. Ibid., p. 5.

3. Lucille Kallen, *The Piano Bird* (New York: Ballantine Books, 1985), p. 90.

4. Lilian Jackson Braun, *The Cat Who Ate Danish Modern* (New York: Jove Publications, 1986), p. 9.

MURDER BETWEEN THE PAGES (cont.)

5. Gwen Bristow and Bruce Manning, *The Mardi Gras Murders* (New York: The Mystery League, 1932), p. 37.

6. Nancy Barr Mavity, *The Body On the Floor* (Garden City, N.Y.: The Crime Club, Doubleday, Doran & Co., 1932), p. 11.

7. Mignon Eberhart, *The Cases of Susan Dare* (New York: Popular Library, 1961), p. 9.

8. Ann Bridge, *The Lighthearted Quest* (New York: Berkley Medallion Books, 1964), p. 243.

9. Orania Papazoglou, *Sweet, Savage Death* (New York: Penguin Books, 1985), p. 20.

10. John Stephen Strange, *Rope Enough* (New York: The Crime Club, Doubleday, Doran & Co., 1938), p. 52.

11. Leslie Grant-Adamson, *Death on Widow's Walk* (New York: Charles Scribner's Sons, 1985), pp. 25–26.

12. Leela Cutter, *Who Stole Stonehenge?* (New York: St. Martin's Press, 1983), p. 31.

13. Susan Kelly, *The Gemini Man* (New York: Ballantine Books, 1986), pp. 172–173.

MUSEUM PIECES

1. Dorothy L. Sayers, *The Nine Tailors* (New York: A Harvest/HBJ Book, 1962), p. 6.

2. M. K. Wren, *Oh Bury Me Not* (Garden City, N.Y.: Doubleday & Co., 1976), p. 72.

3. M. K. Wren, *Seasons of Death* (Garden City, N.Y.: Doubleday & Co., 1981), pp. 1–2.

4. Elizabeth Peters, *Silhouette in Scarlet* (New York: Congdon & Weed, 1983), pp. 5–6.

5. Elizabeth Peters, *Street of the Five Moons* (New York: Dodd, Mead & Co., 1978), p. 4.

6. Marcia Muller, *The Tree of Death* (New York: Walker & Co., 1983), pp. 29–30.

7. Charlotte MacLeod, *The Withdrawing Room* (New York: Avon Books, 1981), p. 59.

8. Lady Harriette R. Campbell, *The Porcelain Fish Mystery* (New York: Alfred A. Knopf, 1937), p. 26.

9. Elizabeth Daly, *The Book of the Crime* (New York: Bantam Books, 1983), pp. 21–22.

LEGAL EAGLES

1. Sara Woods, *The Windy Side of the Law* (New York: Popular Library, Harper & Row, 1965), pp. 25–26.
2. E. X. Giroux, *A Death for Adonis* (New York: Ballantine Books, 1986), p. 5.
3. Ibid., p. 103.
4. Sarah Caudwell, *Thus Was Adonis Murdered* (New York: Penguin Books, 1985), p. 12.
5. Sarah Caudwell, *The Shortest Way to Hades* (New York: Penguin Books, 1986), p. 7.
6. Anthony Gilbert, *Dark Death* (New York: Pyramid Books, 1963), pp. 127–128.
7. Anthony Gilbert, *The Looking Glass Murder* (New York: Pyramid Books, 1968), p. 117.
8. Craig Rice, *But the Doctor Died* (New York: Lancer Books, 1967), pp. 11–12.
9. The Gordons, *Night Before the Wedding* (Roslyn, N.Y.: Walter J. Black, Detective Book Club, 1969), p. 13.
10. Karin Berne, *Shock Value* (New York: Popular Library, Warner Books, 1985), p. 13.
11. Margaret Millar, *The Murder of Miranda* (New York: Random House, 1979), pp. 44–45.
12. Carolyn Wheat, *Dead Man's Thoughts* (New York: St. Martin's Press, 1983), p. 12.
13. Ibid., p. 228.
14. Chelsea Quinn Yarbro, *Music When Sweet Voices Die* (New York: G. P. Putnam's Sons, 1979), pp. 214–215.
15. Julie Smith, *The Sourdough Wars* (New York: Walker & Co., 1984), p. 100.

MURDER BETWEEN THE PAGES

1. Lucille Kallen, *Introducing C. B. Greenfield* (New York: Ballantine Books, 1983), p. 2.
2. Ibid., p. 5.
3. Lucille Kallen, *The Piano Bird* (New York: Ballantine Books, 1985), p. 90.
4. Lilian Jackson Braun, *The Cat Who Ate Danish Modern* (New York: Jove Publications, 1986), p. 9.
5. Gwen Bristow and Bruce Manning, *The Mardi Gras Murders* (New York: The Mystery League, 1932), p. 37.

MURDER BETWEEN THE PAGES (cont.)

6. Nancy Barr Mavity, *The Body On the Floor* (Garden City, N.Y.: The Crime Club, Doubleday, Doran & Co., 1932), p. 11.

7. Mignon Eberhart, *The Cases of Susan Dare* (New York: Popular Library, 1961), p. 9.

8. Ann Bridge, *The Lighthearted Quest* (New York: Berkley Medallion Books, 1964), p. 243.

9. Orania Papazoglou, *Sweet, Savage Death* (New York: Penguin Books, 1985), p. 20.

10. John Stephen Strange, *Rope Enough* (New York: The Crime Club, Doubleday, Doran & Co., 1938), p. 52.

11. Leslie Grant-Adamson, *Death on Widow's Walk* (New York: Charles Scribner's Sons, 1985), pp. 25–26.

12. Leela Cutter, *Who Stole Stonehenge?* (New York: St. Martin's Press, 1983), p. 31.

13. Susan Kelly, *The Gemini Man* (New York: Ballantine Books, 1986), pp. 172–173.

MUSEUM PIECES

1. Dorothy L. Sayers, *The Nine Tailors* (New York: A Harvest/HBJ Book, 1962), p. 6.

2. M. K. Wren, *Oh Bury Me Not* (Garden City, N.Y.: Doubleday & Co., 1976), p. 72.

3. M. K. Wren, *Seasons of Death* (Garden City, N.Y.: Doubleday & Co., 1981), pp. 1–2.

4. Elizabeth Peters, *Silhouette in Scarlet* (New York: Congdon & Weed, 1983), pp. 5–6.

5. Elizabeth Peters, *Street of the Five Moons* (New York: Dodd, Mead & Co., 1978), p. 4.

6. Marcia Muller, *The Tree of Death* (New York: Walker & Co., 1983), pp. 29–30.

7. Charlotte MacLeod, *The Withdrawing Room* (New York: Avon Books, 1981), p. 59.

8. Lady Harriette R. Campbell, *The Porcelain Fish Mystery* (New York: Alfred A. Knopf, 1937), p. 26.

9. Elizabeth Daly, *The Book of the Crime* (New York: Bantam Books, 1983), pp. 21–22.

PORTRAITS IN CRIME

1. Clarissa Watson, *The Fourth Stage of Gainsborough Brown* (New York: David McKay Co., 1977), pp. vii–viii.

2. Ngaio Marsh, *Artists in Crime* (New York: Jove Publications, 1980), p. 6.

3. Kelley Roos, *Sailor Take Warning* (New York: Dell Publishing, 1944), introduction.

4. Kelley Roos, *Murder in Any Language* (New York: Dell Publishing, 1948), p. 55.

5. Barbara Ninde Byfield, *A Parcel of Their Fortunes* (Garden City, N.Y.: Doubleday & Co., 1979), p. 27.

6. Barbara Ninde Byfield, *Solemn High Murder* (Garden City, N.Y.: Doubleday & Co., 1975), p. 65.

7. Clarissa Watson, *Runaway* (New York: Atheneum, 1985), pp. 29–30.

8. Dorothy Dunnett, *Dolly and the Doctor Bird* (New York: Vintage Books, 1982), pp. 30–31.

9. Dorothy Dunnett, *Dolly and the Cookie Bird* (New York: Vintage Books, 1982), p. 261.

10. W. A. Barber and R. F. Schabelitz, *Drawn Conclusion* (New York: Penguin Books, 1943), pp. 50–51.

PRIVATE EYES

1. Agatha Christie, *The Murder of Roger Ackroyd* (New York: Pocket Books, 1939), pp. 90–91.

2. Carolyn Wells, *Prillilgirl* (Philadelphia: Lippincott Co., 1924), pp. 291–292.

3. Lee Thayer, *Dead Men's Shoes* (New York: J. H. Sears & Co., 1929), pp. 22–23.

4. Patricia Wentworth, *Grey Mask* (Sevenoaks: Coronet, 1981), p. 64.

5. Patricia Wentworth, *The Clock Strikes Twelve* (London: Coronet, 1980), pp. 95–96.

6. Agatha Christie, *The Secret Adversary* (Frogmore, St. Albans: Triad/Panther, 1979), p. 13.

7. Frances Crane, *Horror on the Ruby X* (New York: Random House, 1956), p. 192.

8. Gale Gallagher, *I Found Him Dead* (New York: Collier Books, 1962), p. 7.

9. P. D. James, *An Unsuitable Job for a Woman* (New York: Fawcett Popular Library, 1972), p. 88.

10. Ibid., p. 144.

PRIVATE EYES (cont.)

11. Marcia Muller, *Games to Keep the Dark Away* (New York: St. Martin's Press, 1984), pp. 105–106.
12. Liza Cody, *Stalker* (New York: Warner Books, 1984), p. 35.
13. Sara Paretsky, *Indemnity Only* (New York: Ballantine Books, 1982), p. 163.
14. Sue Grafton, *B is for Burglar* (New York: Holt, Rinehart and Winston, 1985), p. 27.

STRANGE BEDFELLOWS IN BRASS BEDS

1. Manning Coles, *Drink to Yesterday* (London: J. M. Dent & Sons, 1984), p. 69.
2. Ibid., pp. 59–60.
3. Leslie Ford, *Siren in the Night* (New York: Bantam Books, 1948), pp. 68–69.
4. Hildegarde Tolman Teilhet, *The Assassins* (Garden City, N.Y.: Doubleday & Co., 1946), pp. 65–67.
5. R. B. Dominic, *Murder in High Place* (Garden City, N.Y.: Doubleday & Co., 1970), p. 3.
6. R. B. Dominic, *Epitaph for a Lobbyist* (New York: PaperJacks, 1986), p. 13.
7. Dorothy Gilman, *The Unexpected Mrs. Pollifax* (New York: Fawcett Crest Books, 1970), p. 56.
8. Evelyn Anthony, *Albatross* (New York: G. P. Putnam's Sons, 1983), pp. 233–234.
9. Ibid., p. 110.
10. Joyce Porter, *The Chinks in the Curtain* (New York: Charles Scribner's Sons, 1968), p. 188.

THEY PICK UP THE PIECES AND HOLD DOWN THE FORT

1. Patricia Moyes, *Death and the Dutch Uncle* (New York: Holt, Rinehart and Winston, 1968), pp. 165–166.
2. Martha Grimes, *The Man with a Load of Mischief* (New York: Dell Publishing, 1981), pp. 29–30.
3. Margaret Scherf, *The Cautious Overshoes* (Garden City, N.Y.: Doubleday & Co., 1956), pp. 139–140.
4. Emma Lathen, *The Longer the Thread* (New York: Pocket Books, 1971), pp. 11–12.

THEY PICK UP THE PIECES AND HOLD DOWN THE FORT (cont.)

5. Linda Barnes, *Dead Heat* (New York: Ballantine Books, 1984) pp. 105–107.

UNEXPECTED DETECTIVES

1. Agatha Christie, *Nemesis* (Anstey: F. A. Thorpe, 1971), p. 39.
2. Agatha Christie, *Mr. Parker Pyne, Detective* (New York: Dell Publishing, 1974), p. 7.
3. D. B. Olsen, *Death Walks on Cat Feet* (New York: Popular Library, 1956), pp. 56–57.
4. Amber Dean, *Chanticleer's Muffled Crow* (Garden City, N.Y.: Doubleday, Doran & Co., 1945), p. 11.
5. Hildegarde Dolson, *To Spite Her Face* (New York: J. P. Lippincott Co., 1971), pp. 224–225.
6. Mignon Warner, *A Medium for Murder* (New York: Dell Publishing, 1980), p. 26.
7. Dorothy Salisbury Davis, *A Death in the Life* (New York: Avon Books, 1977), p. 23.
8. Baroness Emmuska Orczy, *The Old Man in the Corner* (New York: International Polygonics, 1977), p. 3. (first published 1909)
9. David Frome, *Mr. Pinkerton Has the Clue* (New York: Popular Library, 1964), pp. 8–9.
10. Phoebe Atwood Taylor, *Figure Away* (Taftsville: A Foul Play Press Book, The Countryman Press, 1979), p. 113.
11. Alisa Craig, *The Grub-and-Stakers Quilt a Bee* (Garden City, N.Y.: Doubleday and Co., 1985), p. 18.
12. Susan Dunlap, *The Last Annual Slugfest* (New York: St. Martin's Press, 1986), p. 42.
13. Shelley Singer, *Spit in the Ocean* (New York: St. Martin's Press, 1987), p. 12.

MASTER LIST

1. Mary Fitt, *Death and Mary Dazill* (West Dreighton & Middlesex: Penguin Books, 1948)

Susan Thompson has done research in biochemistry and bacteriology at one of the nation's leading hospitals, worked as a chef, seamstress, school administrator and is the mother of two adolescents.

Victoria Nichols has research experience in the pathology and surgical departments at a major medical school, has been a ship's cook, travel guide, independent film project coordinator, and is the mother of three grown children.

Collectively, they bring over sixty years of mystery reading to this first project. They live in Palo Alto, California.